井 上 雄 彦

Takehiko Inoue

I WANT TO BE BETTER AT BASKETBALL.
I WANT TO BE A BETTER DRIBBLER.
I WANT TO BE MORE AMBIDEXTROUS.
I WANT TO BE A BETTER PASSER.
I WANT BETTER COURT VISION.
I WANT TO BE A BETTER SHOOTER.
I JUST WANT TO MAKE MORE BASKETS.
I WANT TO BE BETTER DEFENSIVELY.
I WANT TO BE ABLE TO PLAY A FULL 40 MINUTES.
WHAT ABOUT YOU GUYS?

Takehiko Inoue's *Slam Dunk* is one of the most popular manga of all time, having sold over 100 million copies worldwide. He followed that series up with two titles lauded by critics and fans alike—*Vagabond*, a fictional account of the life of Miyamoto Musashi, and *Real*, a manga about wheelchair basketball.

SLAM DUNK
Vol. 24: For Victory

SHONEN JUMP Manga Edition

STORY AND ART BY TAKEHIKO INOUE

English Adaptation/Stan!
Translation/Joe Yamazaki
Touch-up Art & Lettering/James Gaubatz
Cover & Graphic Design/Matt Hinrichs
Editor/Mike Montesa

© 1990 - 2012 Takehiko Inoue and I.T. Planning, Inc.
Originally published in Japan in 1995 by Shueisha
Inc., Tokyo. English translation rights arranged with
I.T. Planning, Inc. All rights reserved.

The SLAM DUNK U.S. trademark is used with
permission from NBA Properties, Inc.

Some scenes have been modified from the original
Japanese edition.

The stories, characters and incidents mentioned in this
publication are entirely fictional.

Printed in Canada

Published by VIZ Media, LLC
P.O. Box 77010
San Francisco, CA 94107

10 9 8 7 6 5 4 3 2 1
First printing, October 2012

THE WORLD'S
MOST POPULAR MANGA
www.shonenjump.com

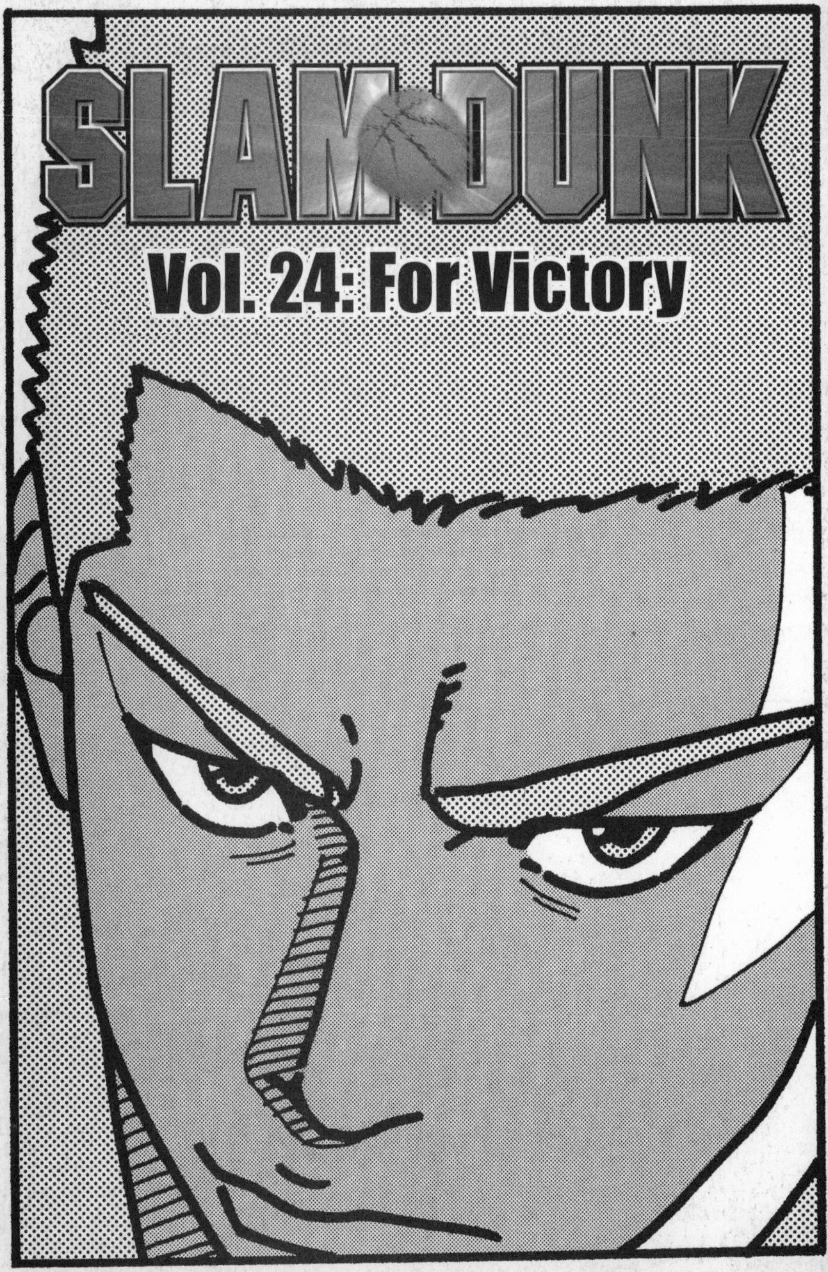
SLAM DUNK
Vol. 24: For Victory

STORY AND ART BY TAKEHIKO INOUE

Character Introduction

Hanamichi Sakuragi
A first-year at Shohoku High School, Sakuragi is in love with Haruko Akagi.

Haruko Akagi
Also a first-year at Shohoku, Takenori Akagi's little sister has a crush on Kaede Rukawa.

Takenori Akagi
A third-year and the basketball team's captain, Akagi has an intense passion for his sport.

Kaede Rukawa
The object of Haruko's affection (and that of many of Shohoku's female students!), this first-year has been a star player since junior high.

Minami

Kishimoto

Ryota Miyagi
A problem child with
a thing for Ayako.

Ayako
Basketball Team
Manager

Hisashi Mitsui
An MVP during
junior high.

Our Story Thus Far

Hanamichi Sakuragi is rejected by close to 50 girls during his three years in junior high. He joins the basketball team to be closer to Haruko Akagi, but his frustration mounts when all he does is practice day after day.

Shohoku advances through the Prefectural Tournament and earns a spot in the Nationals.

In a weeklong secret training session, Sakuragi makes 20,000 shots to prepare for the Nationals.

Shohoku's first round opponent is Osaka's Toyotama High. Between Rukawa's injury early in the game and Toyotama's overwhelming "run and gun" offense, Shohoku finds itself down by six points at halftime.

Vol. 24:
For Victory

Table of Contents

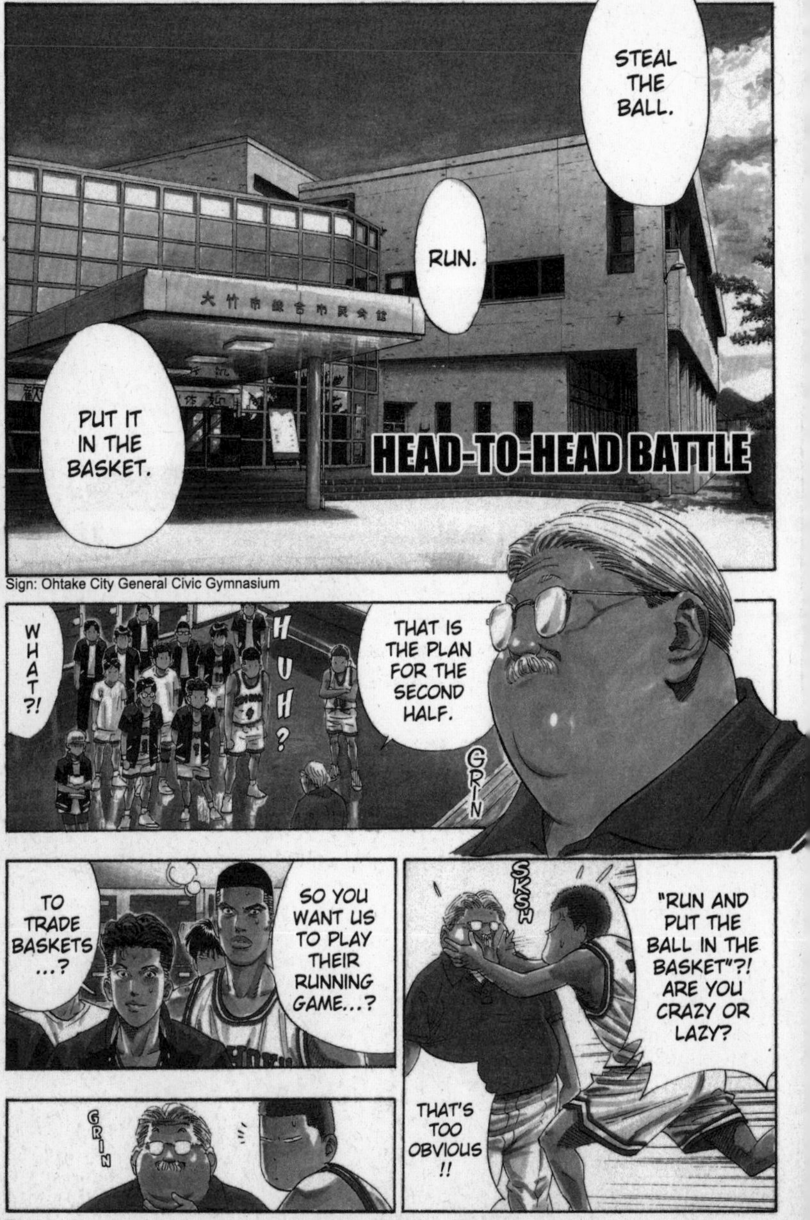
STEAL THE BALL.
RUN.
PUT IT IN THE BASKET.
HEAD-TO-HEAD BATTLE
GRIN
THAT IS THE PLAN FOR THE SECOND HALF.
HUH?
WHAT?!
"RUN AND PUT THE BALL IN THE BASKET"?! ARE YOU CRAZY OR LAZY?
SKSH
THAT'S TOO OBVIOUS!!
SO YOU WANT US TO PLAY THEIR RUNNING GAME...?
TO TRADE BASKETS...?
GRIN

Sign: Ohtake City General Civic Gymnasium

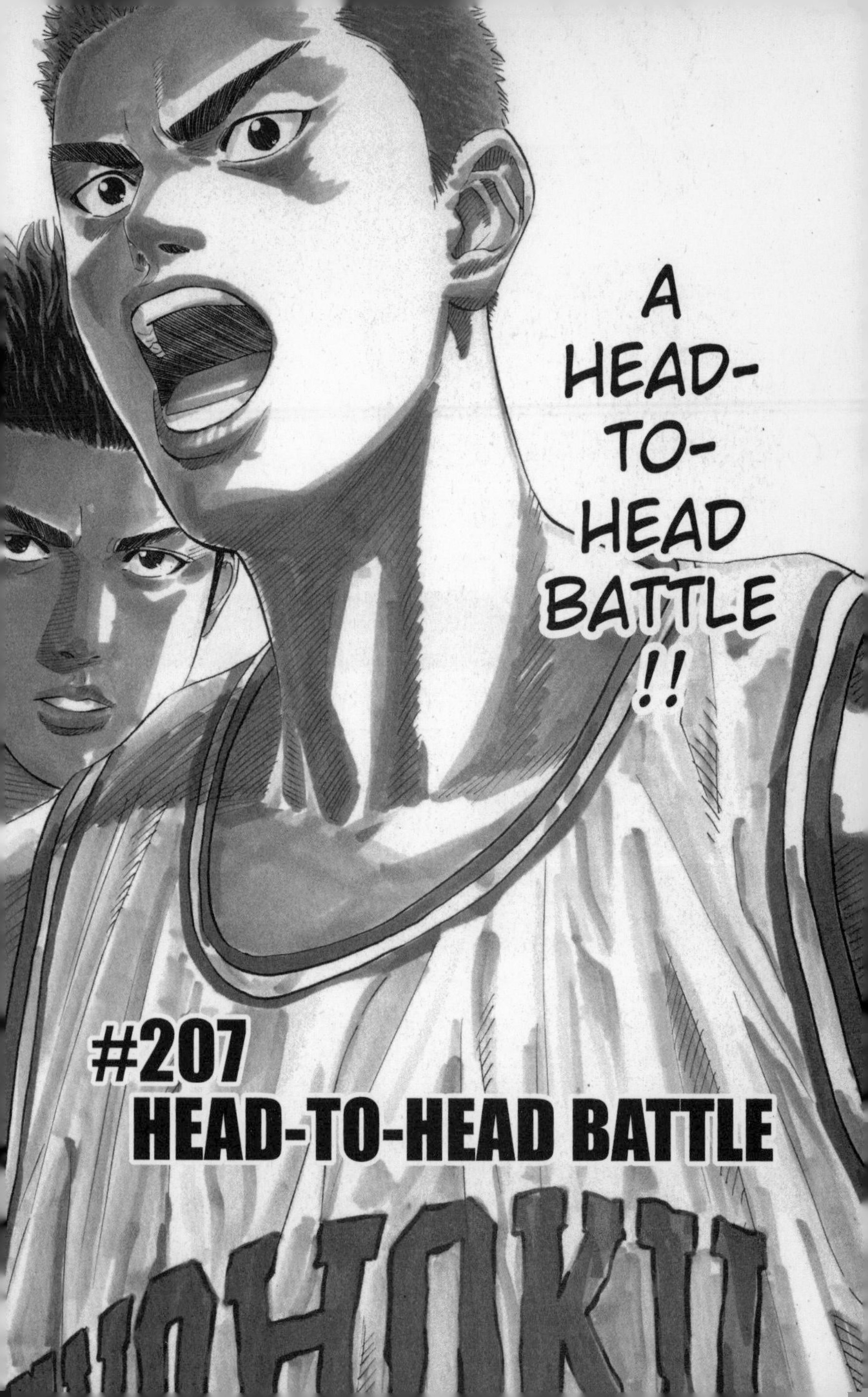
A HEAD-TO-HEAD BATTLE!!
#207
HEAD-TO-HEAD BATTLE

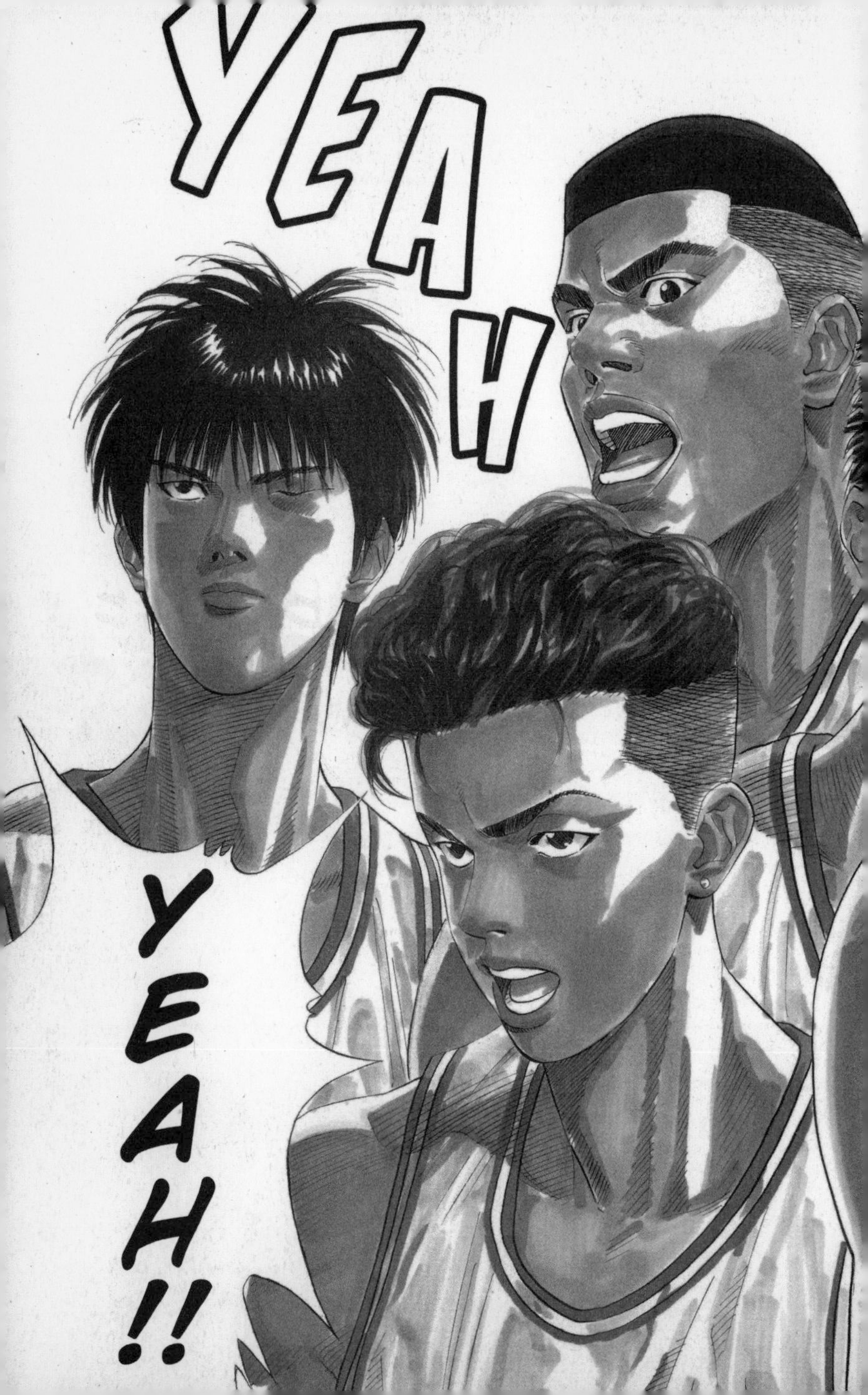
YEAH
YEAH!!

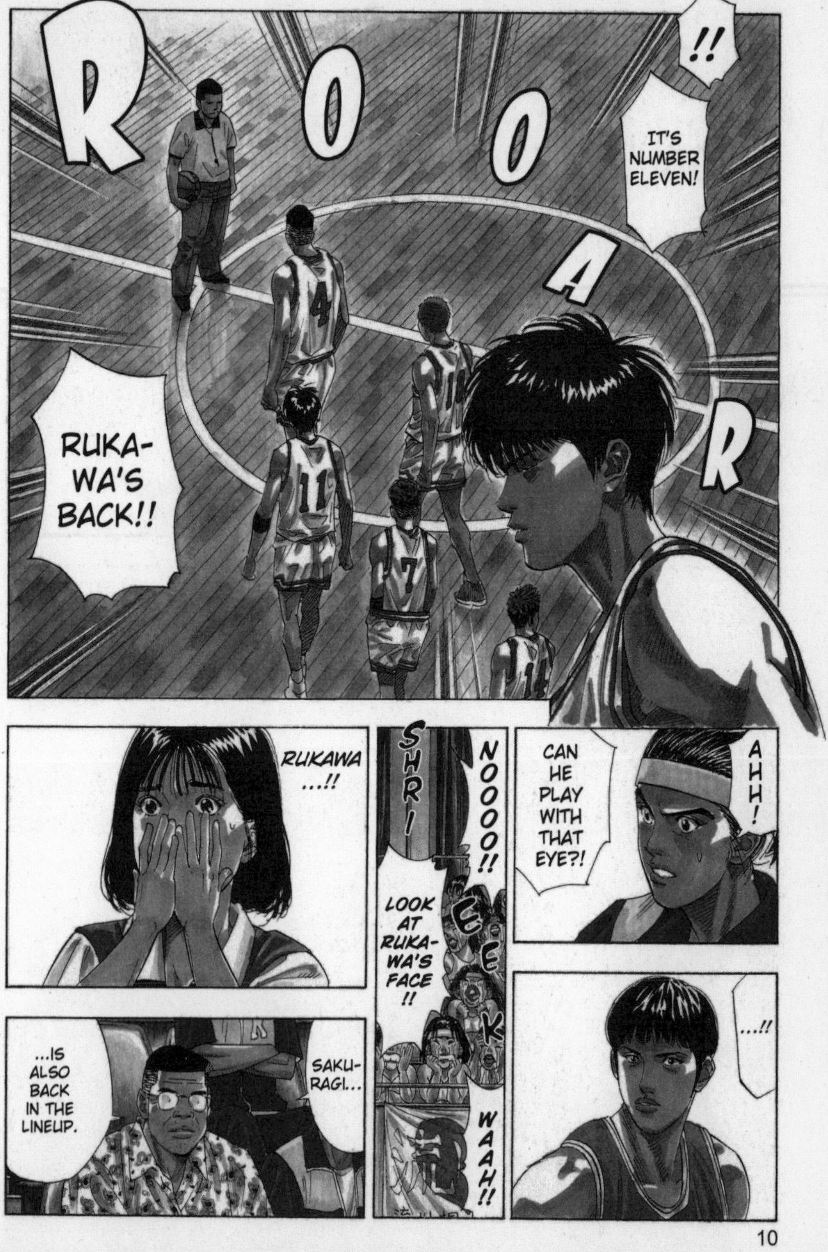
!!
IT'S NUMBER ELEVEN!
ROOOAR
RUKAWA'S BACK!!
AHH!
CAN HE PLAY WITH THAT EYE?!
...!!
NOOOOO!!
SHRI
LOOK AT RUKAWA'S FACE!!
EEEK
WAAAH!!
RUKAWA ...!!
SAKURAGI...
...IS ALSO BACK IN THE LINEUP.

READ THIS WAY

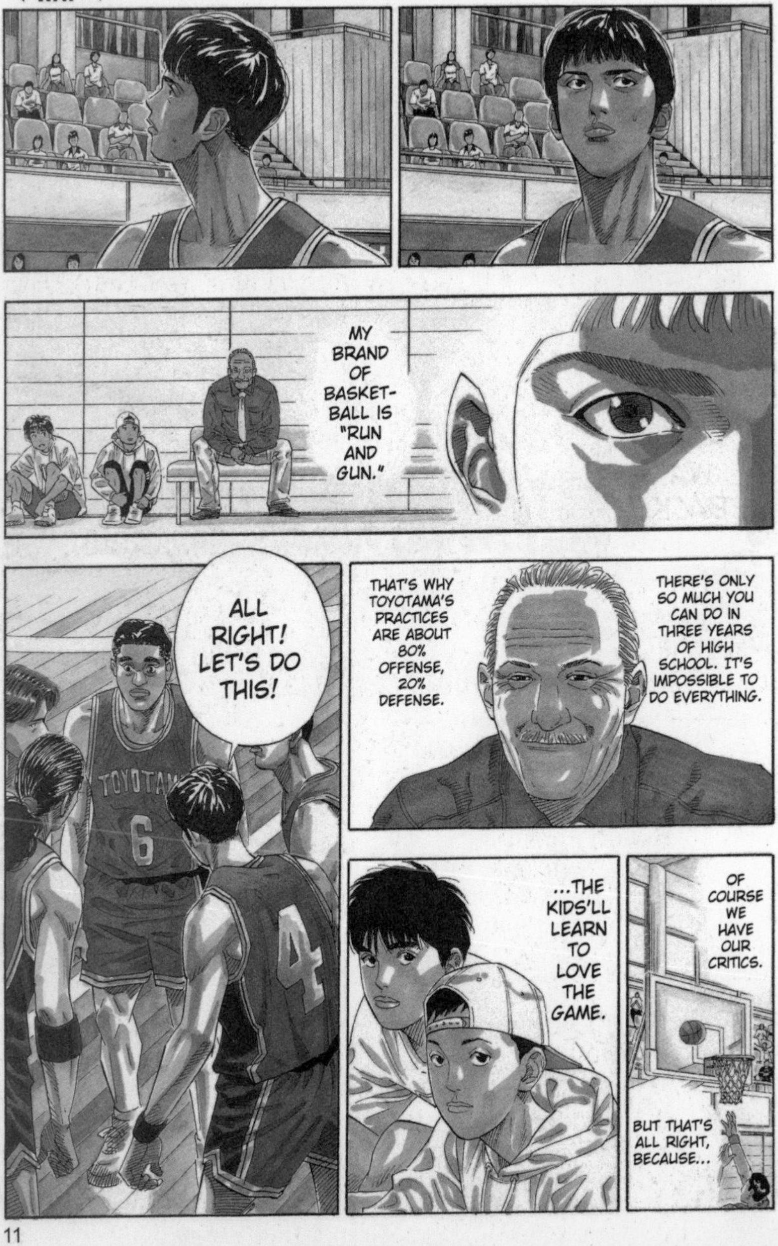
MY BRAND OF BASKET-BALL IS "RUN AND GUN."
THERE'S ONLY SO MUCH YOU CAN DO IN THREE YEARS OF HIGH SCHOOL. IT'S IMPOSSIBLE TO DO EVERYTHING.
THAT'S WHY TOYOTAMA'S PRACTICES ARE ABOUT 80% OFFENSE, 20% DEFENSE.
OF COURSE WE HAVE OUR CRITICS.
BUT THAT'S ALL RIGHT, BECAUSE...
...THE KIDS'LL LEARN TO LOVE THE GAME.
ALL RIGHT! LET'S DO THIS!
TOYOTAMA

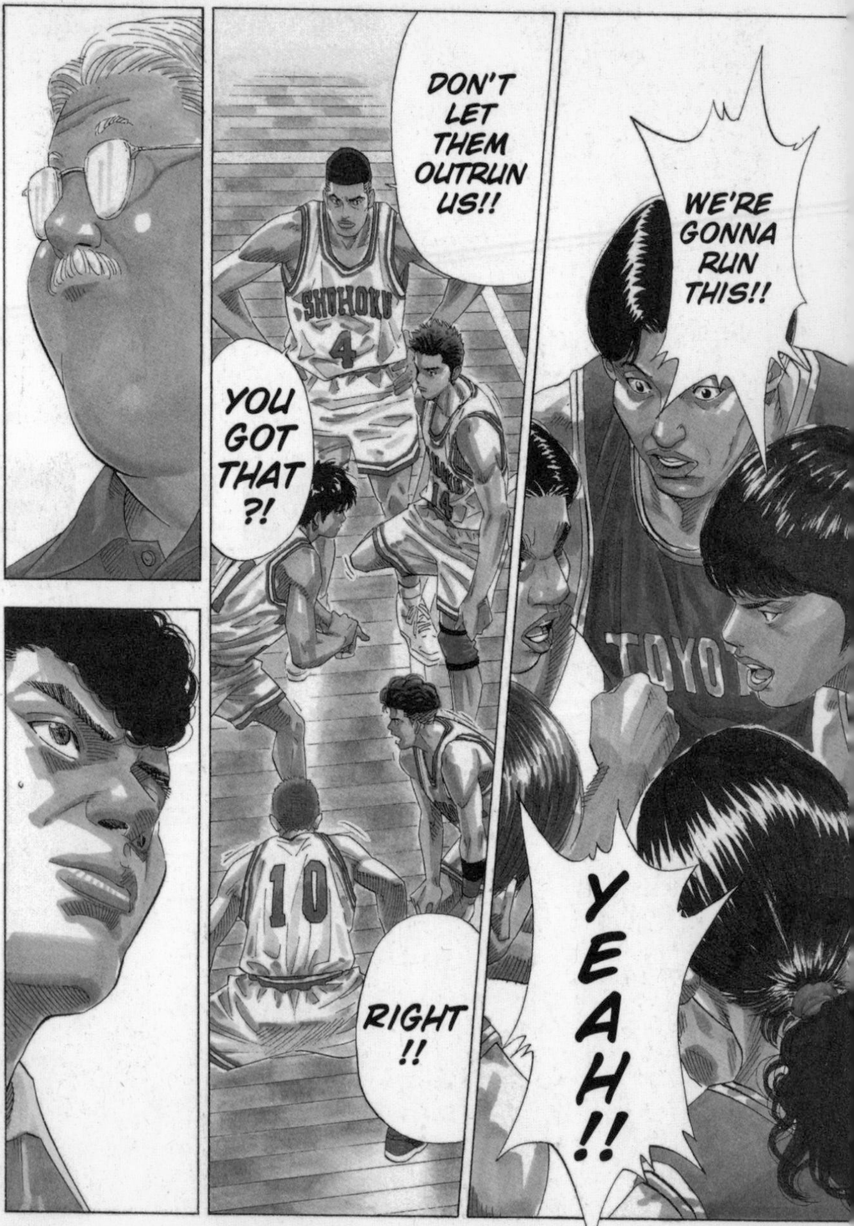
WE'RE GONNA RUN THIS!!
YEAH!!
DON'T LET THEM OUTRUN US!!
YOU GOT THAT?!
RIGHT!!

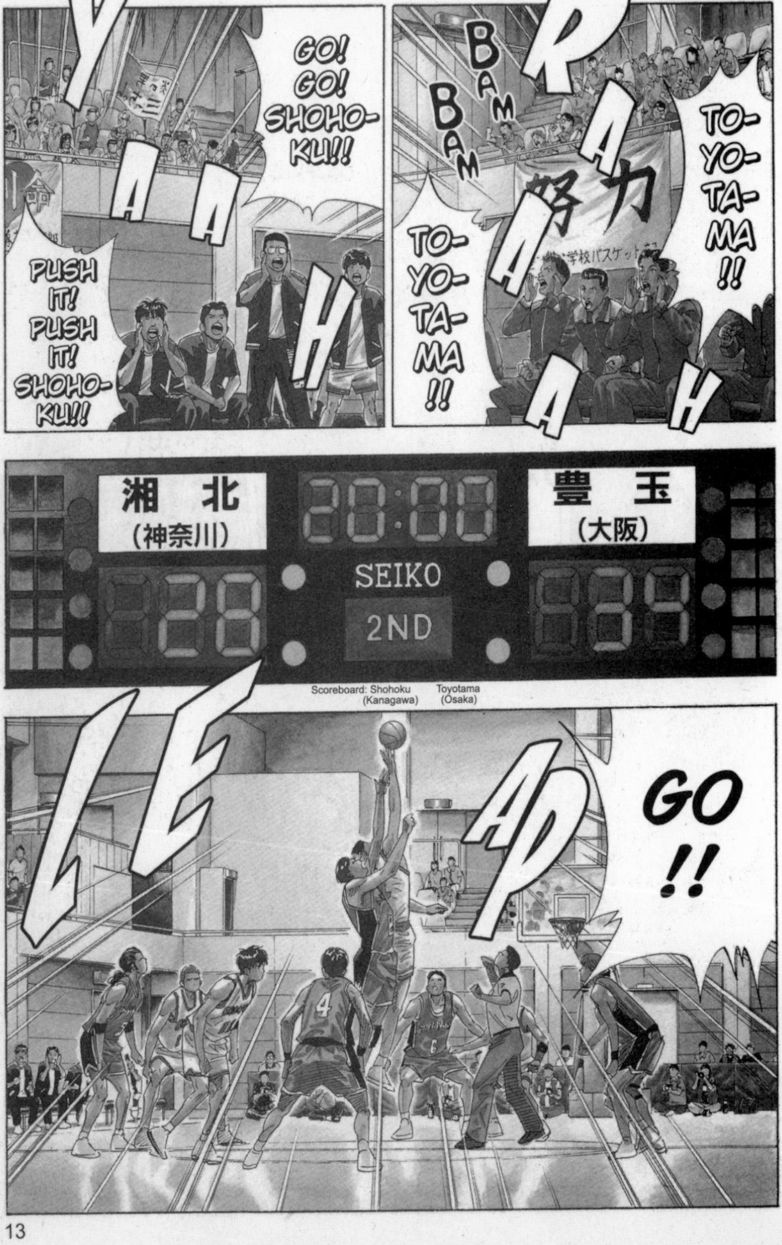
RAAAAH
BAM BAM
TO-YO-TA-MA!!
TO-YO-TA-MA!!
YAAAH
GO! GO! SHOHO-KU!!
PUSH IT! PUSH IT! SHOHO-KU!!
湘北 (神奈川)
豊玉 (大阪)
SEIKO
2ND
LEAP
GO!!

Scoreboard: Shohoku (Kanagawa) Toyotama (Osaka)

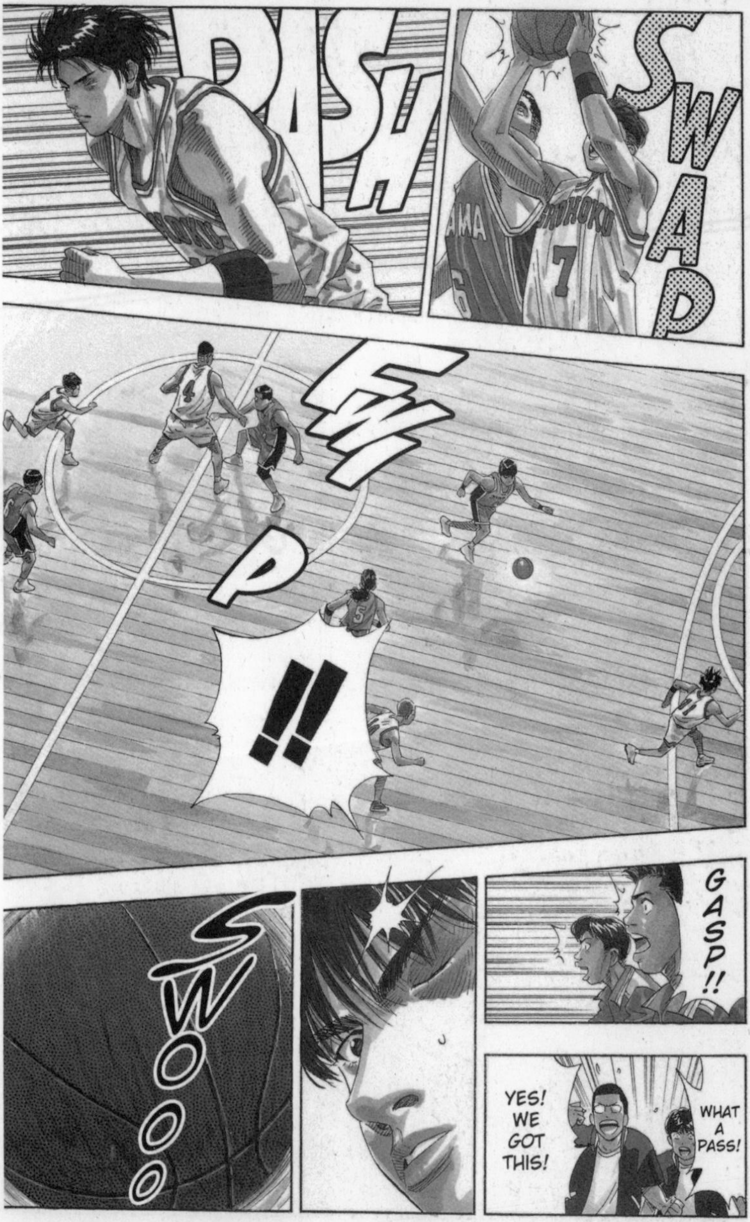
SWAP
DASH
FWIP
!!
GASP!!
WHAT A PASS!
YES! WE GOT THIS!
SWOOOO

READ THIS WAY

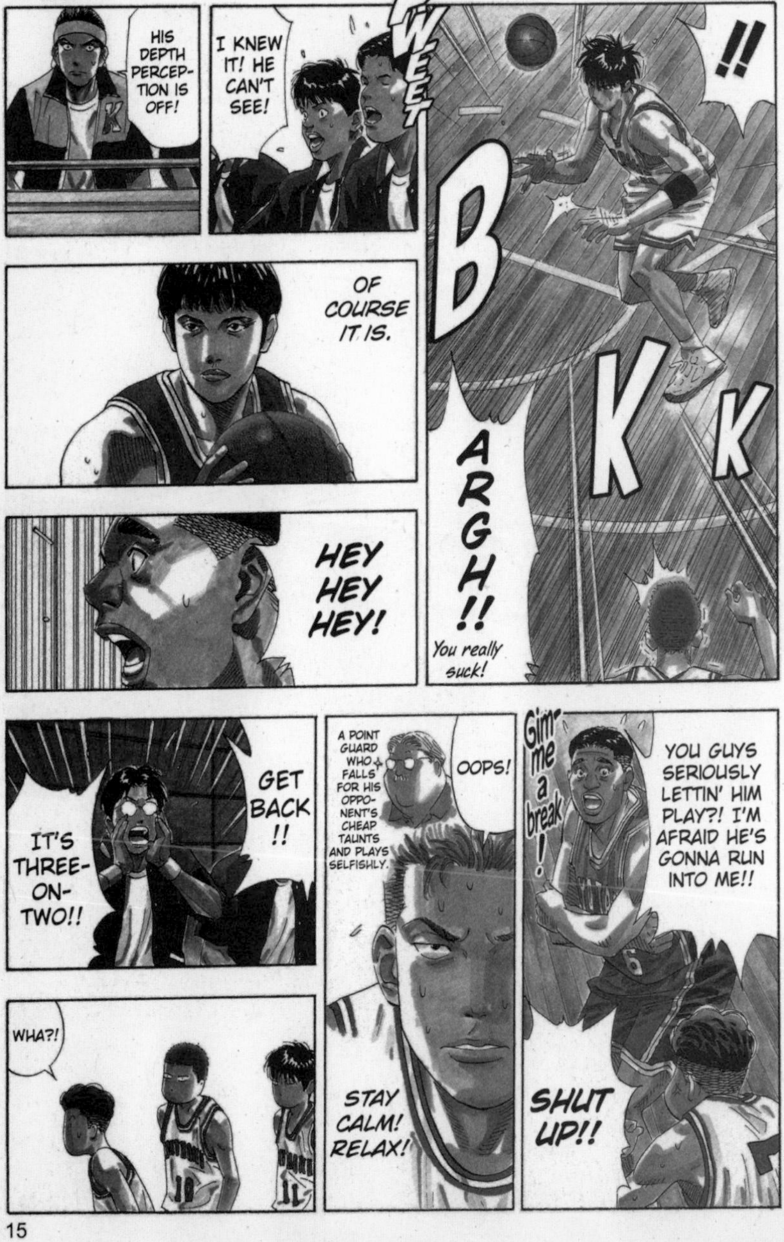
FWEET
!!
BAKK K
ARGH!!
You really suck!
I KNEW IT! HE CAN'T SEE!
HIS DEPTH PERCEPTION IS OFF!
OF COURSE IT IS.
HEY HEY HEY!
YOU GUYS SERIOUSLY LETTIN' HIM PLAY?! I'M AFRAID HE'S GONNA RUN INTO ME!!
Gimme a break!
SHUT UP!!
OOPS!
A POINT GUARD WHO FALLS FOR HIS OPPONENT'S CHEAP TAUNTS AND PLAYS SELFISHLY.
STAY CALM! RELAX!
GET BACK!!
IT'S THREE-ON-TWO!!
WHA?!

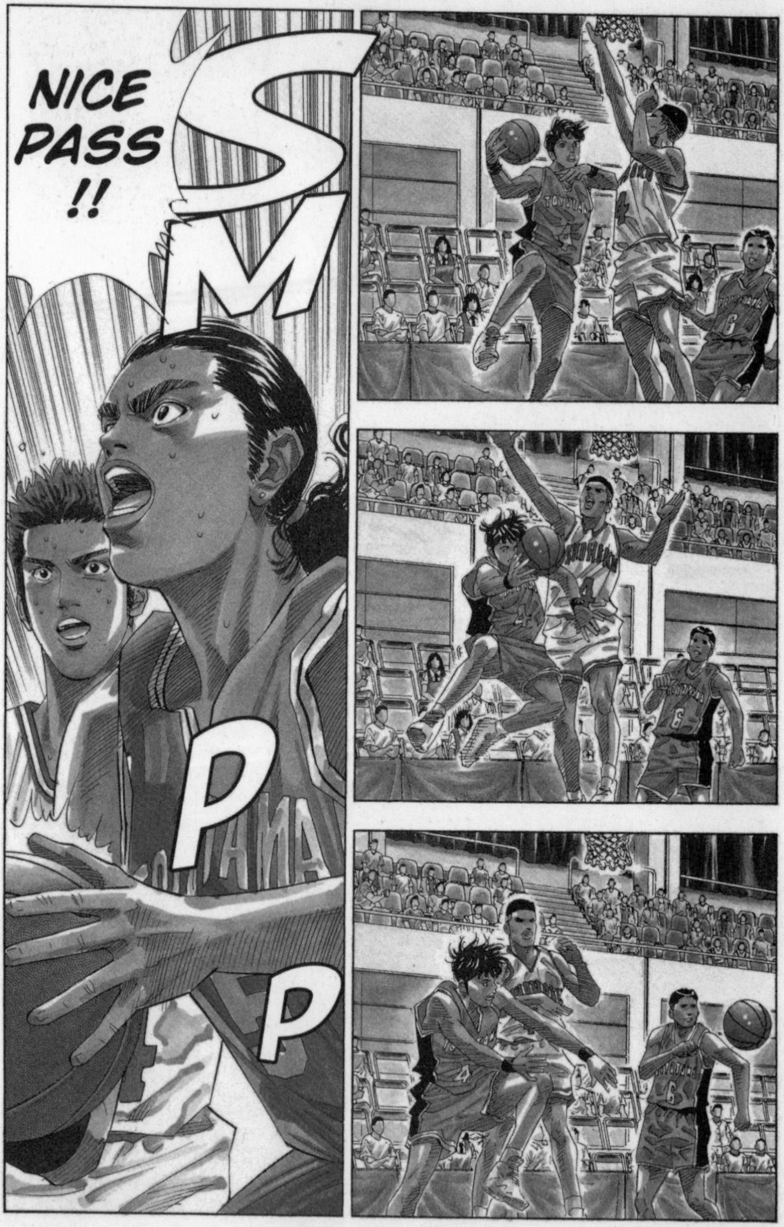
SM
PP
NICE PASS !!

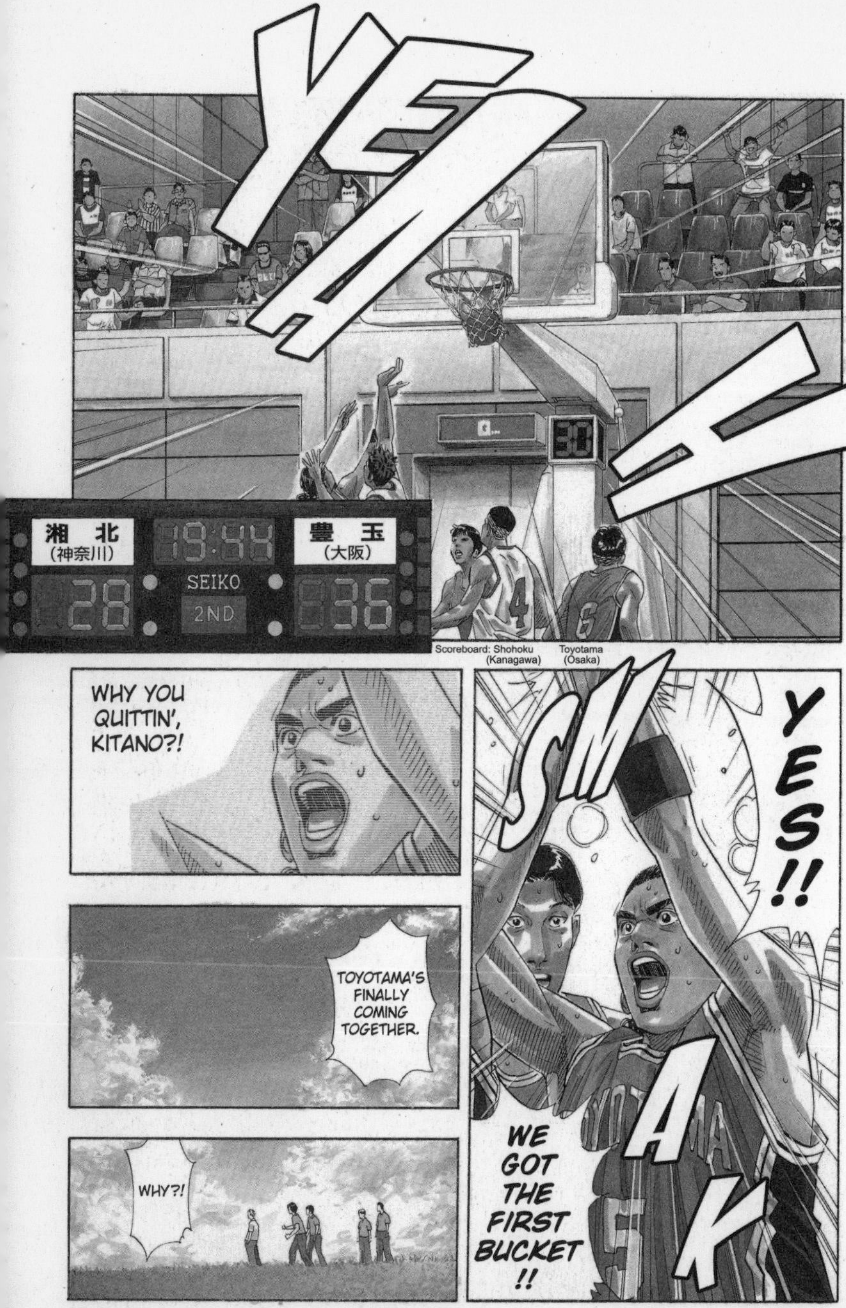
YEAH
湘北
(神奈川)
19:44
豊玉
(大阪)
28
SEIKO
2ND
36
Scoreboard: Shohoku (Kanagawa) Toyotama (Osaka)
SMAK
YES!!
WE GOT THE FIRST BUCKET!!
WHY YOU QUITTIN', KITANO?!
TOYOTAMA'S FINALLY COMING TOGETHER.
WHY?!

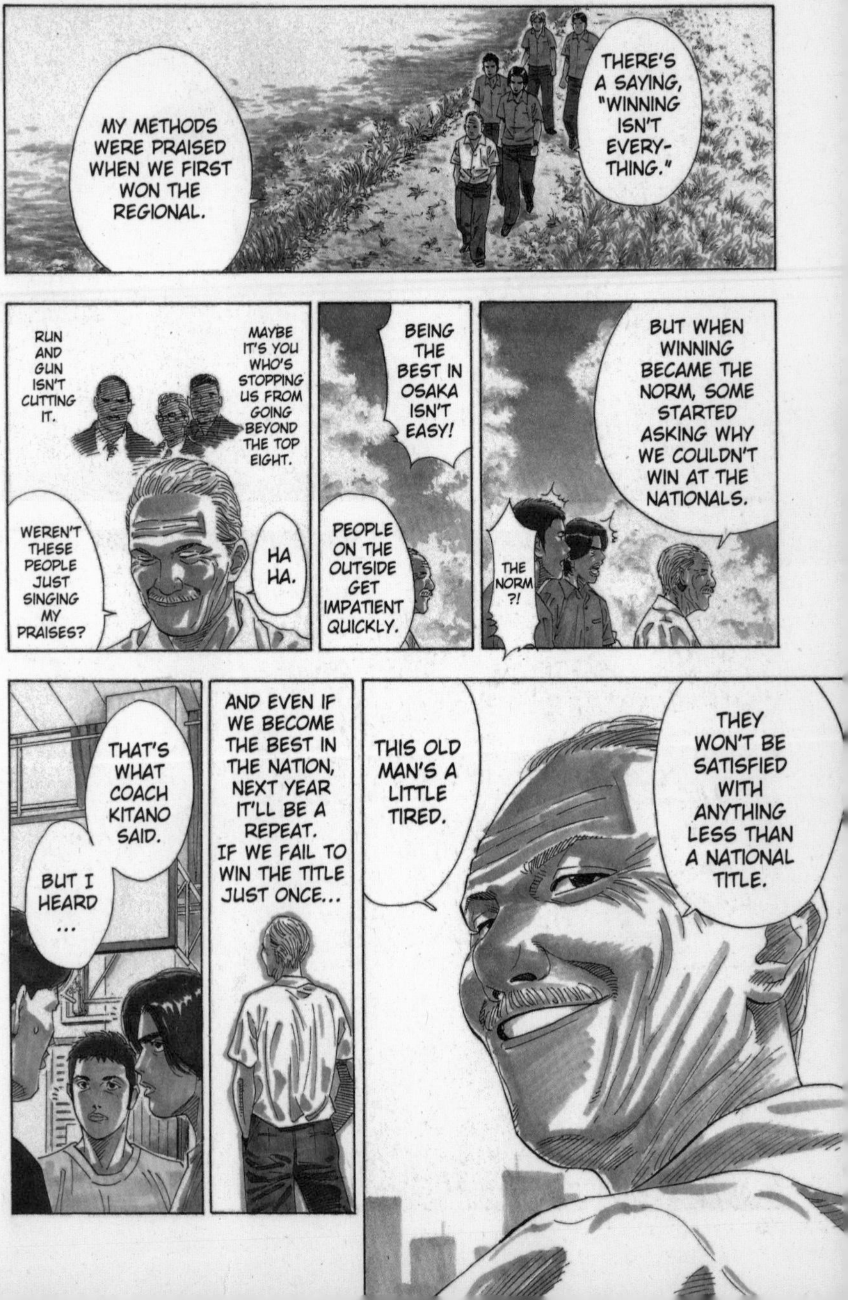
THERE'S A SAYING, "WINNING ISN'T EVERYTHING."
MY METHODS WERE PRAISED WHEN WE FIRST WON THE REGIONAL.
BUT WHEN WINNING BECAME THE NORM, SOME STARTED ASKING WHY WE COULDN'T WIN AT THE NATIONALS.
THE NORM ?!
BEING THE BEST IN OSAKA ISN'T EASY!
PEOPLE ON THE OUTSIDE GET IMPATIENT QUICKLY.
MAYBE IT'S YOU WHO'S STOPPING US FROM GOING BEYOND THE TOP EIGHT.
RUN AND GUN ISN'T CUTTING IT.
HA HA.
WEREN'T THESE PEOPLE JUST SINGING MY PRAISES?
THEY WON'T BE SATISFIED WITH ANYTHING LESS THAN A NATIONAL TITLE.
THIS OLD MAN'S A LITTLE TIRED.
AND EVEN IF WE BECOME THE BEST IN THE NATION, NEXT YEAR IT'LL BE A REPEAT. IF WE FAIL TO WIN THE TITLE JUST ONCE...
THAT'S WHAT COACH KITANO SAID.
BUT I HEARD ...

READ THIS WAY

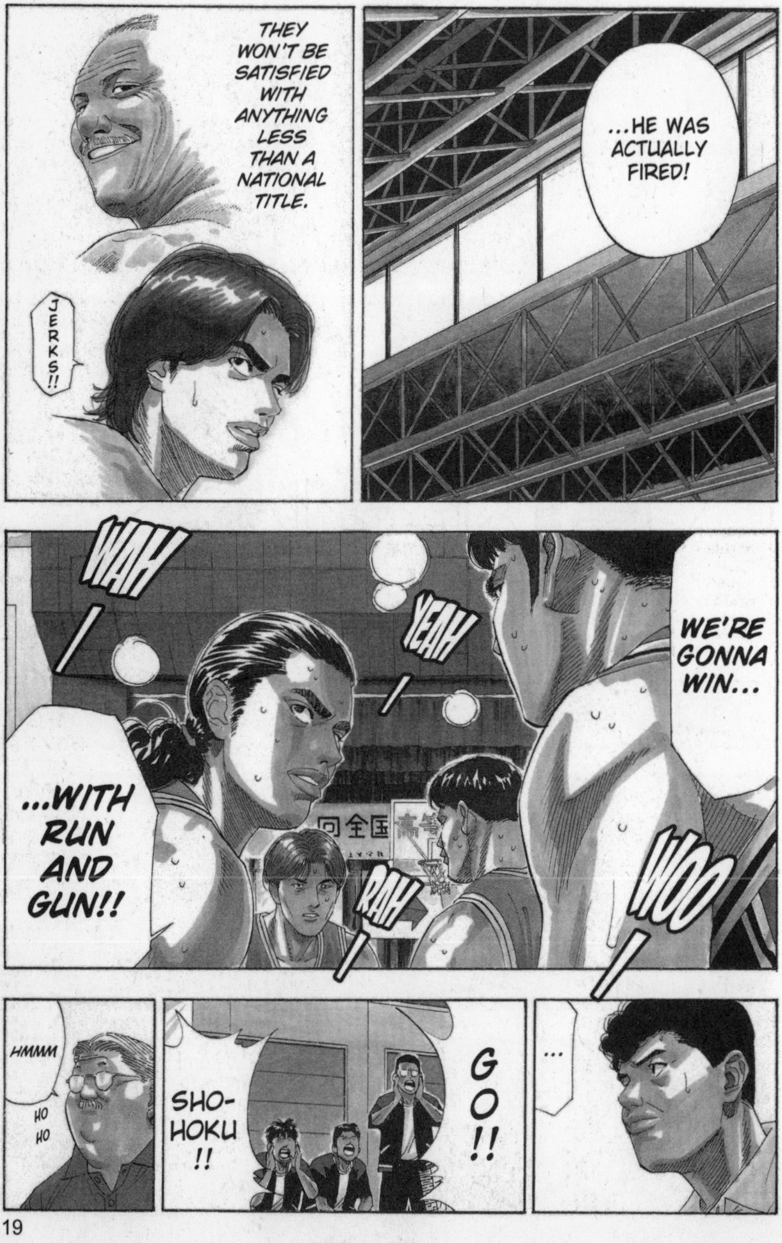
...HE WAS ACTUALLY FIRED!
THEY WON'T BE SATISFIED WITH ANYTHING LESS THAN A NATIONAL TITLE.
JERKS!!
WE'RE GONNA WIN...
YEAH
WAH
WOO
...WITH RUN AND GUN!!
RAH
...
GO!!
SHO-HOKU!!
HMMM
HO HO

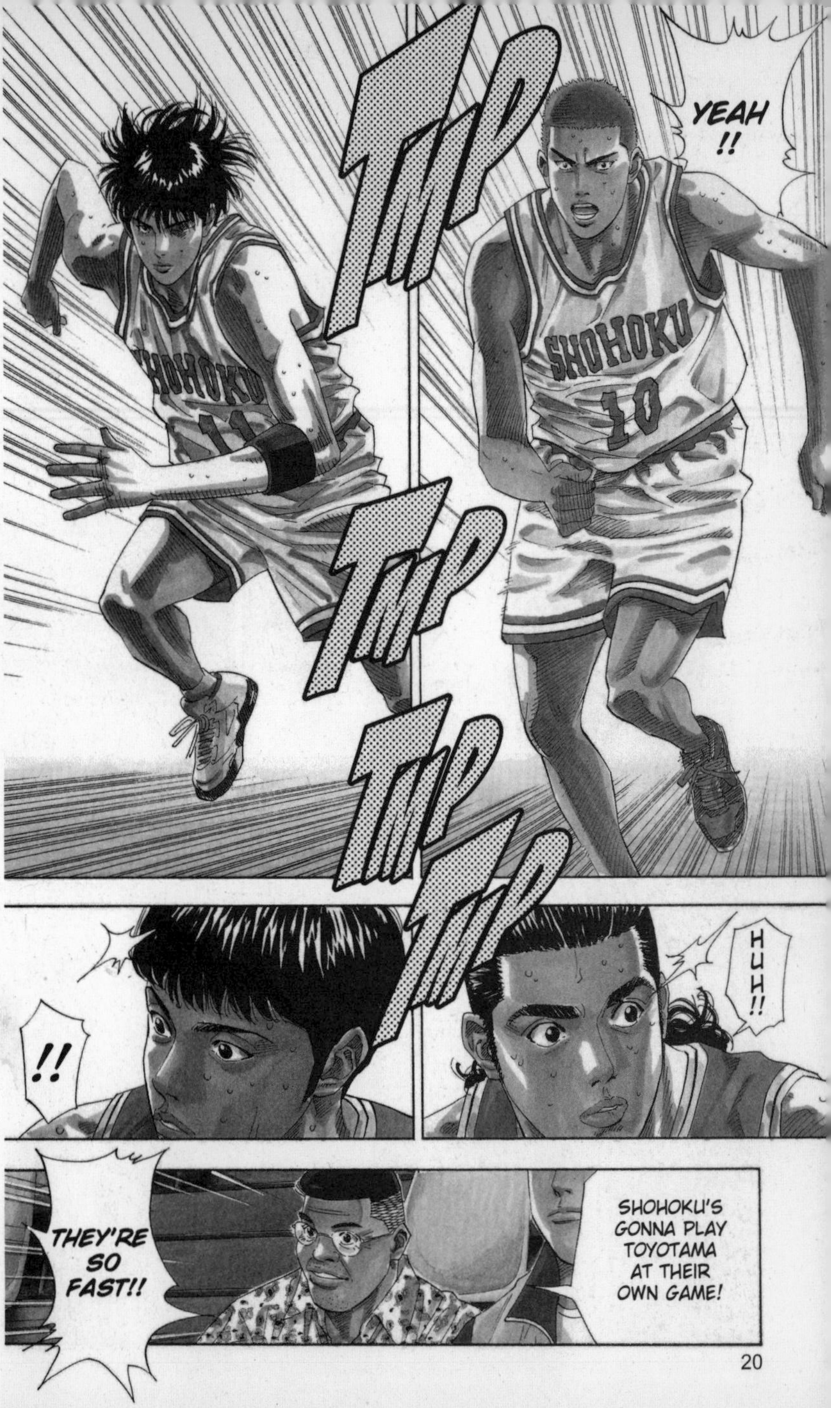
YEAH !!
TMP
TMP
TMP
TMP
HUH!!
!!
SHOHOKU'S GONNA PLAY TOYOTAMA AT THEIR OWN GAME!
THEY'RE SO FAST!!

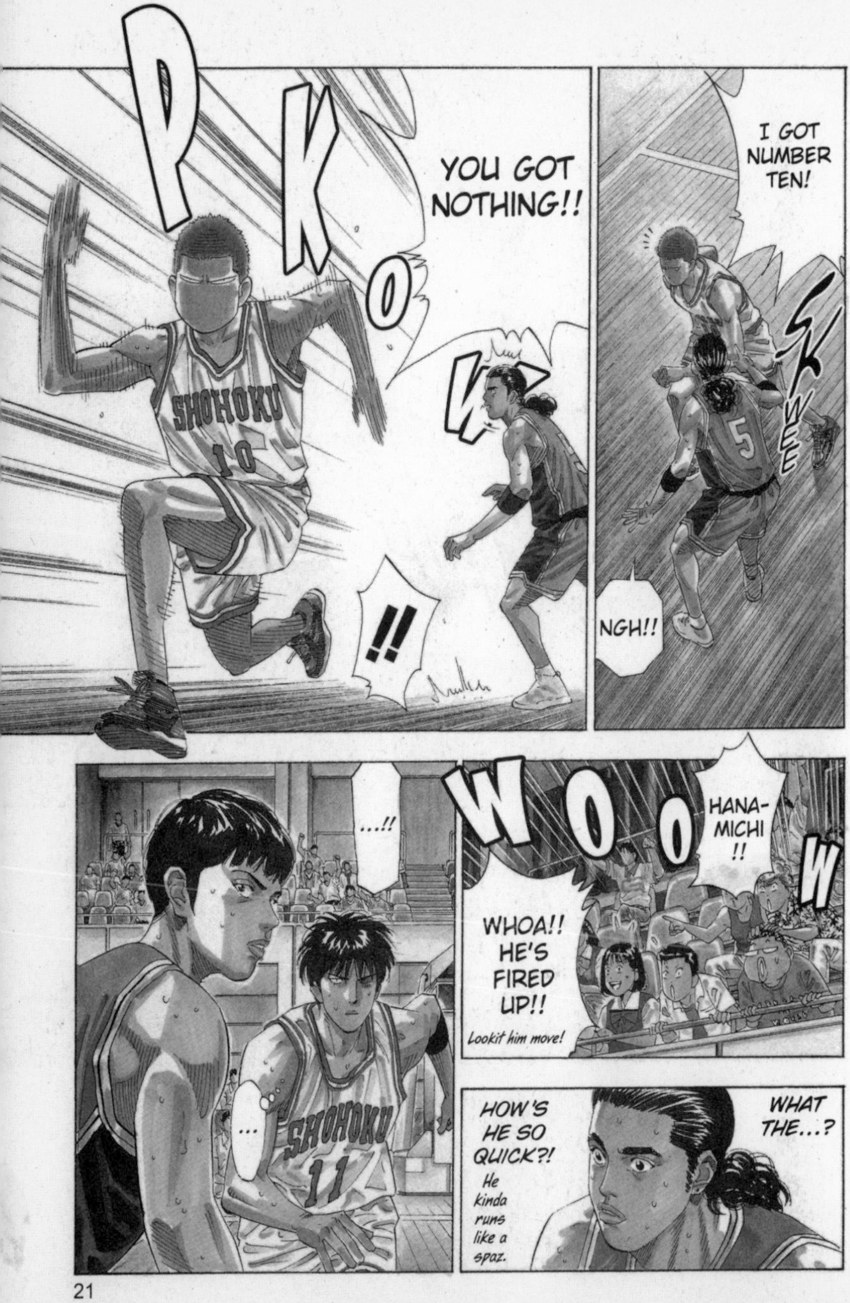
I GOT NUMBER TEN!
SKWEE
NGH!!
PKO
YOU GOT NOTHING!!
WK
!!
HANA-MICHI!!
WOOOW
WHOA!! HE'S FIRED UP!!
Lookit him move!
WHAT THE...?
HOW'S HE SO QUICK?!
He kinda runs like a spaz.
...!!
...

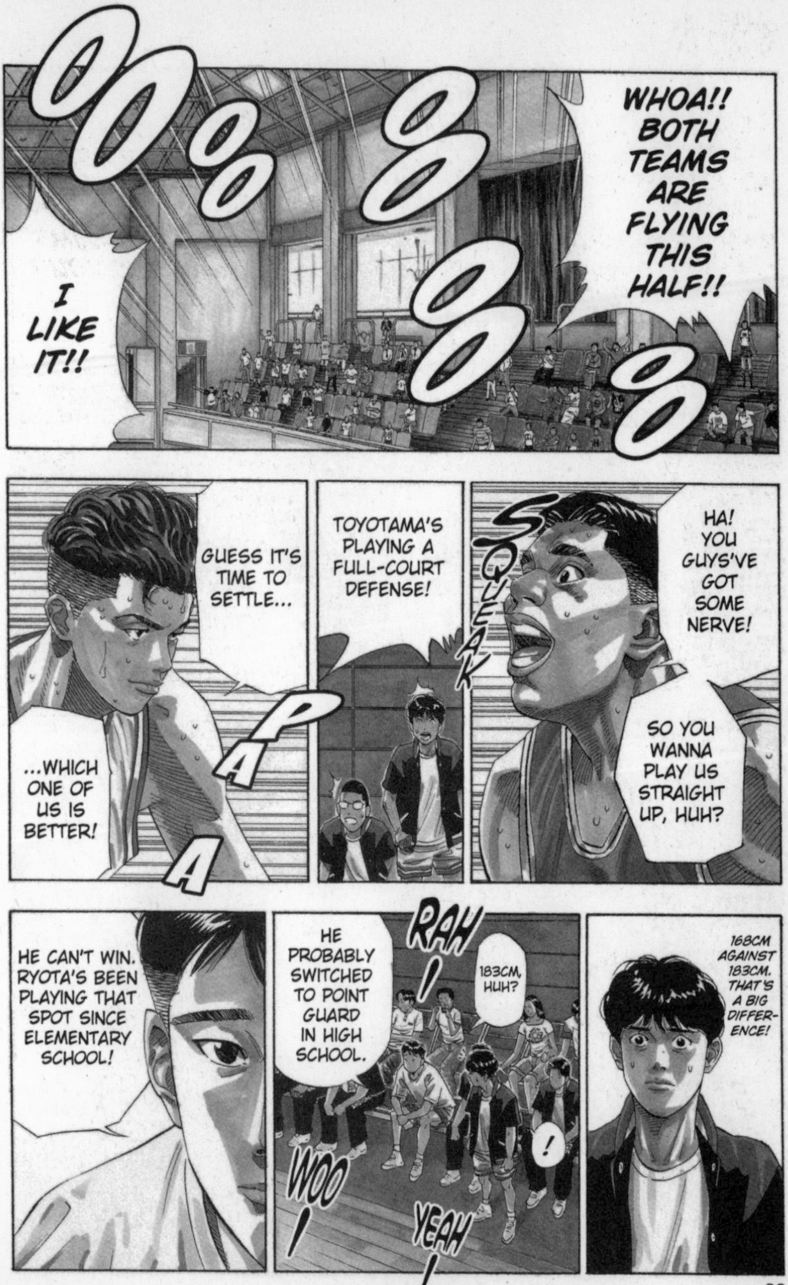

WHOA!! BOTH TEAMS ARE FLYING THIS HALF!!
I LIKE IT!!
HA! YOU GUYS'VE GOT SOME NERVE!
SQUEAK
SO YOU WANNA PLAY US STRAIGHT UP, HUH?
TOYOTAMA'S PLAYING A FULL-COURT DEFENSE!
GUESS IT'S TIME TO SETTLE...
PAA
...WHICH ONE OF US IS BETTER!
168CM AGAINST 183CM. THAT'S A BIG DIFFERENCE!
RAH!
183CM, HUH?
HE PROBABLY SWITCHED TO POINT GUARD IN HIGH SCHOOL.
!
WOO!
YEAH!
HE CAN'T WIN. RYOTA'S BEEN PLAYING THAT SPOT SINCE ELEMENTARY SCHOOL!

READ THIS WAY

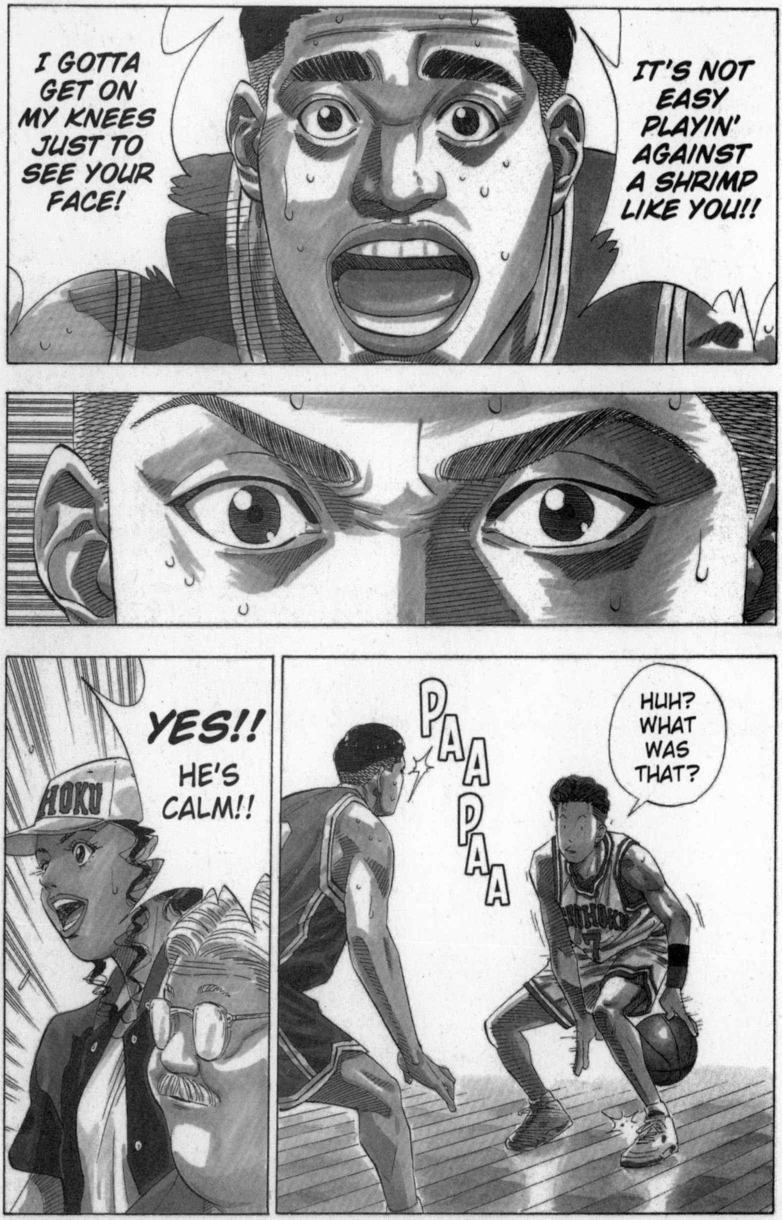
IT'S NOT EASY PLAYIN' AGAINST A SHRIMP LIKE YOU!!
I GOTTA GET ON MY KNEES JUST TO SEE YOUR FACE!
HUH? WHAT WAS THAT?
PAAAPAAA
YES!!
HE'S CALM!!

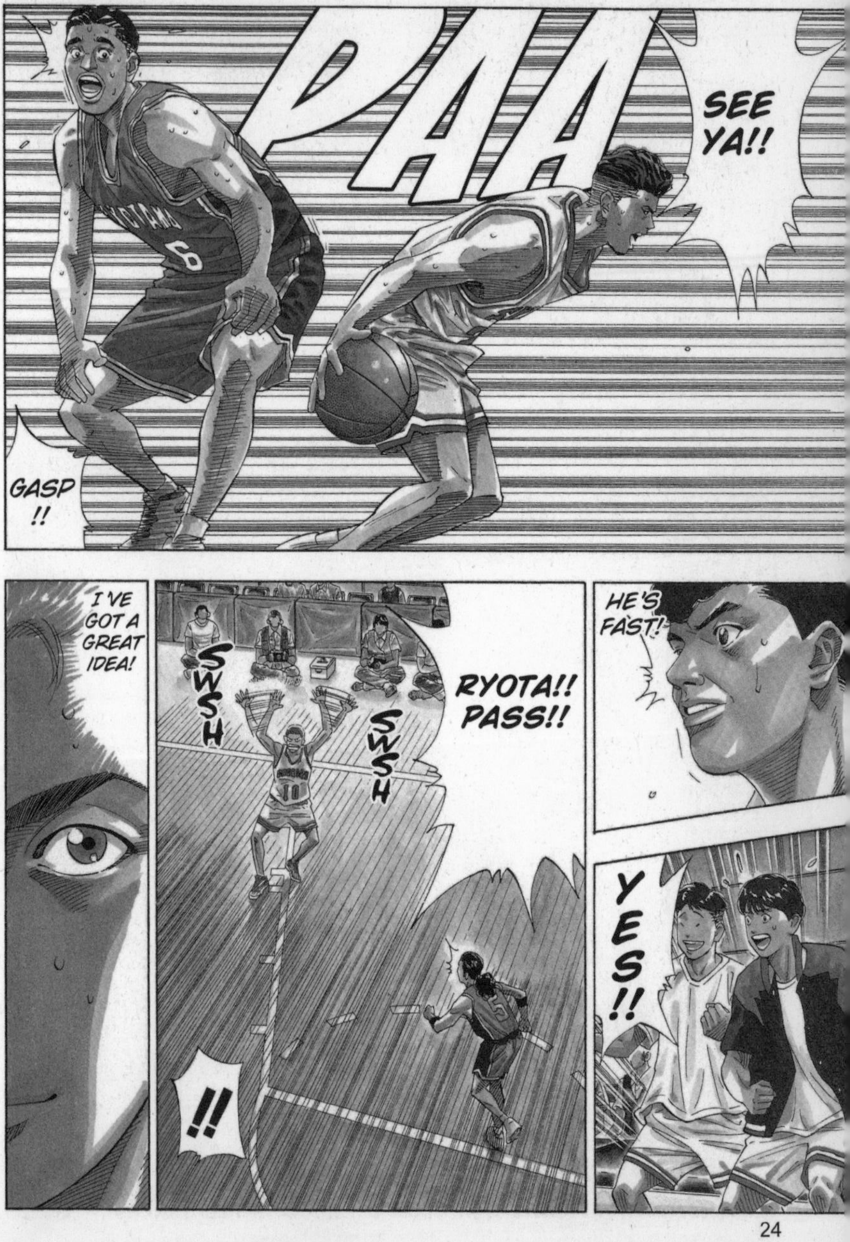
SEE YA!!
GASP !!
HE'S FAST!
YES!!
RYOTA!! PASS!!
SWSH
SWSH
!!
I'VE GOT A GREAT IDEA!

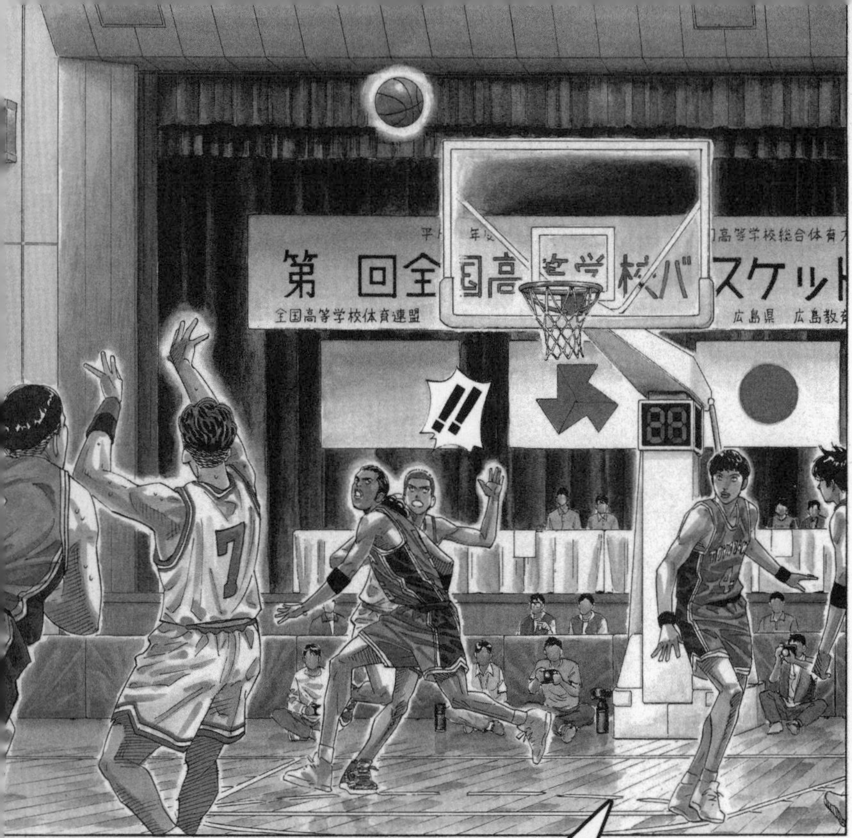
全国高等学校体育連盟
!!

Sign: National High School Basketball Championship Tournament

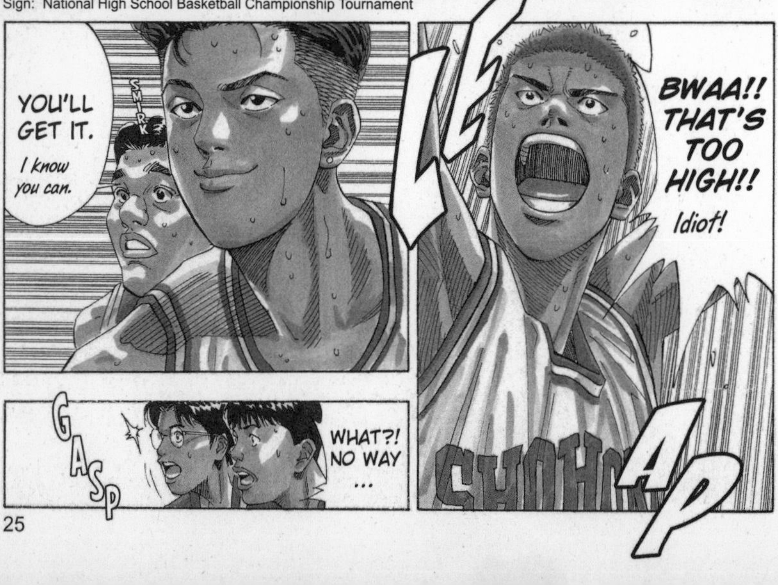
BWAA!! THAT'S TOO HIGH!!
Idiot!
AP
YOU'LL GET IT.
I know you can.
SMIRK
GASP
WHAT?! NO WAY ...

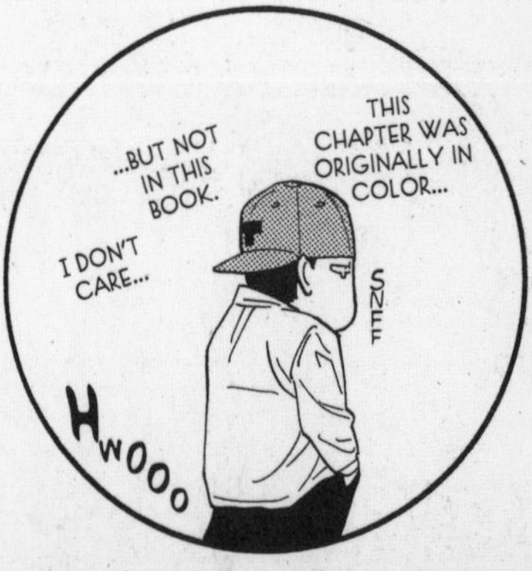
THIS CHAPTER WAS ORIGINALLY IN COLOR...
...BUT NOT IN THIS BOOK.
SNFF
I DON'T CARE...
HWOOO

SLAM DUNK

PROOF OF AN ACE

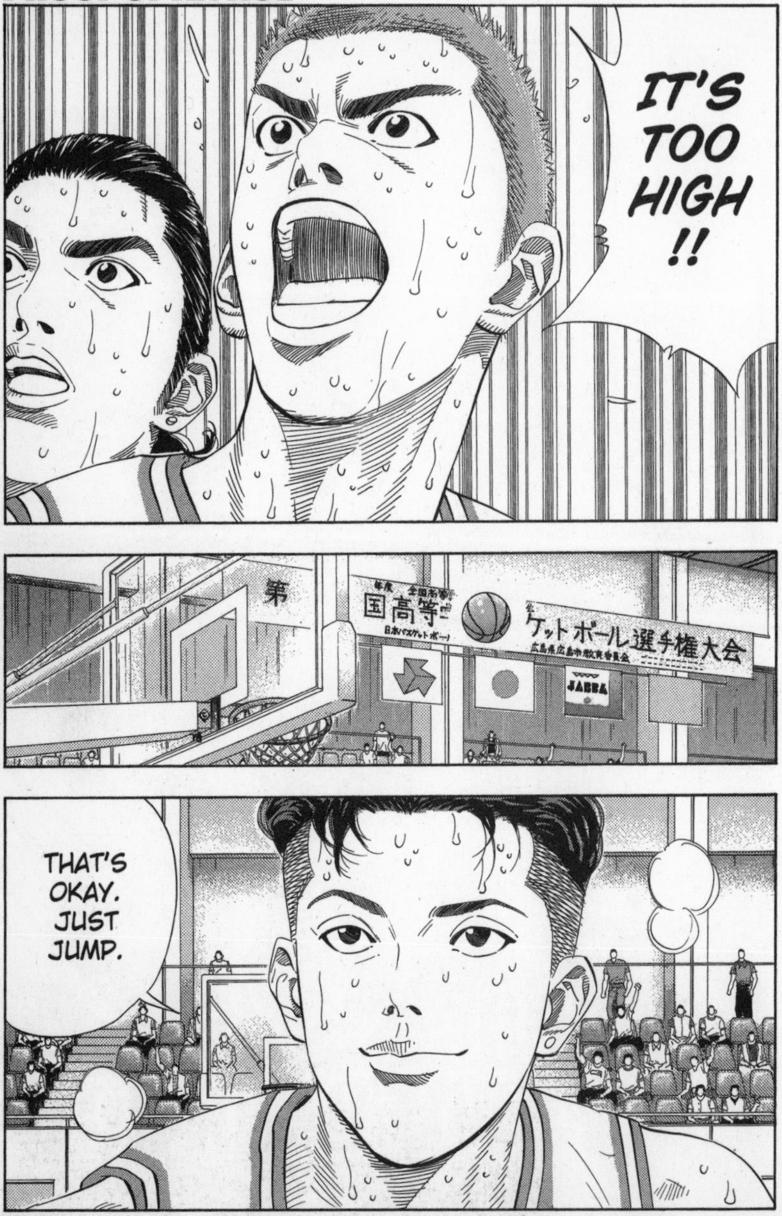
IT'S TOO HIGH!!
第
国高等
ケットボール選手権大会
JABBA
THAT'S OKAY. JUST JUMP.

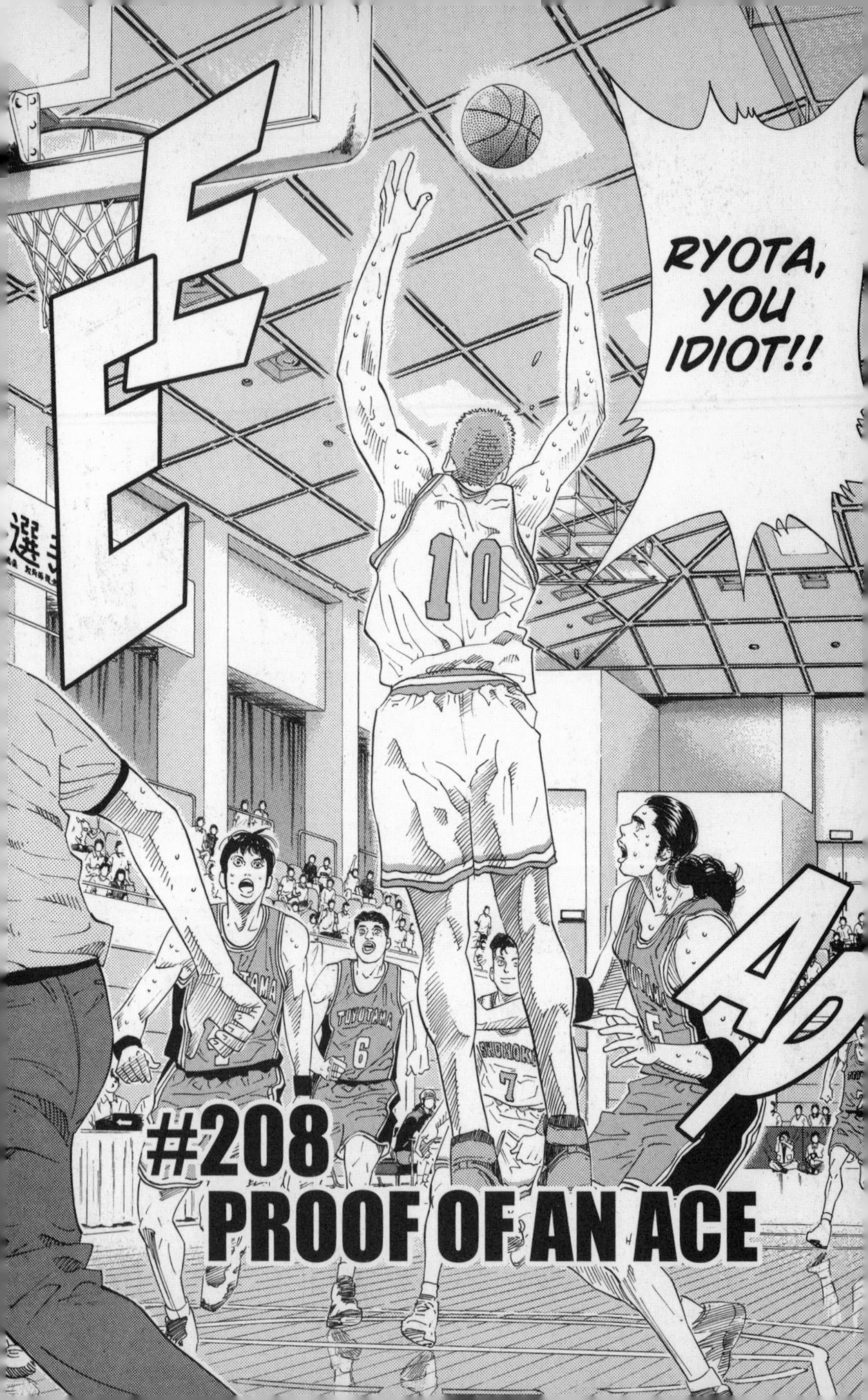
RYOTA, YOU IDIOT!!

#208 PROOF OF AN ACE

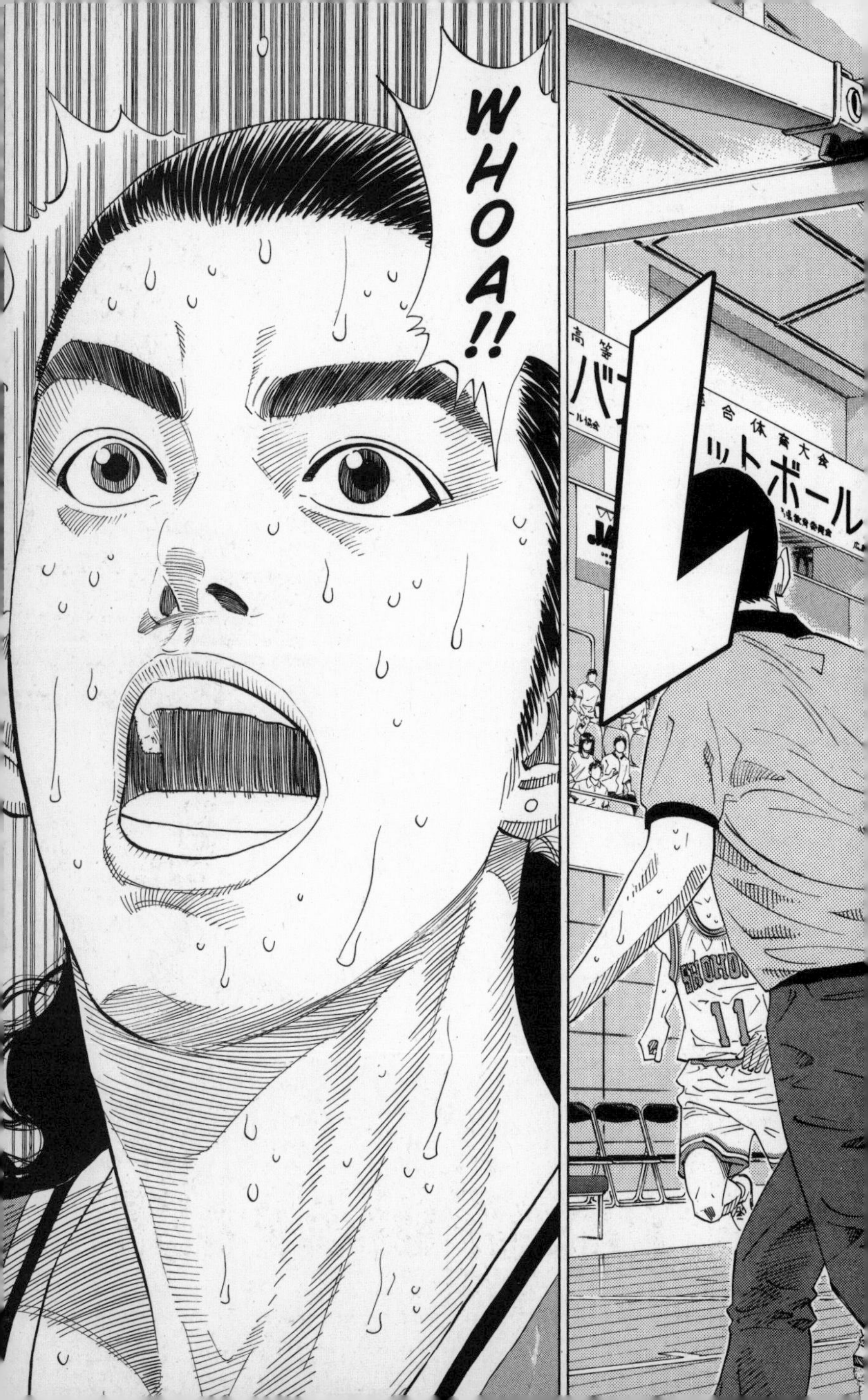
WHOA!!

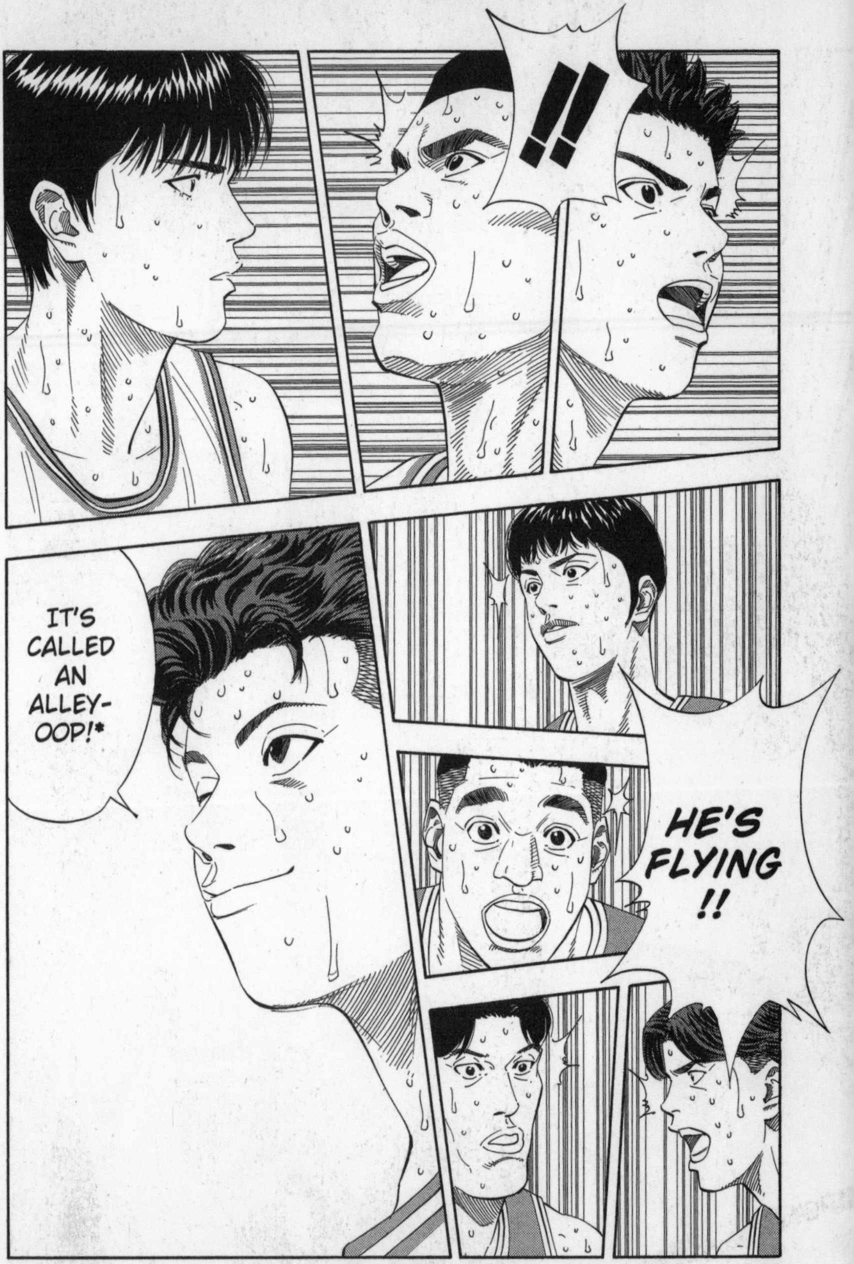
!!
HE'S FLYING !!
IT'S CALLED AN ALLEY-OOP!*

* ALLEY-OOP: TO CATCH A PASS THROWN ABOVE THE BASKET AND DUNK IT IN A SINGLE MOVE.

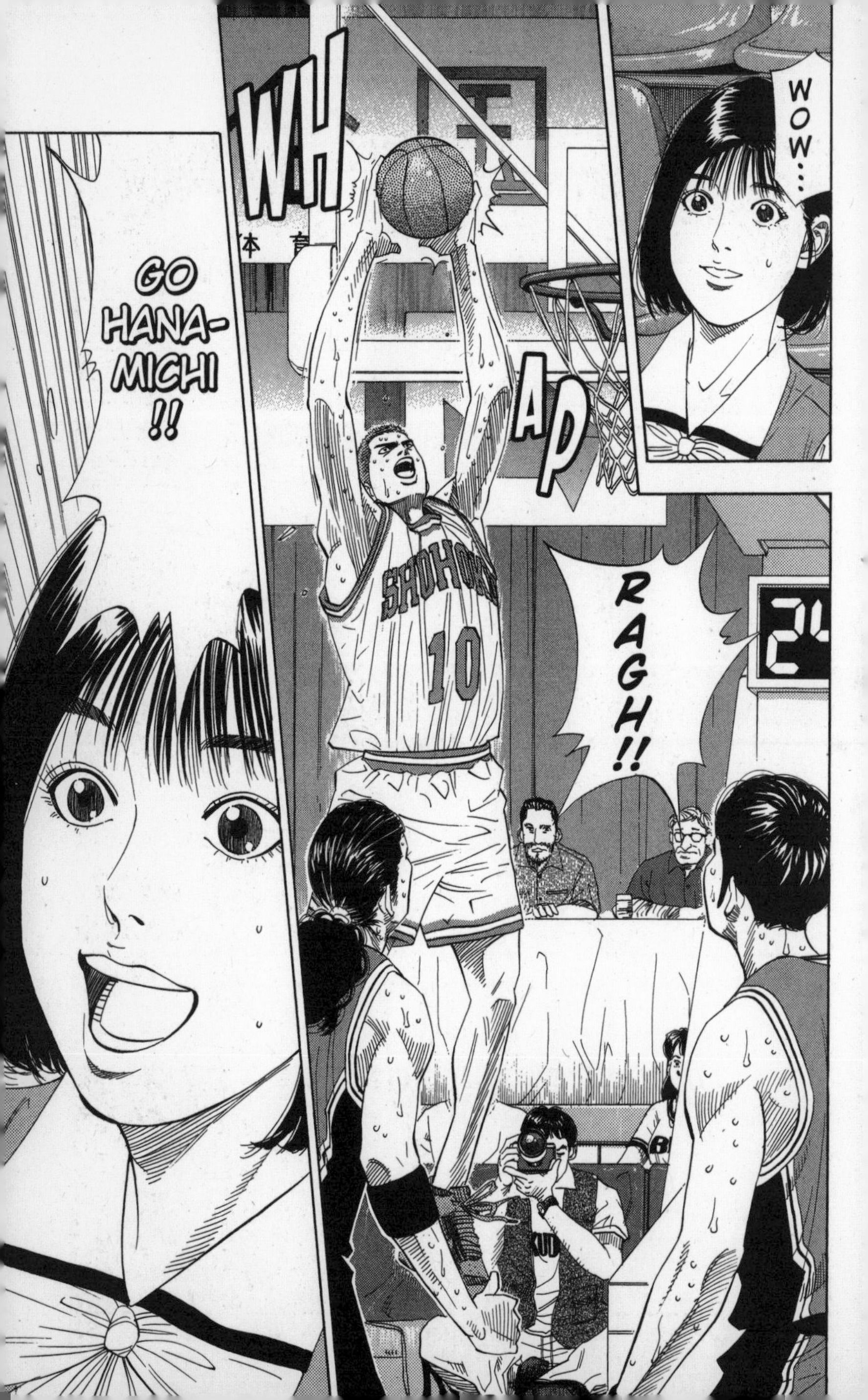
WOW...
WHAP
RAGH!!
GO HANA-MICHI!!

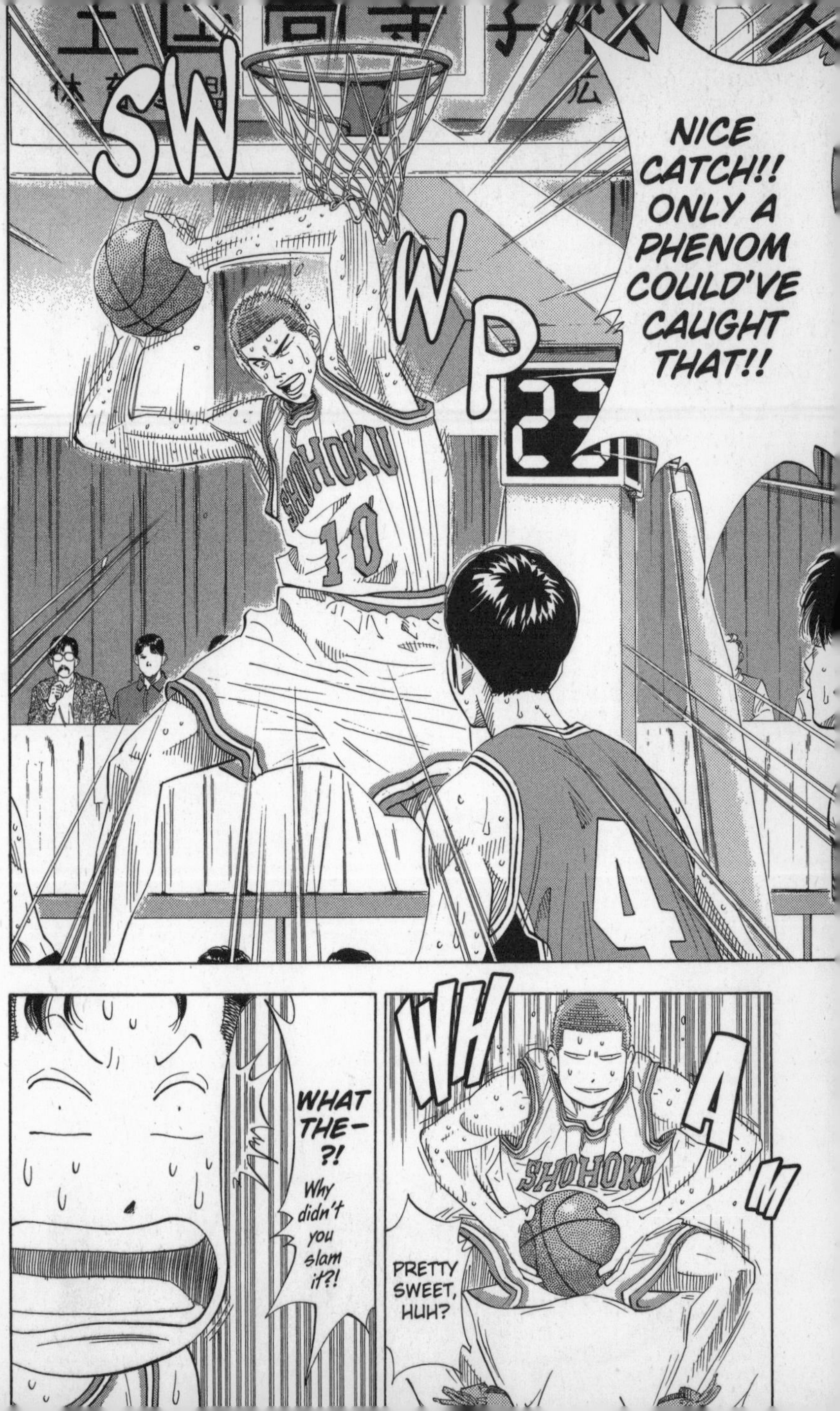
NICE CATCH!! ONLY A PHENOM COULD'VE CAUGHT THAT!!
SW
WP
WH
A
M
PRETTY SWEET, HUH?
WHAT THE-?!
Why didn't you slam it?!

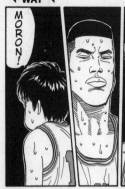

READ THIS WAY

GASP!!
!!
MORON!
BENEATH THE BASKET SHOT!
FWEET FWEET FWEET
HMPH!
YES!! IT'S IN!!
GOAL-TENDING!!
HUH?!
GOALTENDING (OFFENSIVE)
WHETHER IT'S A SHOT OR A PASS, ONCE THE BALL IS ON A DOWNWARD FLIGHT AFTER IT HAS REACHED ITS HIGHEST POINT, IT MAY NOT BE TOUCHED ABOVE THE RIM.
THAT'S RIGHT.
HAVE I MENTIONED THIS RULE BEFORE?
DR. T'S HANDY BASKETBALL TIPS
ACCORDING TO THIS RULE, AN ALLEY-OOP SHOULD BE ILLEGAL.
I HEAR IT'S TACITLY APPROVED.
CUZ IT'D BE BORING OTHERWISE.
BEARDED VERSION

※ IN 1995 A NEW RULE SAID THAT IF IT IS A PASSED BALL IT MAY BE TOUCHED. IN OTHER WORDS, THE ALLEY-OOP IS LEGAL.

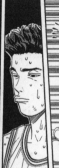

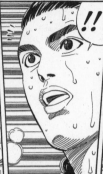

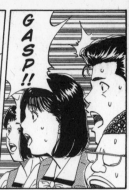

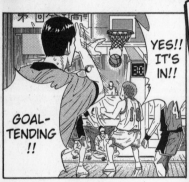

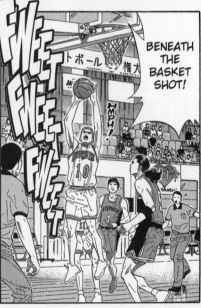

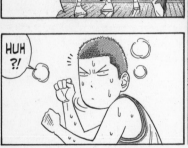

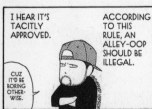

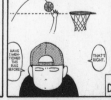

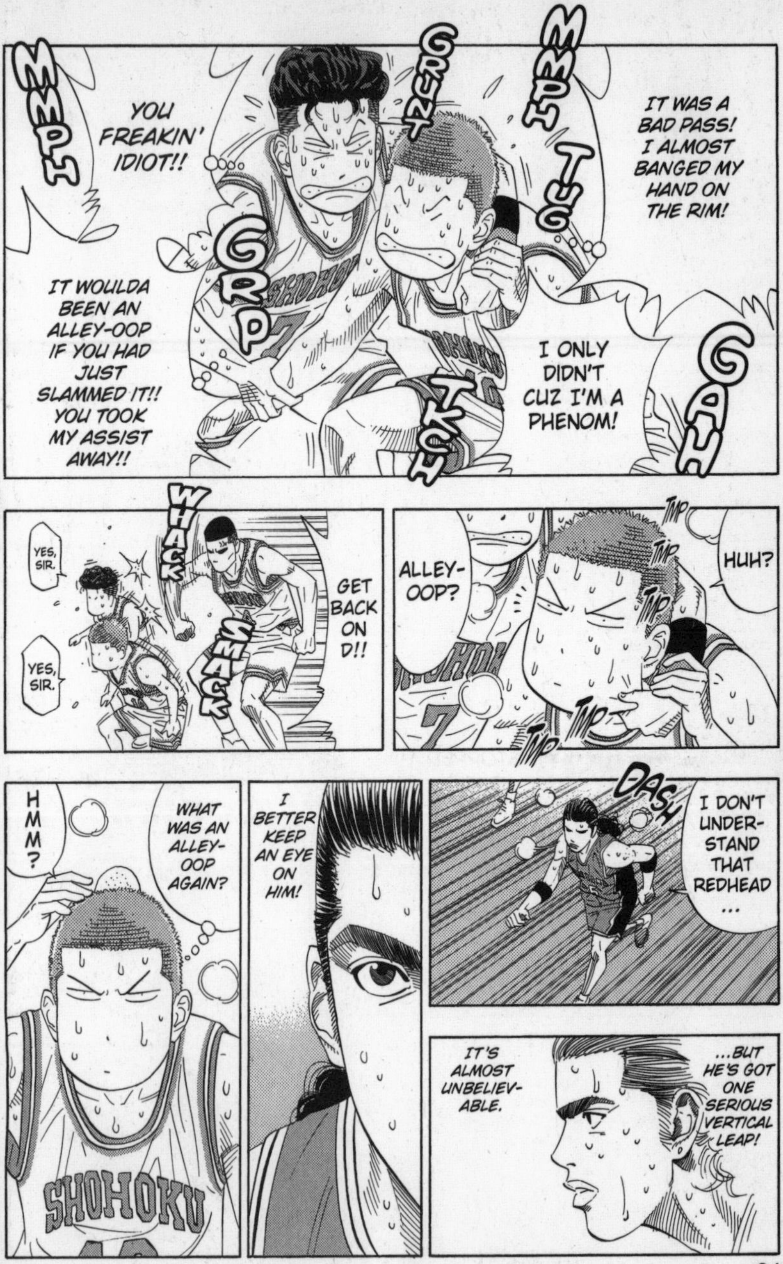
MMMPH
IT WAS A BAD PASS! I ALMOST BANGED MY HAND ON THE RIM!
TUG
GRUNT
GAAH
I ONLY DIDN'T CUZ I'M A PHENOM!
TKCH
YOU FREAKIN' IDIOT!!
MMMPH
GRP
IT WOULDA BEEN AN ALLEY-OOP IF YOU HAD JUST SLAMMED IT!! YOU TOOK MY ASSIST AWAY!!
TMP
TMP
TMP
HUH?
ALLEY-OOP?
TMP
TMP
GET BACK ON D!!
WHACK
SMACK
YES, SIR.
YES, SIR.
DASH
I DON'T UNDER-STAND THAT REDHEAD ...
IT'S ALMOST UNBELIEV-ABLE.
...BUT HE'S GOT ONE SERIOUS VERTICAL LEAP!
I BETTER KEEP AN EYE ON HIM!
WHAT WAS AN ALLEY-OOP AGAIN?
HMM?

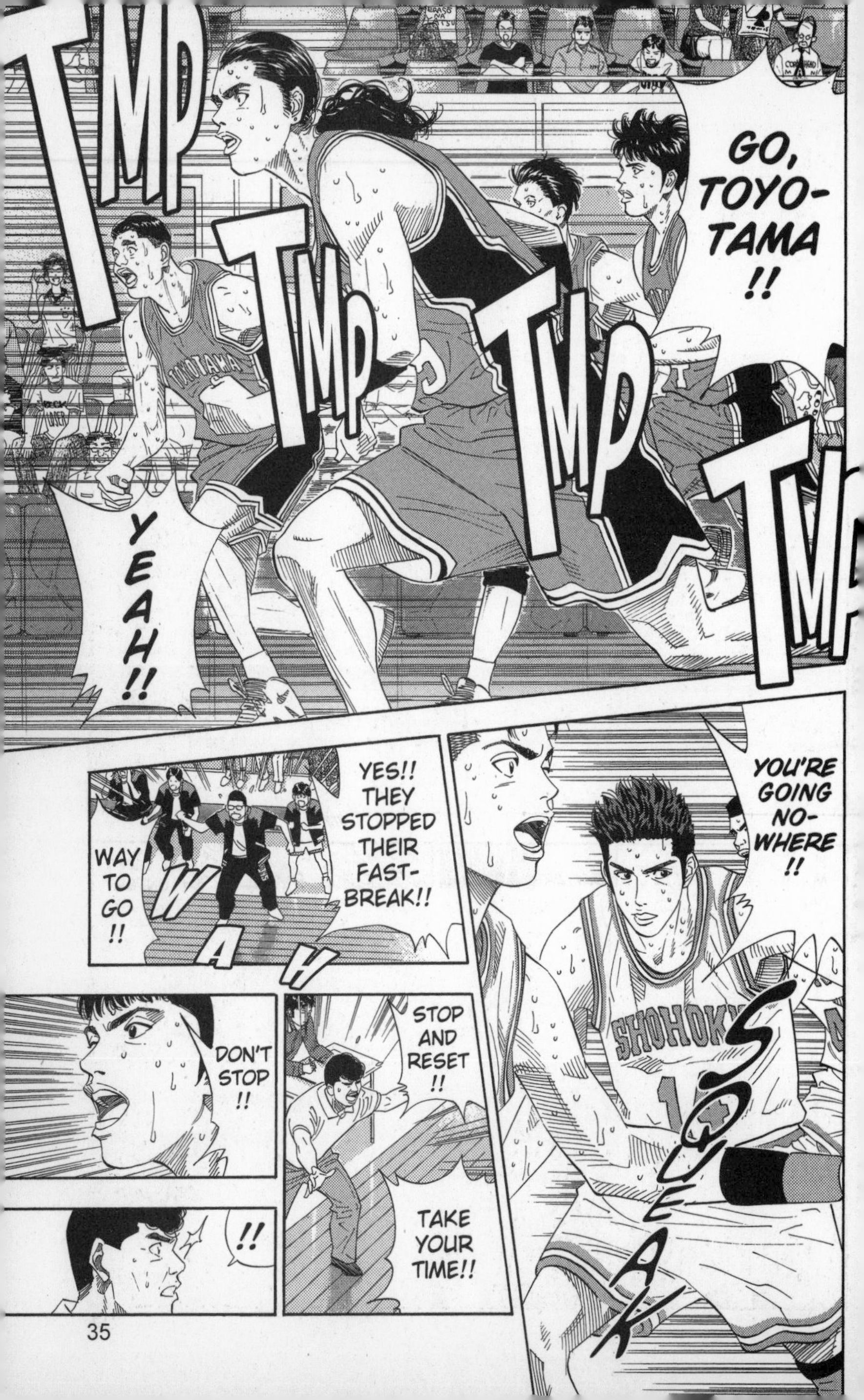
GO, TOYO-TAMA!!
TMP TMP TMP TMP TMP
YEAH!!
YOU'RE GOING NO-WHERE!!
SQUEAK
YES!! THEY STOPPED THEIR FAST-BREAK!!
WAY TO GO!!
WAH
STOP AND RESET!!
TAKE YOUR TIME!!
DON'T STOP!!
!!

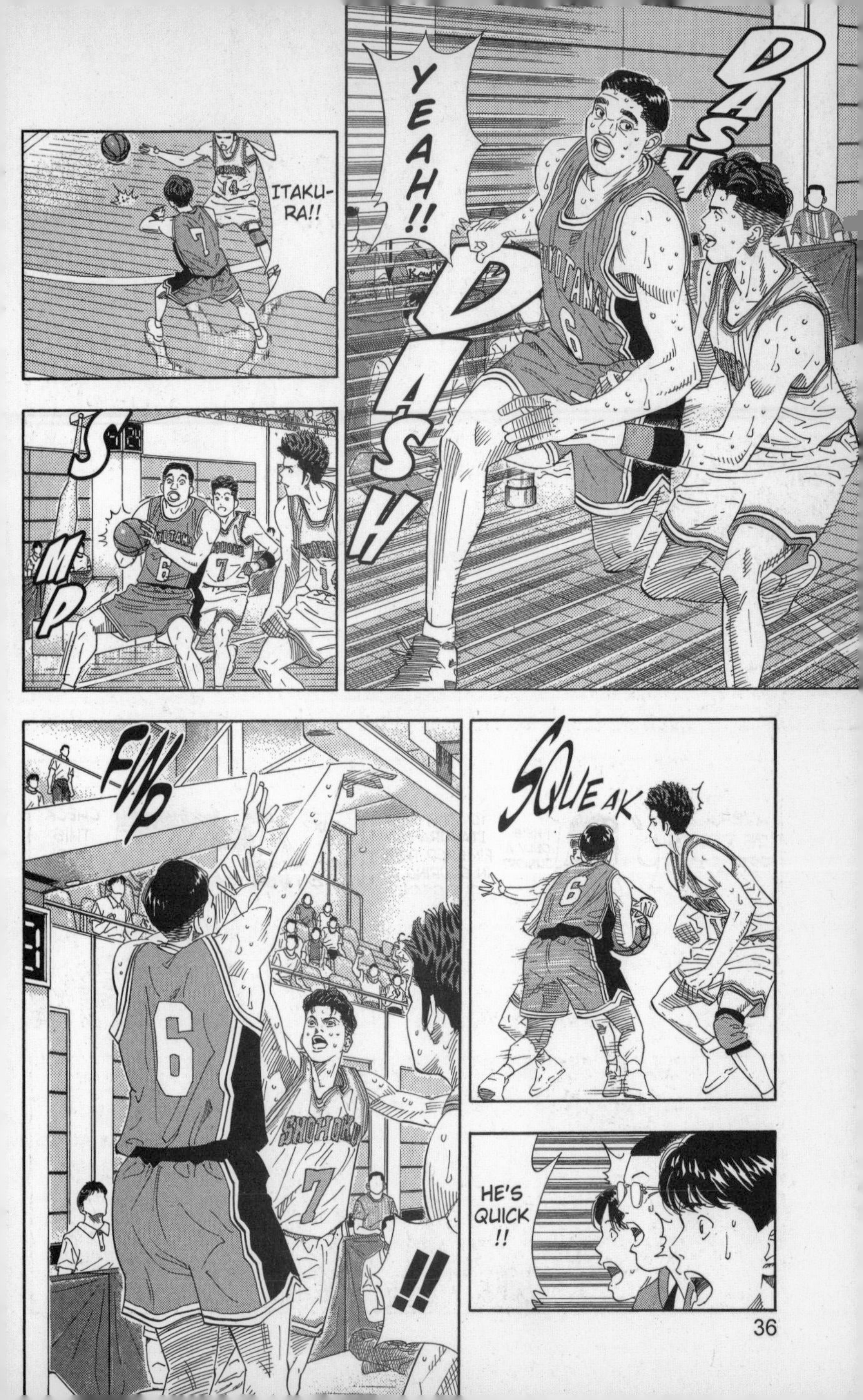
DASH
YEAH!!
DASH
ITAKURA!!
SQUEAK
HE'S QUICK!!
FWP
!!

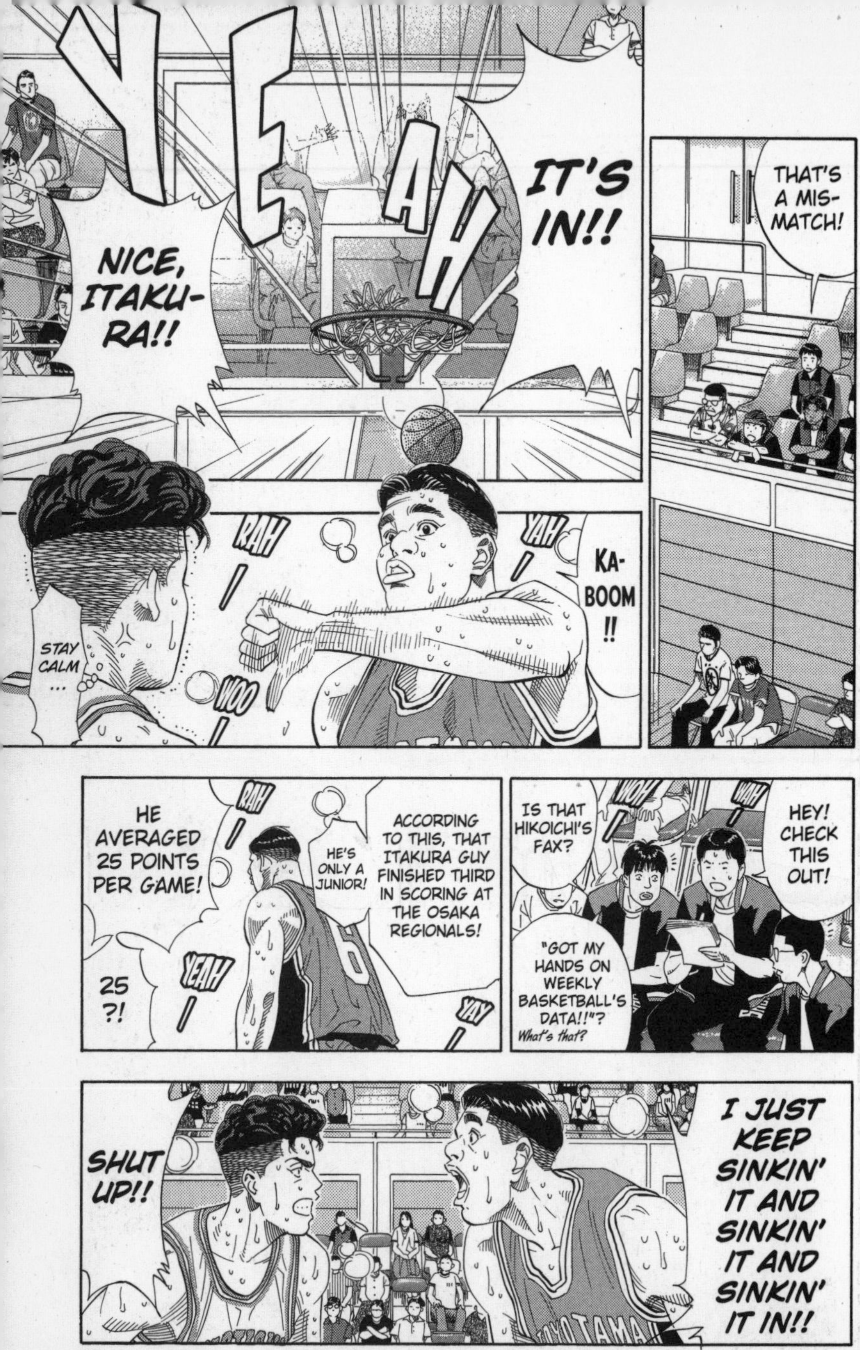
YEAH
IT'S IN!!
NICE, ITAKU-RA!!
THAT'S A MIS-MATCH!
YAH
KA-BOOM !!
RAH
WOO
STAY CALM ...
HEY! CHECK THIS OUT!
YAH
IS THAT HIKOICHI'S FAX?
WOH
"GOT MY HANDS ON WEEKLY BASKETBALL'S DATA!!"?
What's that?
ACCORDING TO THIS, THAT ITAKURA GUY FINISHED THIRD IN SCORING AT THE OSAKA REGIONALS!
HE'S ONLY A JUNIOR!
YAY
RAH
HE AVERAGED 25 POINTS PER GAME!
YEAH
25 ?!
I JUST KEEP SINKIN' IT AND SINKIN' IT AND SINKIN' IT IN!!
SHUT UP!!

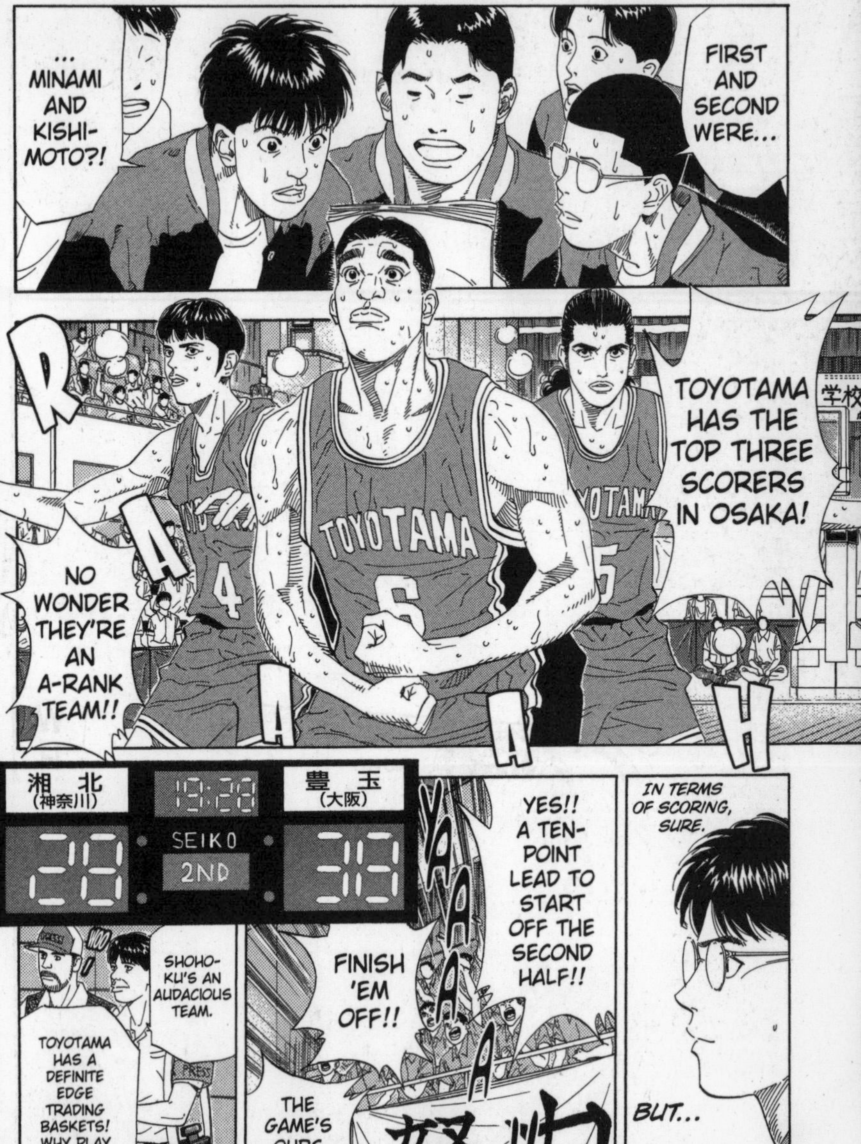
FIRST AND SECOND WERE...
... MINAMI AND KISHI-MOTO?!
RAAAAH
TOYOTAMA HAS THE TOP THREE SCORERS IN OSAKA!
NO WONDER THEY'RE AN A-RANK TEAM!!
IN TERMS OF SCORING, SURE.
BUT...
YES!! A TEN-POINT LEAD TO START OFF THE SECOND HALF!!
FINISH 'EM OFF!!
YAAAAA
THE GAME'S OURS AT THIS RATE!
努力
湘北 (神奈川)
19:28
豊玉 (大阪)
23
SEIKO
2ND
33
SHOHO-KU'S AN AUDACIOUS TEAM.
TOYOTAMA HAS A DEFINITE EDGE TRADING BASKETS! WHY PLAY THEIR KIND OF GAME?!

Scoreboard: Shohoku (Kanagawa) Toyotama (Osaka)

Banner: *Doryoku* (effort/hard work)

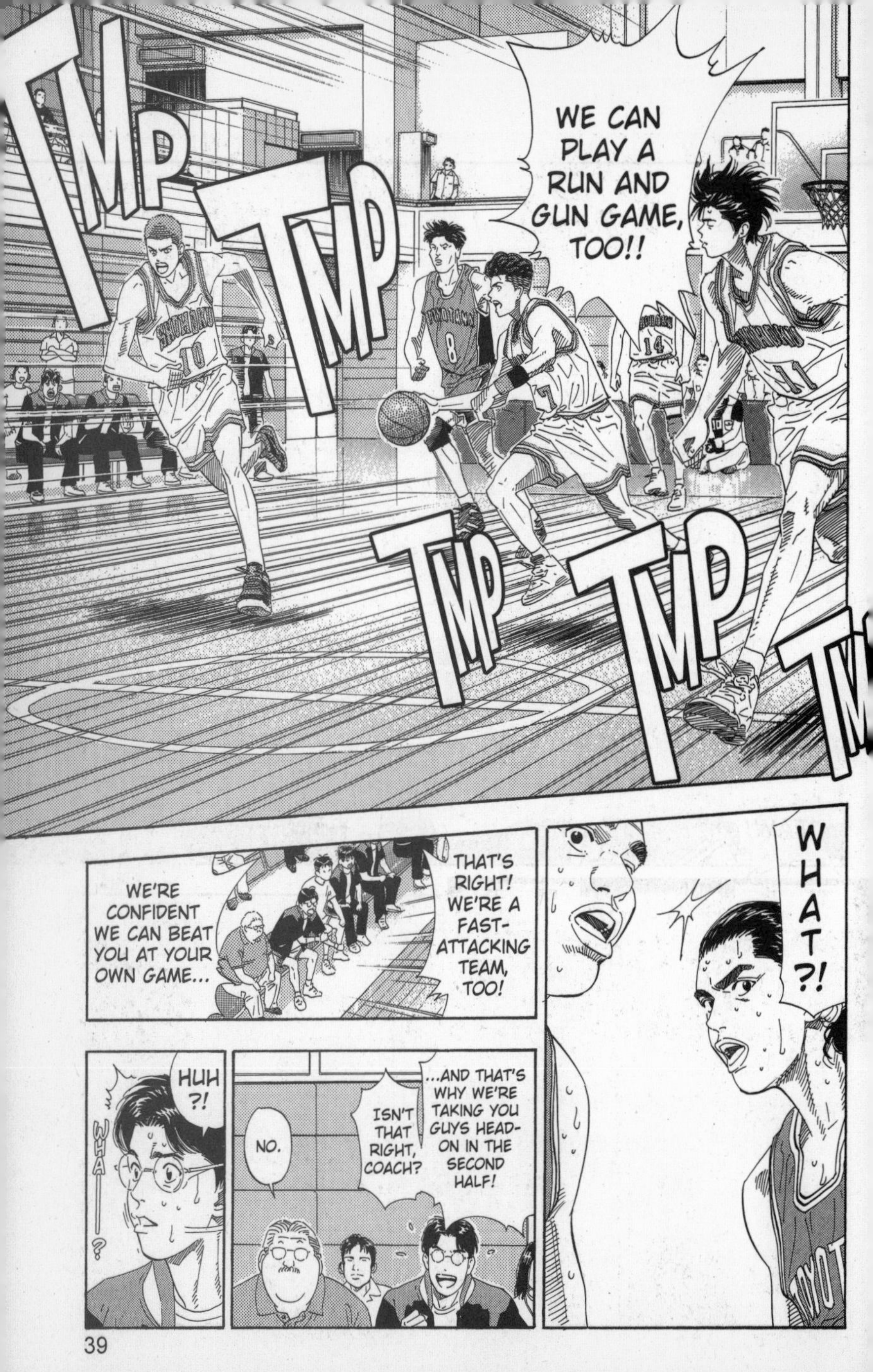
WE CAN PLAY A RUN AND GUN GAME, TOO!!
TMP
TMP
TMP
TMP
TM
WHAT?!
THAT'S RIGHT! WE'RE A FAST-ATTACKING TEAM, TOO!
WE'RE CONFIDENT WE CAN BEAT YOU AT YOUR OWN GAME...
...AND THAT'S WHY WE'RE TAKING YOU GUYS HEAD-ON IN THE SECOND HALF!
ISN'T THAT RIGHT, COACH?
NO.
HUH?!
WHA—?

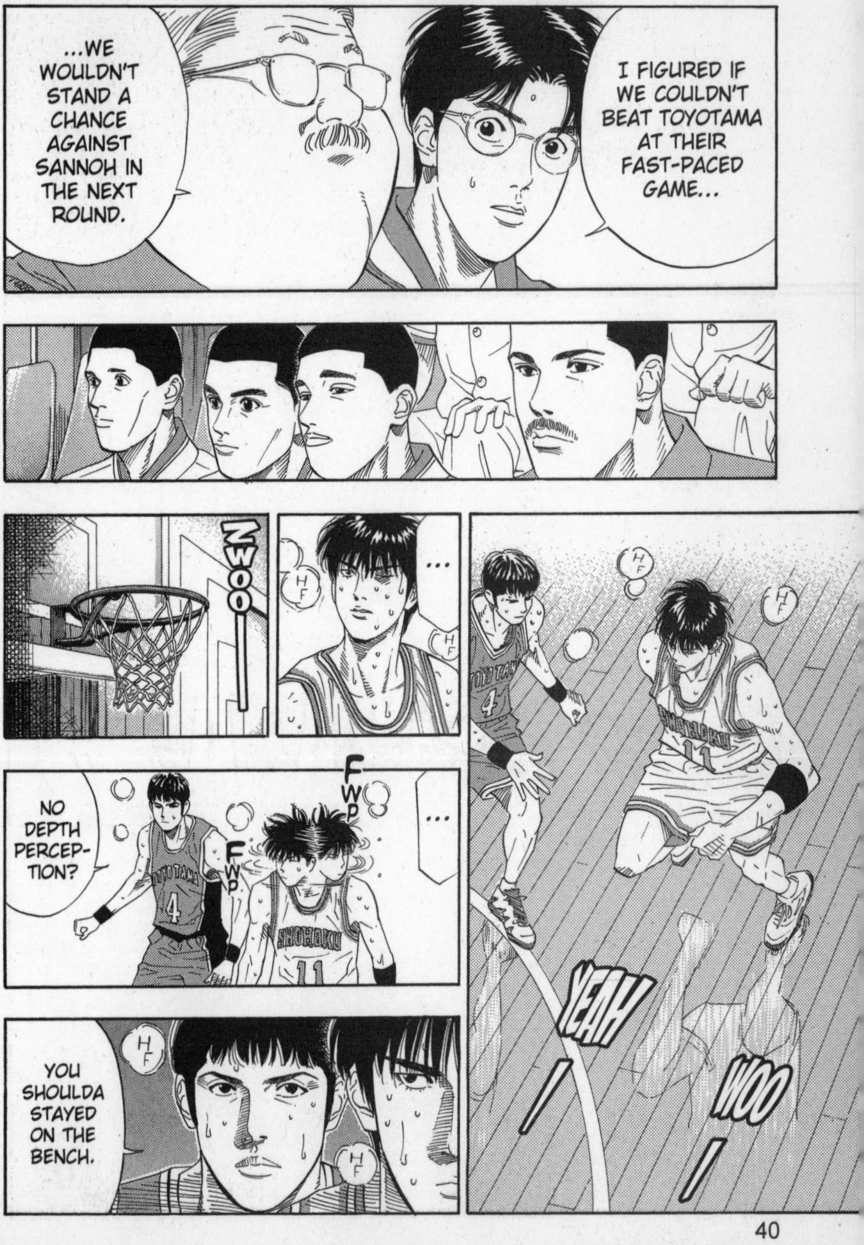
I FIGURED IF WE COULDN'T BEAT TOYOTAMA AT THEIR FAST-PACED GAME...
...WE WOULDN'T STAND A CHANCE AGAINST SANNOH IN THE NEXT ROUND.
HF
HF
YEAH
WOO
...
HF
HF
ZWOO
...
FWP
FWP
NO DEPTH PERCEPTION?
HF
HF
YOU SHOULDA STAYED ON THE BENCH.

READ THIS WAY

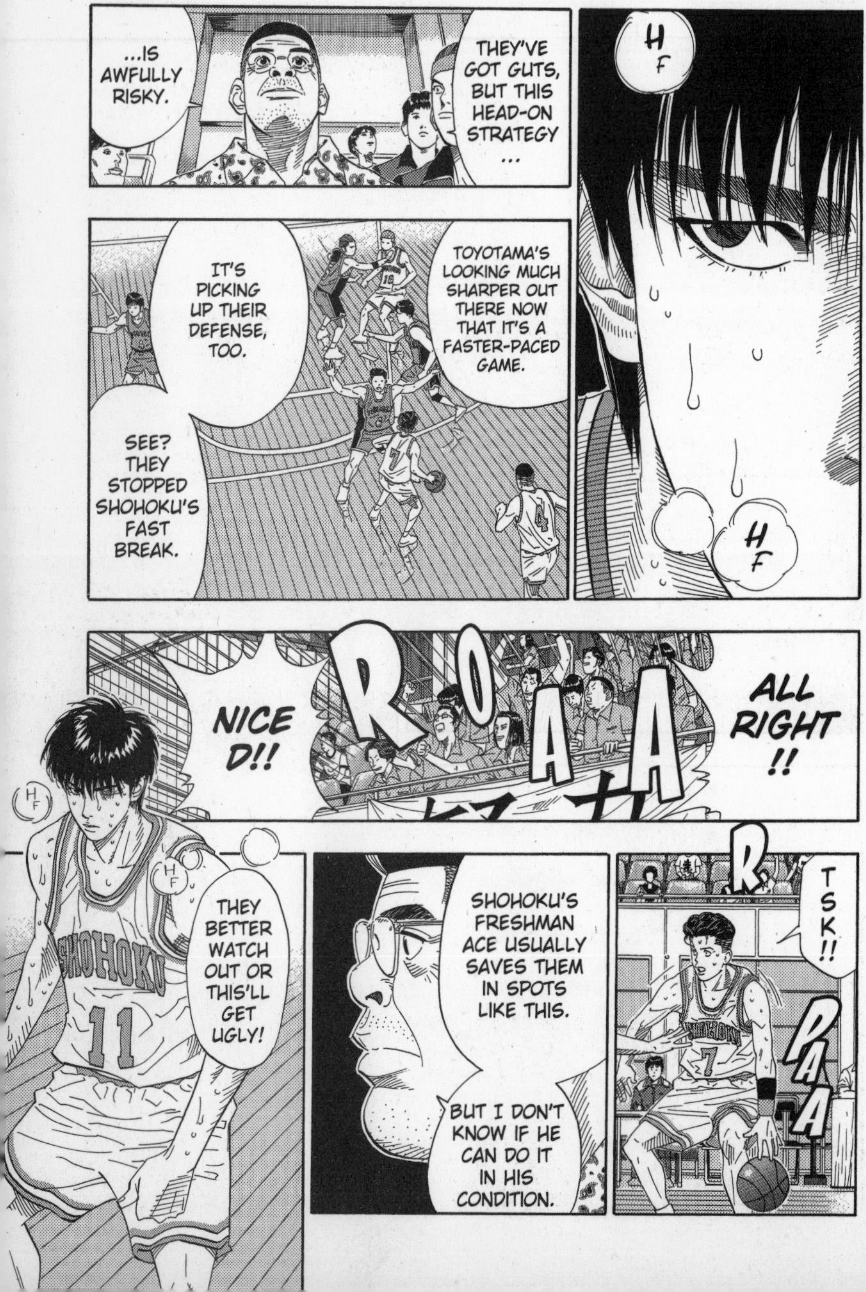
HF
HF
THEY'VE GOT GUTS, BUT THIS HEAD-ON STRATEGY ...
...IS AWFULLY RISKY.
TOYOTAMA'S LOOKING MUCH SHARPER OUT THERE NOW THAT IT'S A FASTER-PACED GAME.
IT'S PICKING UP THEIR DEFENSE, TOO.
SEE? THEY STOPPED SHOHOKU'S FAST BREAK.
ALL RIGHT!!
ROAAR
NICE D!!
TSK!!
R
PAA
SHOHOKU'S FRESHMAN ACE USUALLY SAVES THEM IN SPOTS LIKE THIS.
BUT I DON'T KNOW IF HE CAN DO IT IN HIS CONDITION.
HF
HF
THEY BETTER WATCH OUT OR THIS'LL GET UGLY!

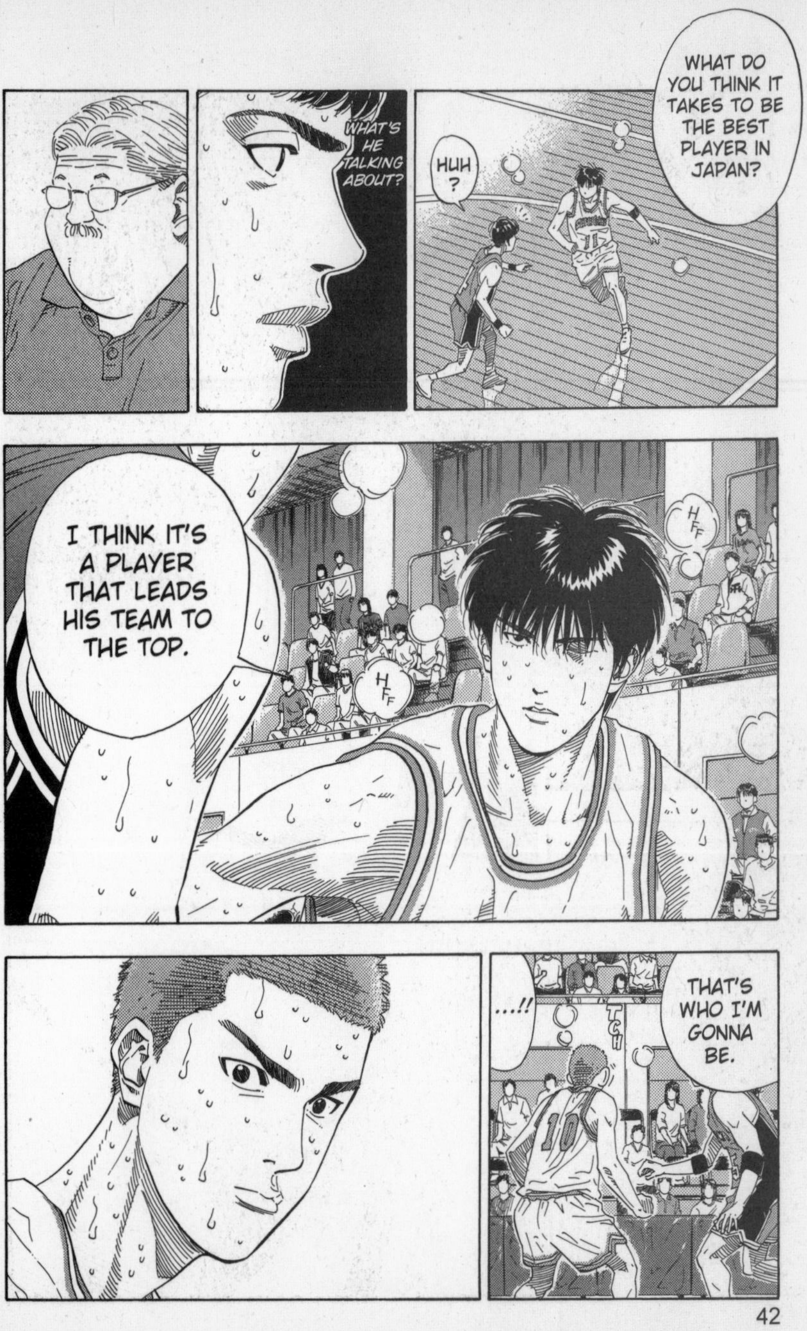
WHAT DO YOU THINK IT TAKES TO BE THE BEST PLAYER IN JAPAN?
HUH ?
WHAT'S HE TALKING ABOUT?
HFF
I THINK IT'S A PLAYER THAT LEADS HIS TEAM TO THE TOP.
HFF
THAT'S WHO I'M GONNA BE.
...!!
TCH

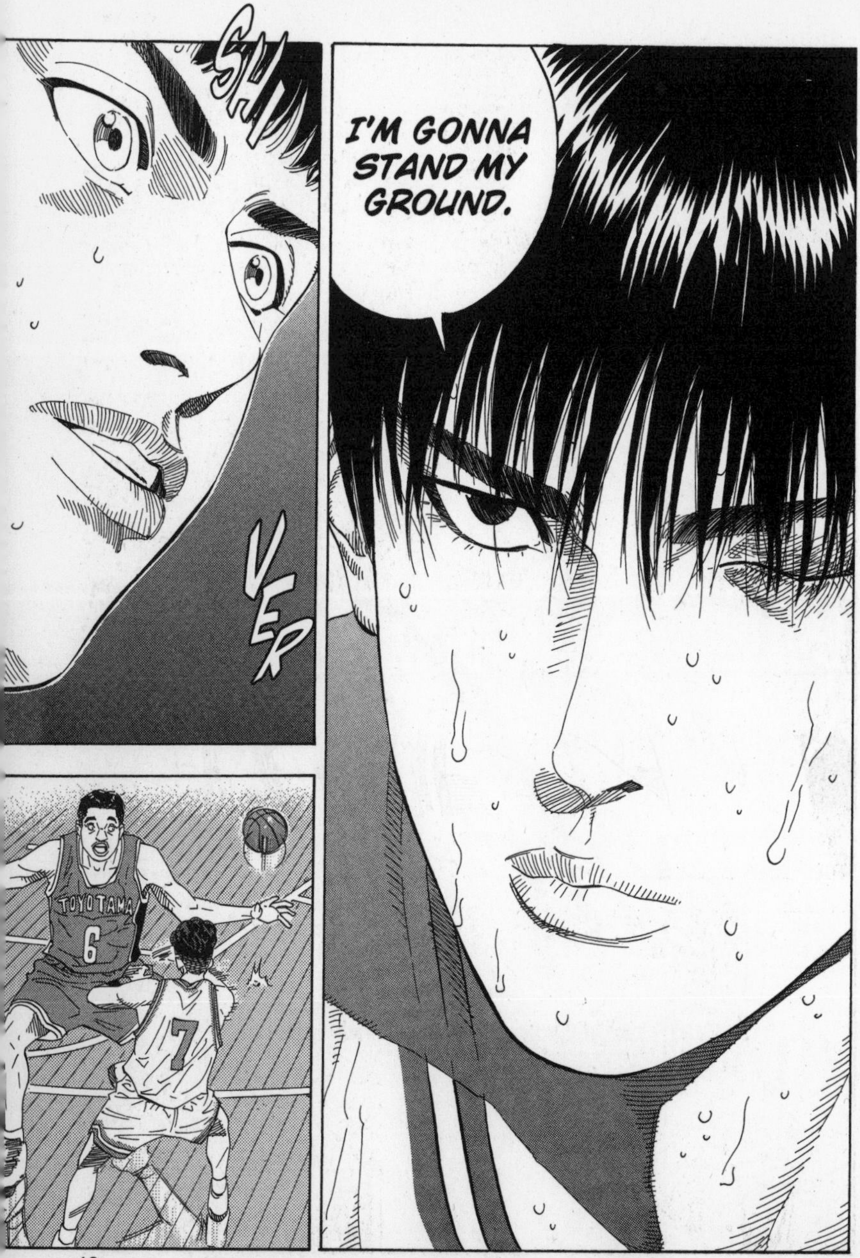
I'M GONNA STAND MY GROUND.
SHI
VER
TOYOTAMA
6
7

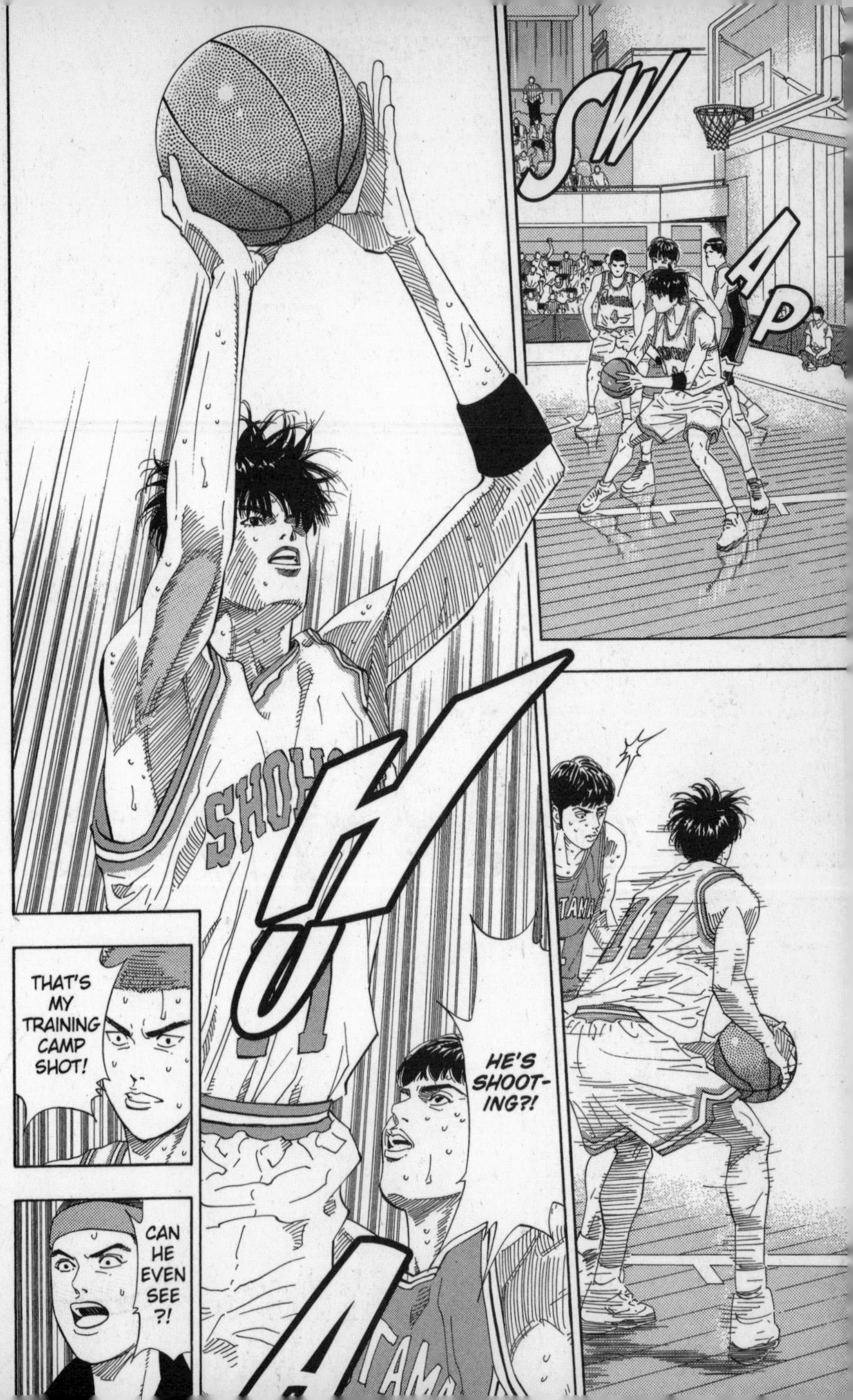
SWAP
HE'S SHOOTING?!
THAT'S MY TRAINING CAMP SHOT!
CAN HE EVEN SEE ?!

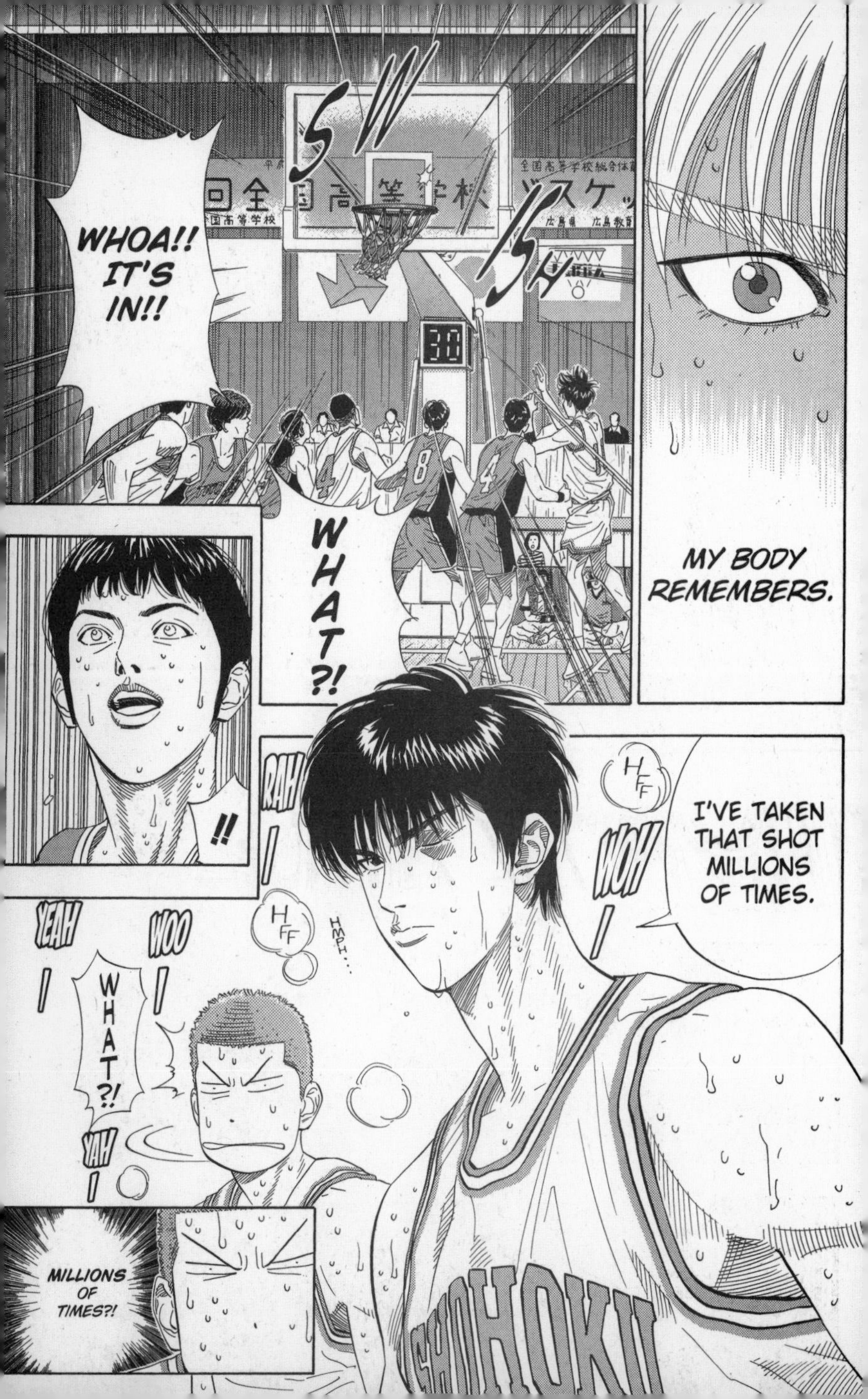
MY BODY REMEMBERS.
SWISH
WHOA!! IT'S IN!!
WHAT?!
I'VE TAKEN THAT SHOT MILLIONS OF TIMES.
HFF
WOH
RAH
HFF
HMPH...
!!
WOO
YEAH
WHAT?!
YAH
MILLIONS OF TIMES?!

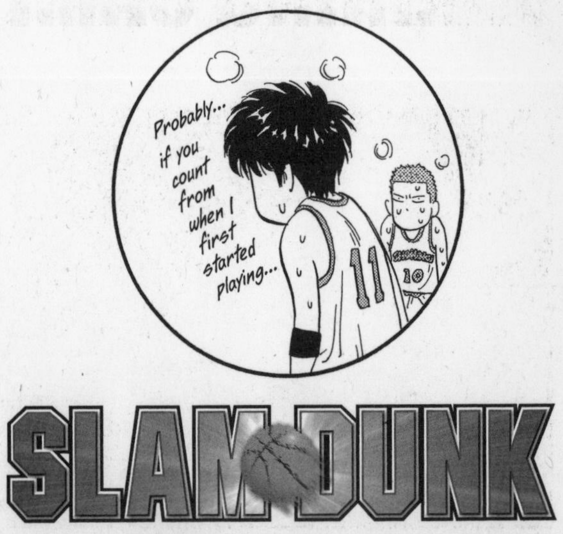
Probably... if you count from when I first started playing...

SLAM DUNK

#209

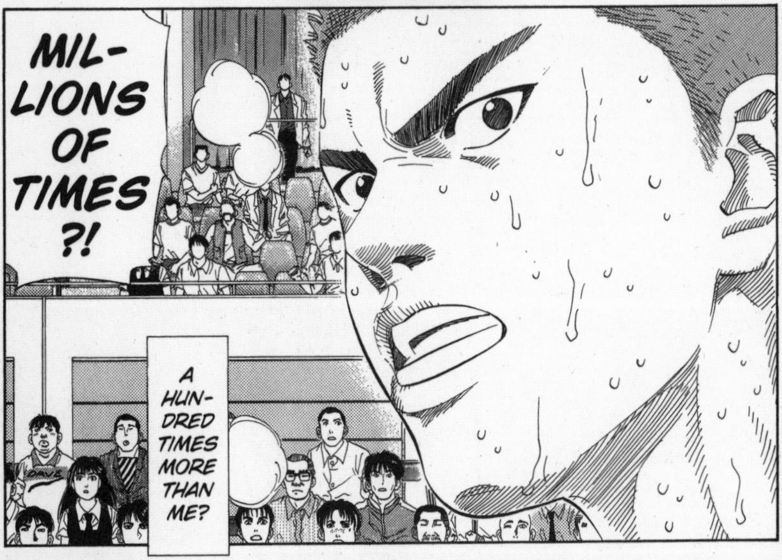
MIL-LIONS OF TIMES ?!
A HUN-DRED TIMES MORE THAN ME?

TRAINING CAMP SHOT

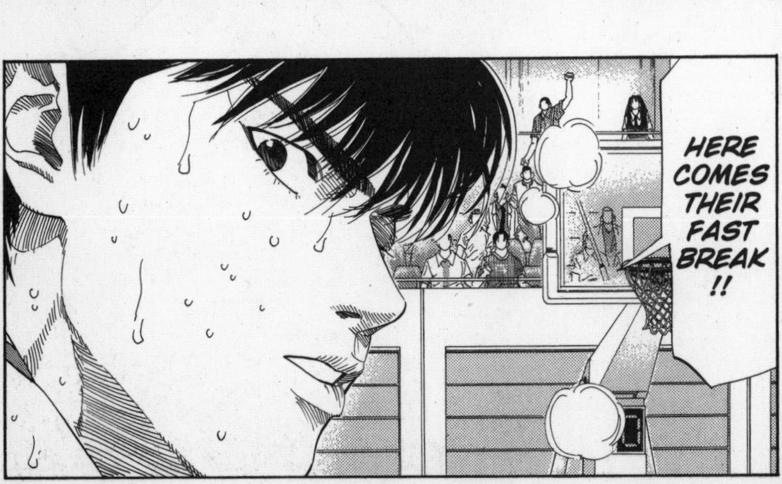
HERE COMES THEIR FAST BREAK !!

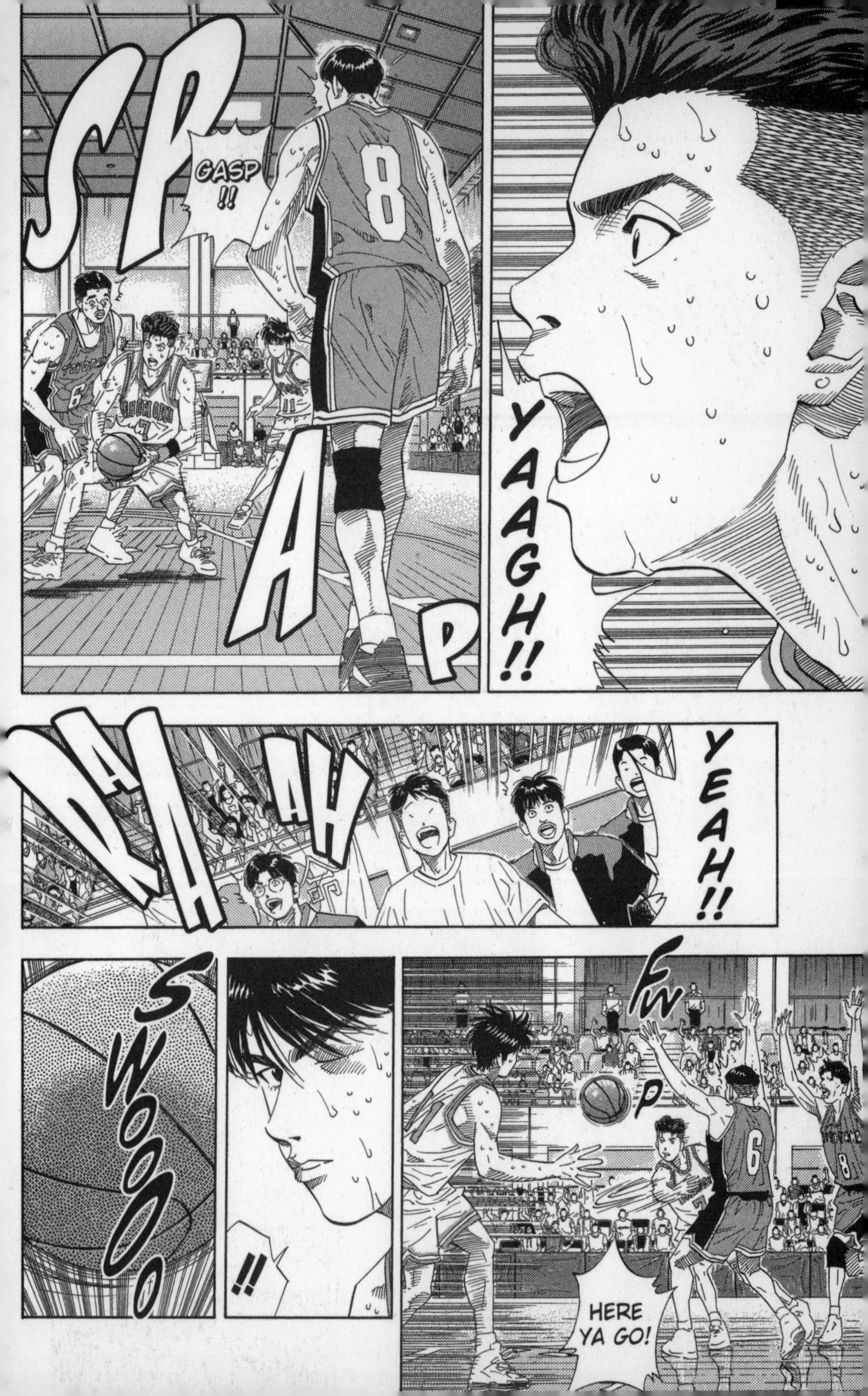
YAAAGH!!
GASP!!
SPAP
YEAH!!
WAAAH
FWP
HERE YA GO!
!!
SWOOOO

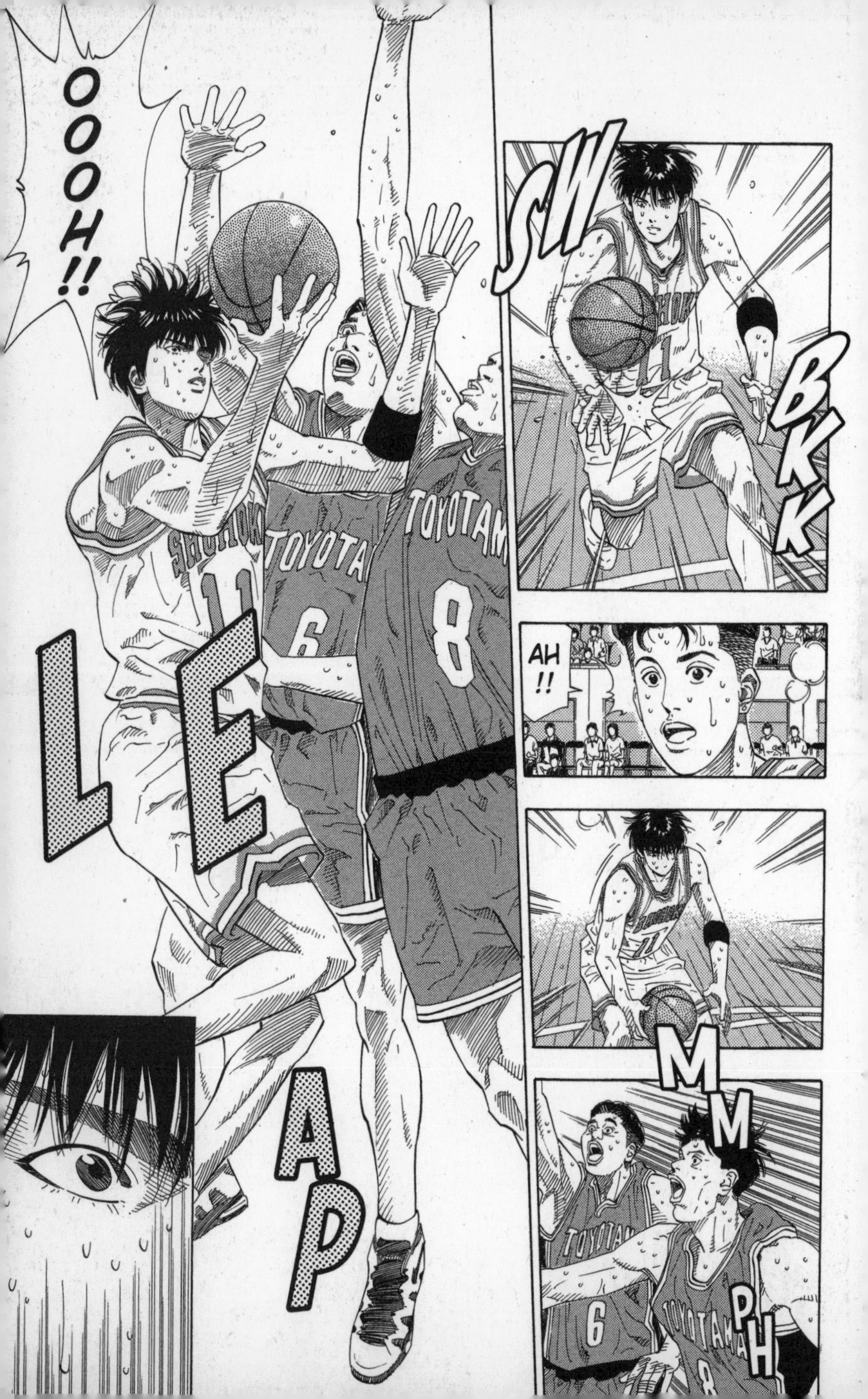
SW
BKK
AH !!
MMMPH
OOOH!!
LEAP

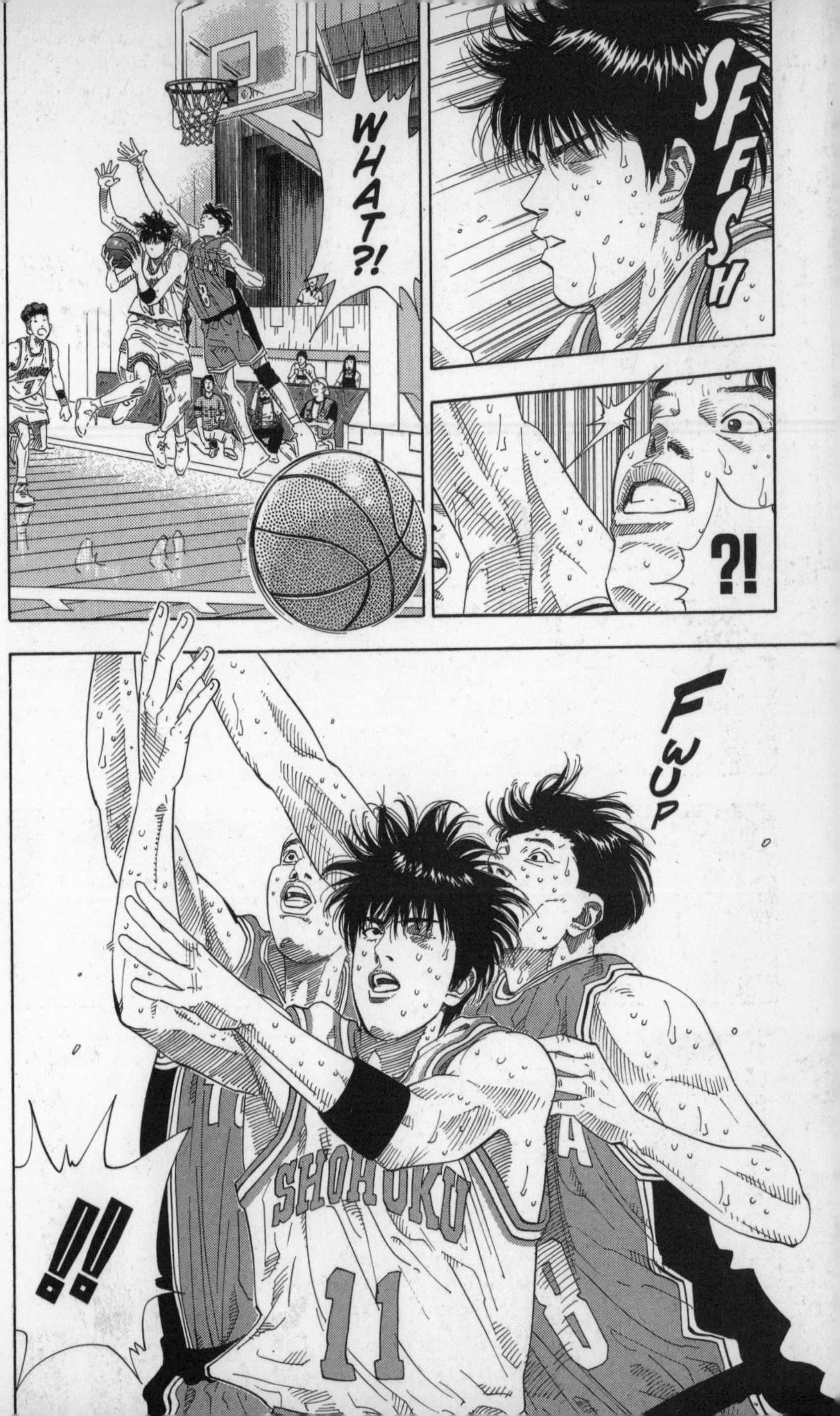
SFFSH
?!
WHAT?!
FWUP
!!

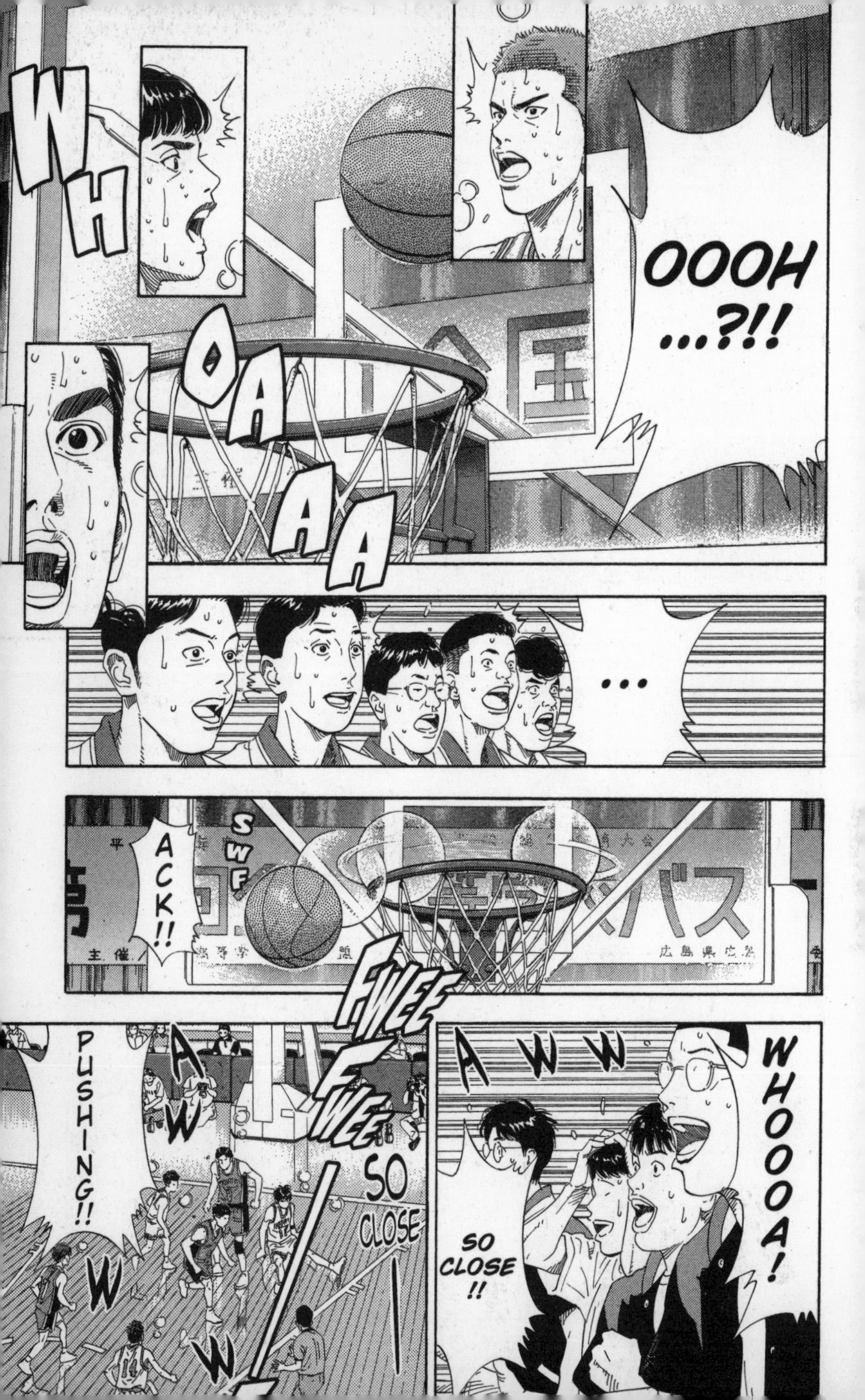
OOOH ...?!!
WHOAAAA
...
SWF
ACK!!
WHOOOOA!
AWW
SO CLOSE !!
FWEE FWEE
SO CLOSE
AWWWW
PUSHING!!

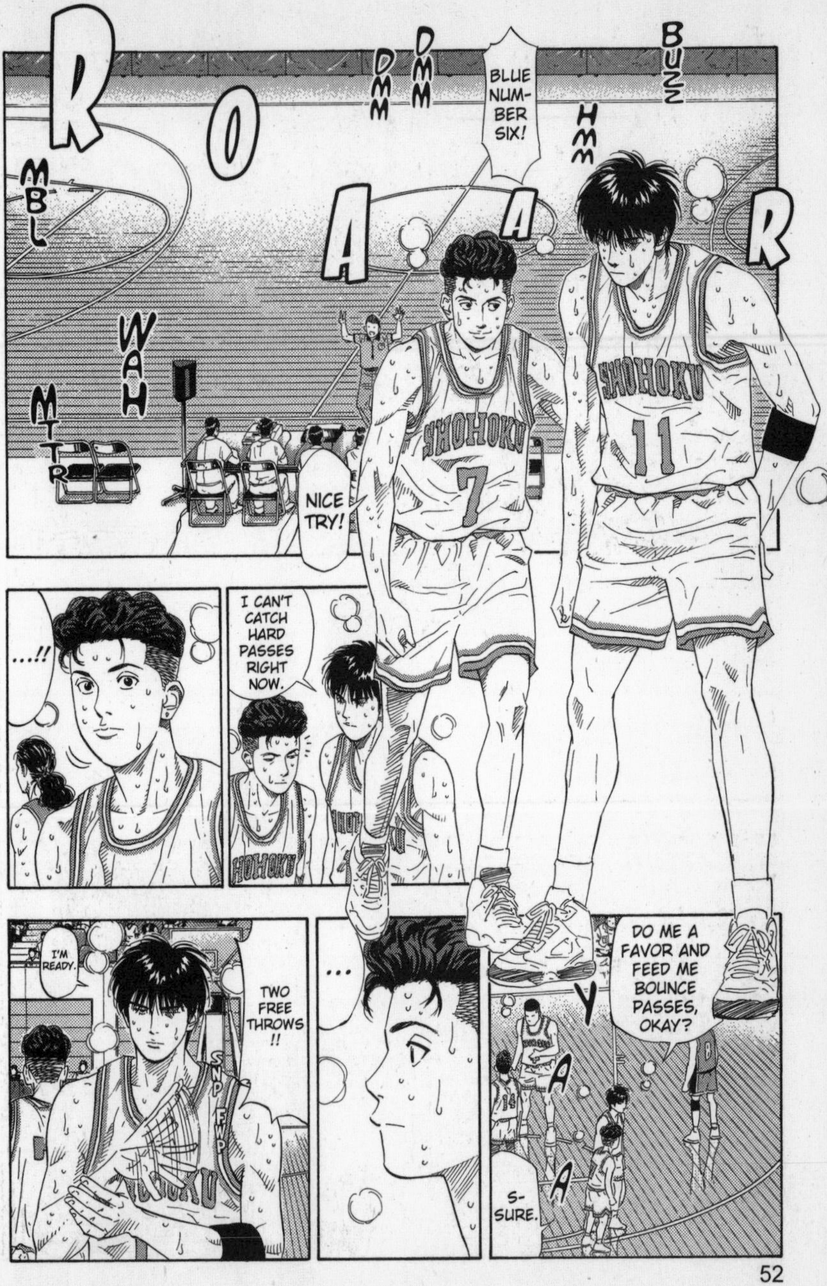
ROAAR
BUZZ
HMM
BLUE NUMBER SIX!
DMM
DMM
MBL
WAH
MTTR
NICE TRY!
I CAN'T CATCH HARD PASSES RIGHT NOW.
...!!
DO ME A FAVOR AND FEED ME BOUNCE PASSES, OKAY?
YAAA
S-SURE.
...
I'M READY.
TWO FREE THROWS !!
SNP
FWP

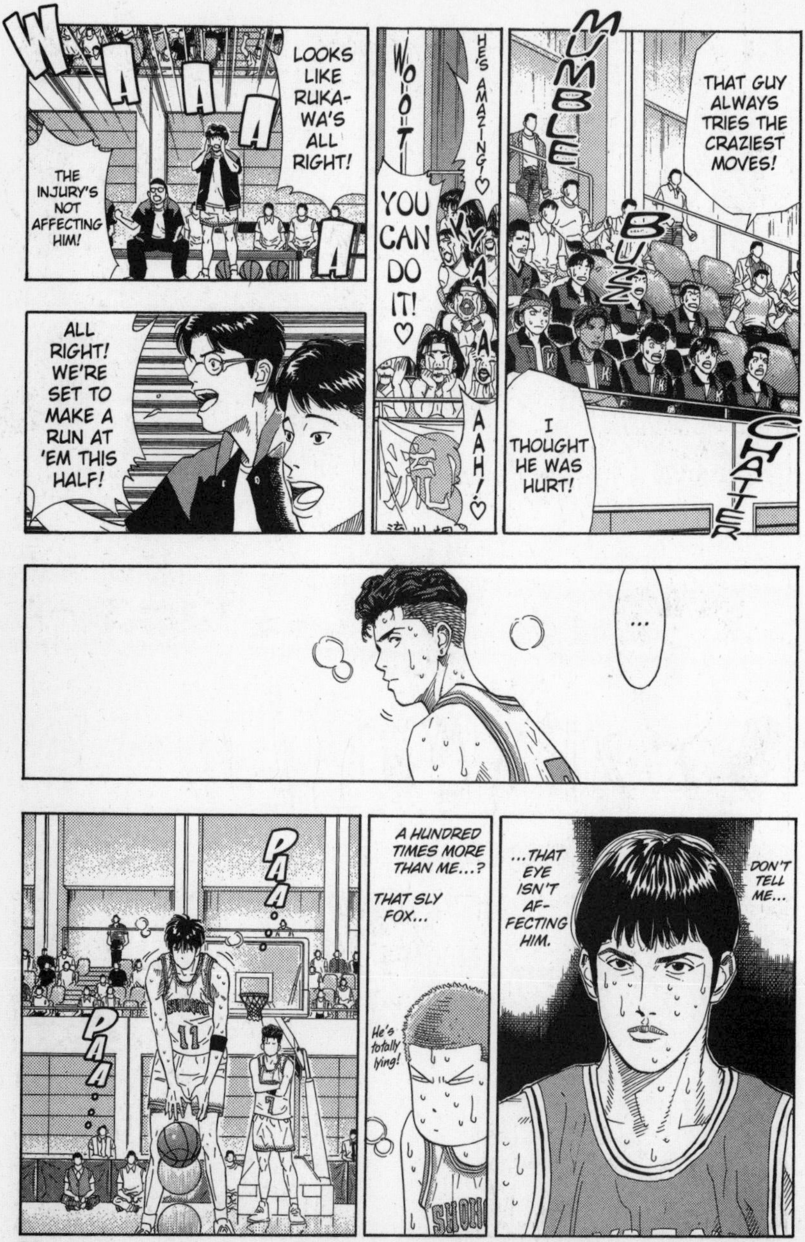
MUMBLE
THAT GUY ALWAYS TRIES THE CRAZIEST MOVES!
BUZZ
I THOUGHT HE WAS HURT!
CHATTER
HE'S AMAZING!♡
WOOT
YOU CAN DO IT!♡
KYAAA
AAH!♡
WAAAAA
LOOKS LIKE RUKAWA'S ALL RIGHT!
THE INJURY'S NOT AFFECTING HIM!
ALL RIGHT! WE'RE SET TO MAKE A RUN AT 'EM THIS HALF!
...
DON'T TELL ME...
...THAT EYE ISN'T AFFECTING HIM.
A HUNDRED TIMES MORE THAN ME...?
THAT SLY FOX...
He's totally lying!
PAA...
PAA...

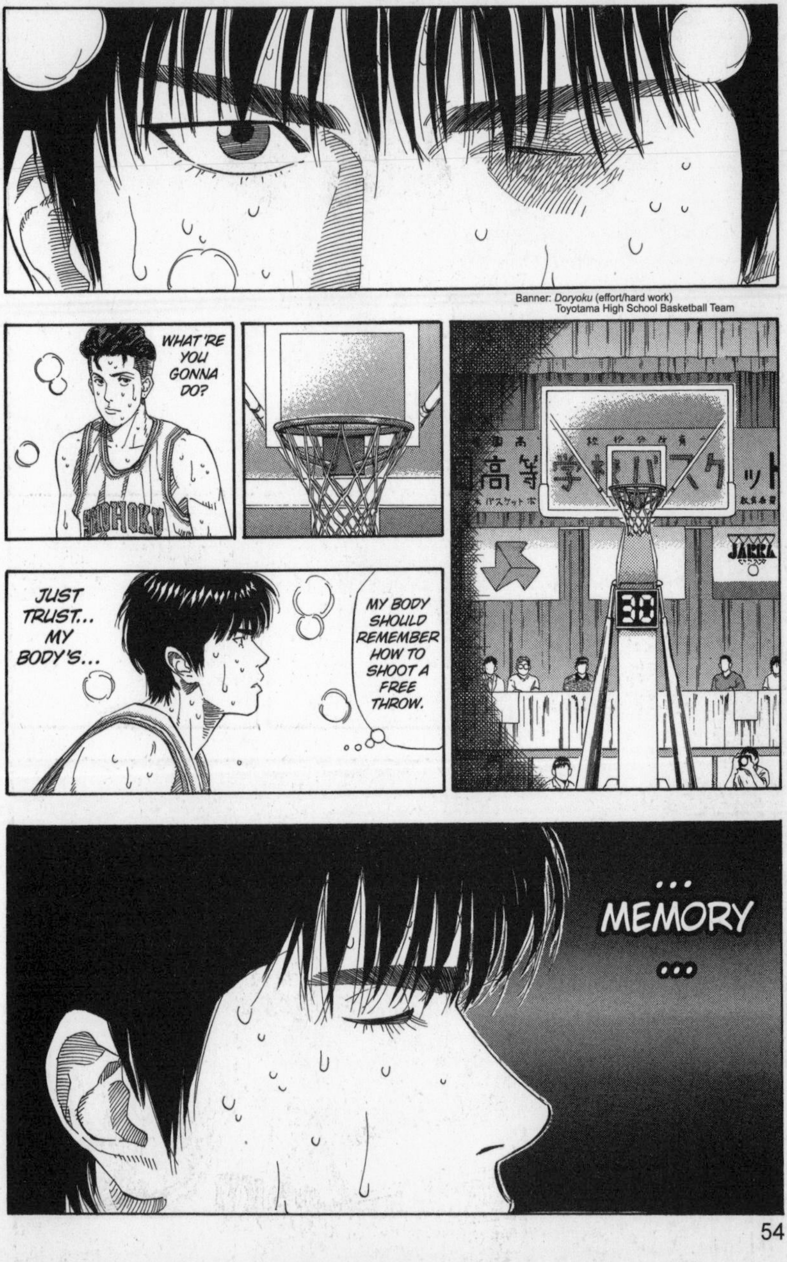
Banner: *Doryoku* (effort/hard work)
Toyotama High School Basketball Team
WHAT'RE YOU GONNA DO?
MY BODY SHOULD REMEMBER HOW TO SHOOT A FREE THROW.
JUST TRUST... MY BODY'S...
... MEMORY ...

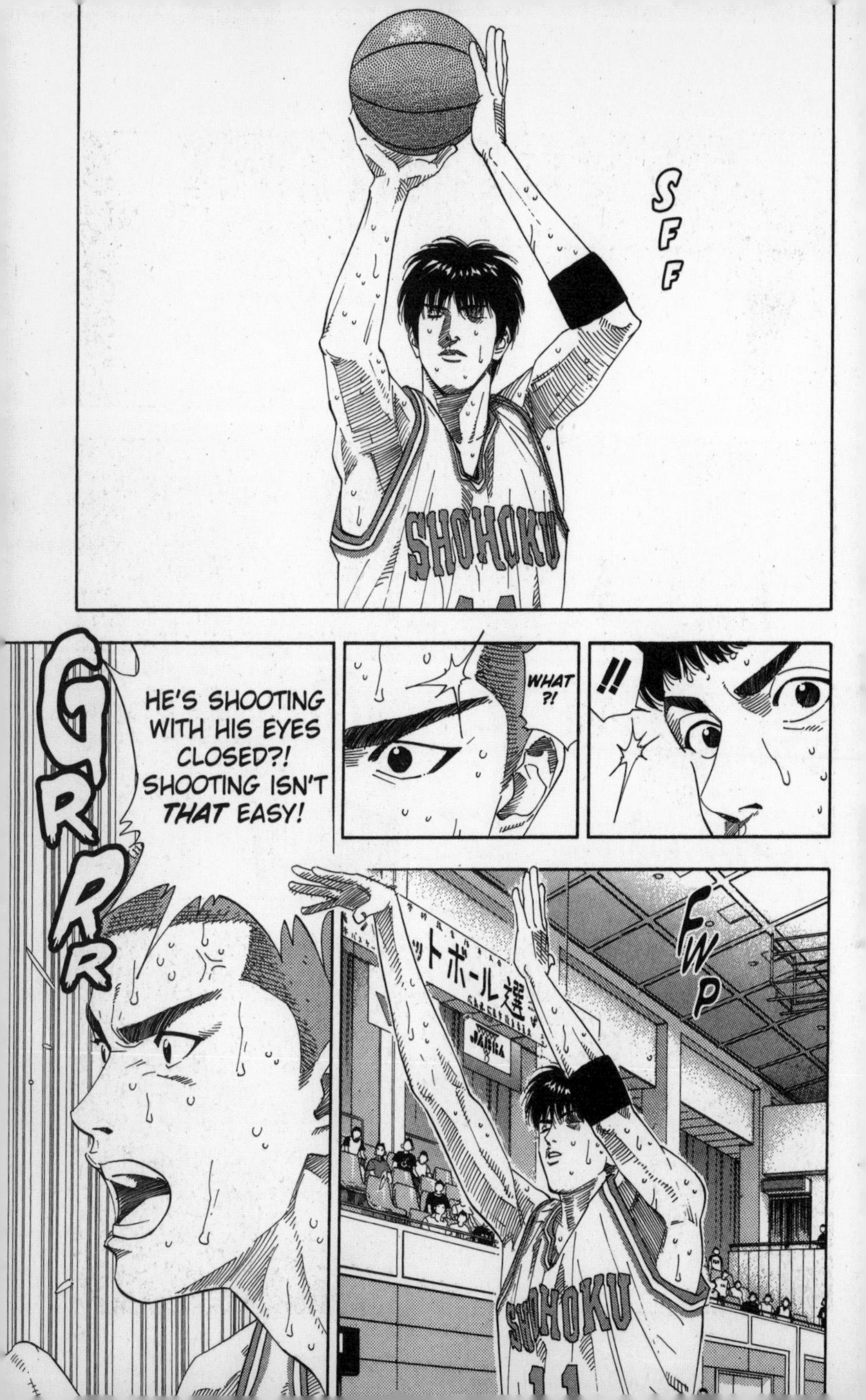
SFF
!!
WHAT ?!
HE'S SHOOTING WITH HIS EYES CLOSED?! SHOOTING ISN'T *THAT* EASY!
FWP
GRRR

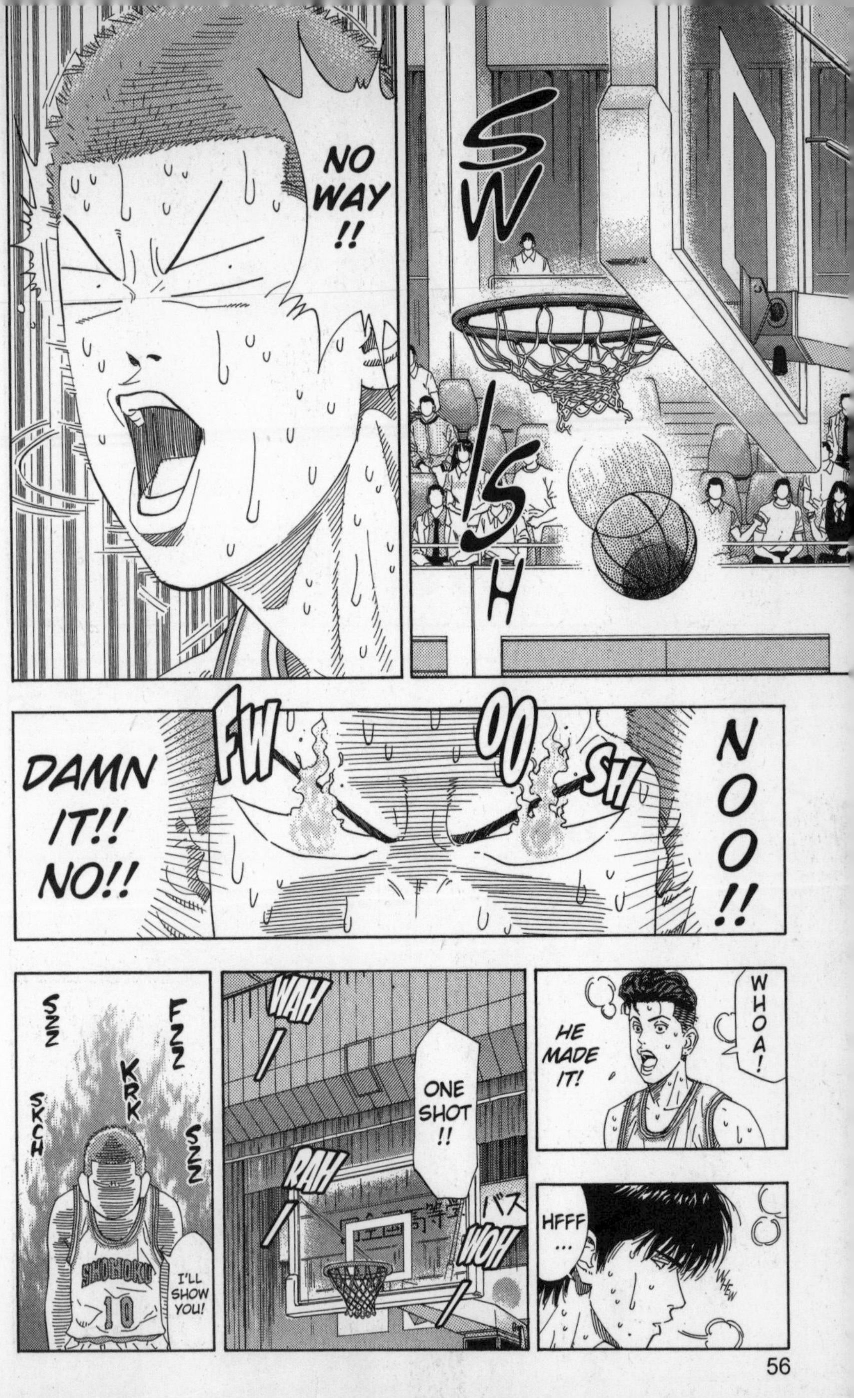
SWISH
NO WAY!!
NOOO!!
FWOOSH
DAMN IT!! NO!!
WHOA!
HE MADE IT!
HFFF...
WHEW
WAH!
ONE SHOT!!
RAH!
バス
WOH!
FZZ
SZZ
KRK
SZZ
SKCH
I'LL SHOW YOU!

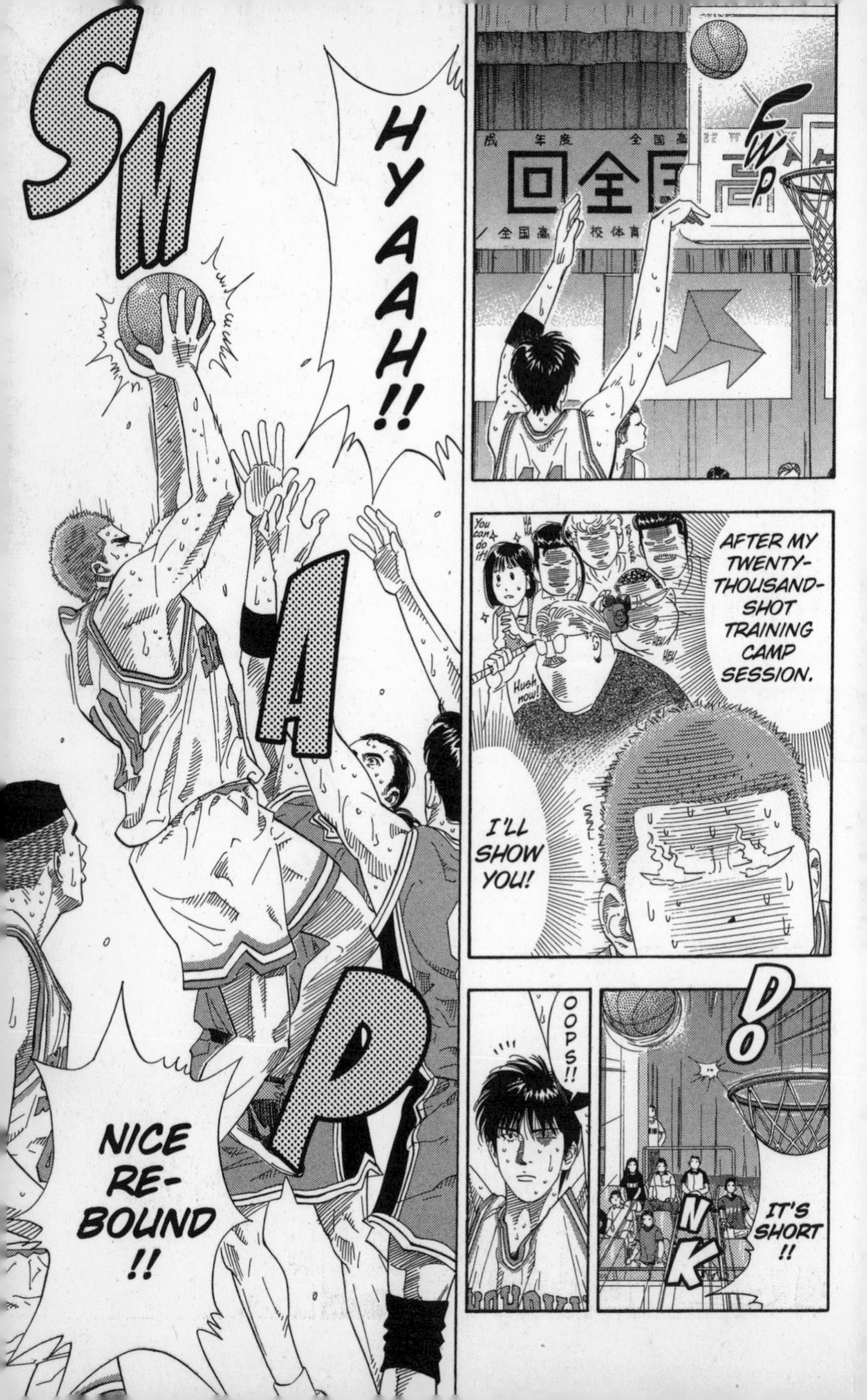
FWP
You can do it!
HA HA
Hush now!
HEH HEH
AFTER MY TWENTY-THOUSAND-SHOT TRAINING CAMP SESSION.
I'LL SHOW YOU!
DONK
IT'S SHORT!!
OOPS!!
SMAP
HYAAAH!!
NICE RE-BOUND!!

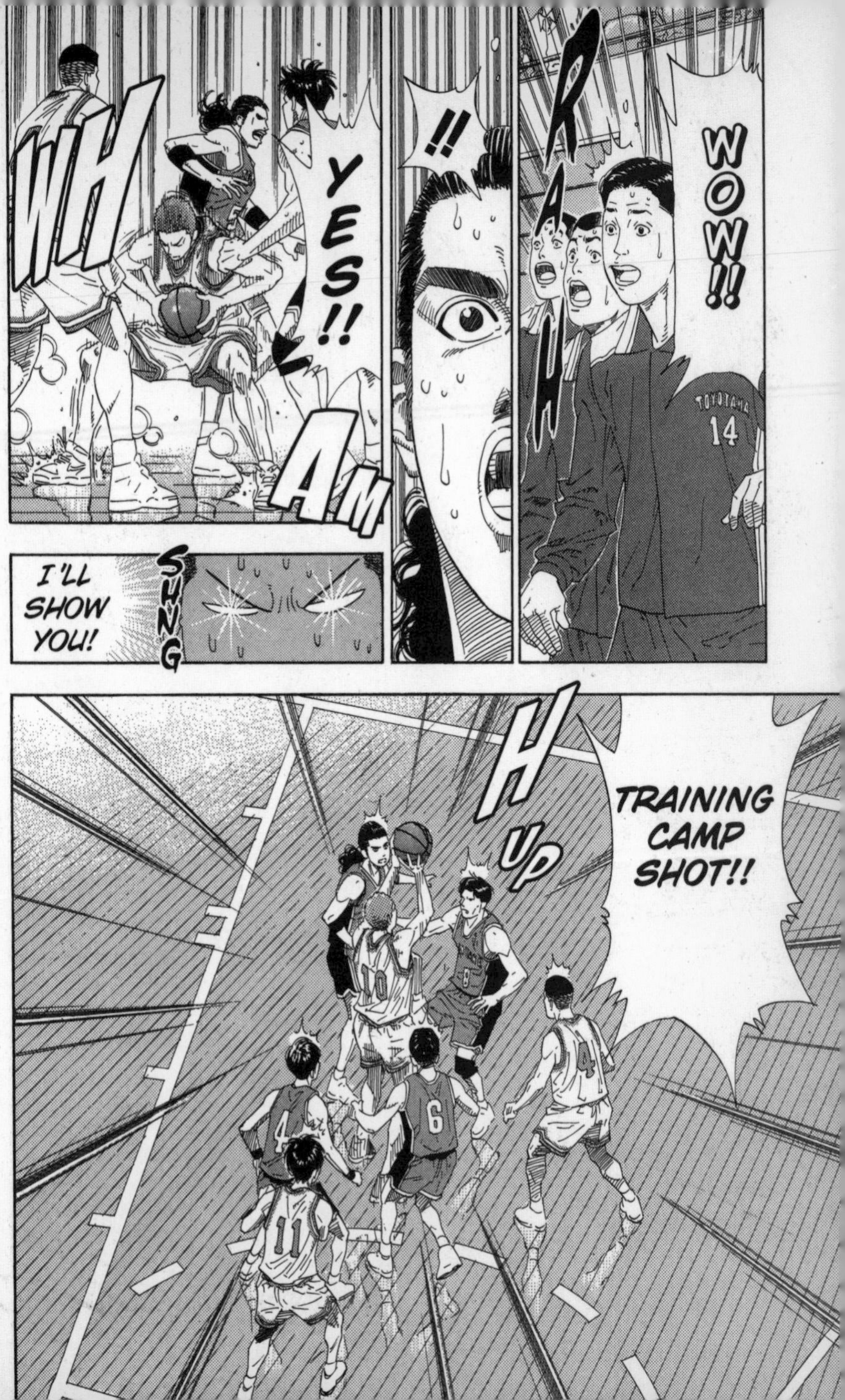

RAAH
WOW!!
TOYOTAMA
14
!!
YES!!
WHAM
I'LL SHOW YOU!
SHING
HUP
TRAINING CAMP SHOT!!

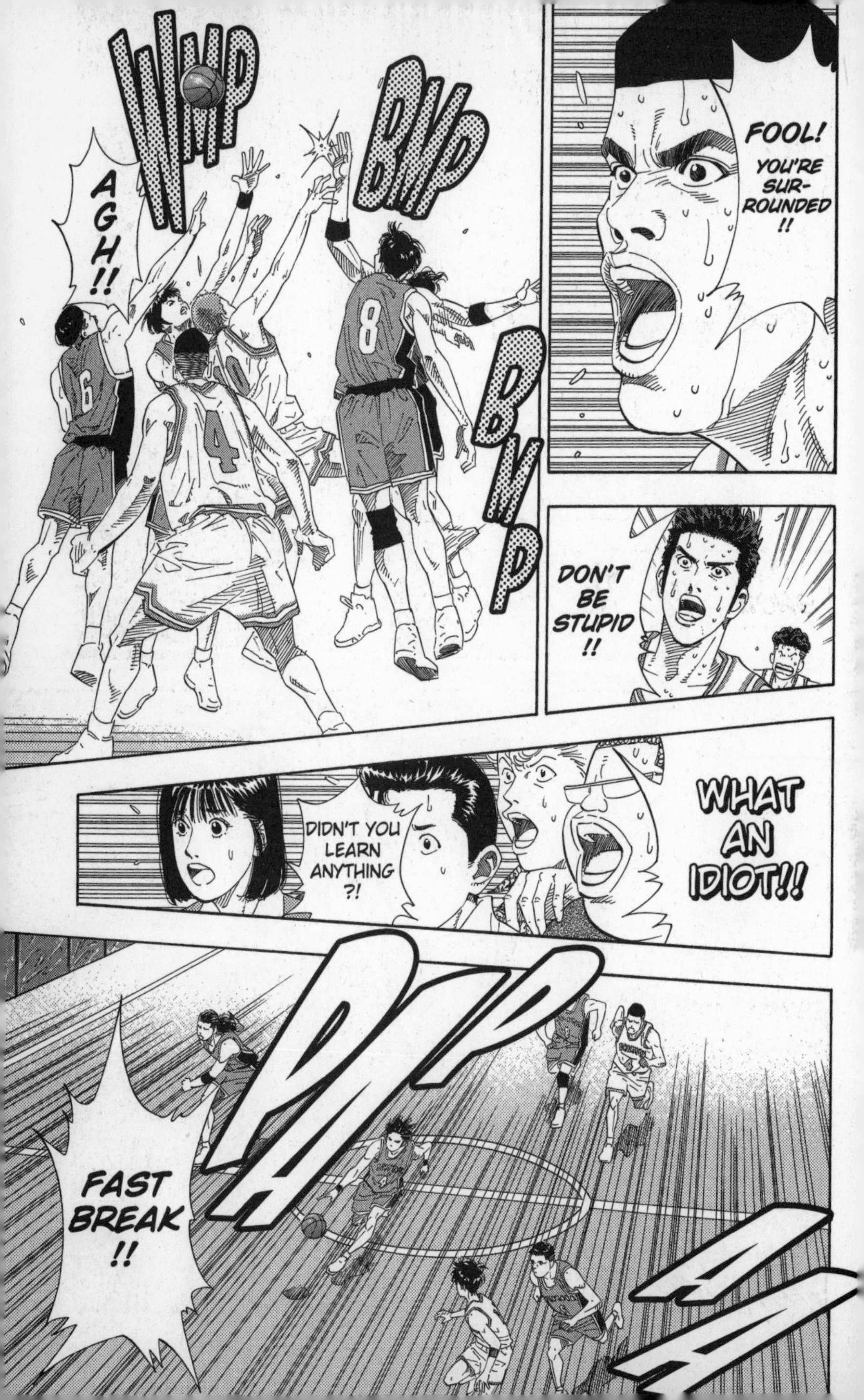
FOOL! YOU'RE SUR-ROUNDED!!
DON'T BE STUPID!!
BMP
WMP
BMP
AGH!!
WHAT AN IDIOT!!
DIDN'T YOU LEARN ANYTHING ?!
FAST BREAK!!

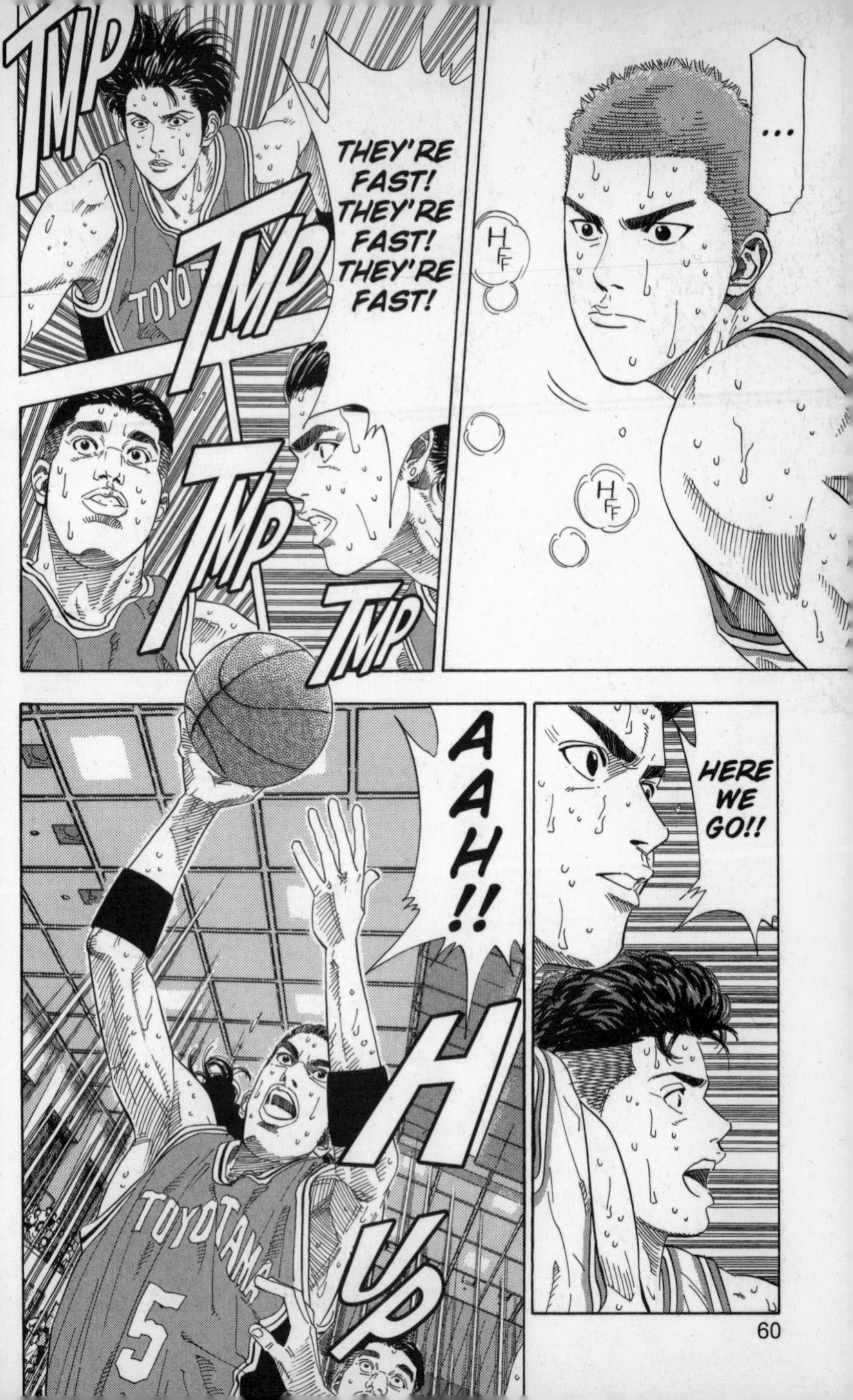
...
HFF
HFF
TMP
THEY'RE FAST! THEY'RE FAST! THEY'RE FAST!
TMP
TMP
TMP
HERE WE GO!!
AAH!!
HUP

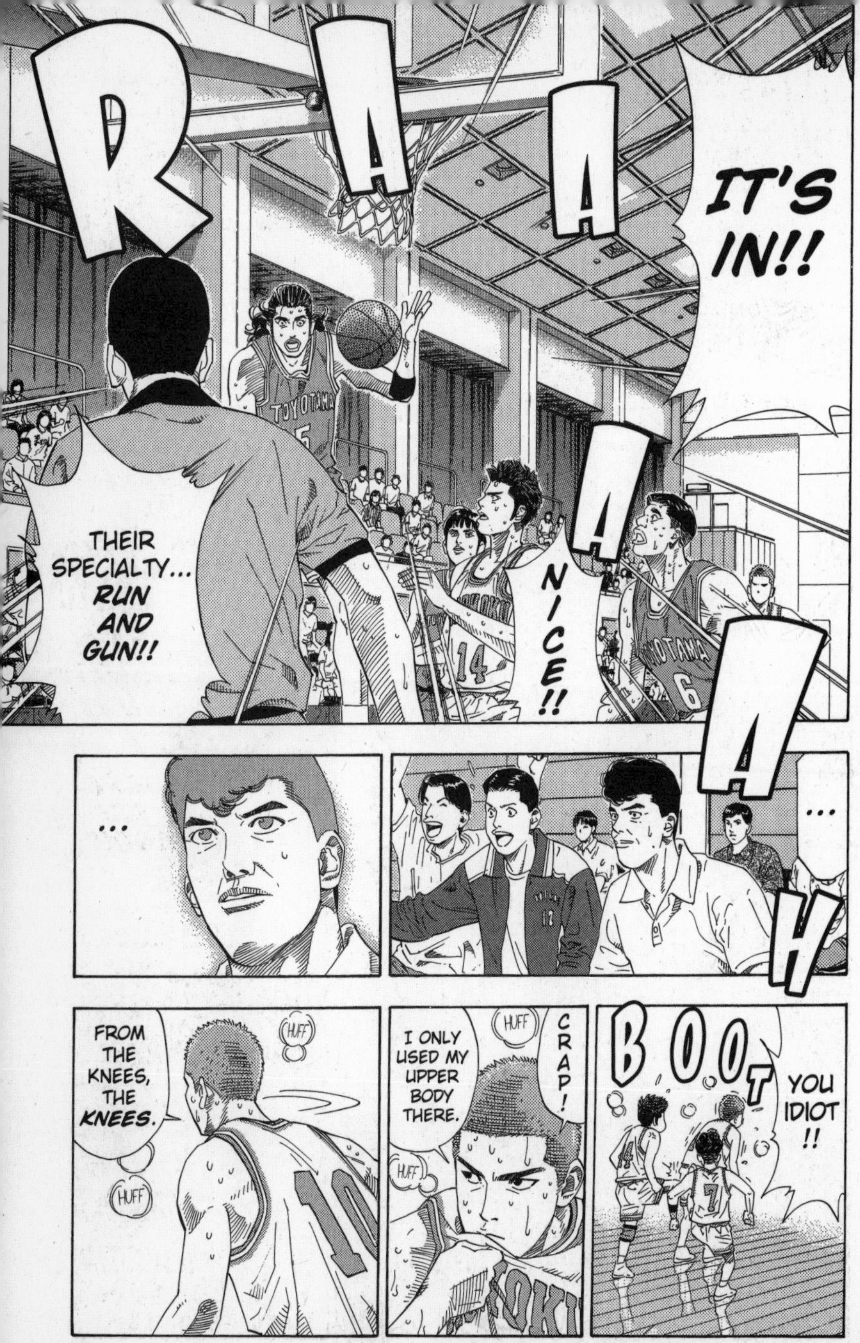

RAAAAH
IT'S IN!!
NICE!!
THEIR SPECIALTY... RUN AND GUN!!
...
...
BOOT
YOU IDIOT!!
CRAP!
HUFF
I ONLY USED MY UPPER BODY THERE.
HUFF
HUFF
FROM THE KNEES, THE KNEES.
HUFF

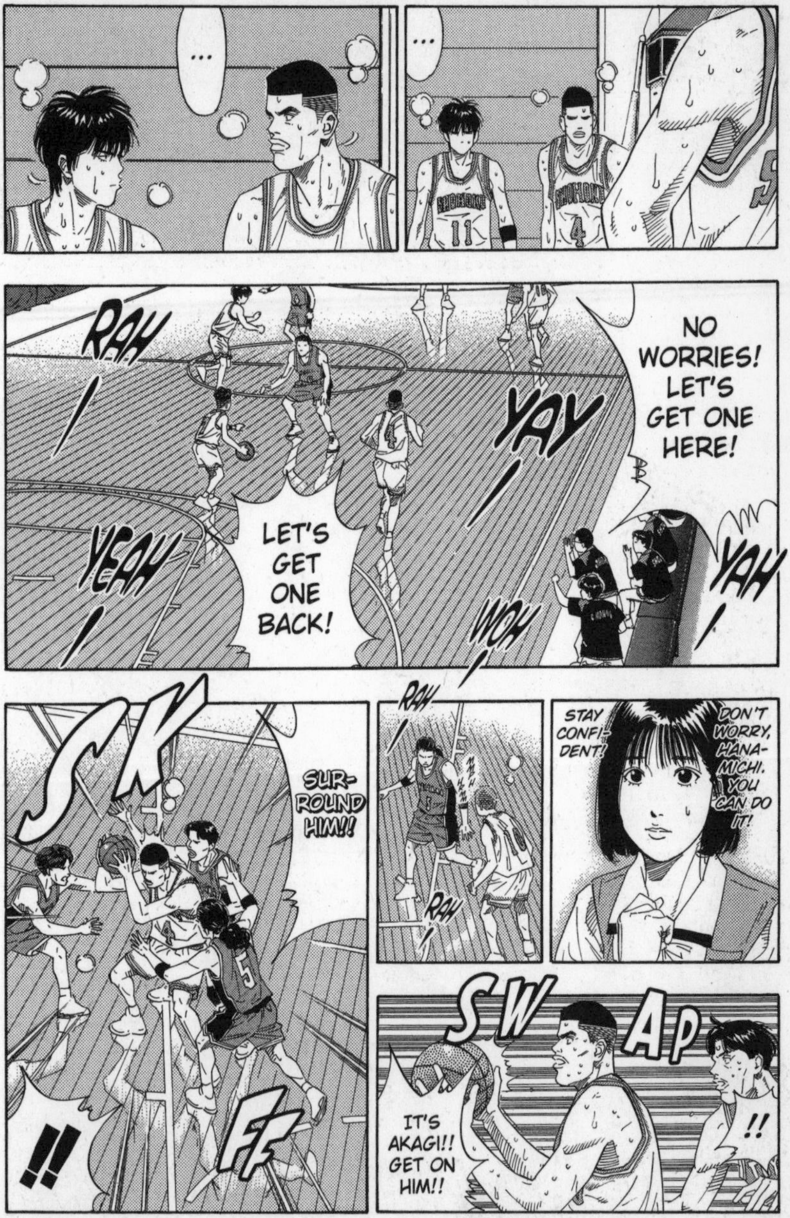
...
...
NO WORRIES! LET'S GET ONE HERE!
YAH!
YAY!
WOH!
RAH!
LET'S GET ONE BACK!
YEAH!
DON'T WORRY, HANAMICHI. YOU CAN DO IT!
STAY CONFIDENT!
RAH!
RAH!
SWAP
!!
IT'S AKAGI!! GET ON HIM!!
SK
SURROUND HIM!!
FF
!!

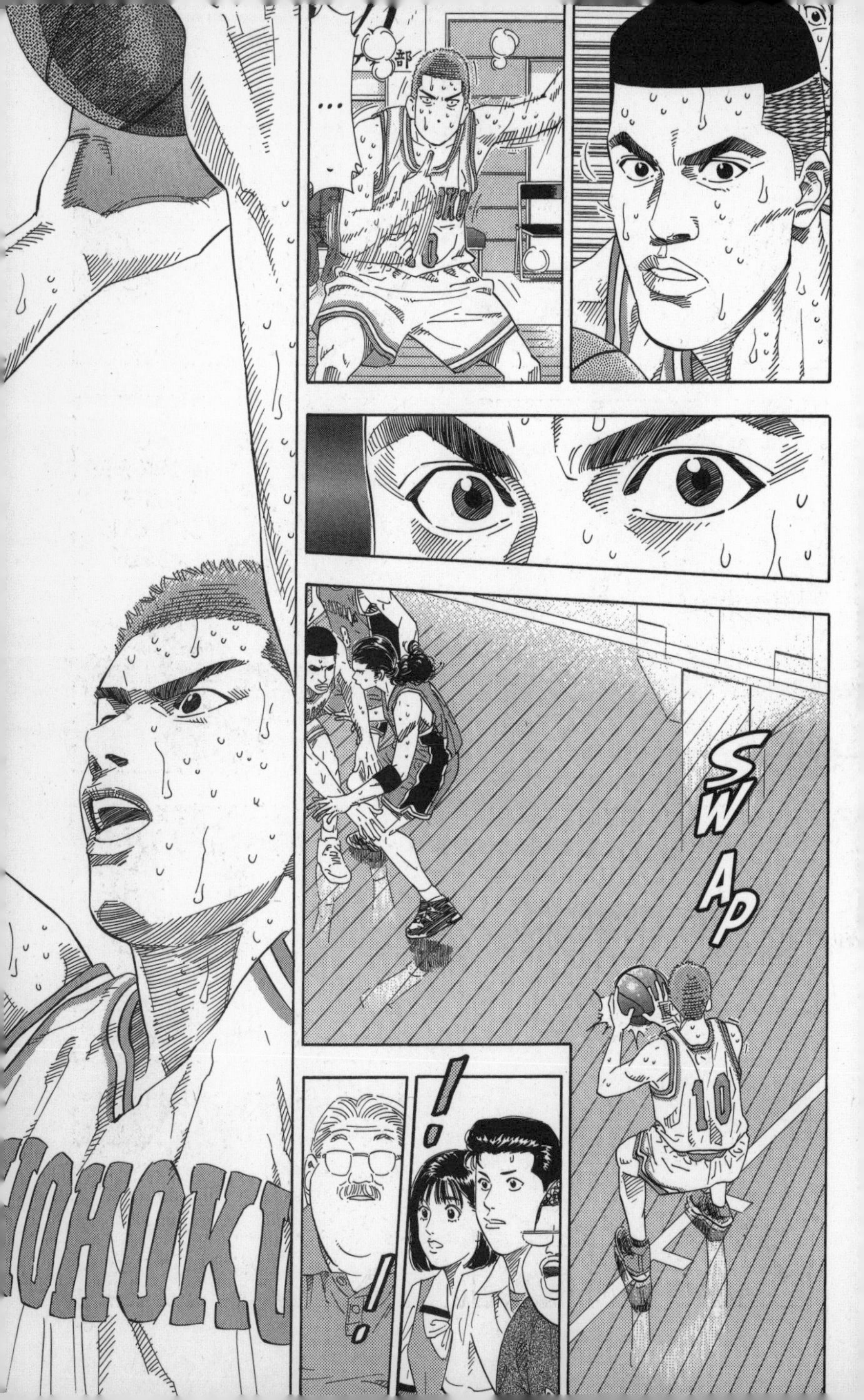
...
SWAP
!
!!

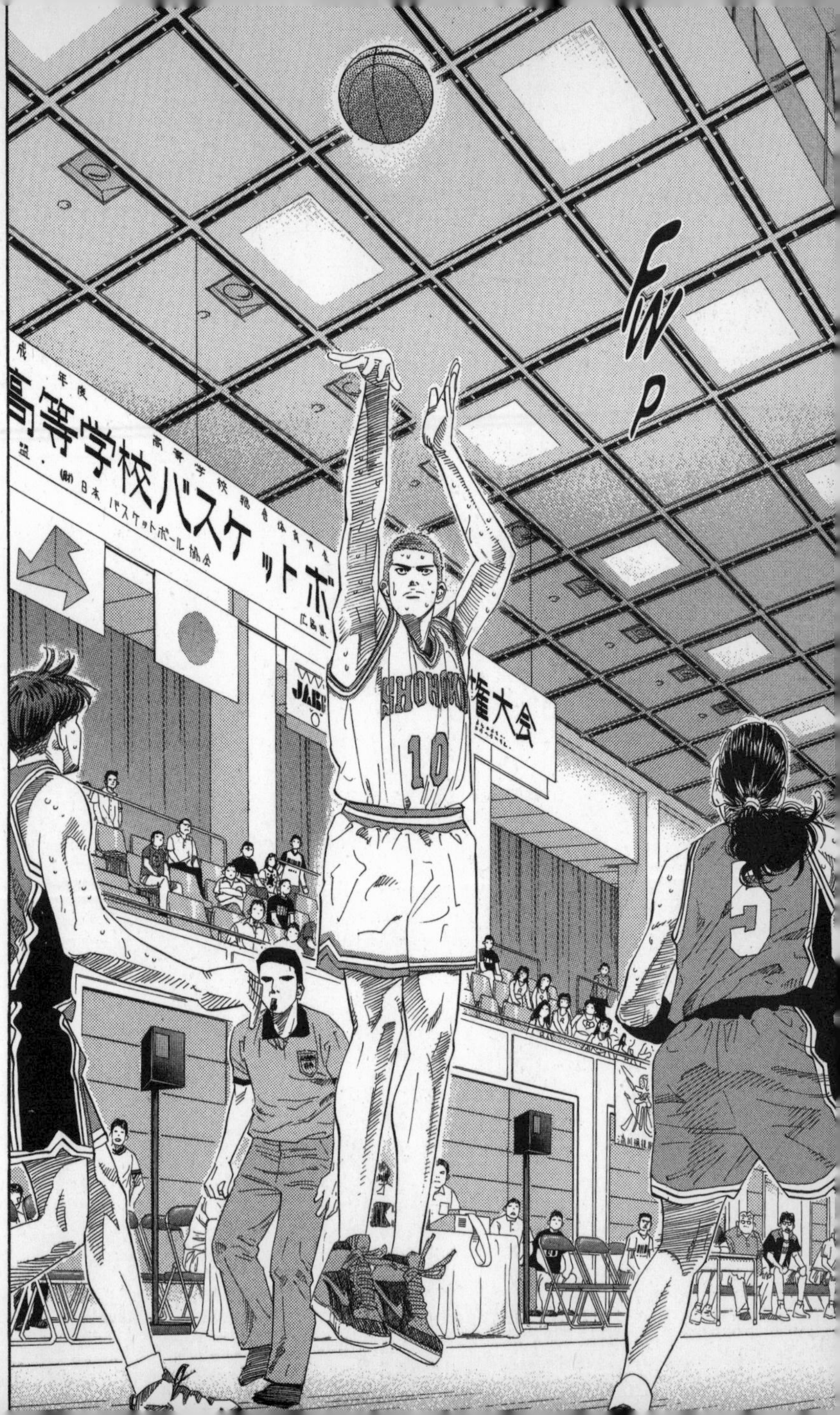
FWP
高等学校バスケットボ
日本 バスケットボール協会
10
5

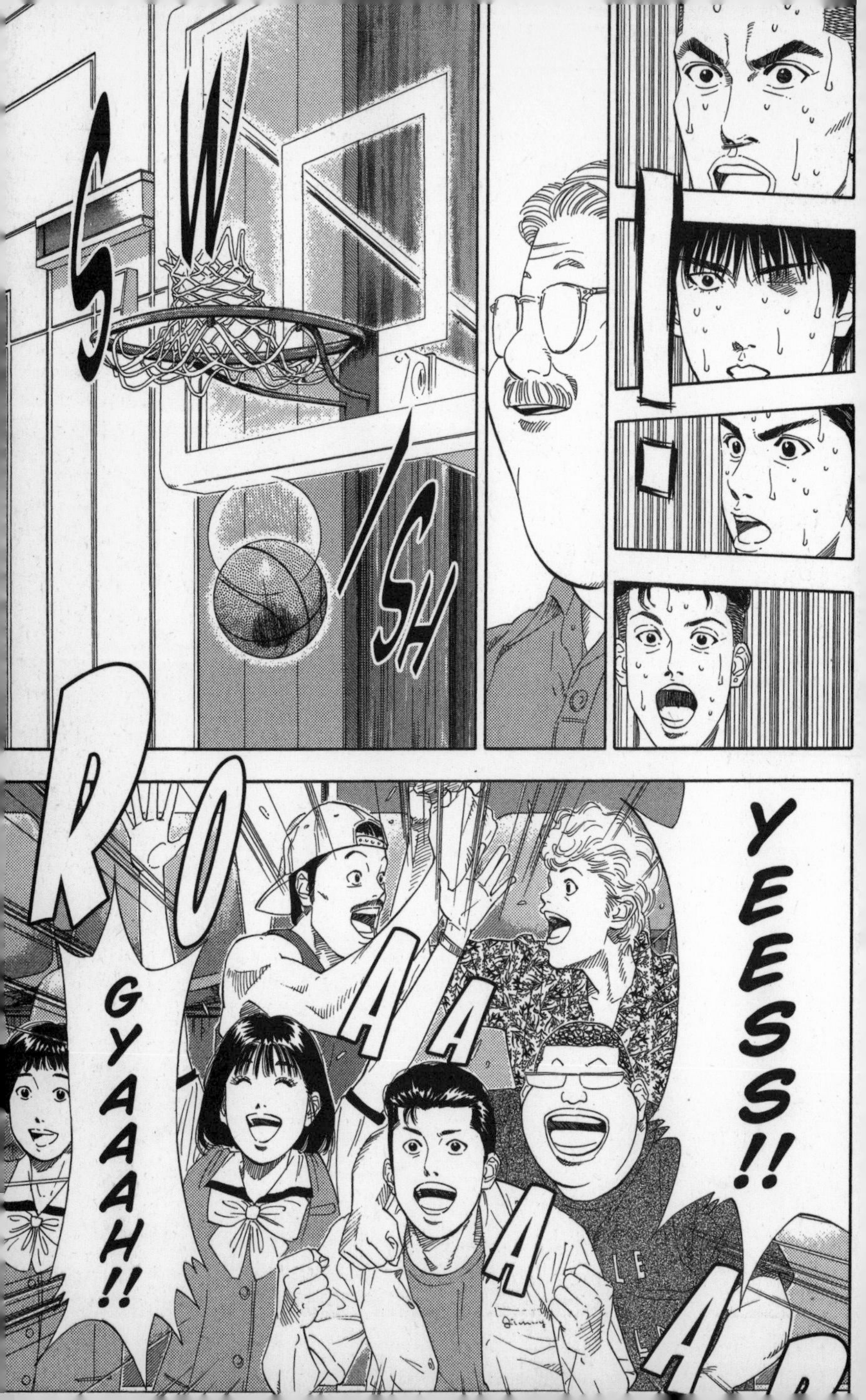
SWISH
YEESS!!
ROAAAA
GYAAAAH!!

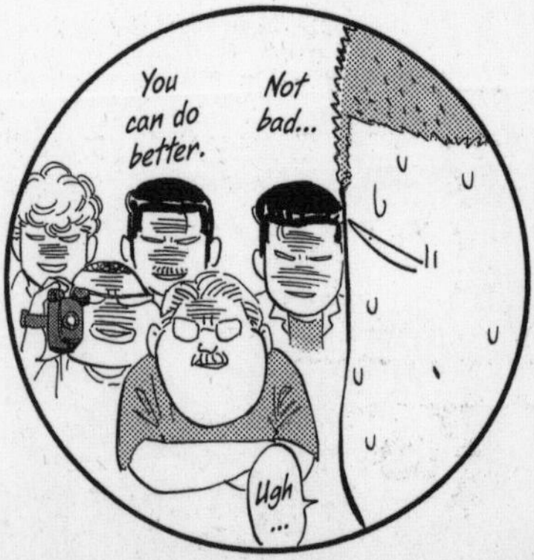
Not bad...
You can do better.
Ugh ...

SLAM DUNK

#210 SHOHOKU'S PURSUIT

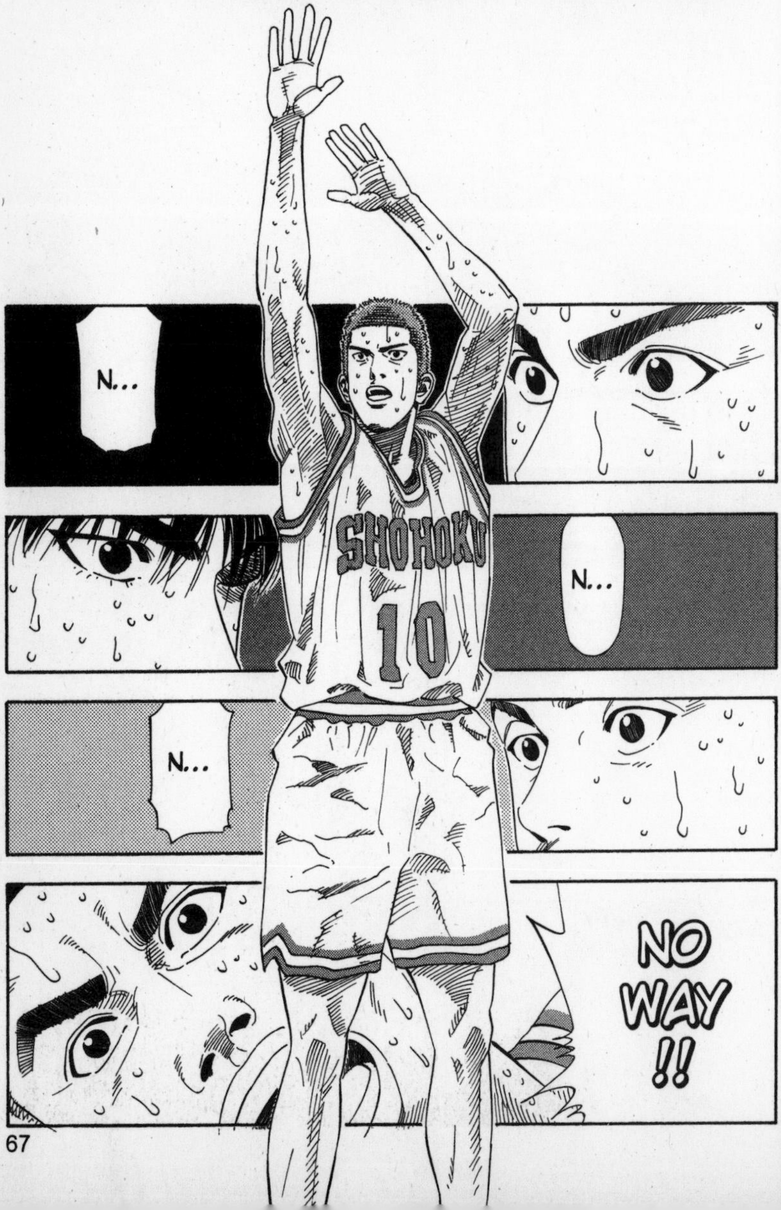
N...
N...
SHOHOKU
10
N...
NO WAY!!

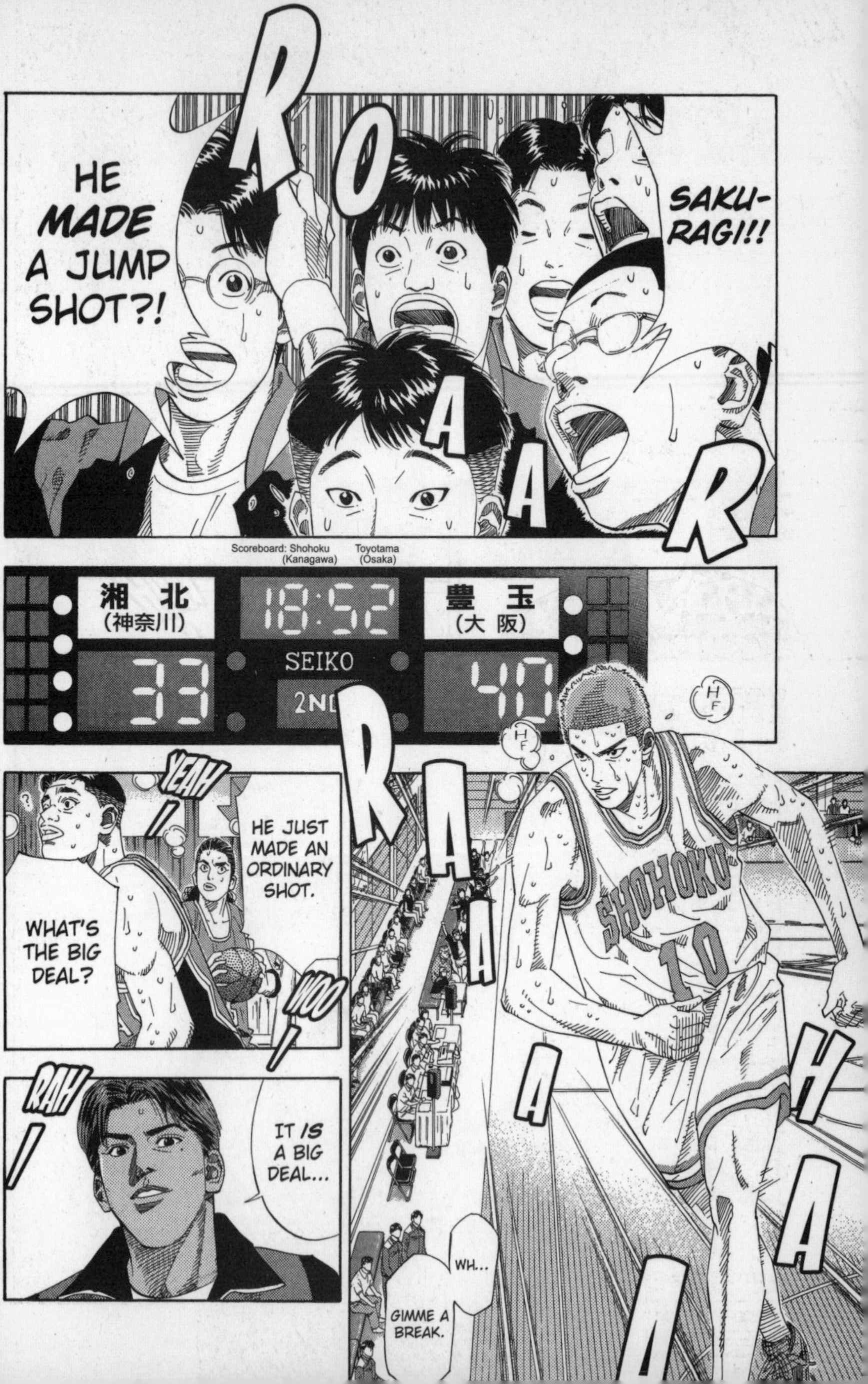
SAKU-RAGI!!
ROAAR
HE MADE A JUMP SHOT?!
Scoreboard: Shohoku (Kanagawa) Toyotama (Osaka)
湘北 (神奈川)
18:52
豊玉 (大阪)
SEIKO
33
40
2ND
RAAA
HAHA
WH...
GIMME A BREAK.
YEAH
HE JUST MADE AN ORDINARY SHOT.
WHAT'S THE BIG DEAL?
WOO
RAH
IT IS A BIG DEAL...

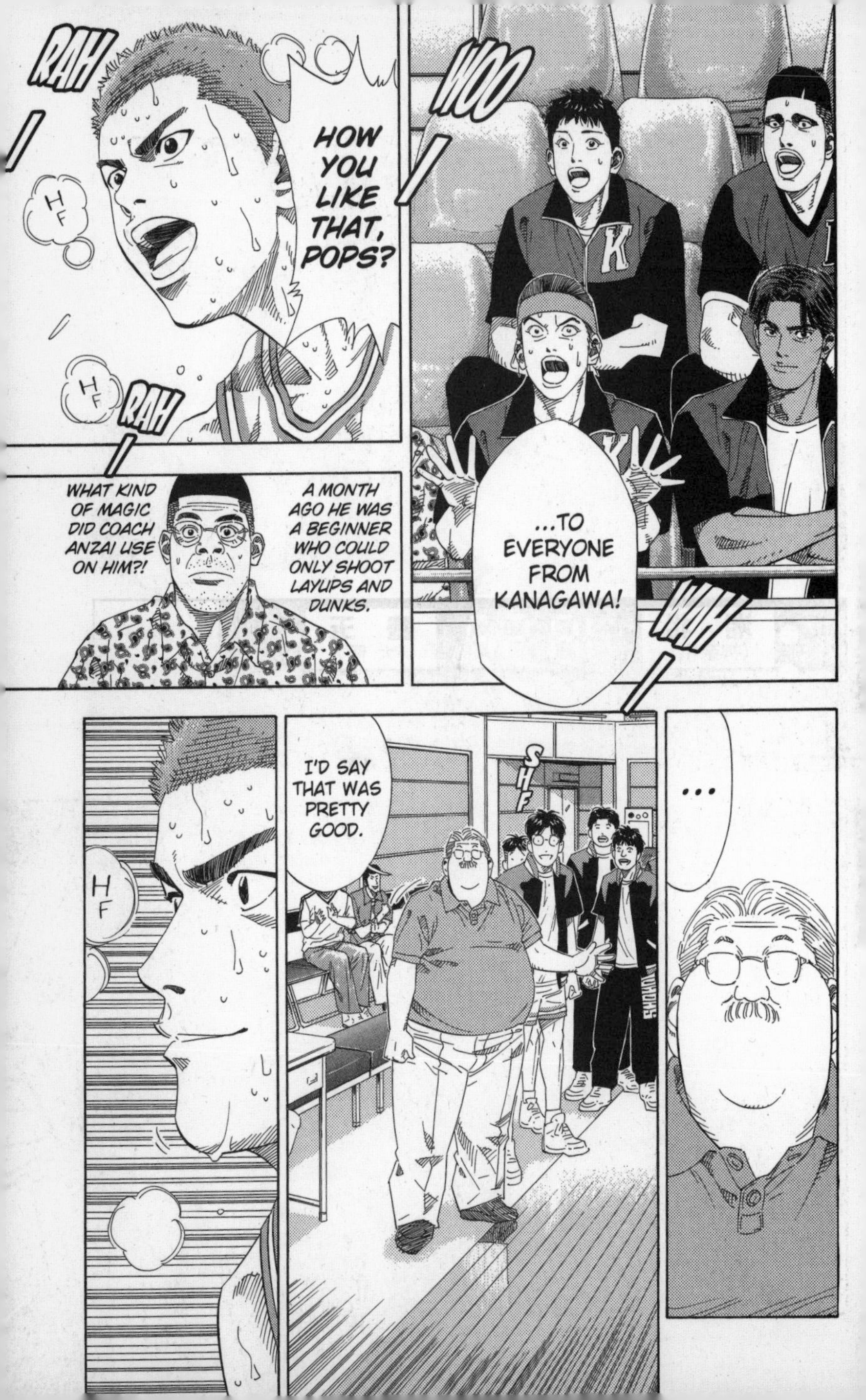
WOO
...TO EVERYONE FROM KANAGAWA!
WAH
RAH
HOW YOU LIKE THAT, POPS?
HF
HF
RAH
A MONTH AGO HE WAS A BEGINNER WHO COULD ONLY SHOOT LAYUPS AND DUNKS.
WHAT KIND OF MAGIC DID COACH ANZAI USE ON HIM?!
...
SHF
I'D SAY THAT WAS PRETTY GOOD.
HF

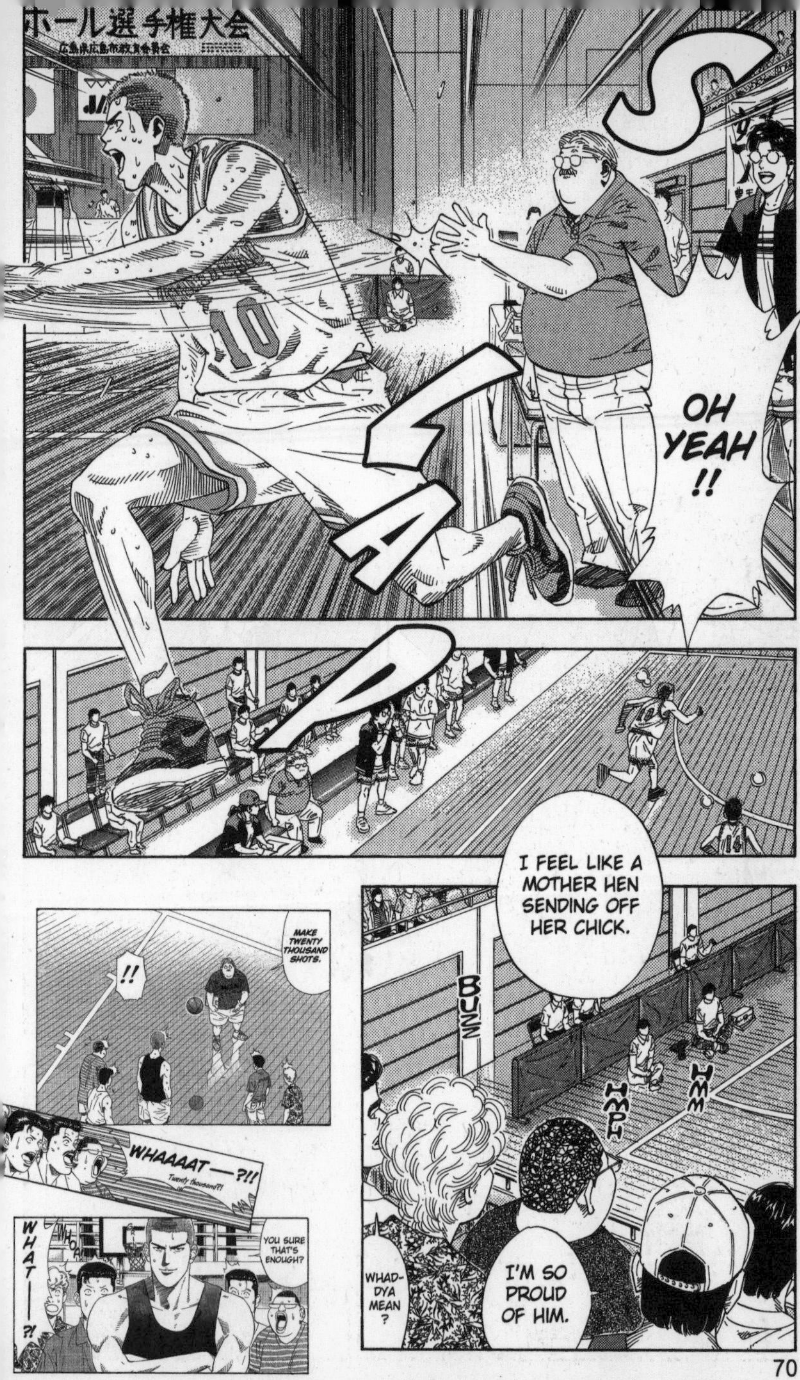
ホール選手権大会
SLAP
OH YEAH !!
I FEEL LIKE A MOTHER HEN SENDING OFF HER CHICK.
BUZZ
HMM
HMPH
I'M SO PROUD OF HIM.
WHADDYA MEAN?
MAKE TWENTY THOUSAND SHOTS.
!!
WHAAAAT——?!!
Twenty thousand?!
YOU SURE THAT'S ENOUGH?
WHOA
WHAT——?!

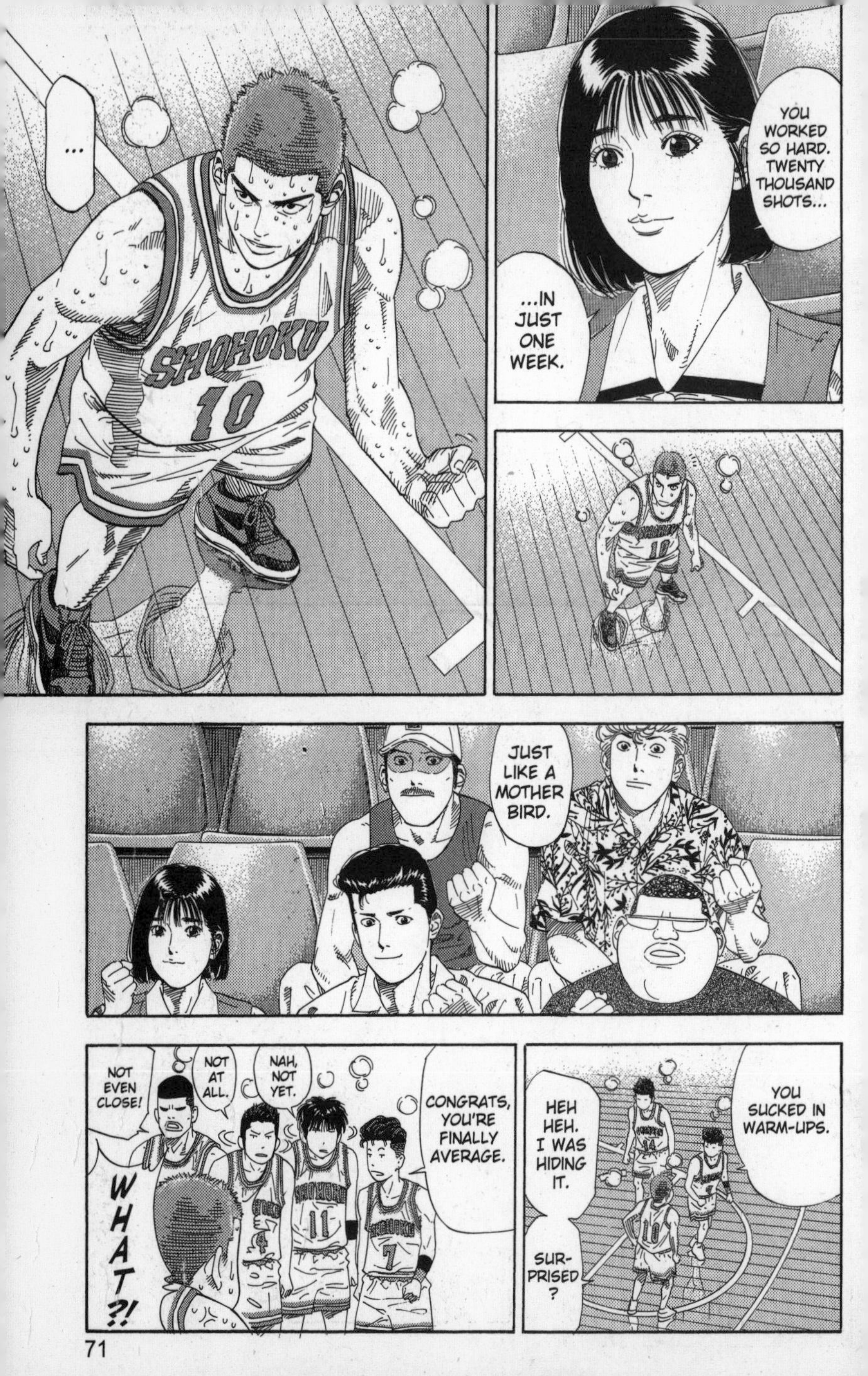
YOU WORKED SO HARD. TWENTY THOUSAND SHOTS...
...IN JUST ONE WEEK.
...
JUST LIKE A MOTHER BIRD.
YOU SUCKED IN WARM-UPS.
HEH HEH. I WAS HIDING IT.
SUR-PRISED?
CONGRATS, YOU'RE FINALLY AVERAGE.
NAH, NOT YET.
NOT AT ALL.
NOT EVEN CLOSE!
WHAT?!

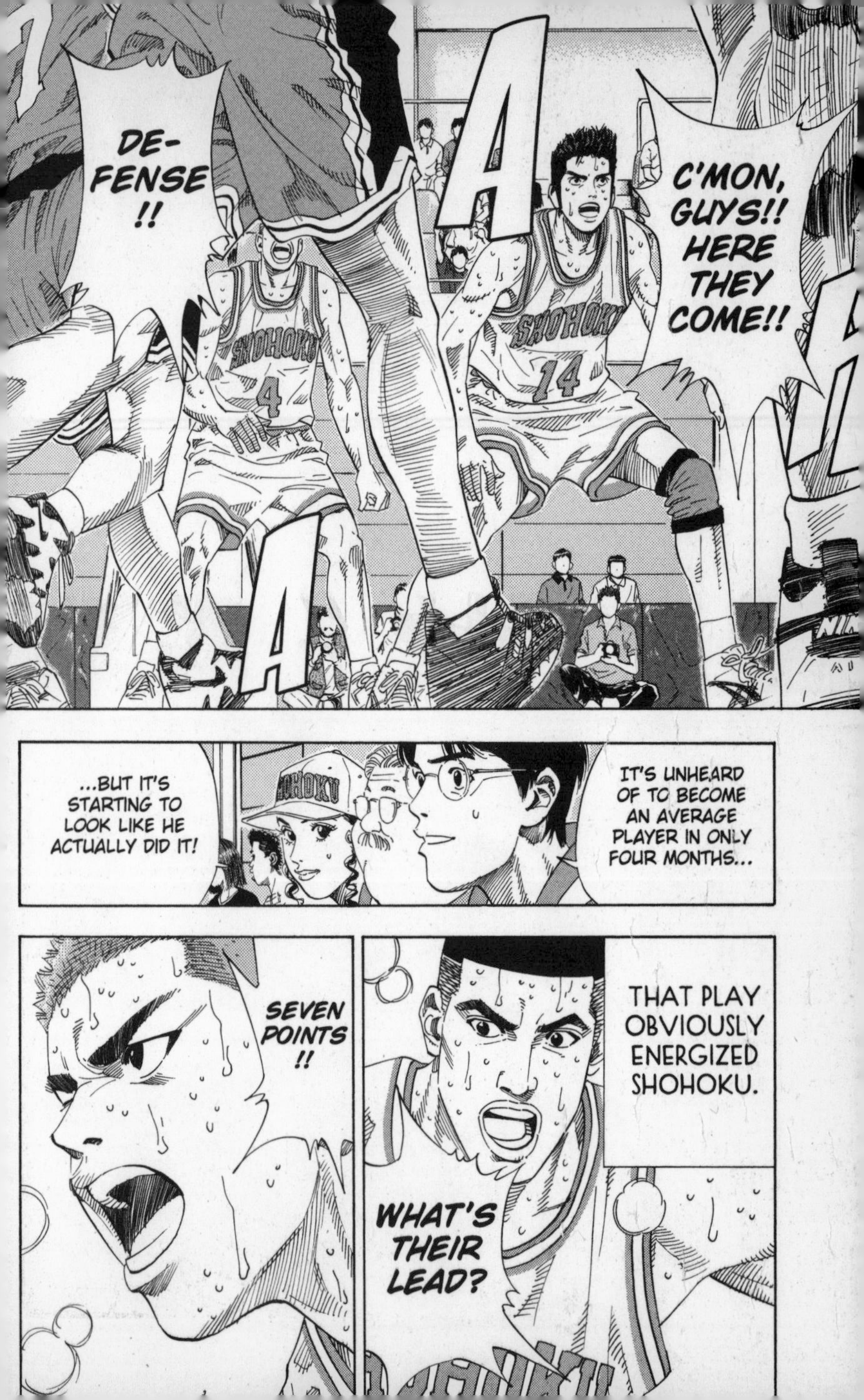
C'MON, GUYS!! HERE THEY COME!!
DE-FENSE!!
A
A
IT'S UNHEARD OF TO BECOME AN AVERAGE PLAYER IN ONLY FOUR MONTHS...
...BUT IT'S STARTING TO LOOK LIKE HE ACTUALLY DID IT!
THAT PLAY OBVIOUSLY ENERGIZED SHOHOKU.
WHAT'S THEIR LEAD?
SEVEN POINTS!!

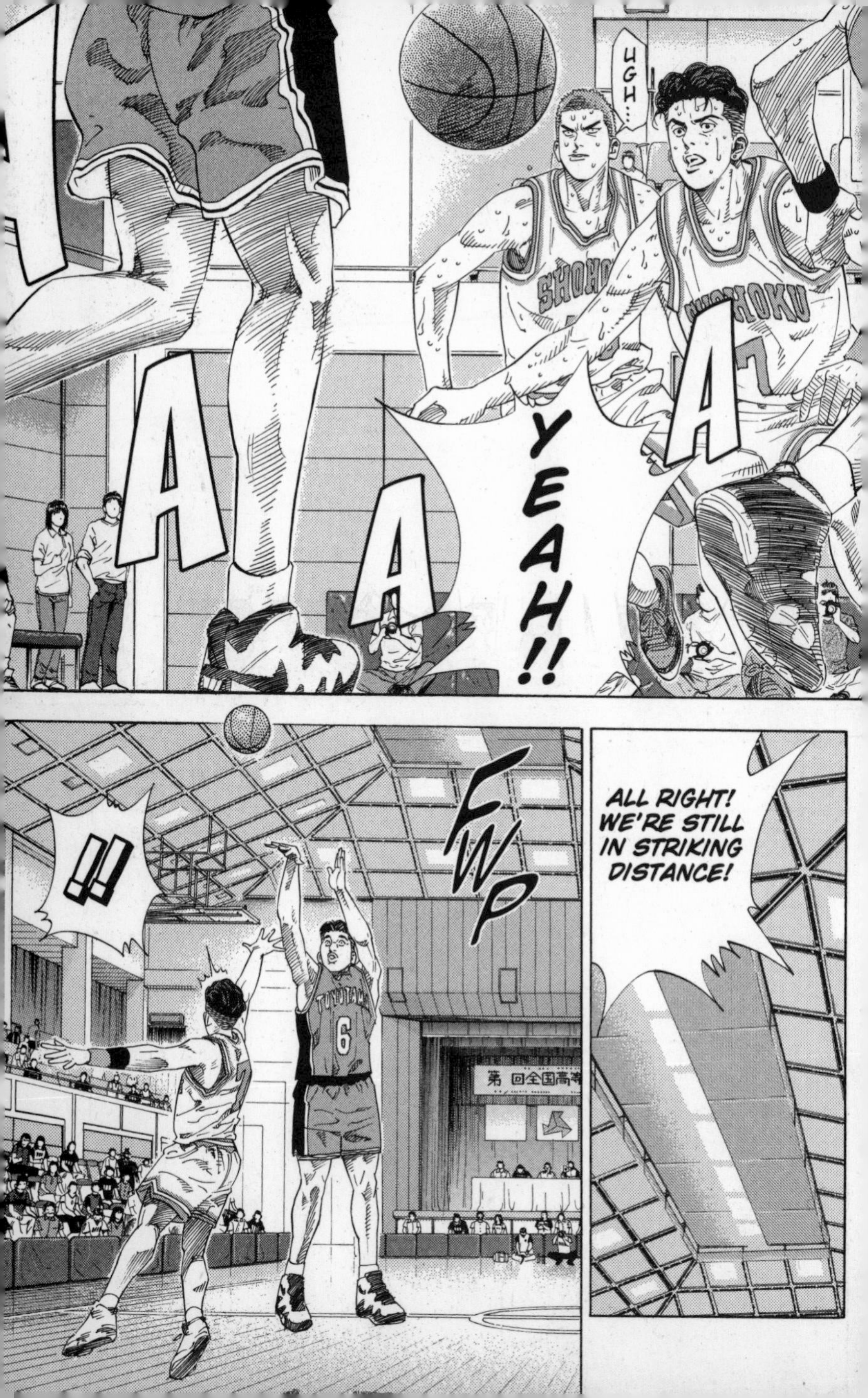
UGH...
A
A
A
YEAH!!
ALL RIGHT! WE'RE STILL IN STRIKING DISTANCE!
FWP
!!
第 回全国高等

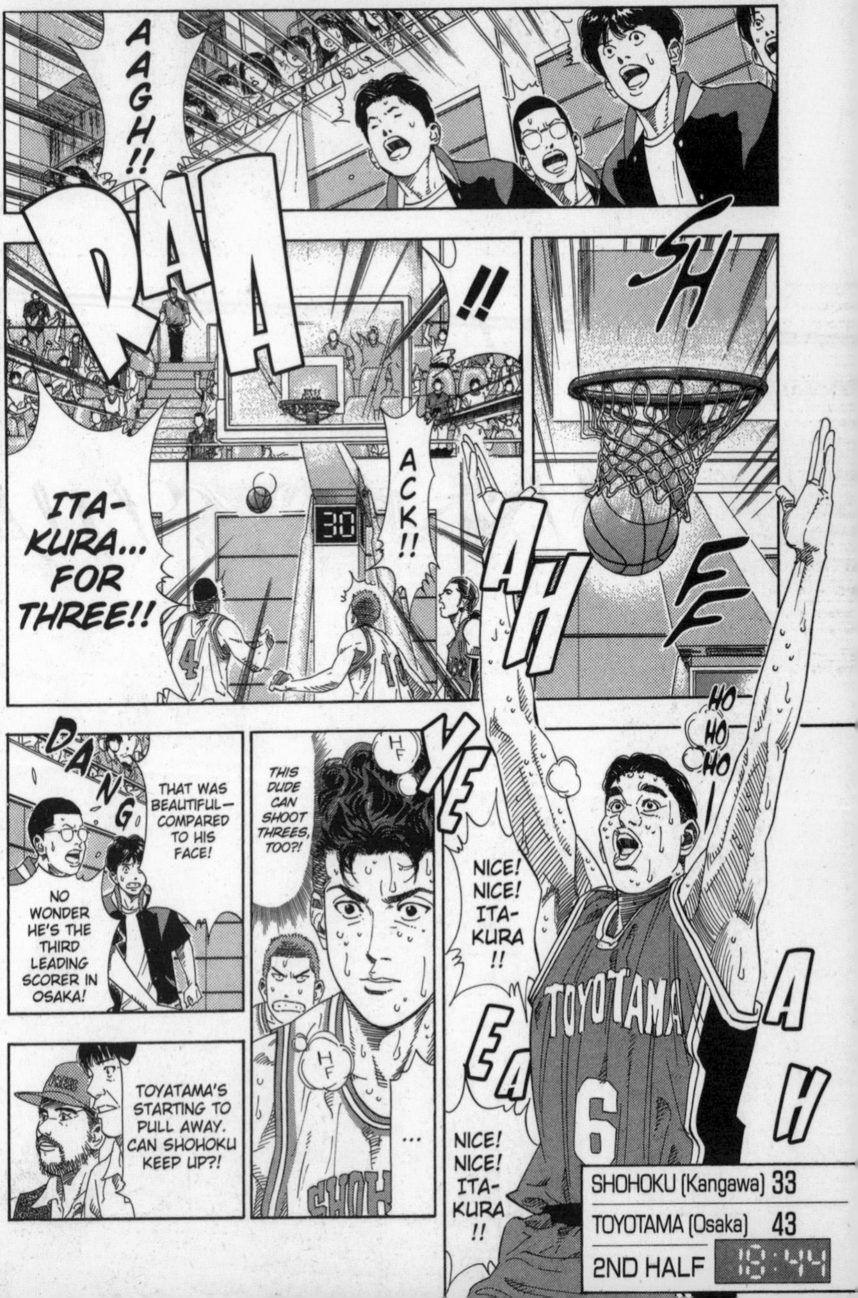
AAGH!!
SH
RAA!!
ACK!!
ITA-KURA... FOR THREE!!
AH
FF
HO HO HO
YE
NICE! NICE! ITA-KURA!!
TOYOTAMA
AH
EA
NICE! NICE! ITA-KURA!!
SHOHOKU (Kangawa) 33
TOYOTAMA (Osaka) 43
2ND HALF 18:44
THIS DUDE CAN SHOOT THREES, TOO?!
HF
HF
...
DANG
THAT WAS BEAUTIFUL—COMPARED TO HIS FACE!
NO WONDER HE'S THE THIRD LEADING SCORER IN OSAKA!
TOYATAMA'S STARTING TO PULL AWAY. CAN SHOHOKU KEEP UP?!

READ THIS WAY

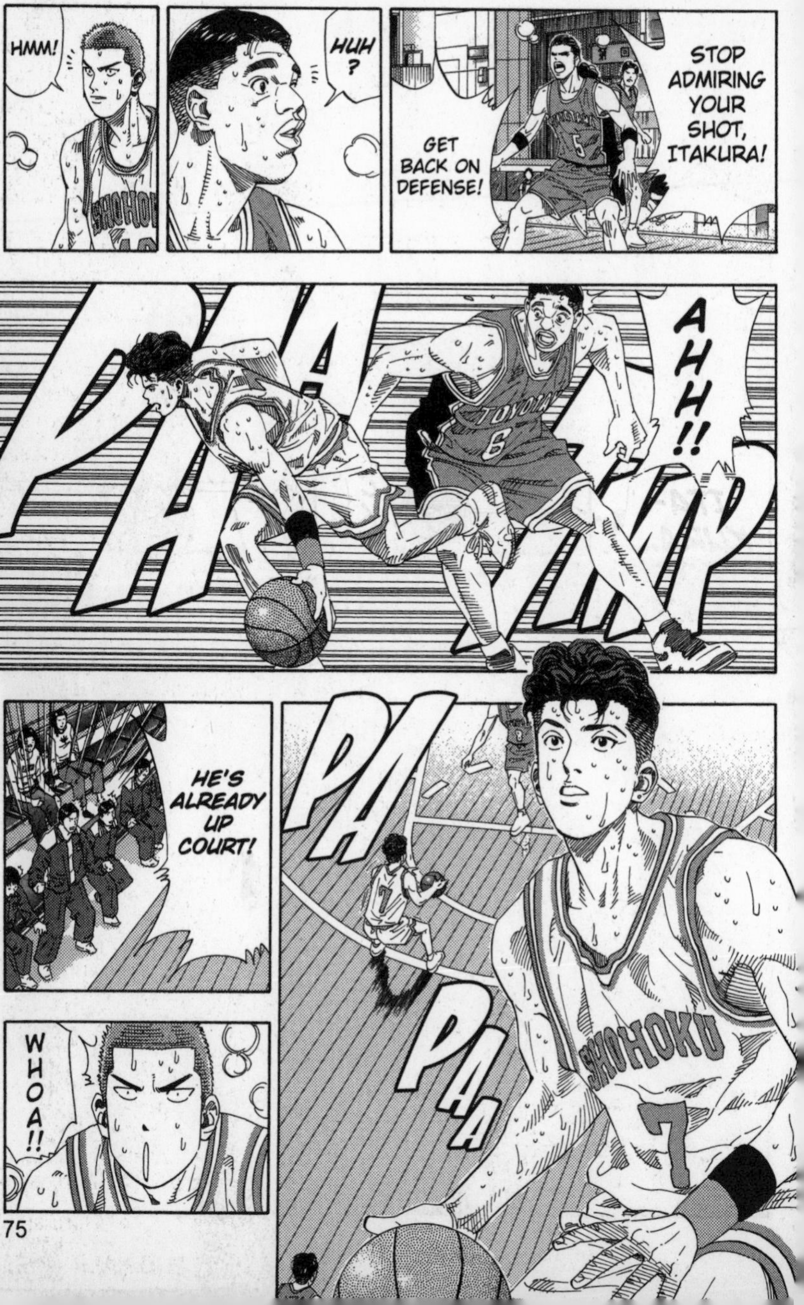
STOP ADMIRING YOUR SHOT, ITAKURA!
GET BACK ON DEFENSE!
HUH?
HMM!
AHH!!
TAP
PA
PA
PAA
HE'S ALREADY UP COURT!
WHOA!!

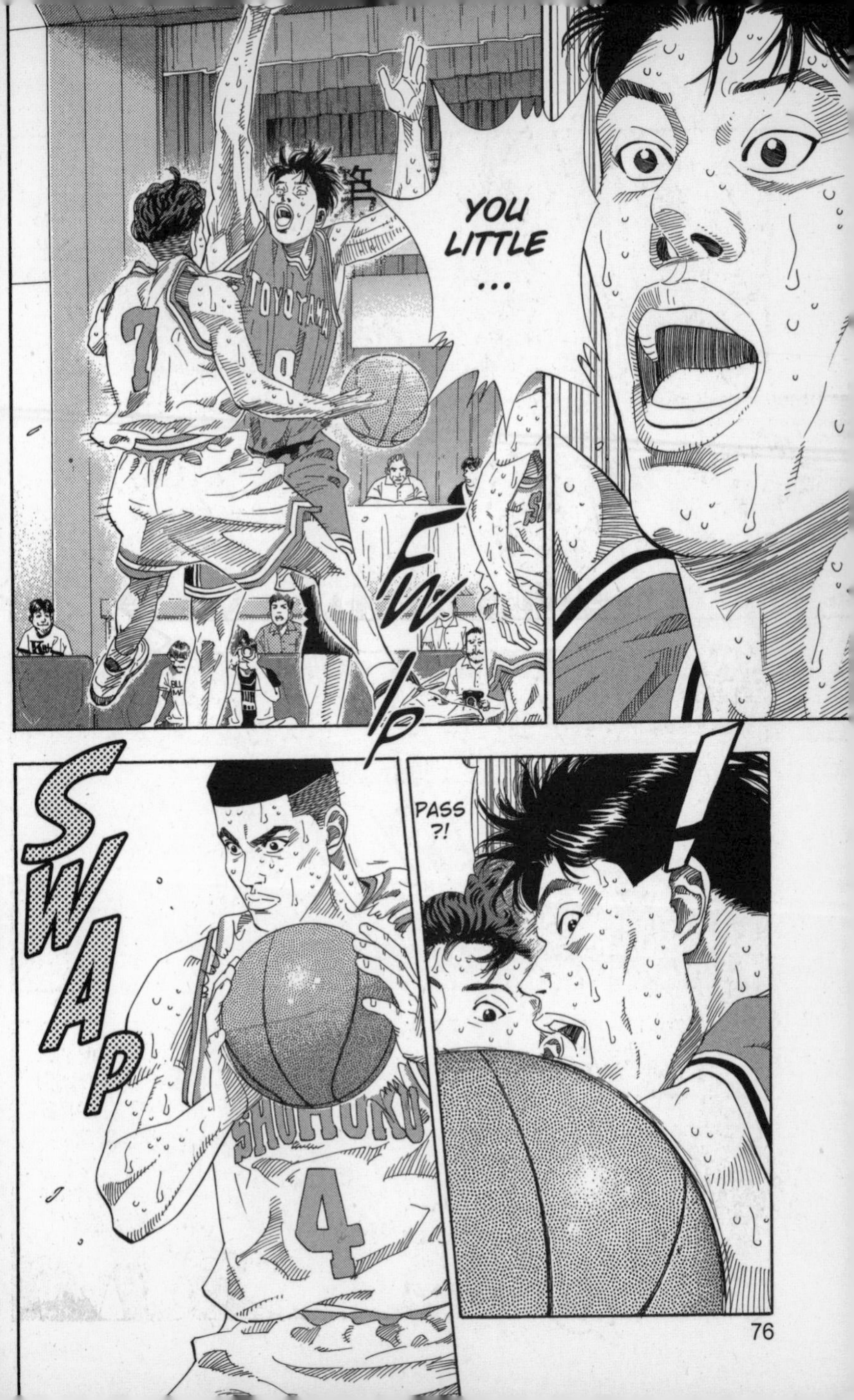
YOU LITTLE ...
FWIP
PASS ?!
SWAP

BRING IT ON, AKAGI!!

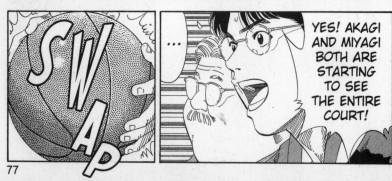

...

YES! AKAGI AND MIYAGI BOTH ARE STARTING TO SEE THE ENTIRE COURT!

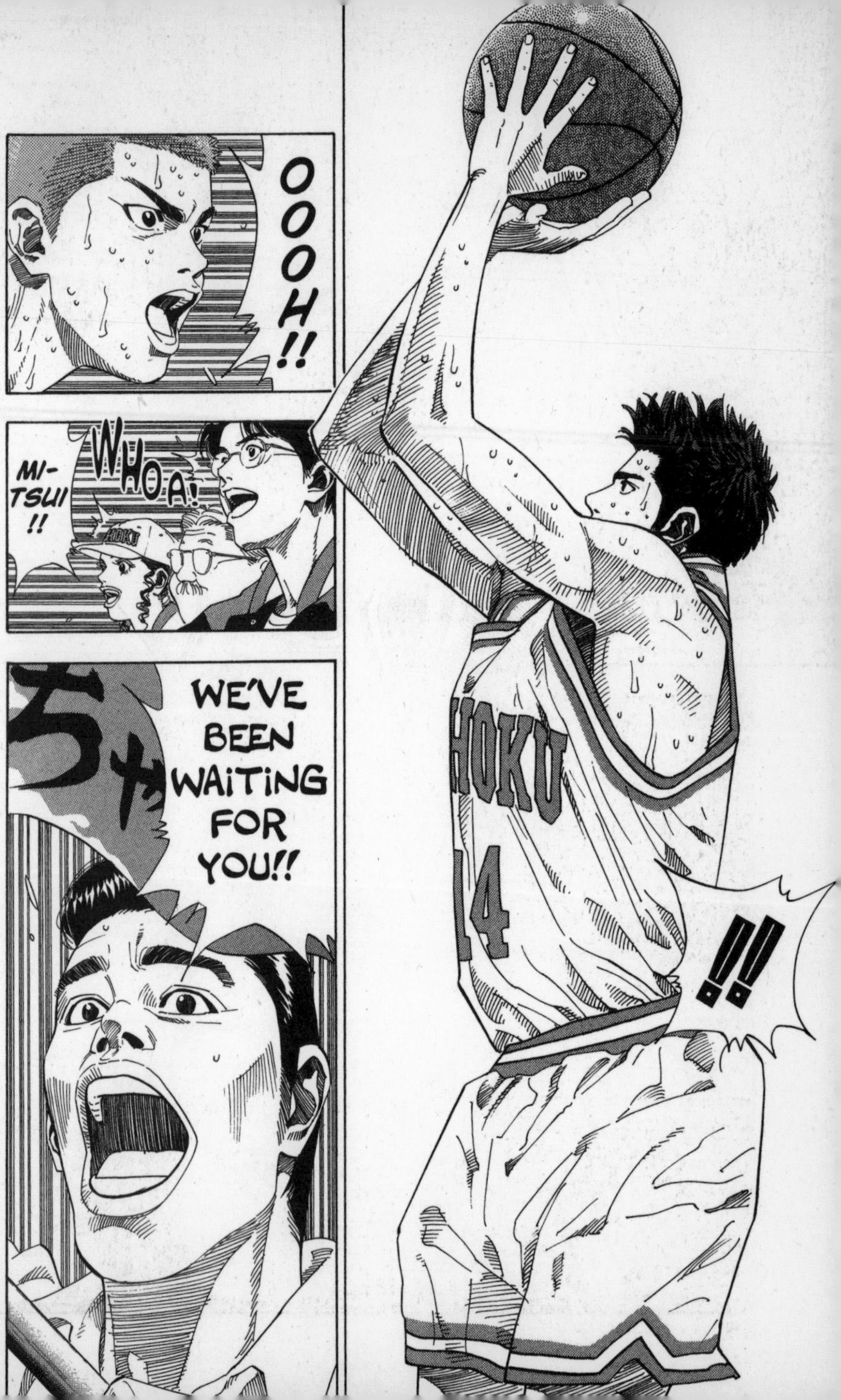
!!
OOOOH!!
WHOA!
MI-TSUI!!
WE'VE BEEN WAITING FOR YOU!!

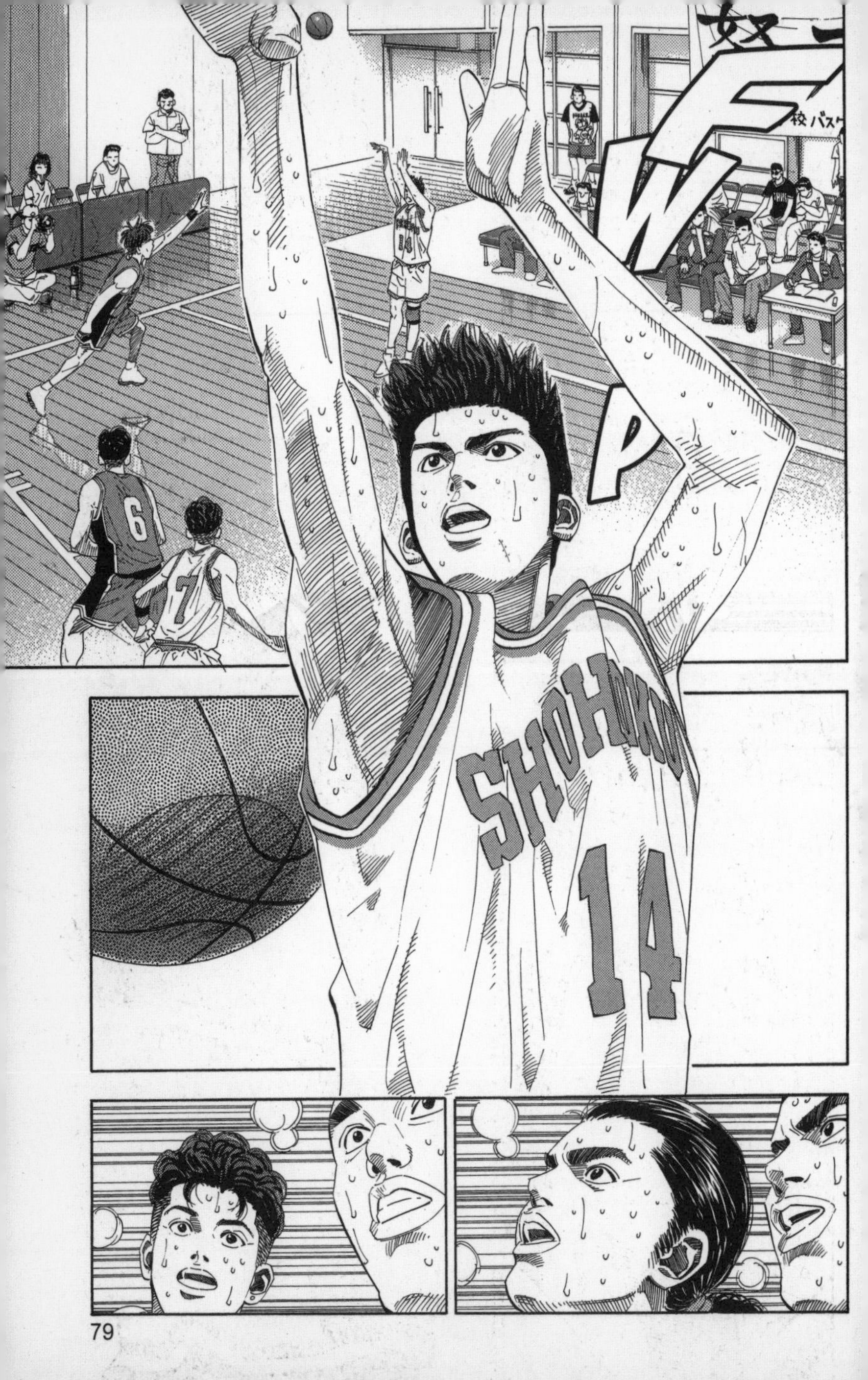
SHOHOKU
14

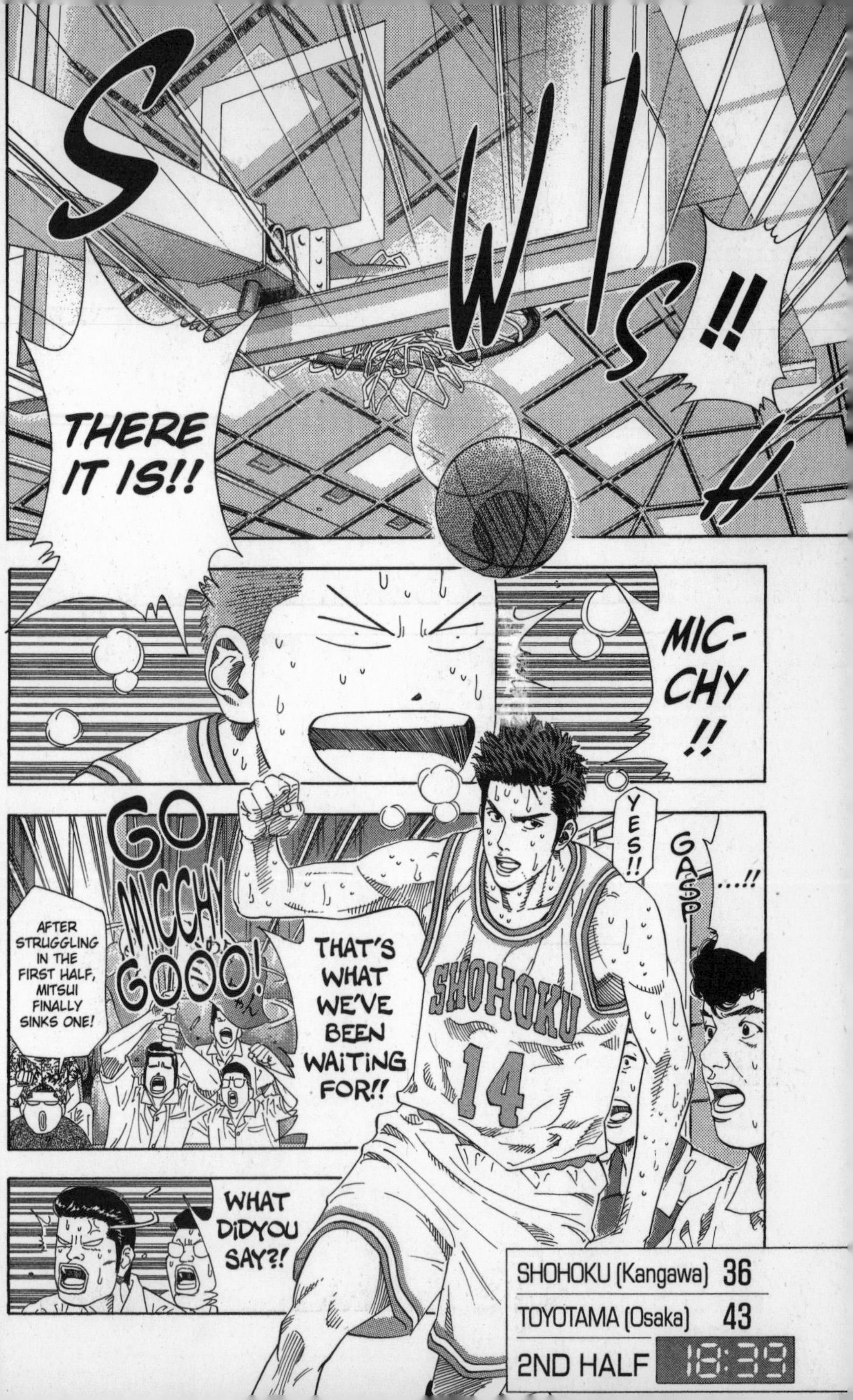
SWISH!!
THERE IT IS!!
MIC-CHY!!
YES!!
GASP
...!!
THAT'S WHAT WE'VE BEEN WAITING FOR!!
GO MICCHY GOOO!
AFTER STRUGGLING IN THE FIRST HALF, MITSUI FINALLY SINKS ONE!
SHOHOKU
14
WHAT DIDYOU SAY?!
SHOHOKU (Kangawa) 36
TOYOTAMA (Osaka) 43
2ND HALF 18:39

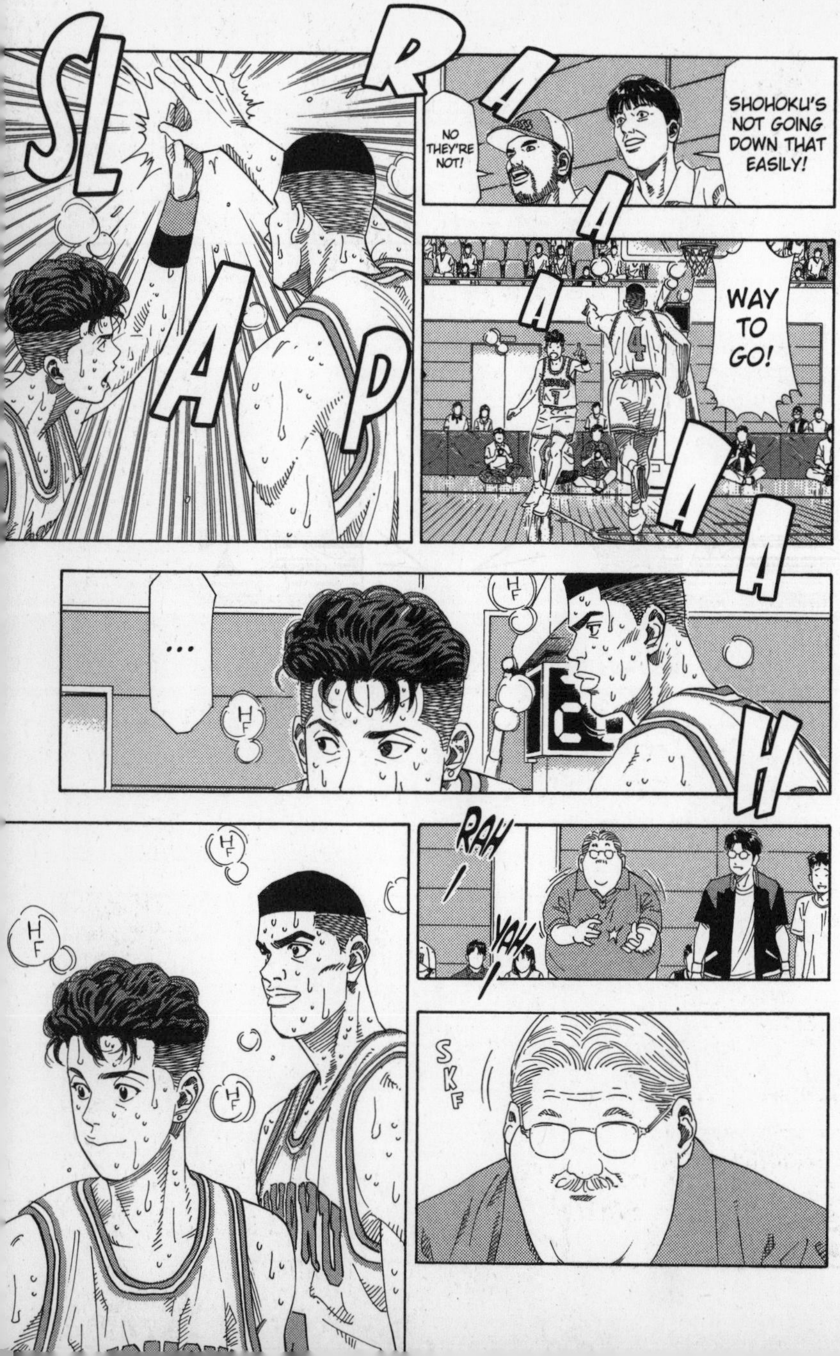
SL
AP
R
A
A
A
AAH
SHOHOKU'S NOT GOING DOWN THAT EASILY!
NO THEY'RE NOT!
WAY TO GO!
HF
...
HF
RAH!
YAH!
SKF
HF
HF
HF

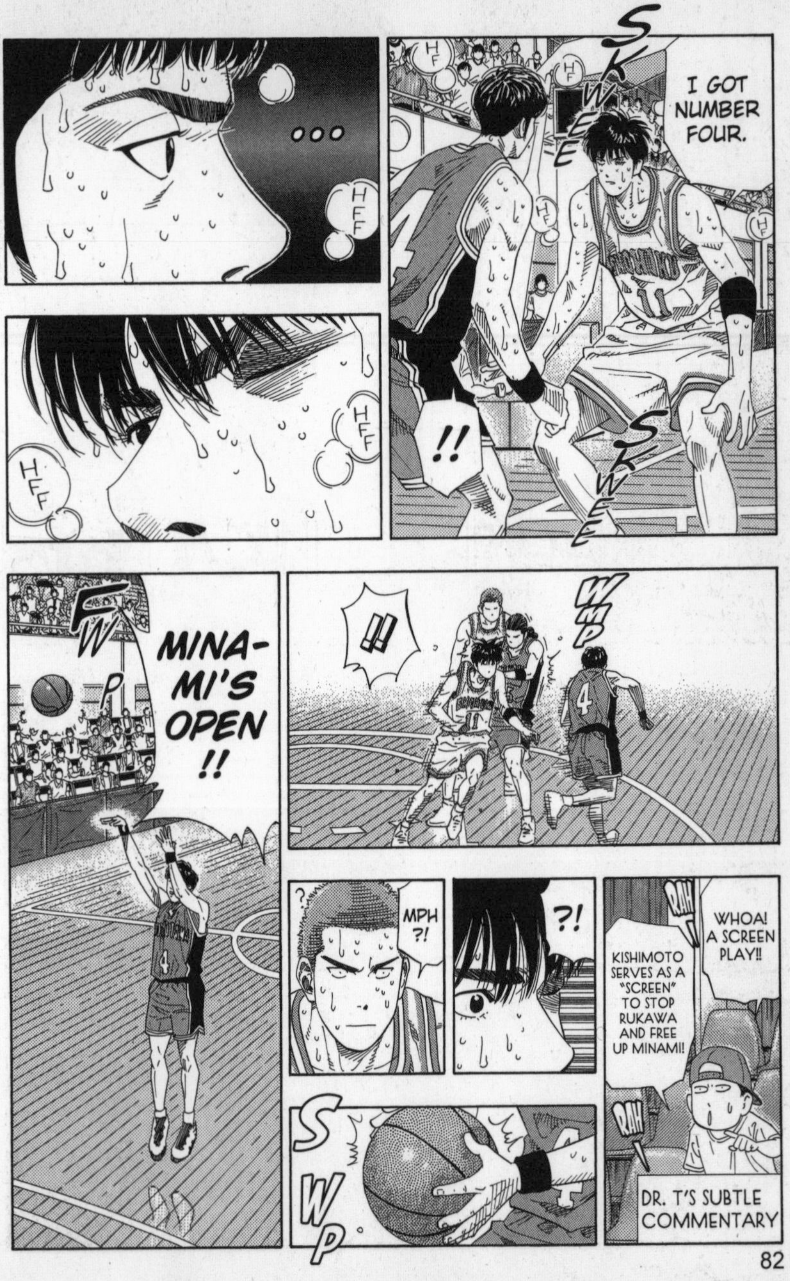
SKWEE
HF
HF
I GOT NUMBER FOUR.
HF
HF
!!
SKWEE
ooo
HFF
HFF
HFF
WMP
!!
RAH
WHOA! A SCREEN PLAY!!
KISHIMOTO SERVES AS A "SCREEN" TO STOP RUKAWA AND FREE UP MINAMI!
RAH
DR. T'S SUBTLE COMMENTARY
?!
MPH ?!
?
SWP
FWP
MINA-MI'S OPEN !!

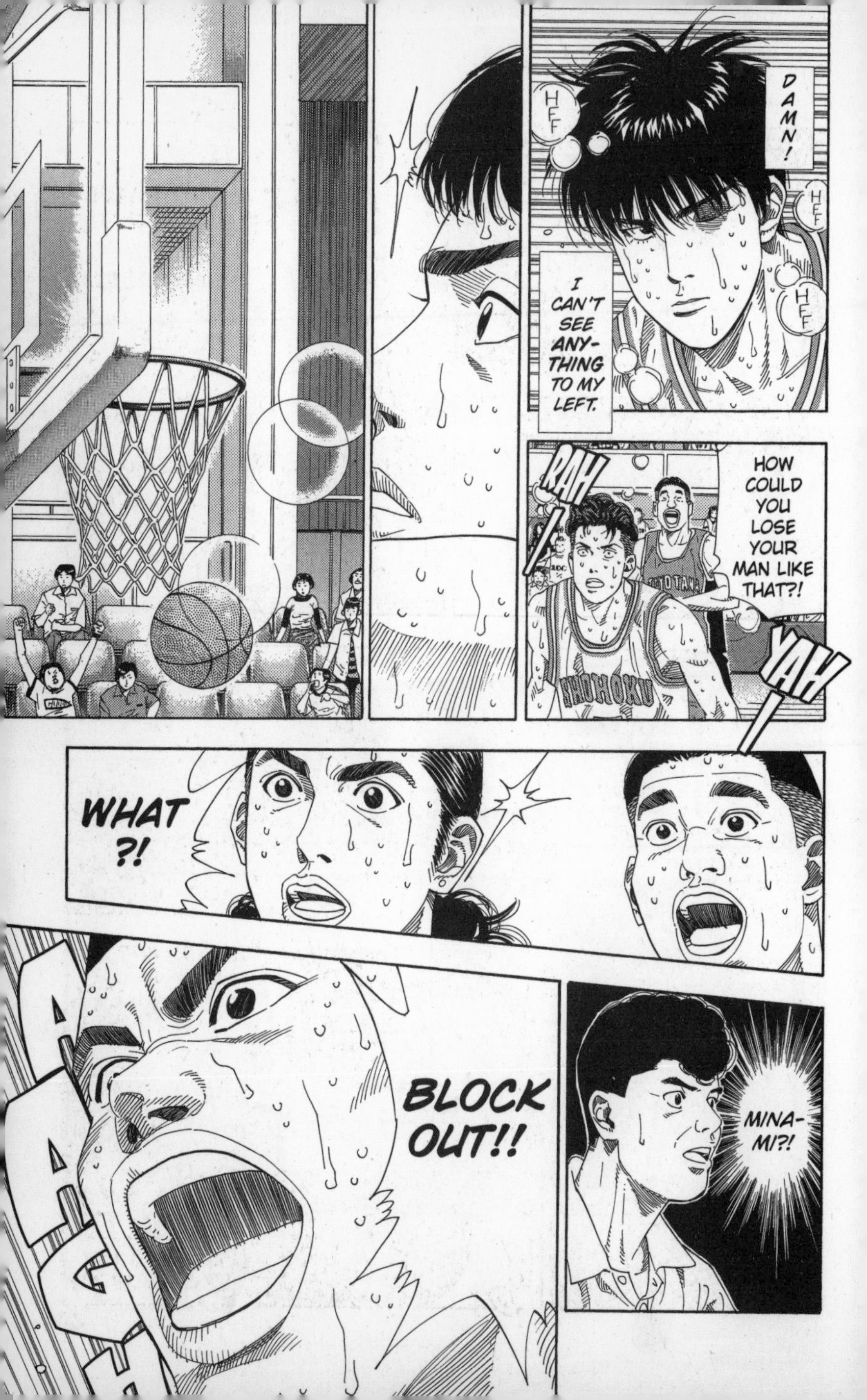
DAMN!
HFF
HFF
I CAN'T SEE ANYTHING TO MY LEFT.
HFF
RAH
HOW COULD YOU LOSE YOUR MAN LIKE THAT?!
YAH
WHAT?!
MINA-MI?!
BLOCK OUT!!

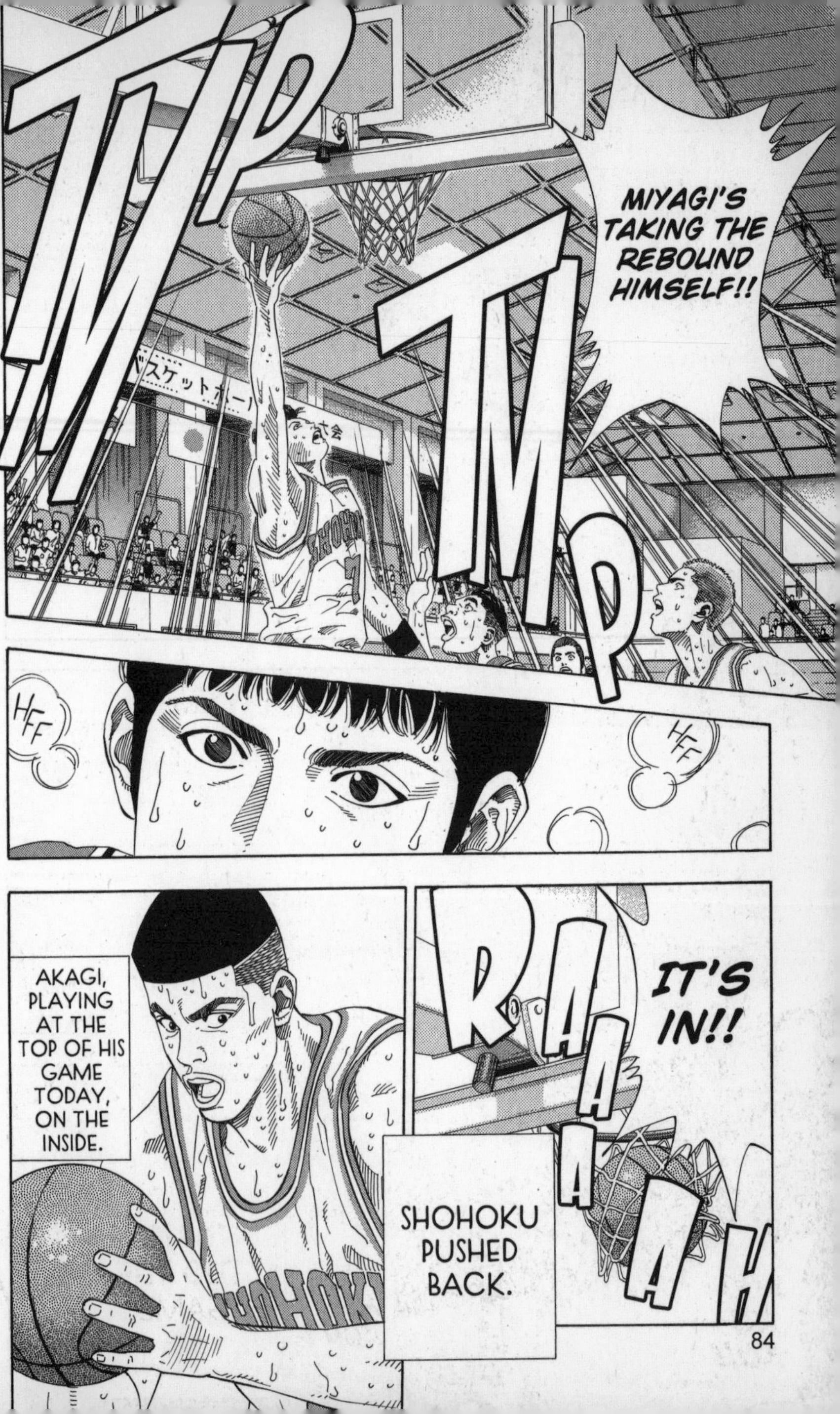
TIP
MIYAGI'S TAKING THE REBOUND HIMSELF!!
TMP
HFF
HFF
RAAAAAH
IT'S IN!!
SHOHOKU PUSHED BACK.
AKAGI, PLAYING AT THE TOP OF HIS GAME TODAY, ON THE INSIDE.

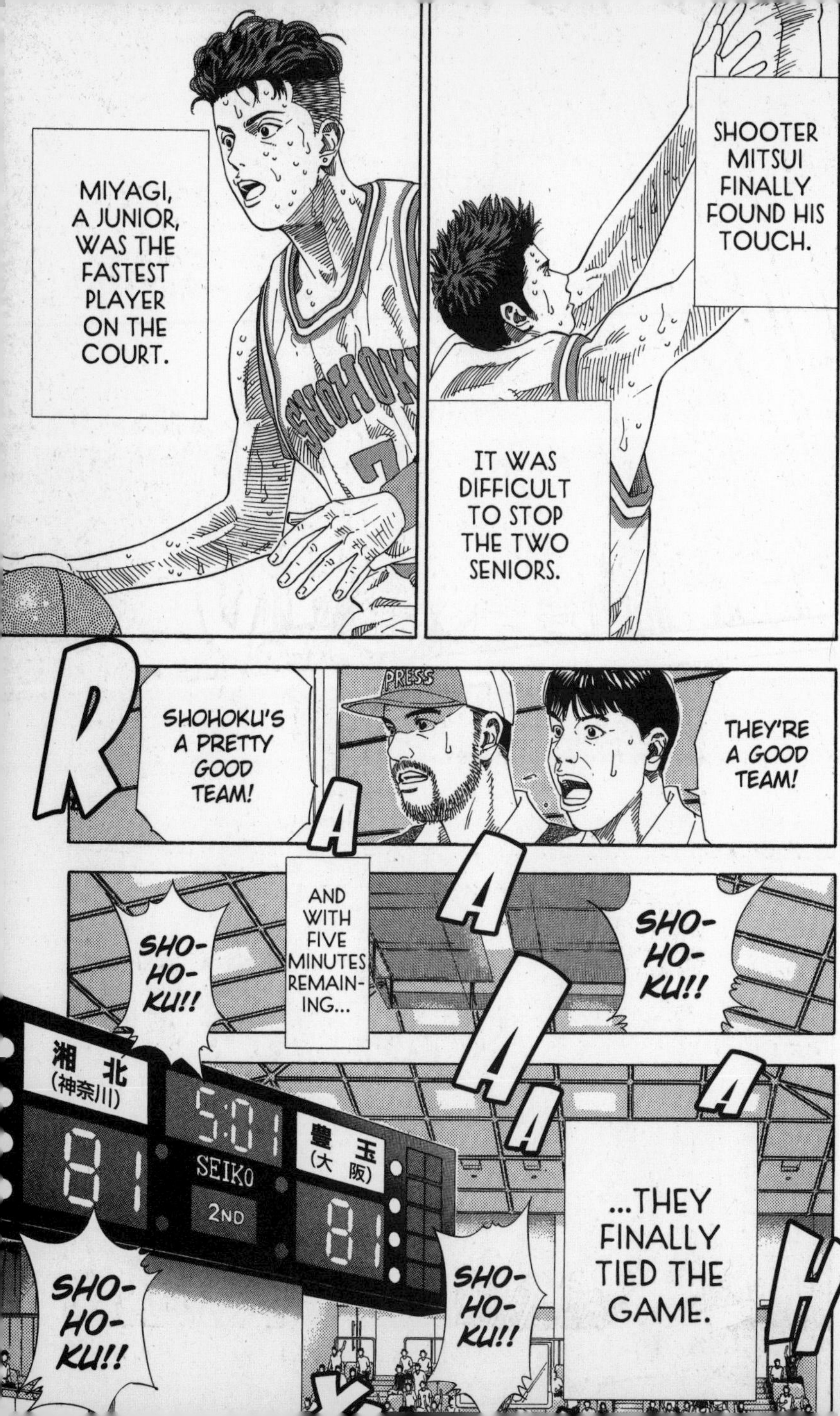
SHOOTER MITSUI FINALLY FOUND HIS TOUCH.
IT WAS DIFFICULT TO STOP THE TWO SENIORS.
MIYAGI, A JUNIOR, WAS THE FASTEST PLAYER ON THE COURT.
PRESS
THEY'RE A GOOD TEAM!
SHOHOKU'S A PRETTY GOOD TEAM!
RAAAAAH
SHO-HO-KU!!
AND WITH FIVE MINUTES REMAINING...
SHO-HO-KU!!
湘北 (神奈川)
81
5:01
SEIKO
2ND
豊玉 (大阪)
81
...THEY FINALLY TIED THE GAME.
SHO-HO-KU!!
SHO-HO-KU!!

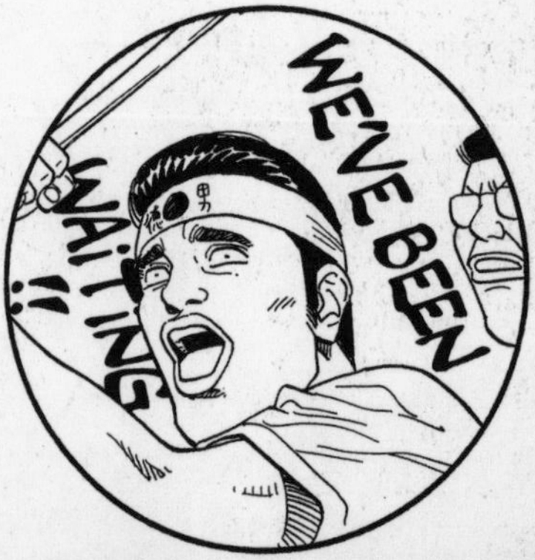
WE'VE BEEN WAITING!!

SLAM DUNK

#211
INTERNAL
COLLAPSE

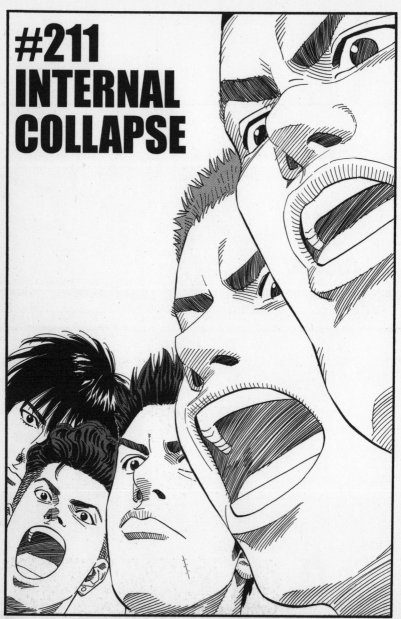

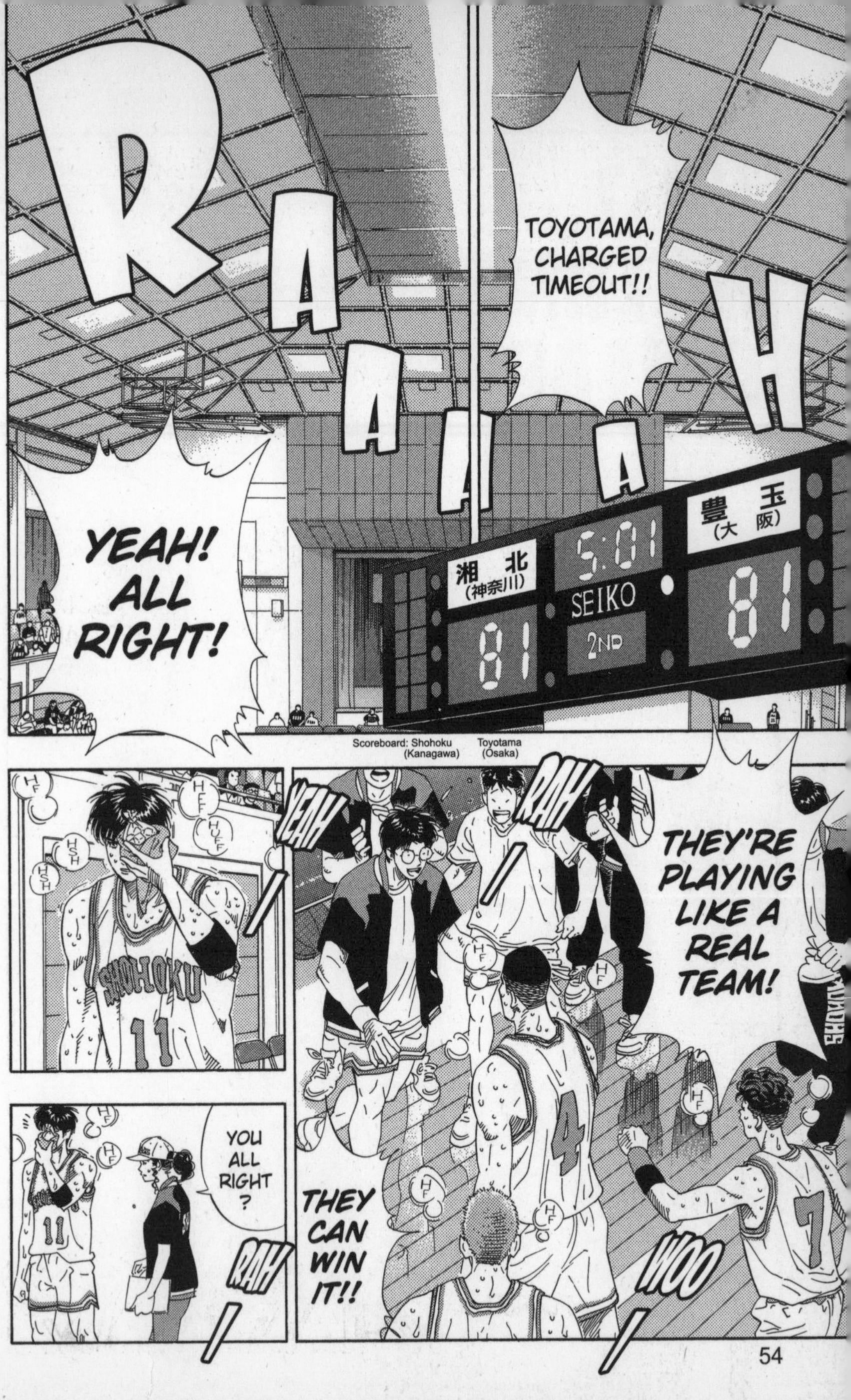
RAAAAH
TOYOTAMA, CHARGED TIMEOUT!!
YEAH! ALL RIGHT!
湘北 (神奈川)
5:01
SEIKO
2ND
豊玉 (大阪)
81
81
Scoreboard: Shohoku (Kanagawa) Toyotama (Osaka)
RAH
THEY'RE PLAYING LIKE A REAL TEAM!
YEAH
WOO
THEY CAN WIN IT!!
RAH
HF
HUFF
HSH
HSH
YOU ALL RIGHT?

READ THIS WAY

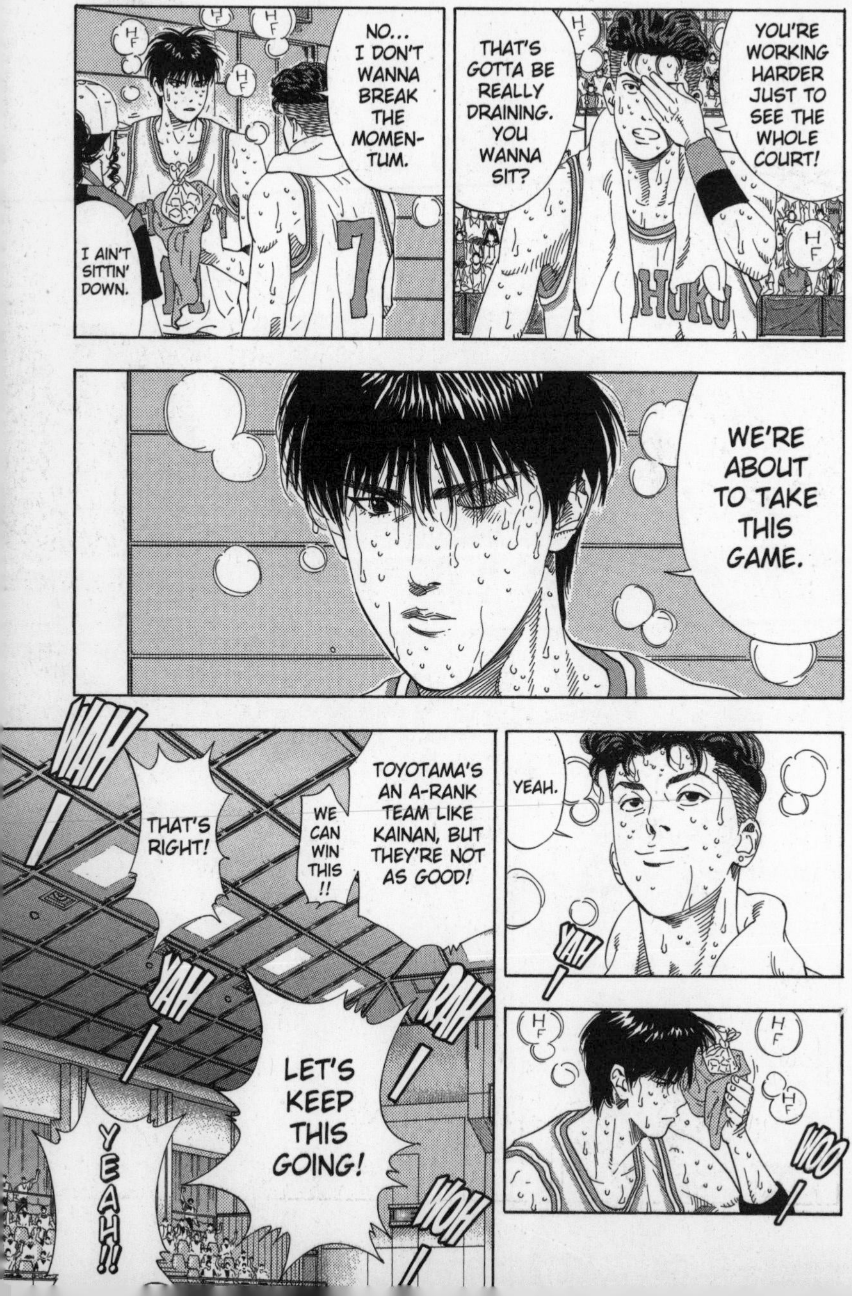

YOU'RE WORKING HARDER JUST TO SEE THE WHOLE COURT!
THAT'S GOTTA BE REALLY DRAINING. YOU WANNA SIT?
HF
NO... I DON'T WANNA BREAK THE MOMENTUM.
I AIN'T SITTIN' DOWN.
HF
WE'RE ABOUT TO TAKE THIS GAME.
YEAH.
YAH
HF
WOO
TOYOTAMA'S AN A-RANK TEAM LIKE KAINAN, BUT THEY'RE NOT AS GOOD!
WE CAN WIN THIS!!
THAT'S RIGHT!
WAH
RAH
YAH
LET'S KEEP THIS GOING!
WOH
YEAH!!

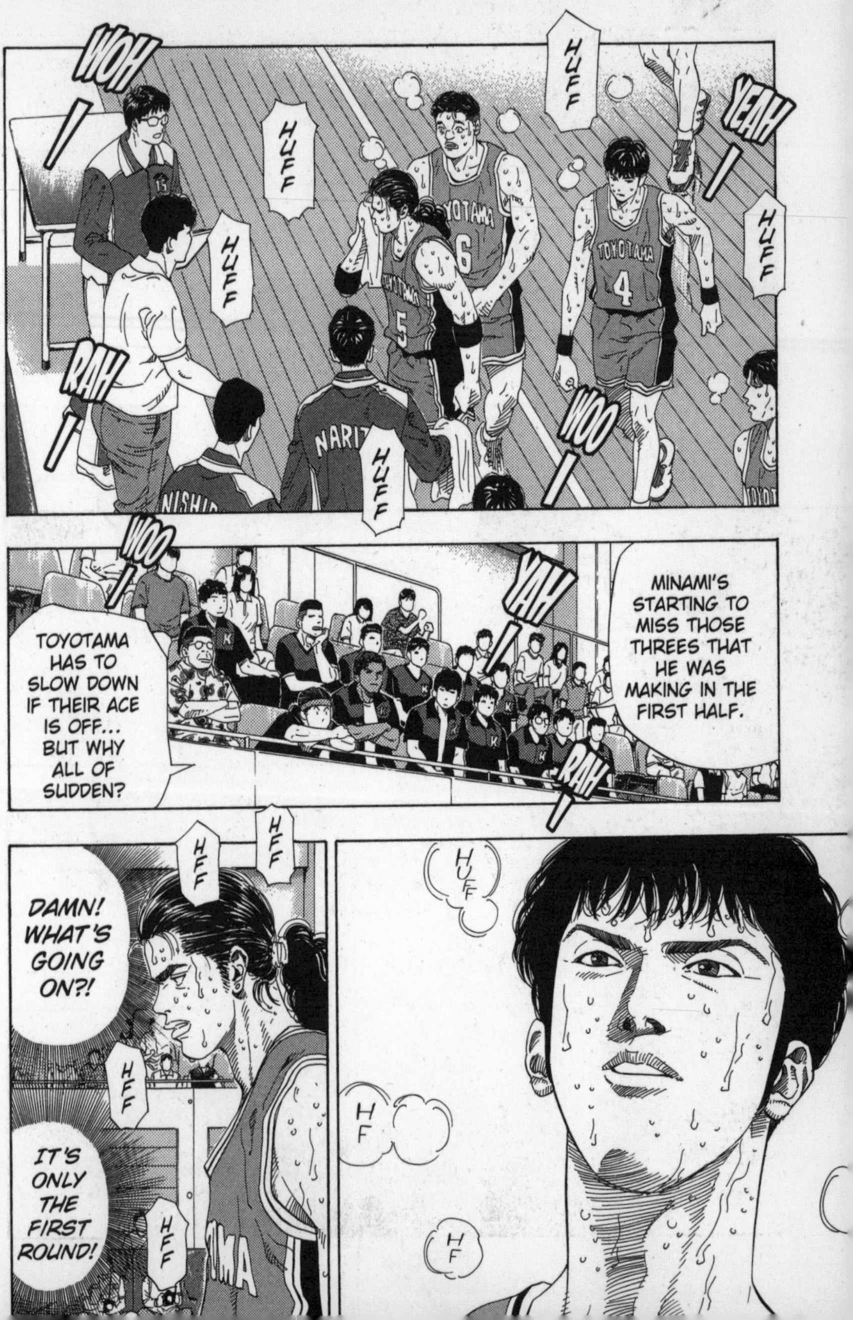

YEAH
HUFF
HUFF
HUFF
WOH
HUFF
WOO
RAH
HUFF
MINAMI'S STARTING TO MISS THOSE THREES THAT HE WAS MAKING IN THE FIRST HALF.
YAH
WOO
RAH
TOYOTAMA HAS TO SLOW DOWN IF THEIR ACE IS OFF... BUT WHY ALL OF SUDDEN?
HUFF
HF
HF
HFF
HFF
DAMN! WHAT'S GOING ON?!
HFF
IT'S ONLY THE FIRST ROUND!
HFF

READ THIS WAY

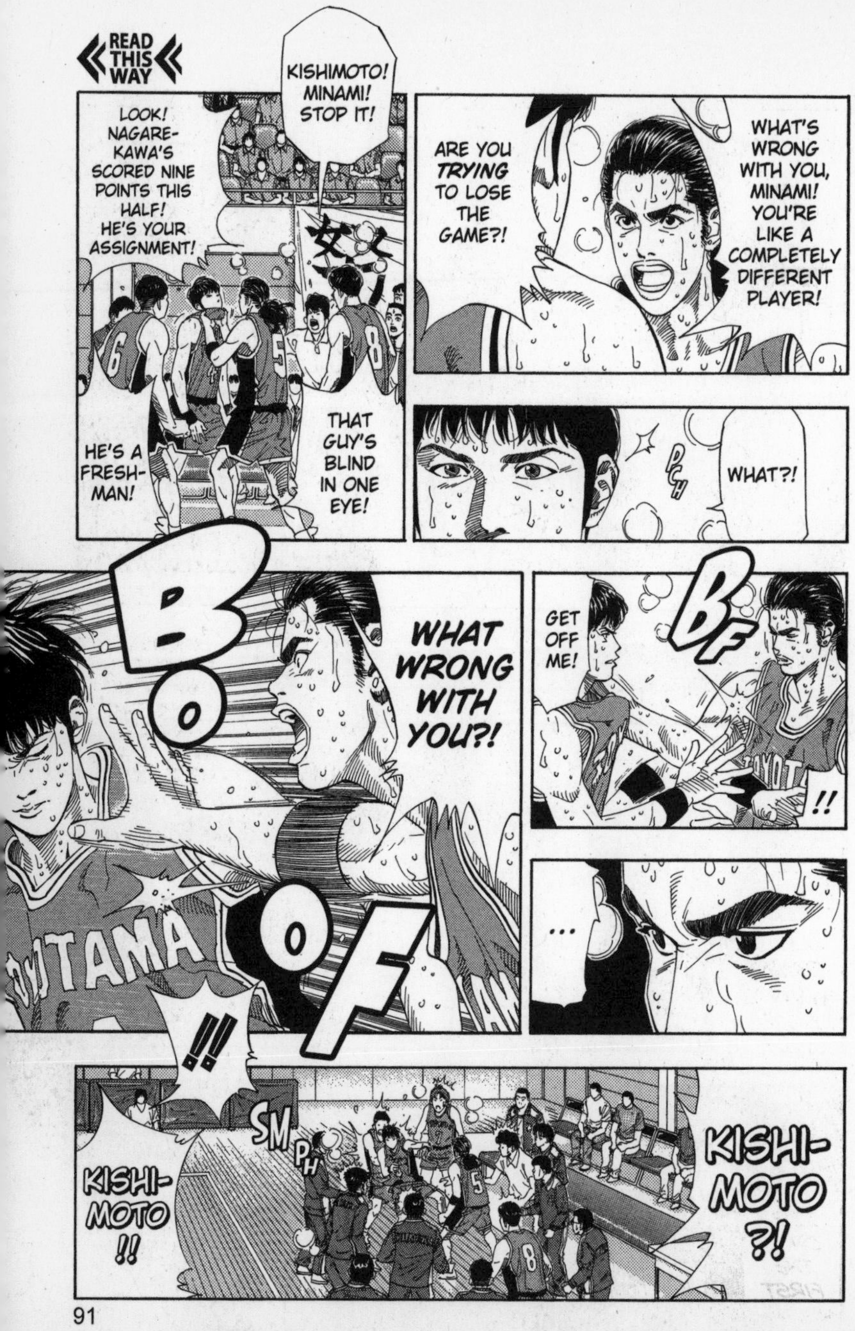
WHAT'S WRONG WITH YOU, MINAMI! YOU'RE LIKE A COMPLETELY DIFFERENT PLAYER!
ARE YOU *TRYING* TO LOSE THE GAME?!
PCH
WHAT?!
KISHIMOTO! MINAMI! STOP IT!
LOOK! NAGARE-KAWA'S SCORED NINE POINTS THIS HALF! HE'S YOUR ASSIGNMENT!
THAT GUY'S BLIND IN ONE EYE!
HE'S A FRESH-MAN!
BF
GET OFF ME!
!!
...
BOOF
WHAT WRONG WITH YOU?!
!!!
KISHI-MOTO?!
SMPH
KISHI-MOTO!!

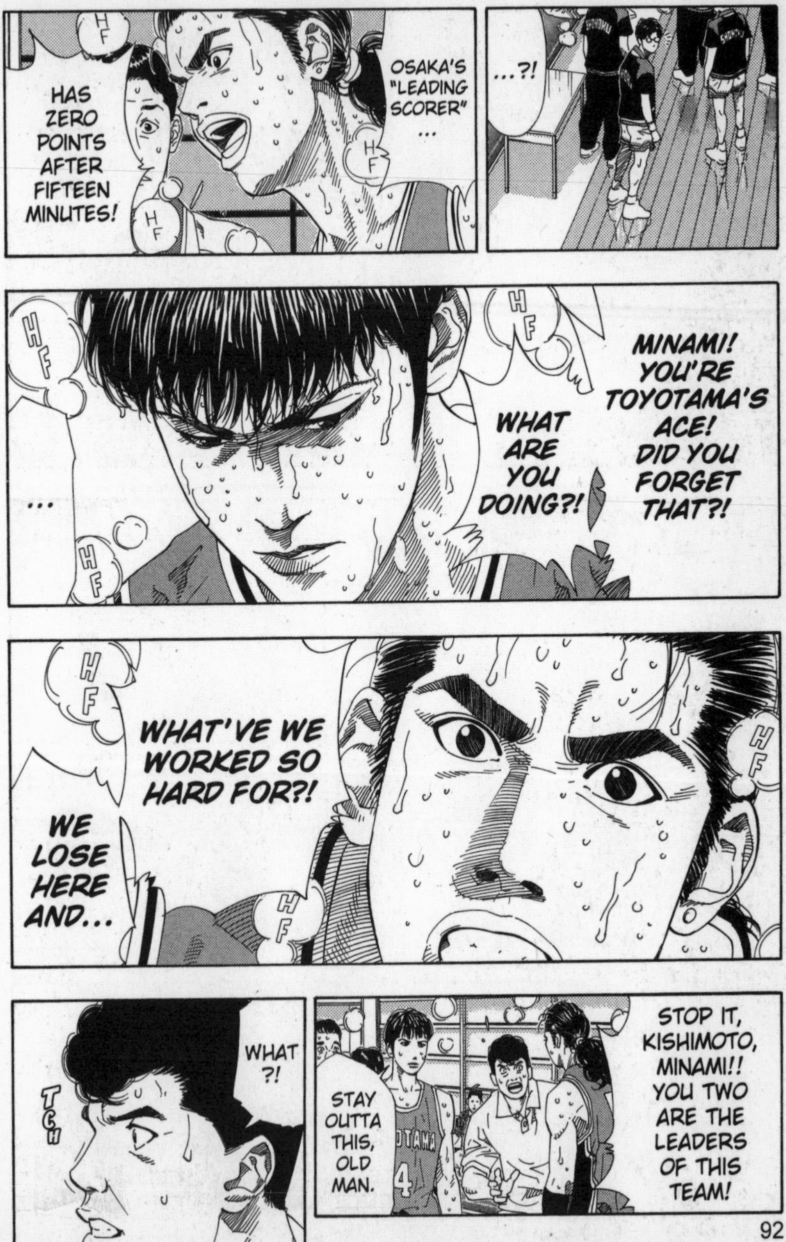
...?!
OSAKA'S "LEADING SCORER"...
HF
HAS ZERO POINTS AFTER FIFTEEN MINUTES!
HF
HF
MINAMI! YOU'RE TOYOTAMA'S ACE! DID YOU FORGET THAT?!
HF
WHAT ARE YOU DOING?!
HF
...
HF
HF
WHAT'VE WE WORKED SO HARD FOR?!
HF
WE LOSE HERE AND...
HF
STOP IT, KISHIMOTO, MINAMI!! YOU TWO ARE THE LEADERS OF THIS TEAM!
STAY OUTTA THIS, OLD MAN.
WHAT ?!
TCH

READ THIS WAY

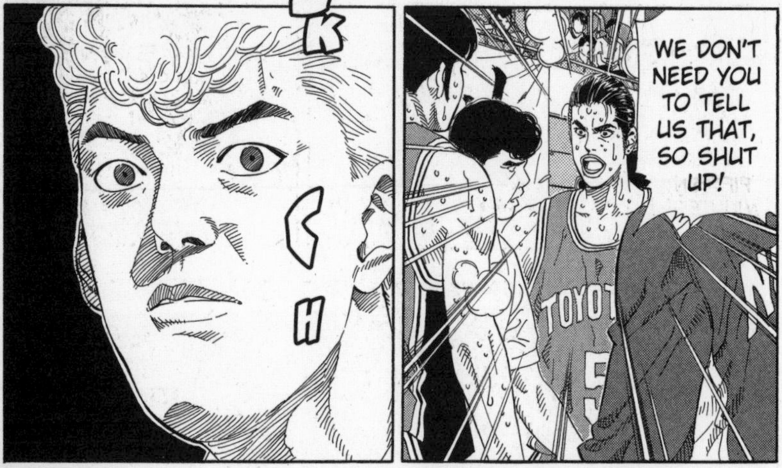
WE DON'T NEED YOU TO TELL US THAT, SO SHUT UP!
SKCH

Banner: *Doryoku* (effort/hard work)

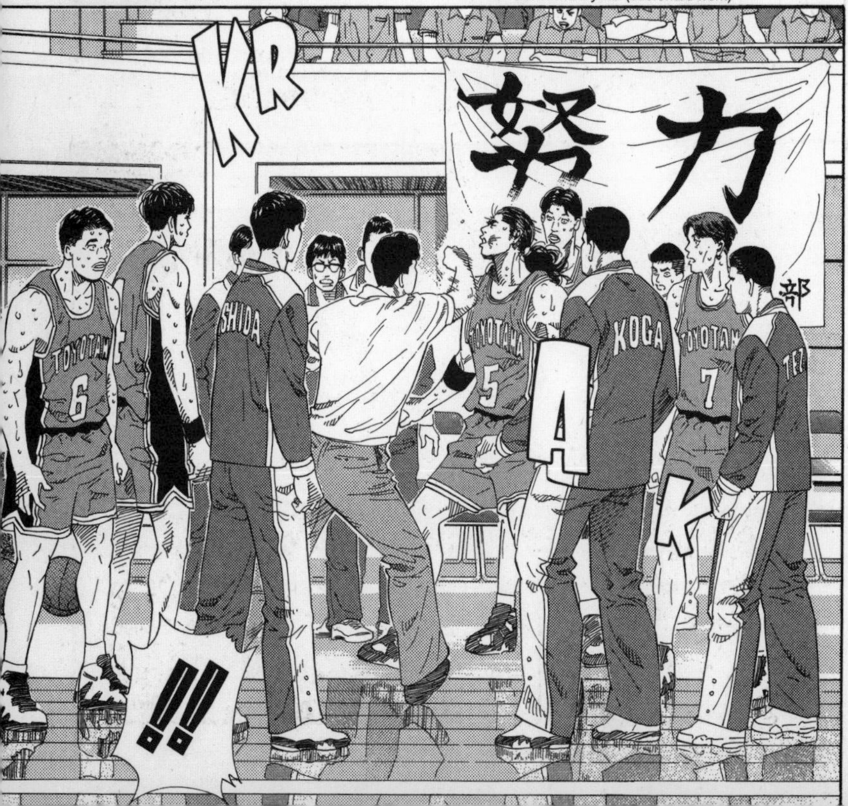
努力
部
KRAK
!!

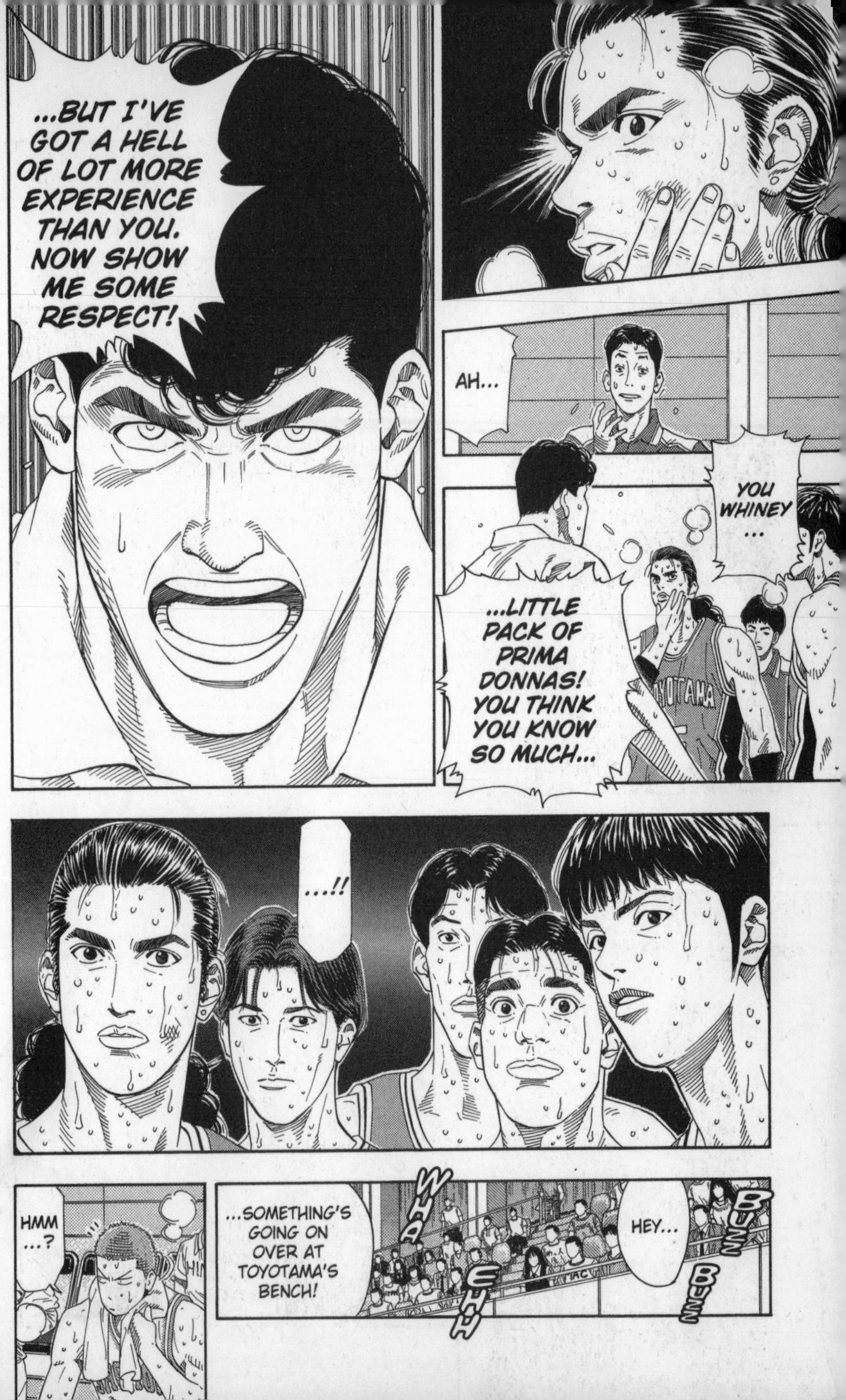
AH...
YOU WHINEY ...
...LITTLE PACK OF PRIMA DONNAS! YOU THINK YOU KNOW SO MUCH...
...BUT I'VE GOT A HELL OF LOT MORE EXPERIENCE THAN YOU. NOW SHOW ME SOME RESPECT!
...!!
BUNN BUNN
HEY...
WHAA EHHH
...SOMETHING'S GOING ON OVER AT TOYOTAMA'S BENCH!
HMM ...?

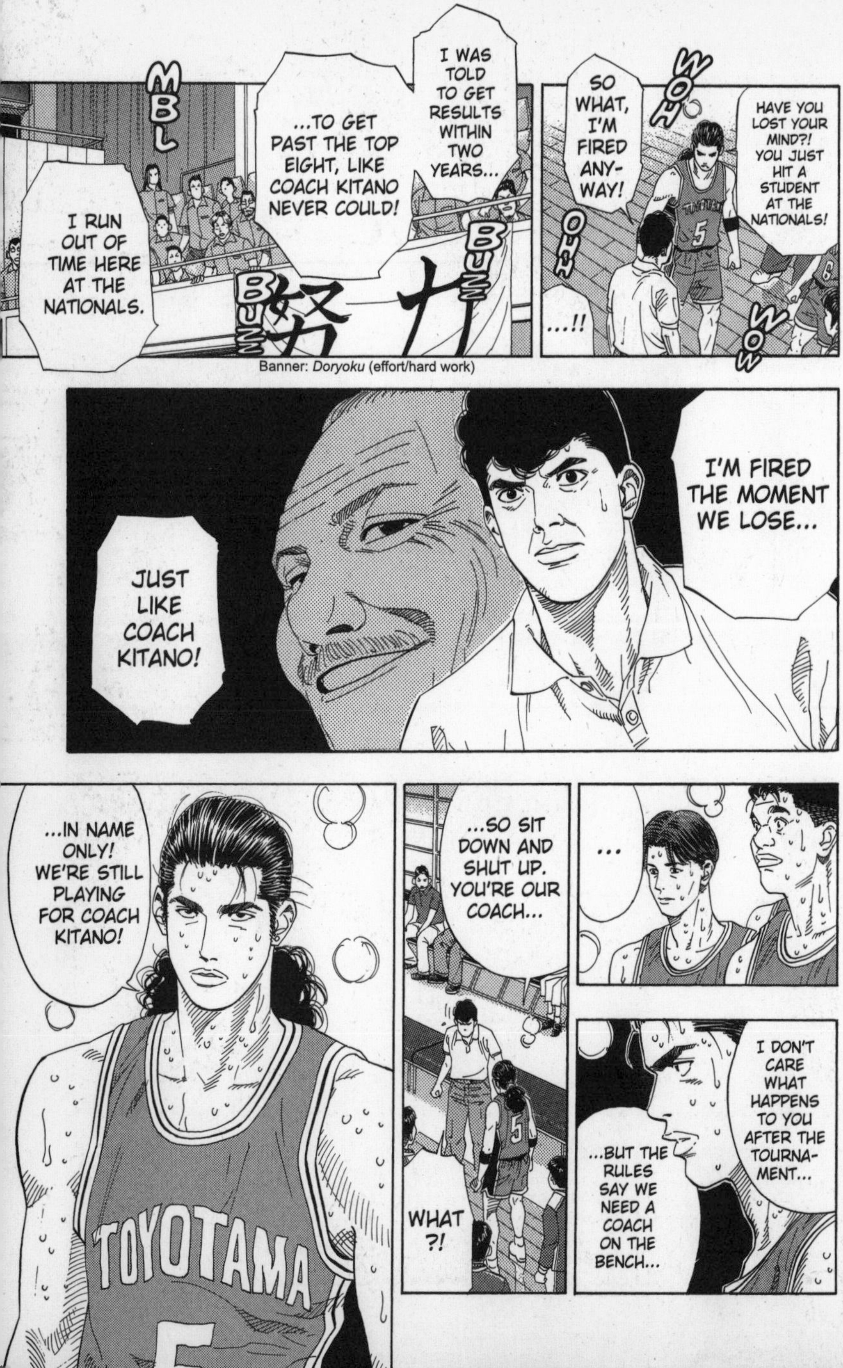
HAVE YOU LOST YOUR MIND?! YOU JUST HIT A STUDENT AT THE NATIONALS!
WOW
OHH
SO WHAT, I'M FIRED ANY-WAY!
WOW
...!!
I WAS TOLD TO GET RESULTS WITHIN TWO YEARS...
...TO GET PAST THE TOP EIGHT, LIKE COACH KITANO NEVER COULD!
BUZZ
MBL
BUZZ
I RUN OUT OF TIME HERE AT THE NATIONALS.
I'M FIRED THE MOMENT WE LOSE...
JUST LIKE COACH KITANO!
...
I DON'T CARE WHAT HAPPENS TO YOU AFTER THE TOURNA-MENT...
...BUT THE RULES SAY WE NEED A COACH ON THE BENCH...
...SO SIT DOWN AND SHUT UP. YOU'RE OUR COACH...
WHAT?!
...IN NAME ONLY! WE'RE STILL PLAYING FOR COACH KITANO!

Banner: *Doryoku* (effort/hard work)

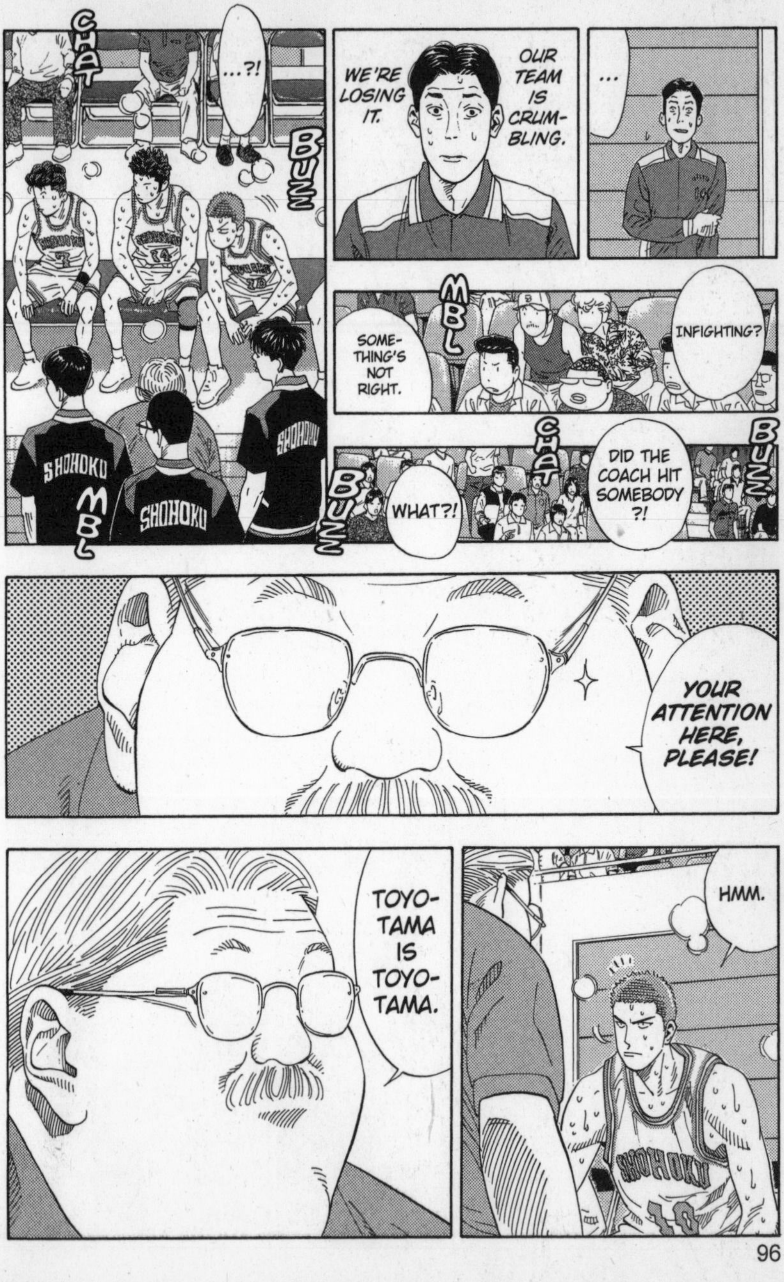
...
OUR TEAM IS CRUM-BLING.
WE'RE LOSING IT.
INFIGHTING?
MBL
SOME-THING'S NOT RIGHT.
BUZZ
DID THE COACH HIT SOMEBODY?!
CHAT
WHAT?!
BUZZ
...?!
BUZZ
CHAT
MBL
YOUR ATTENTION HERE, PLEASE!
HMM.
TOYO-TAMA IS TOYO-TAMA.

READ THIS WAY

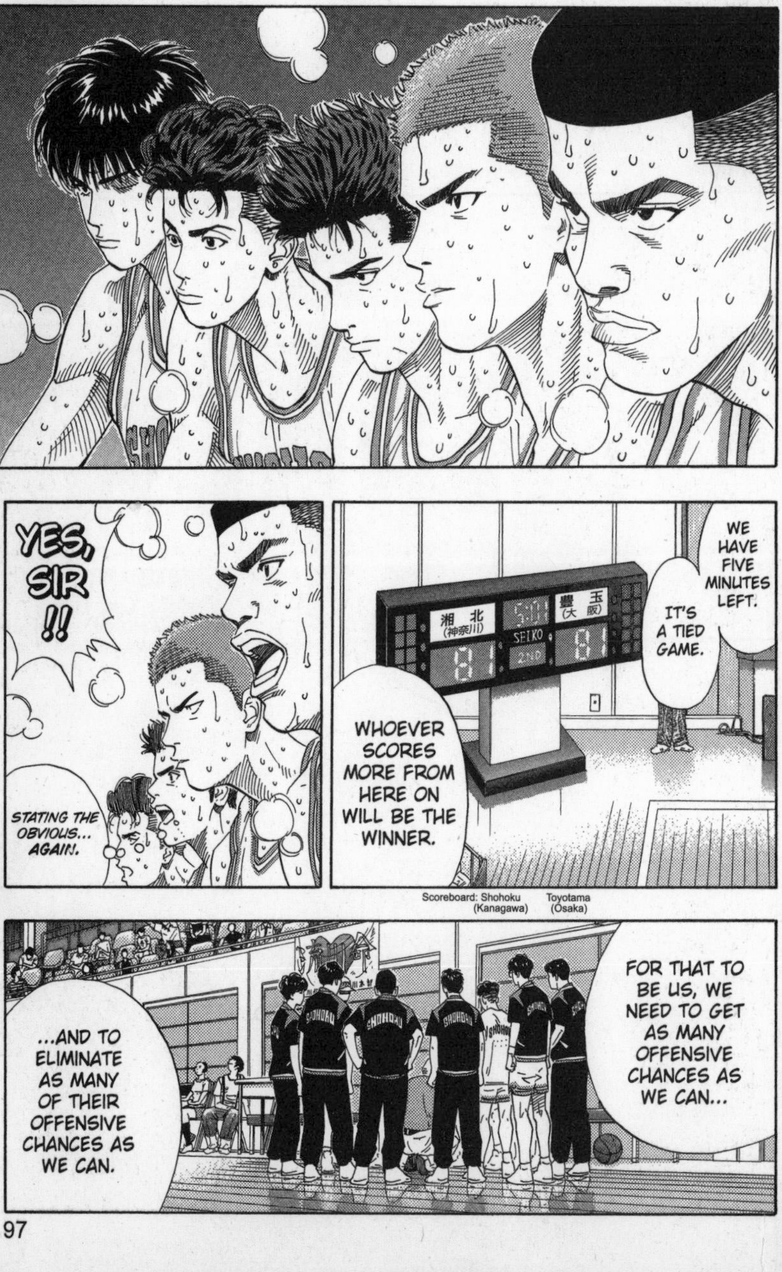
WE HAVE FIVE MINUTES LEFT.
IT'S A TIED GAME.
WHOEVER SCORES MORE FROM HERE ON WILL BE THE WINNER.
YES, SIR!!
STATING THE OBVIOUS... AGAIN.
FOR THAT TO BE US, WE NEED TO GET AS MANY OFFENSIVE CHANCES AS WE CAN...
...AND TO ELIMINATE AS MANY OF THEIR OFFENSIVE CHANCES AS WE CAN.

Scoreboard: Shohoku (Kanagawa) Toyotama (Osaka)

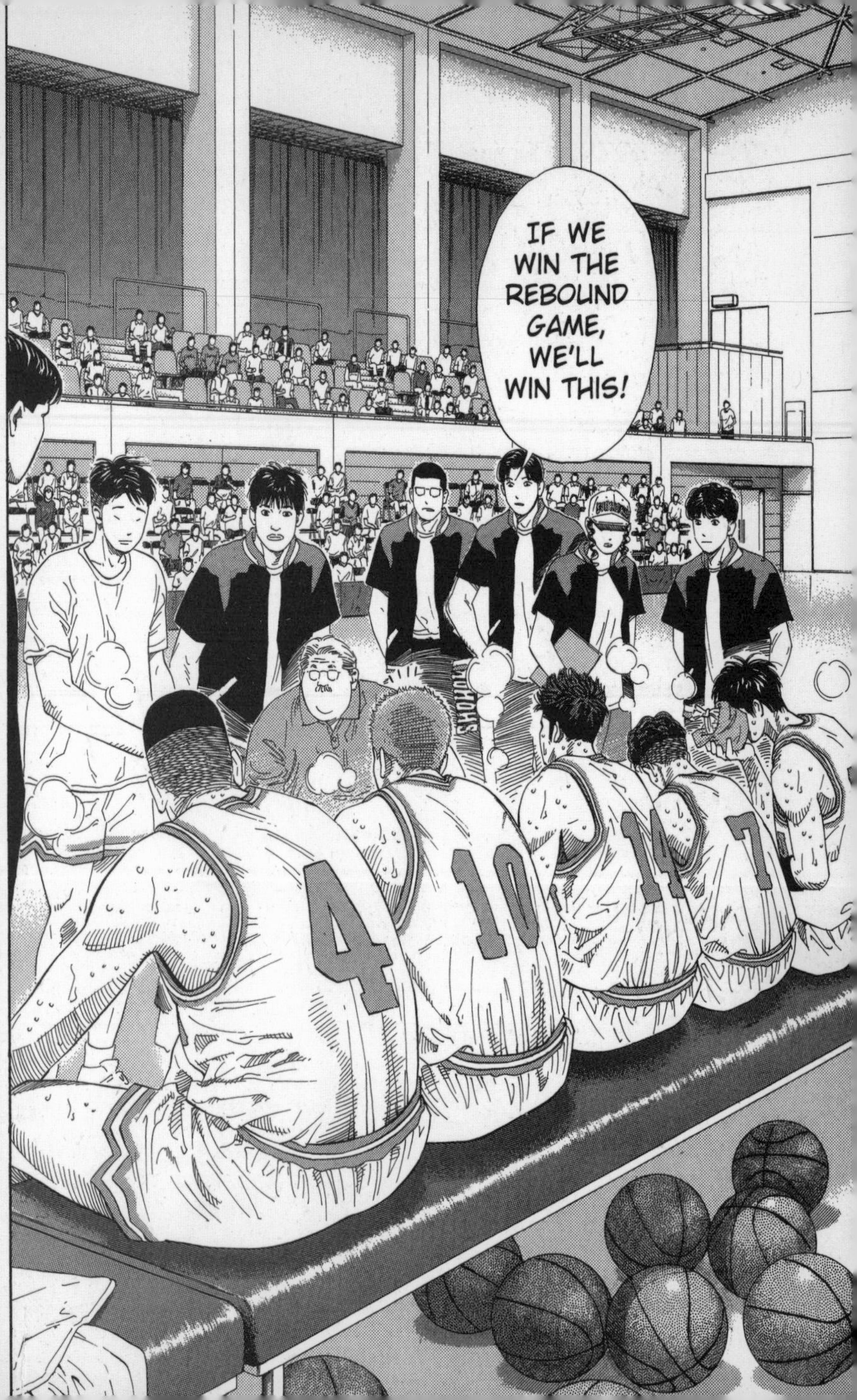
IF WE WIN THE REBOUND GAME, WE'LL WIN THIS!

READ THIS WAY

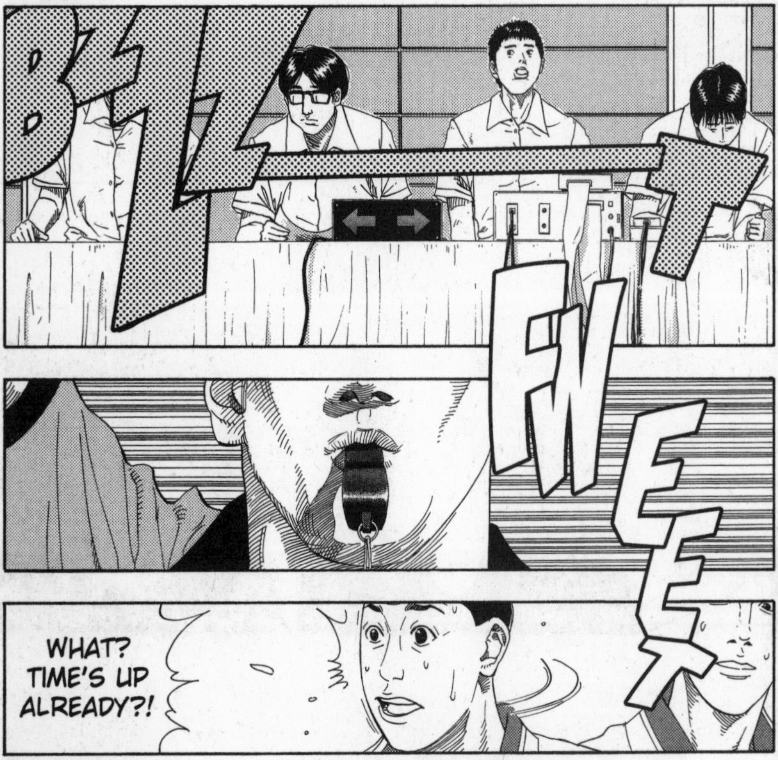
BZZT
FWEEET
WHAT? TIME'S UP ALREADY?!

* BOX OUT: TO USE YOUR BODY TO DELAY OR PREVENT AN OPPOSING PLAYER FROM REACHING A CERTAIN LOCATION.

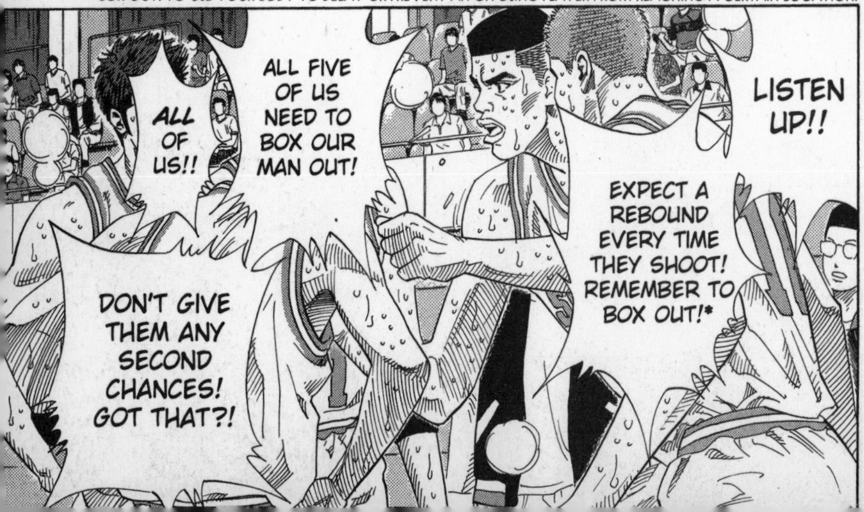
LISTEN UP!!
EXPECT A REBOUND EVERY TIME THEY SHOOT! REMEMBER TO BOX OUT!*
ALL FIVE OF US NEED TO BOX OUR MAN OUT!
ALL OF US!!
DON'T GIVE THEM ANY SECOND CHANCES! GOT THAT?!

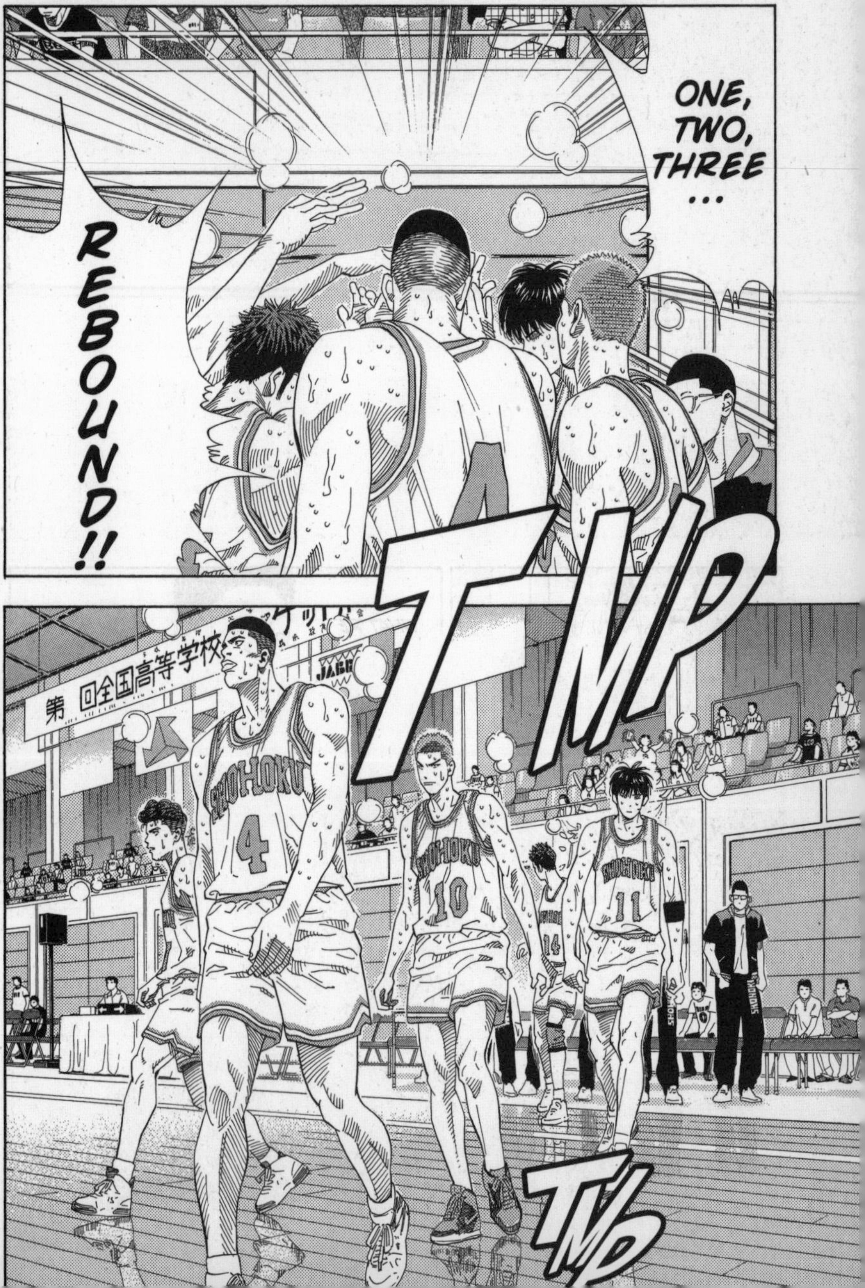
ONE, TWO, THREE...
REBOUND!!
TMP
第 回全国高等学校
TMP

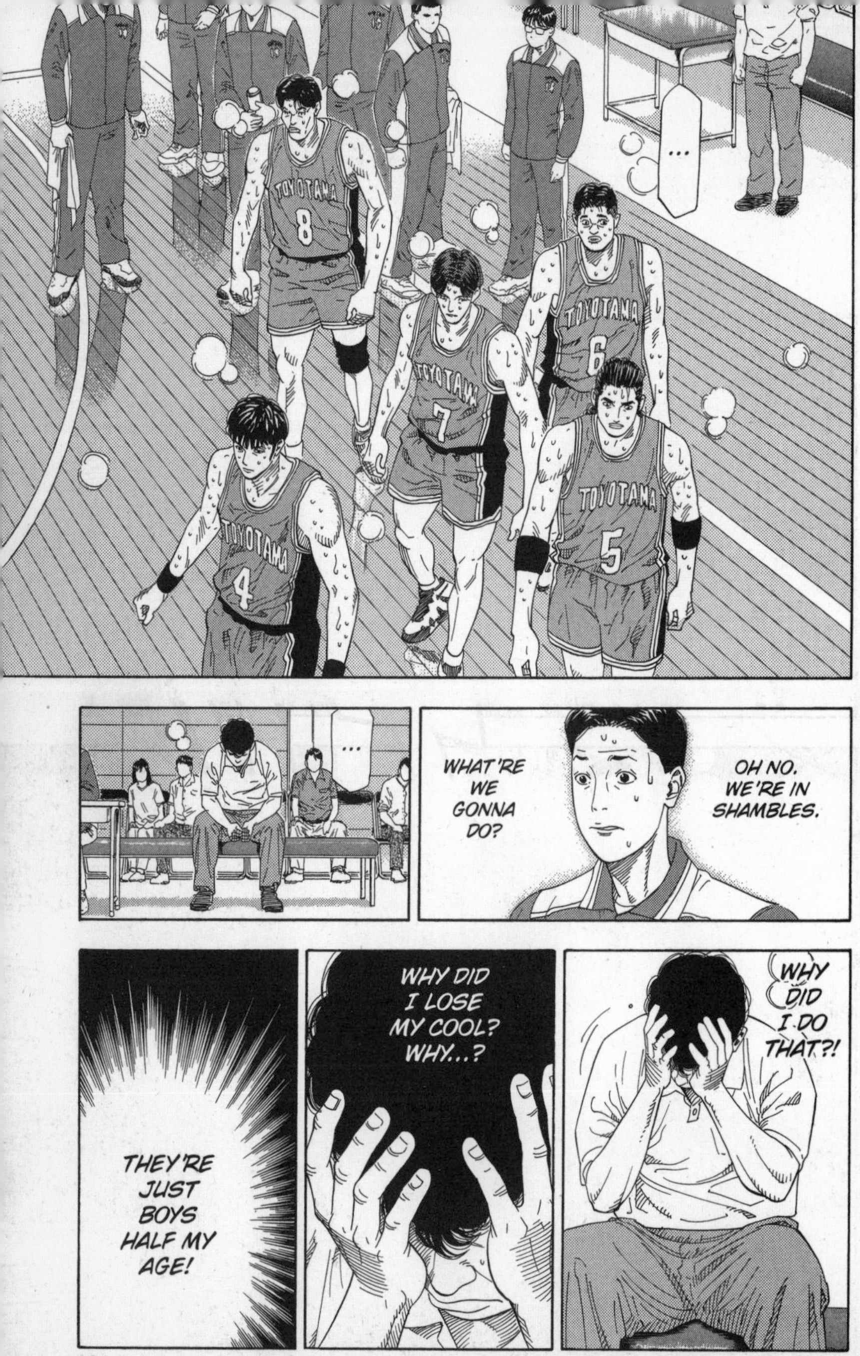
...
OH NO. WE'RE IN SHAMBLES.
WHAT'RE WE GONNA DO?
...
WHY DID I DO THAT?!
WHY DID I LOSE MY COOL? WHY...?
THEY'RE JUST BOYS HALF MY AGE!

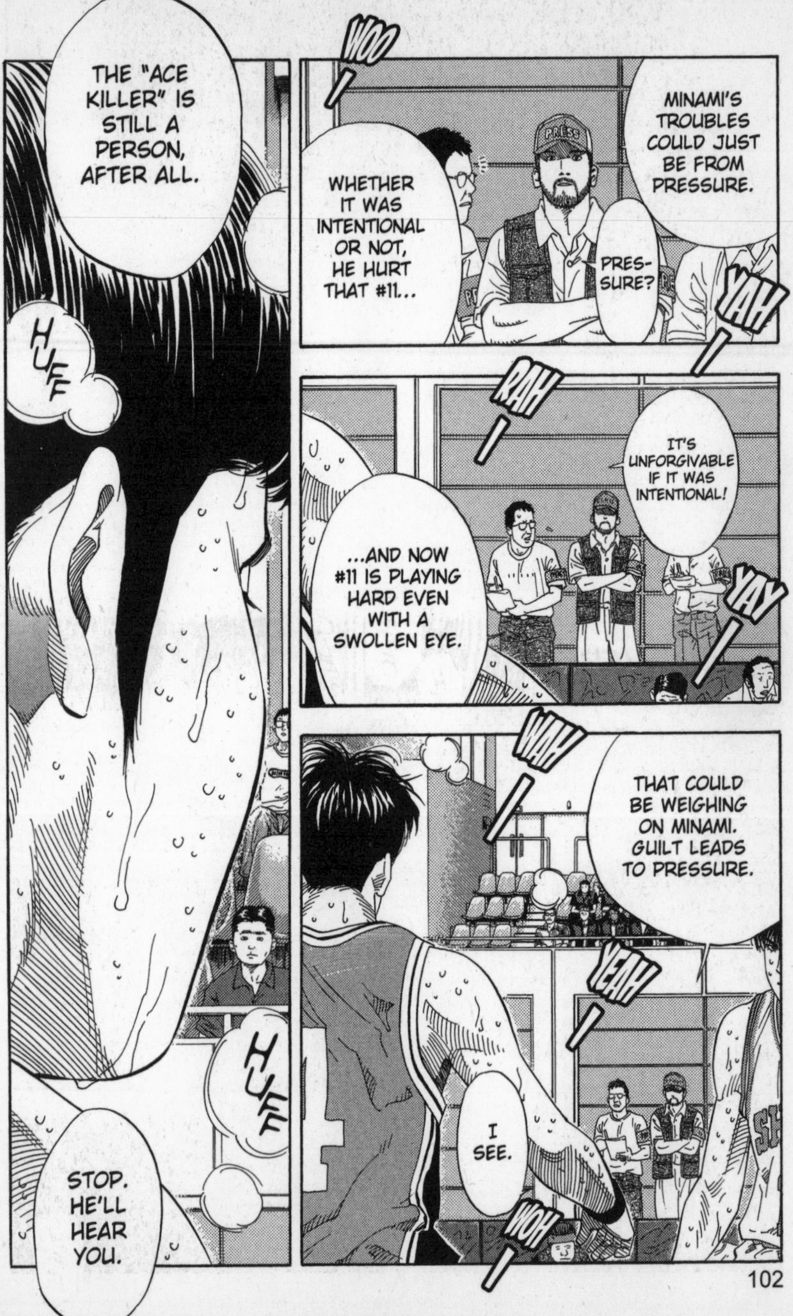
WOO
MINAMI'S TROUBLES COULD JUST BE FROM PRESSURE.
PRES-SURE?
WHETHER IT WAS INTENTIONAL OR NOT, HE HURT THAT #11...
YAH
RAH
IT'S UNFORGIVABLE IF IT WAS INTENTIONAL!
...AND NOW #11 IS PLAYING HARD EVEN WITH A SWOLLEN EYE.
YAY
WAH
THAT COULD BE WEIGHING ON MINAMI. GUILT LEADS TO PRESSURE.
YEAH
I SEE.
WOH
THE "ACE KILLER" IS STILL A PERSON, AFTER ALL.
HUFF
HUFF
STOP. HE'LL HEAR YOU.

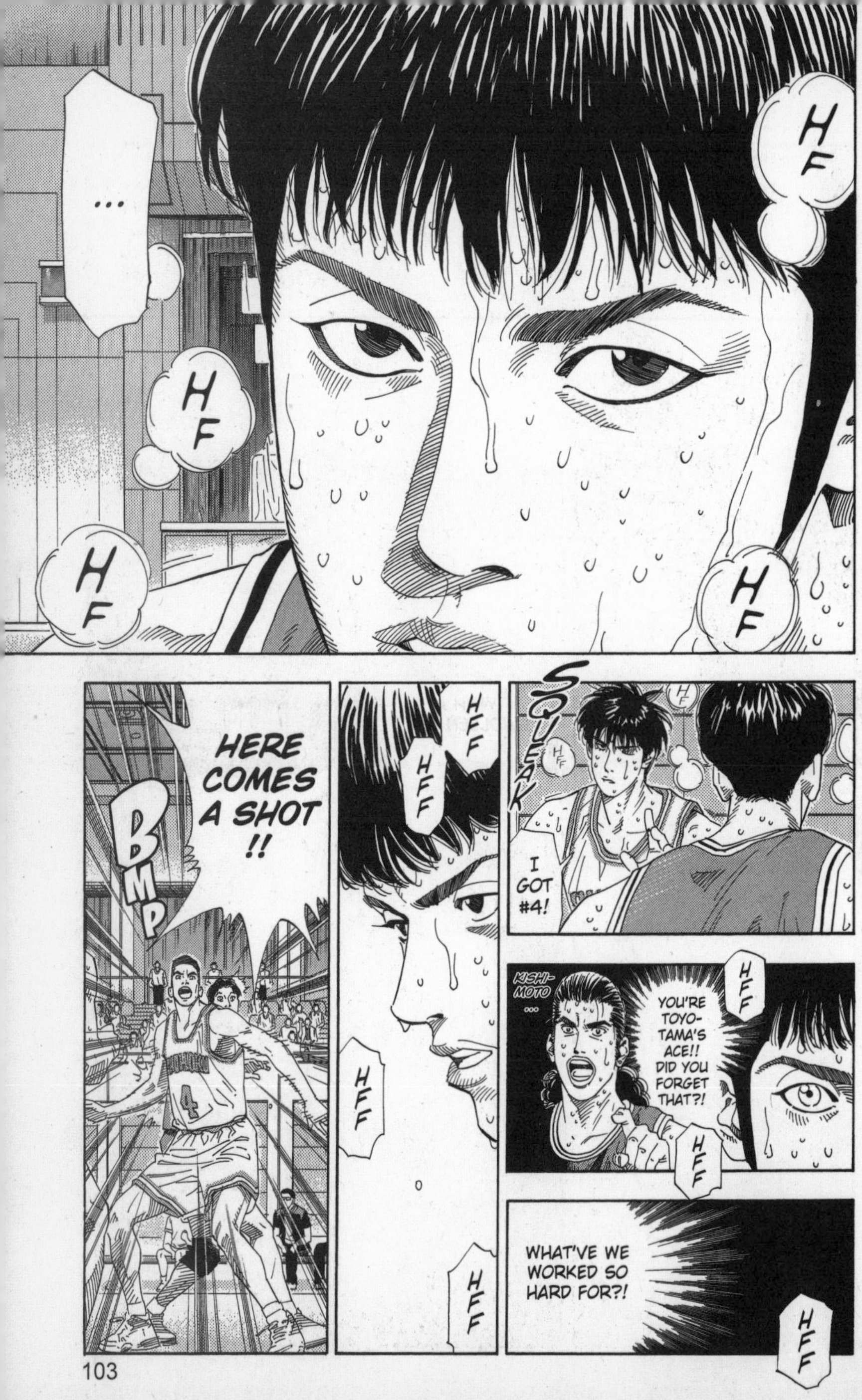
HF
...
HF
HF
HF
SQUEAK
HF
HFF
I GOT #4!
HFF
YOU'RE TOYOTAMA'S ACE!! DID YOU FORGET THAT?!
KISHIMOTO ...
HFF
WHAT'VE WE WORKED SO HARD FOR?!
HFF
HFF
HFF
HFF
HFF
HERE COMES A SHOT !!
BMP

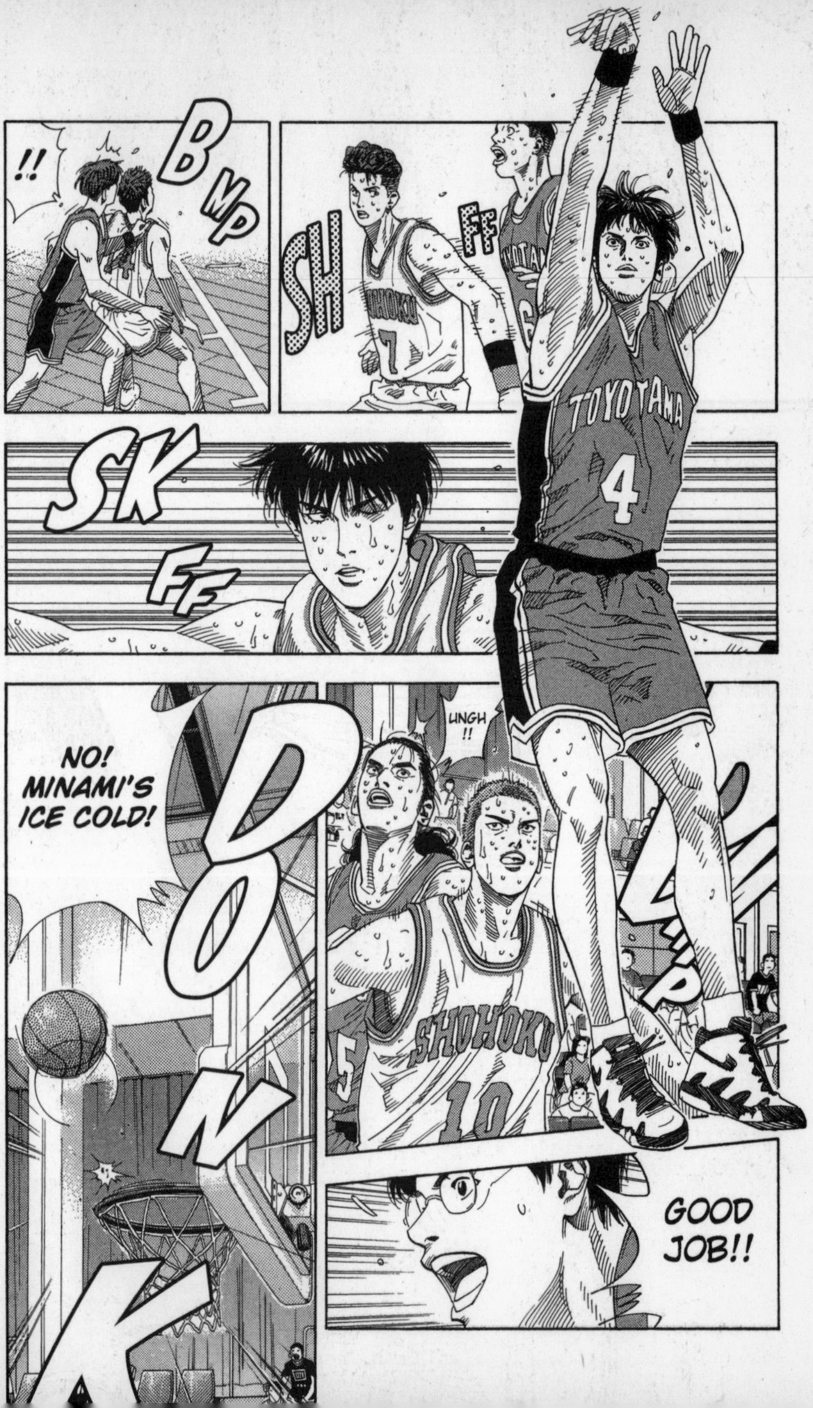
SHFF
!!
BMP
SKFF
UNGH!!
GOOD JOB!!
NO! MINAMI'S ICE COLD!
DONK

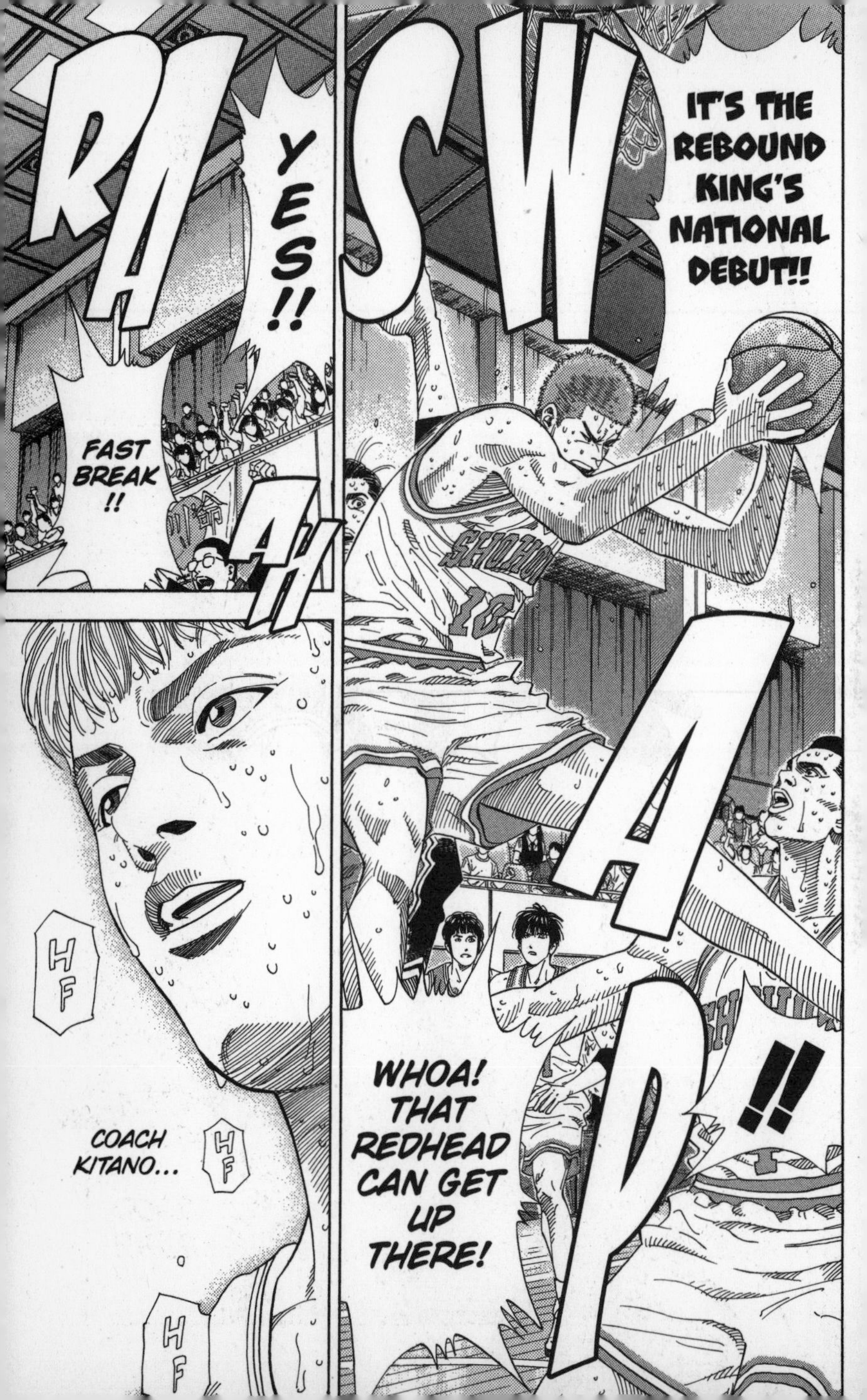
SW
IT'S THE REBOUND KING'S NATIONAL DEBUT!!
A
P!!
WHOA! THAT REDHEAD CAN GET UP THERE!
RA
YES!!
FAST BREAK!!
AH
HF
COACH KITANO...
HF
HF

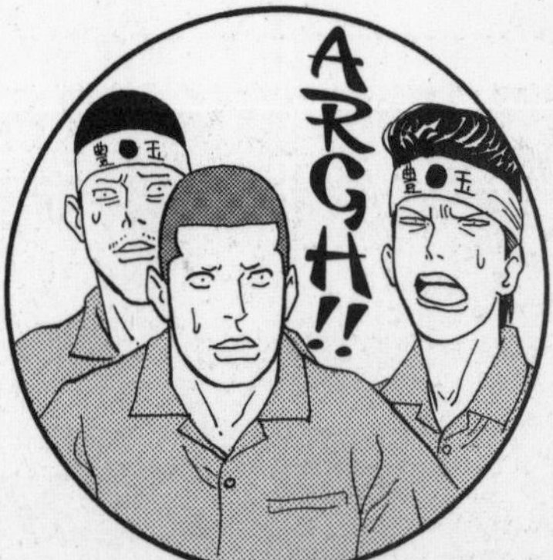
ARGH!!

SLAM DUNK

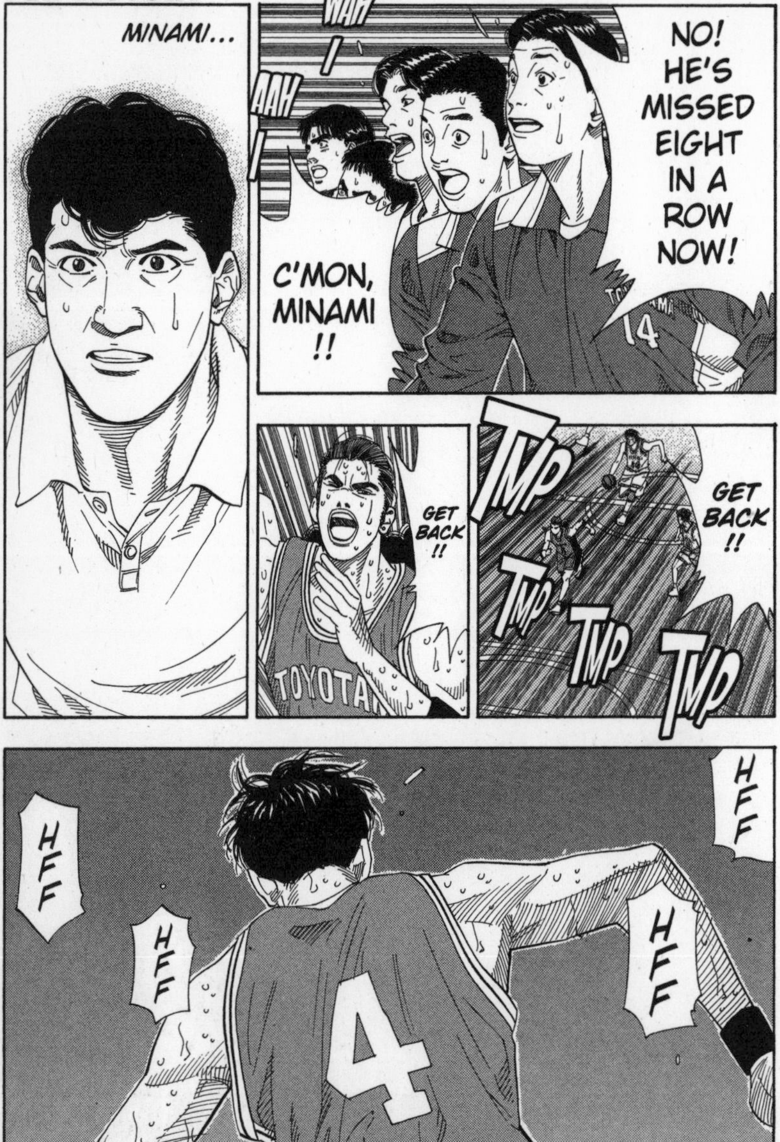
NO! HE'S MISSED EIGHT IN A ROW NOW!
WAH!
AAH!
C'MON, MINAMI!!
TMP TMP TMP TMP
GET BACK!!
GET BACK!!
MINAMI...
HFF
HFF
HFF
HFF

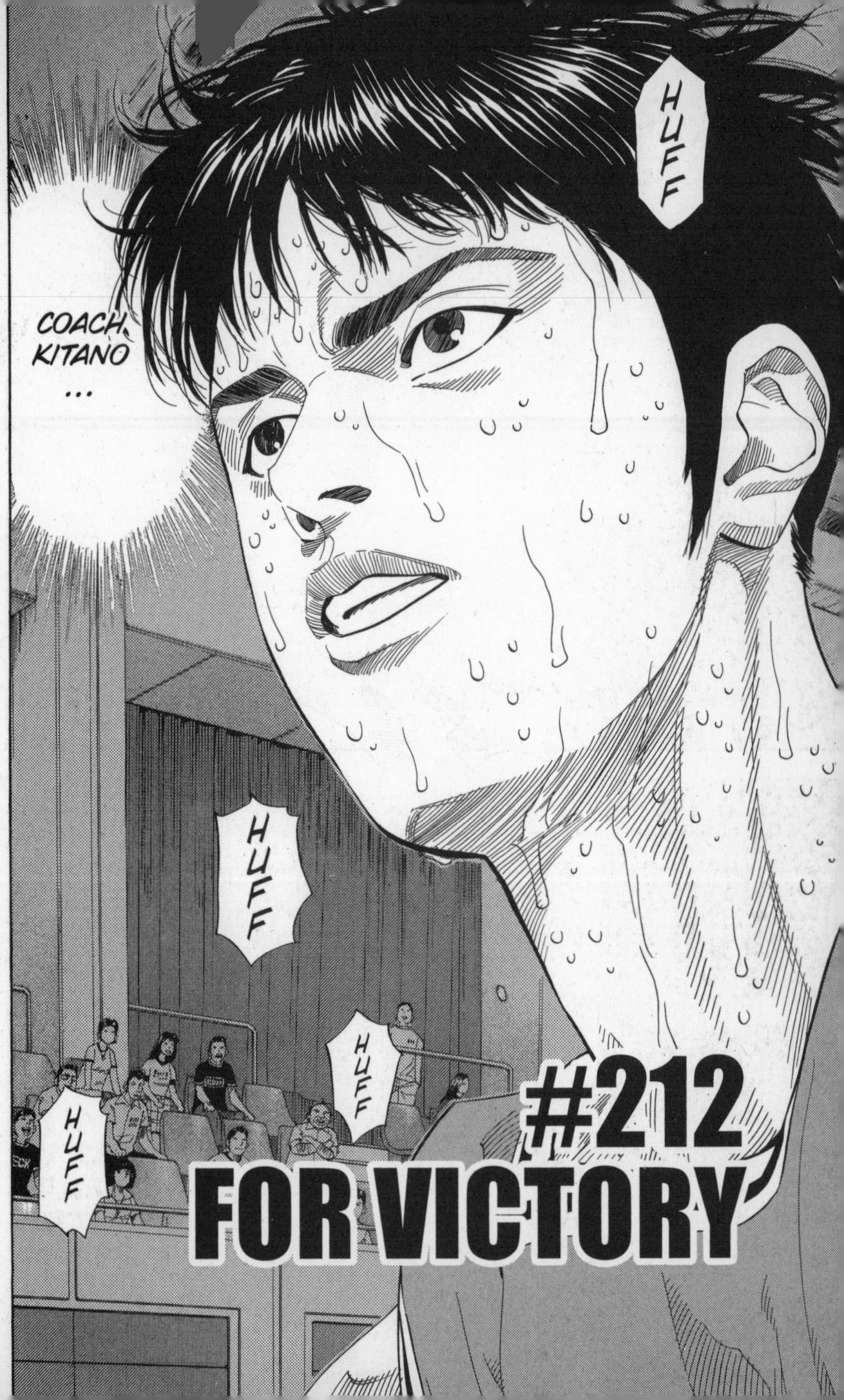
HUFF
COACH KITANO ...
HUFF
HUFF
HUFF
#212
FOR VICTORY

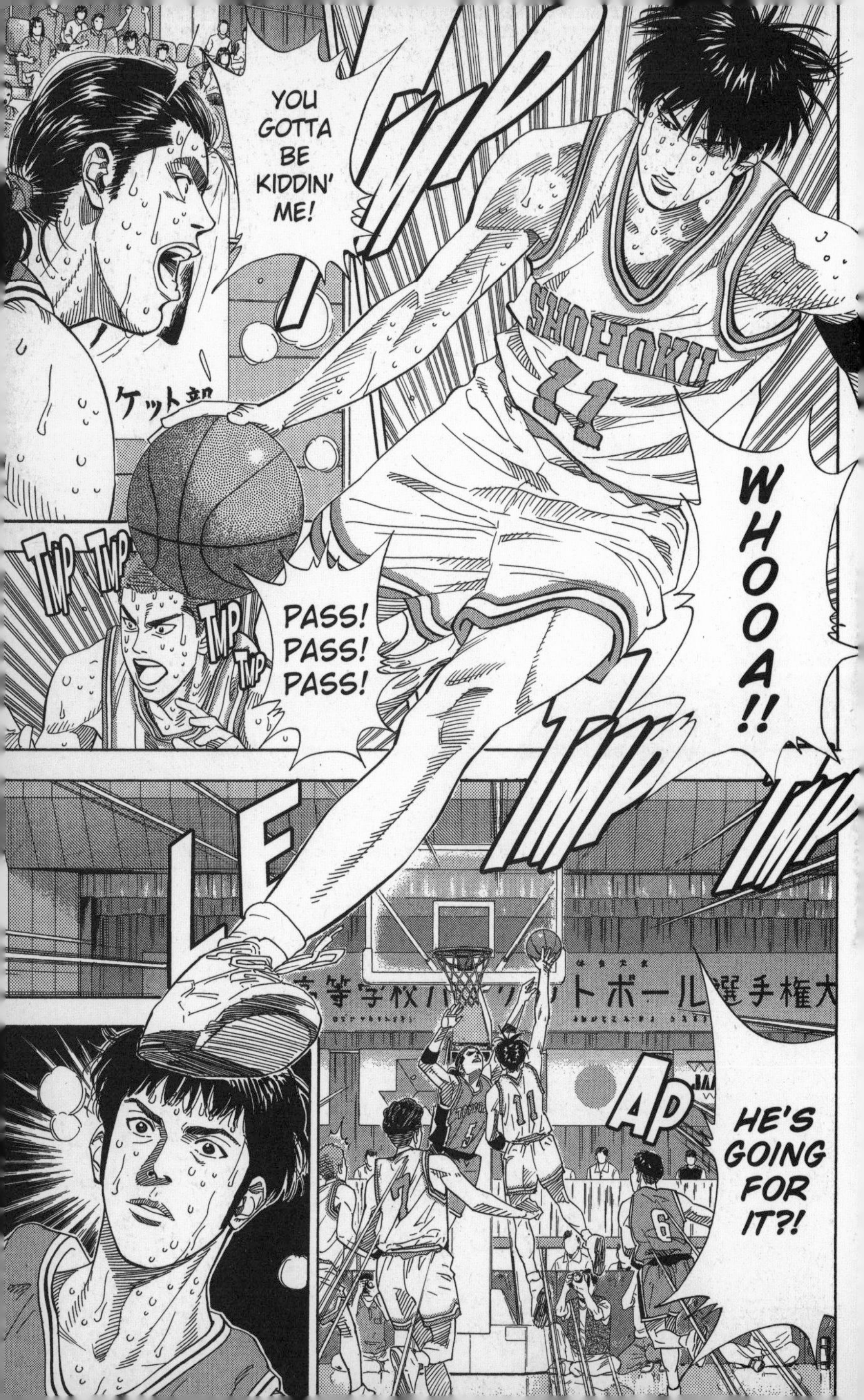
WHOOOA!!
TMP
TMP
YOU GOTTA BE KIDDIN' ME!
PASS! PASS! PASS!
TMP TMP TMP TMP
LE
AP
HE'S GOING FOR IT?!

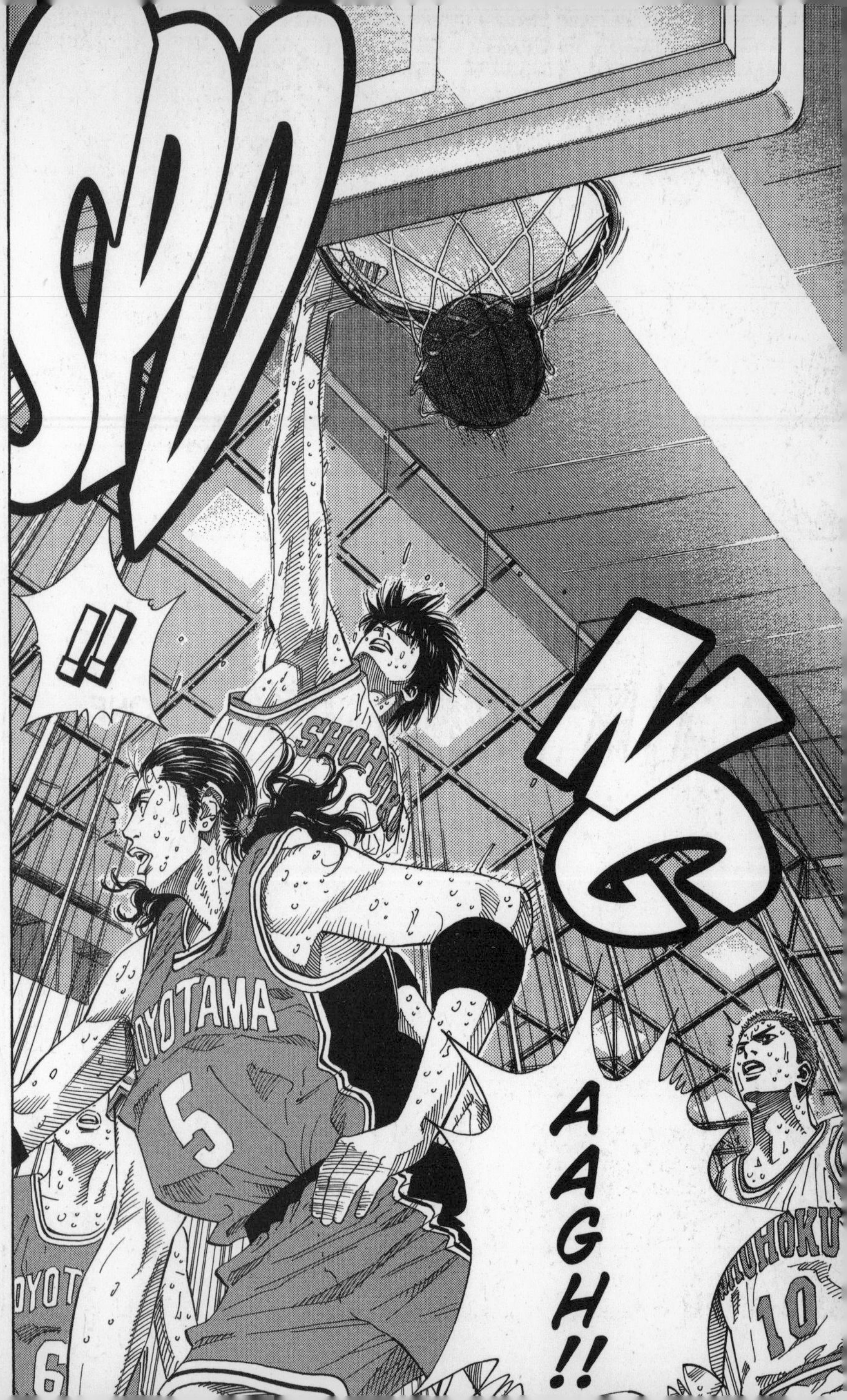
!!
AAGH!!

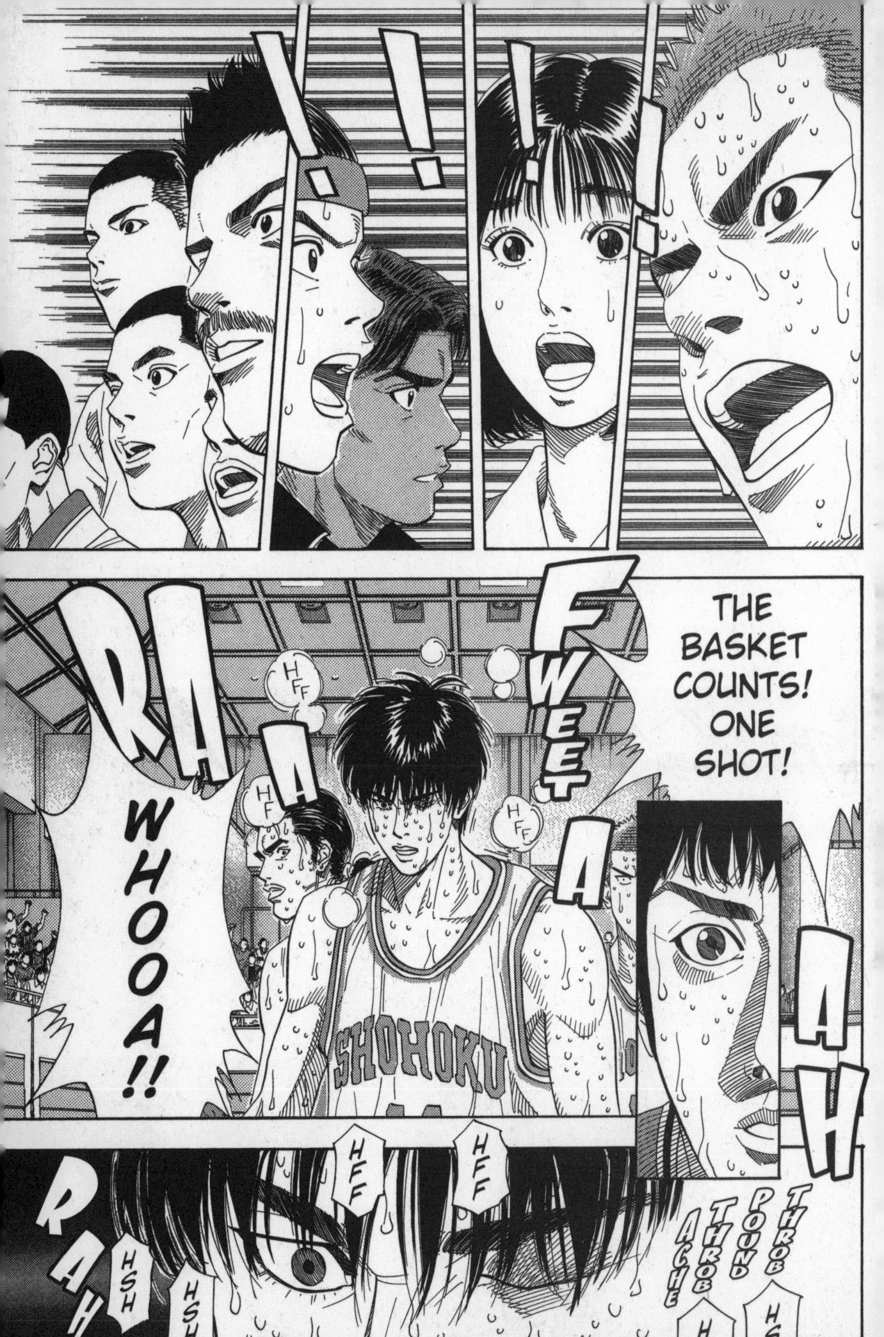
!!
!!
!!
!!
THE BASKET COUNTS! ONE SHOT!
FWEET
RA A A A AH
WHOOOA!!
HFF
HFF
HFF
THROB
HSH
POUND
THROB
HSH
ACHE
HFF
HFF
HSH
HSH
RAH

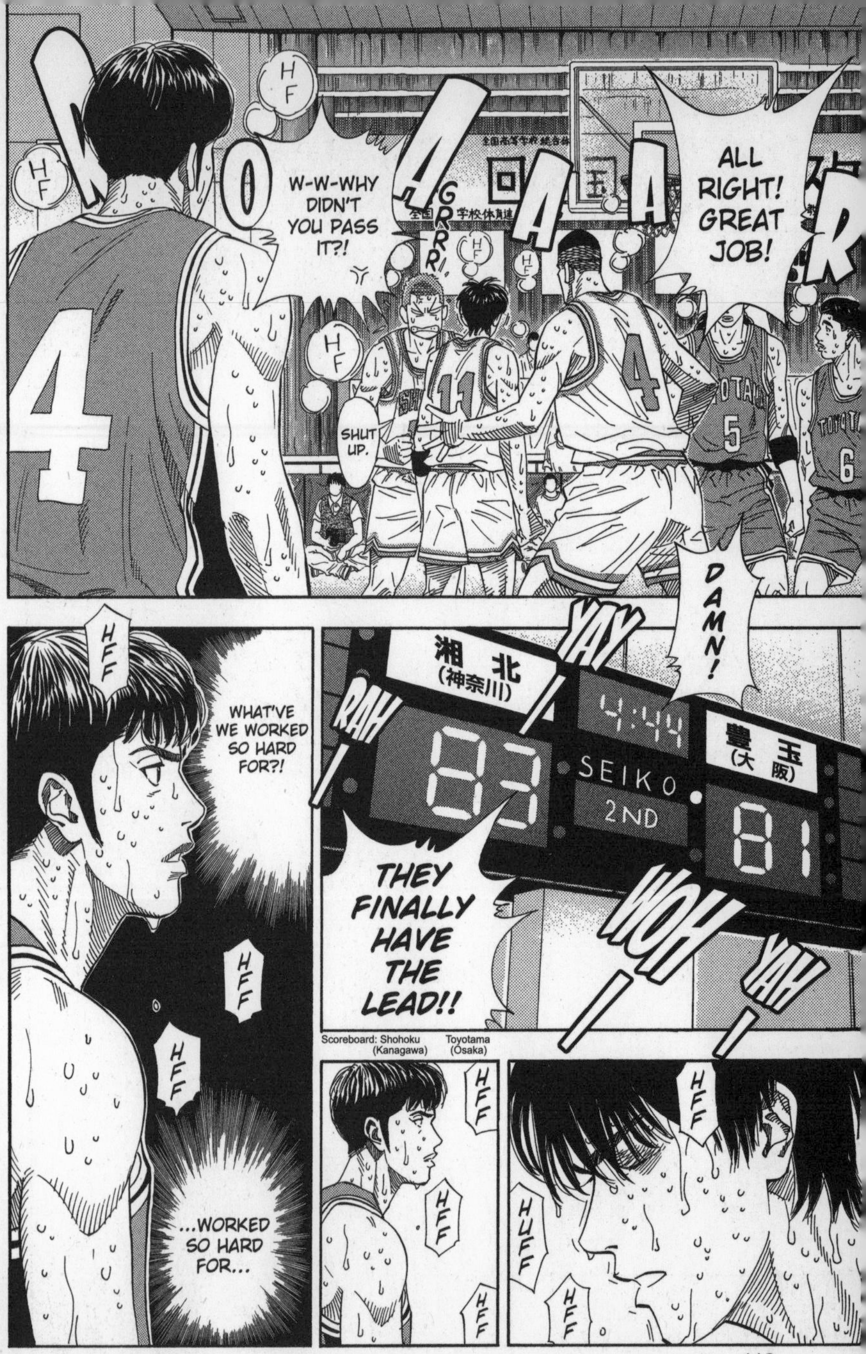
ALL RIGHT! GREAT JOB!
KOAAAR
HF
HF
W-W-WHY DIDN'T YOU PASS IT?!
GRRR
HF
HF
HF
SHUT UP.
DAMN!
湘北 (神奈川)
4:44
SEIKO
2ND
豊玉 (大阪)
83
81
YAY
RAH
THEY FINALLY HAVE THE LEAD!!
WOH
YAH
HFF
HUFF
HFF
HFF
HFF
HFF
WHAT'VE WE WORKED SO HARD FOR?!
HFF
HFF
...WORKED SO HARD FOR...
Scoreboard: Shohoku (Kanagawa) Toyotama (Osaka)

READ THIS WAY

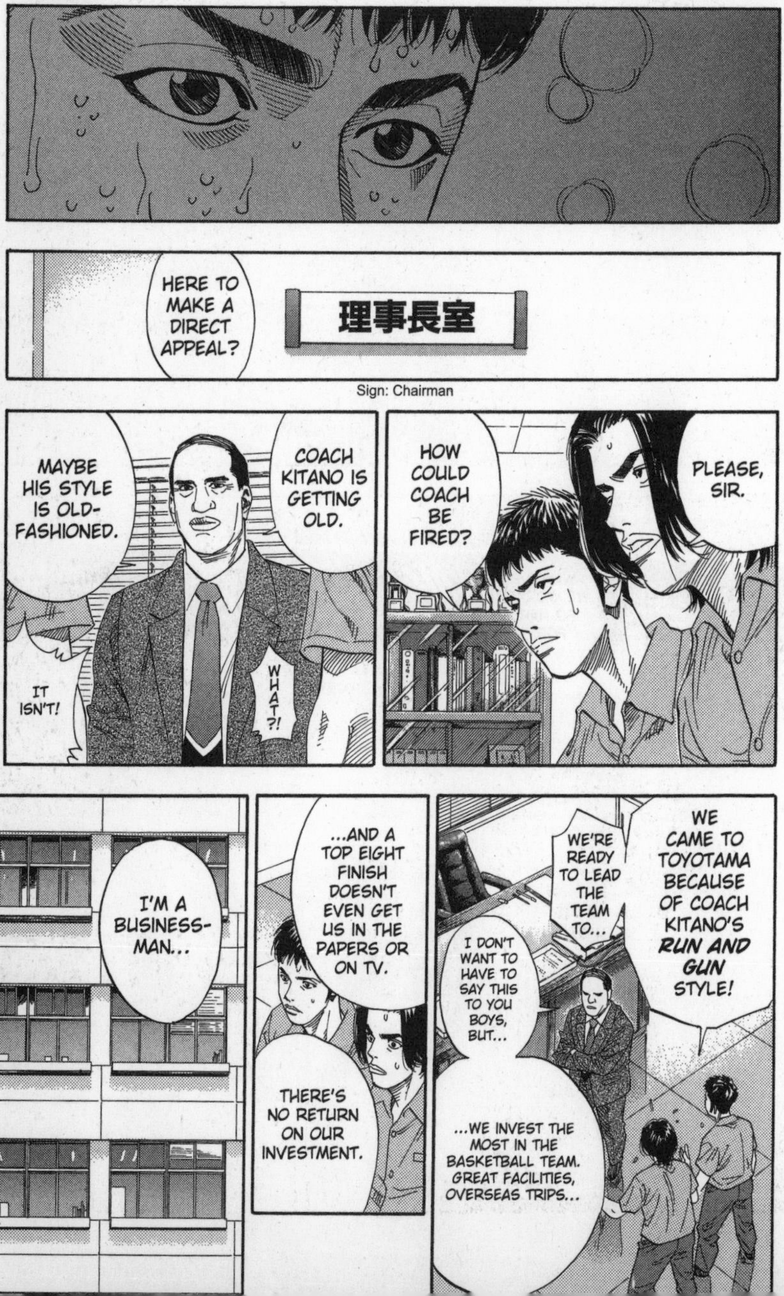
HERE TO MAKE A DIRECT APPEAL?
理事長室
Sign: Chairman
PLEASE, SIR.
HOW COULD COACH BE FIRED?
COACH KITANO IS GETTING OLD.
MAYBE HIS STYLE IS OLD-FASHIONED.
WHAT?!
IT ISN'T!
WE CAME TO TOYOTAMA BECAUSE OF COACH KITANO'S ***RUN AND GUN*** STYLE!
WE'RE READY TO LEAD THE TEAM TO...
I DON'T WANT TO HAVE TO SAY THIS TO YOU BOYS, BUT...
...WE INVEST THE MOST IN THE BASKETBALL TEAM. GREAT FACILITIES, OVERSEAS TRIPS...
...AND A TOP EIGHT FINISH DOESN'T EVEN GET US IN THE PAPERS OR ON TV.
THERE'S NO RETURN ON OUR INVESTMENT.
I'M A BUSINESSMAN...

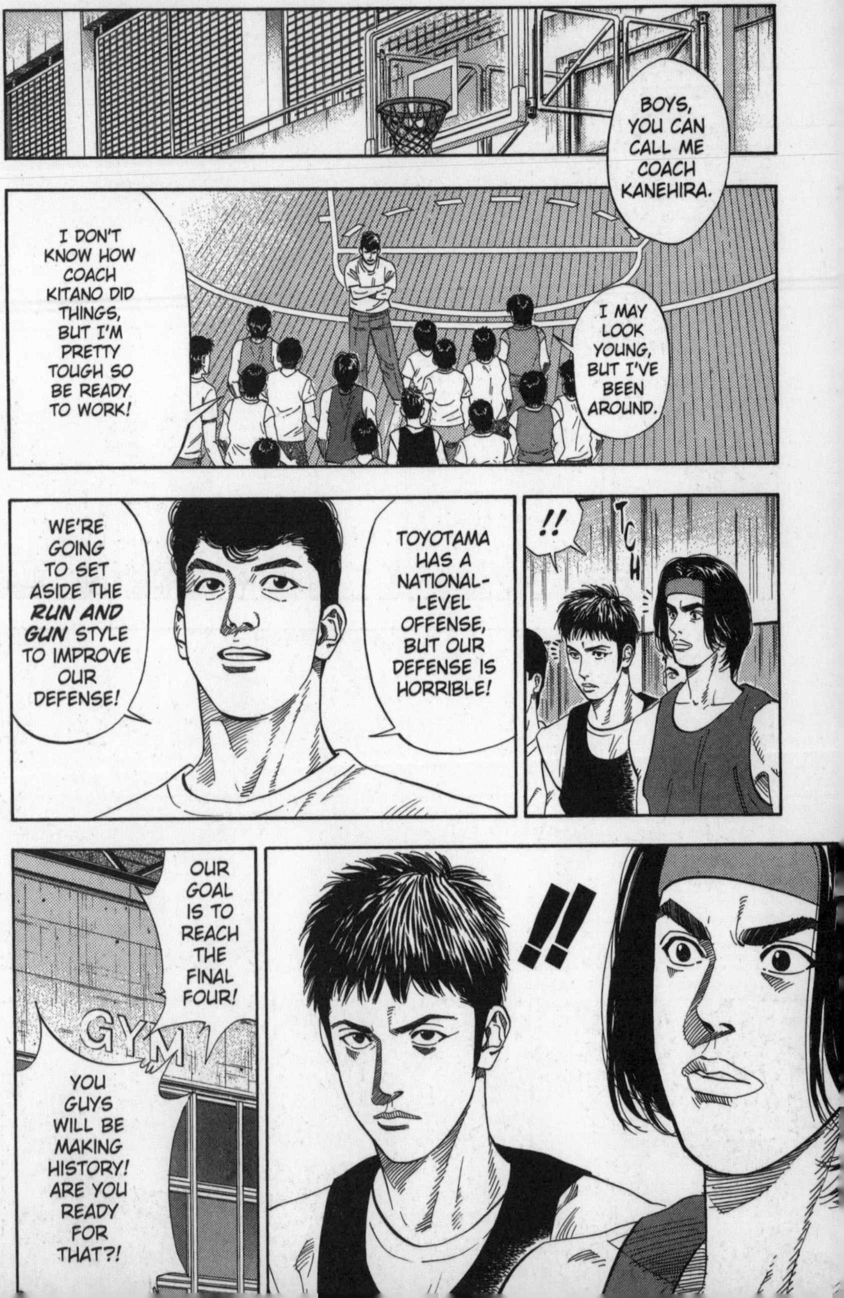
BOYS, YOU CAN CALL ME COACH KANEHIRA.
I MAY LOOK YOUNG, BUT I'VE BEEN AROUND.
I DON'T KNOW HOW COACH KITANO DID THINGS, BUT I'M PRETTY TOUGH SO BE READY TO WORK!
!!
TCH
TOYOTAMA HAS A NATIONAL-LEVEL OFFENSE, BUT OUR DEFENSE IS HORRIBLE!
WE'RE GOING TO SET ASIDE THE ***RUN AND GUN*** STYLE TO IMPROVE OUR DEFENSE!
!!
OUR GOAL IS TO REACH THE FINAL FOUR!
GYM
YOU GUYS WILL BE MAKING HISTORY! ARE YOU READY FOR THAT?!

READ THIS WAY

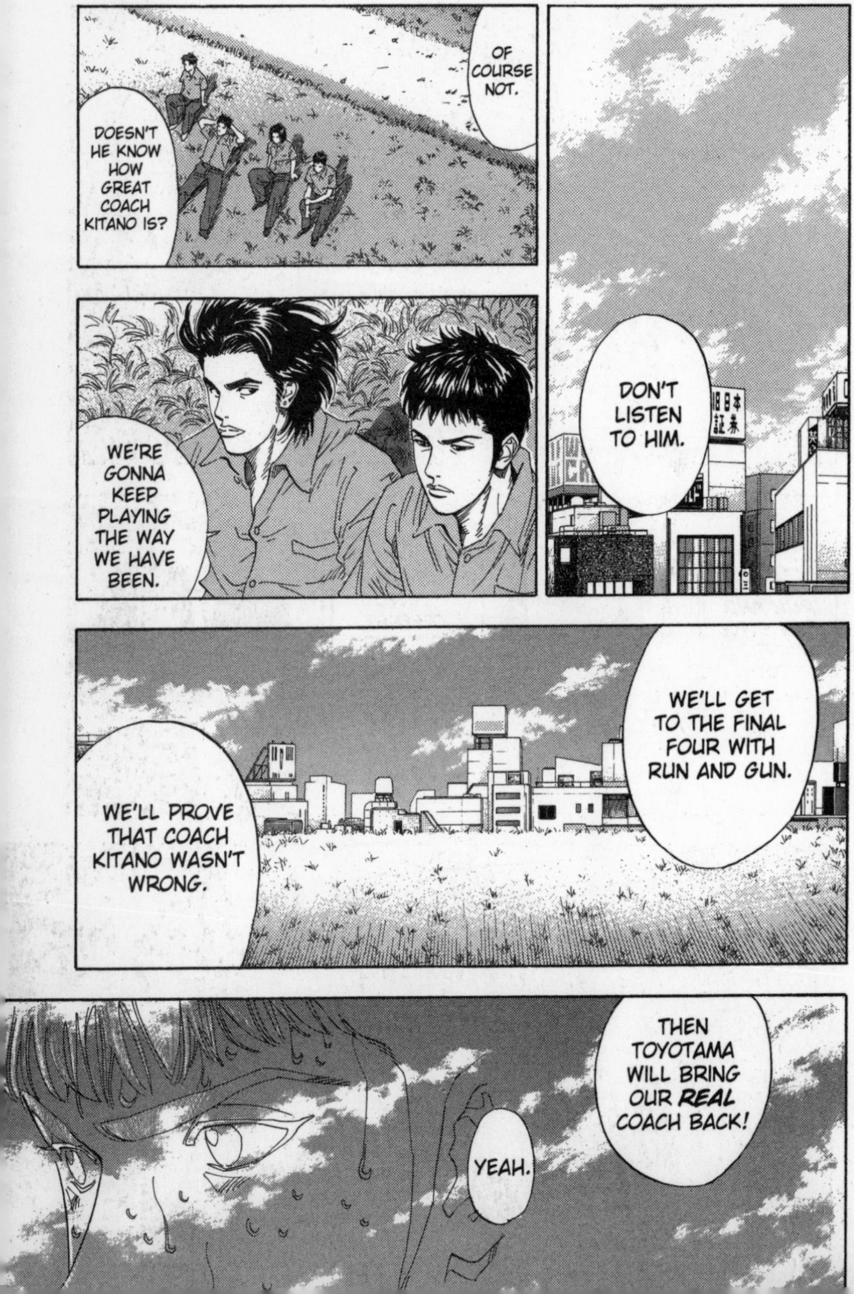

DON'T LISTEN TO HIM.
OF COURSE NOT.
DOESN'T HE KNOW HOW GREAT COACH KITANO IS?
WE'RE GONNA KEEP PLAYING THE WAY WE HAVE BEEN.
WE'LL GET TO THE FINAL FOUR WITH RUN AND GUN.
WE'LL PROVE THAT COACH KITANO WASN'T WRONG.
THEN TOYOTAMA WILL BRING OUR *REAL* COACH BACK!
YEAH.

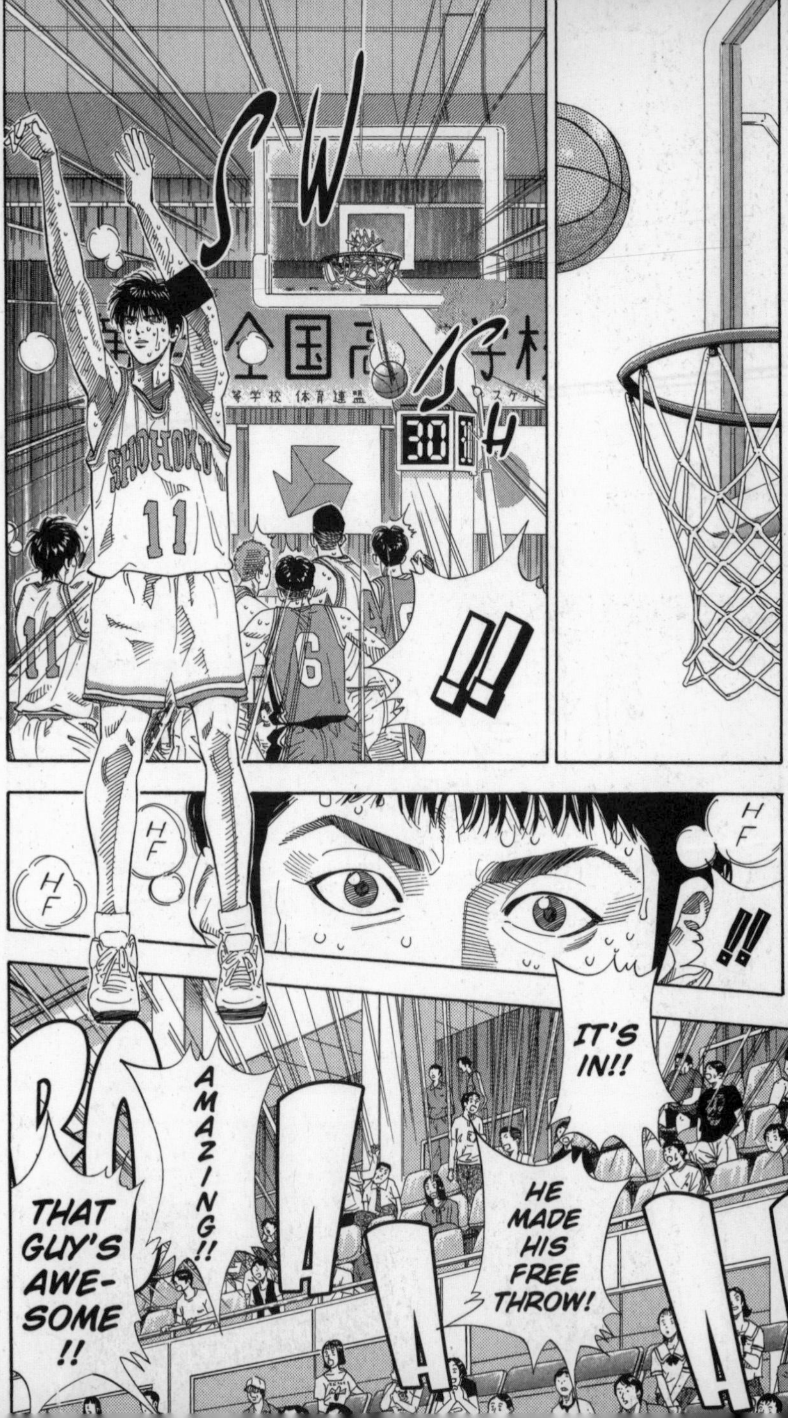
SWISH
!!
HF HF
!!
HF HF
IT'S IN!!
HE MADE HIS FREE THROW!
AMAZING!!
THAT GUY'S AWE-SOME!!
ROAAAR

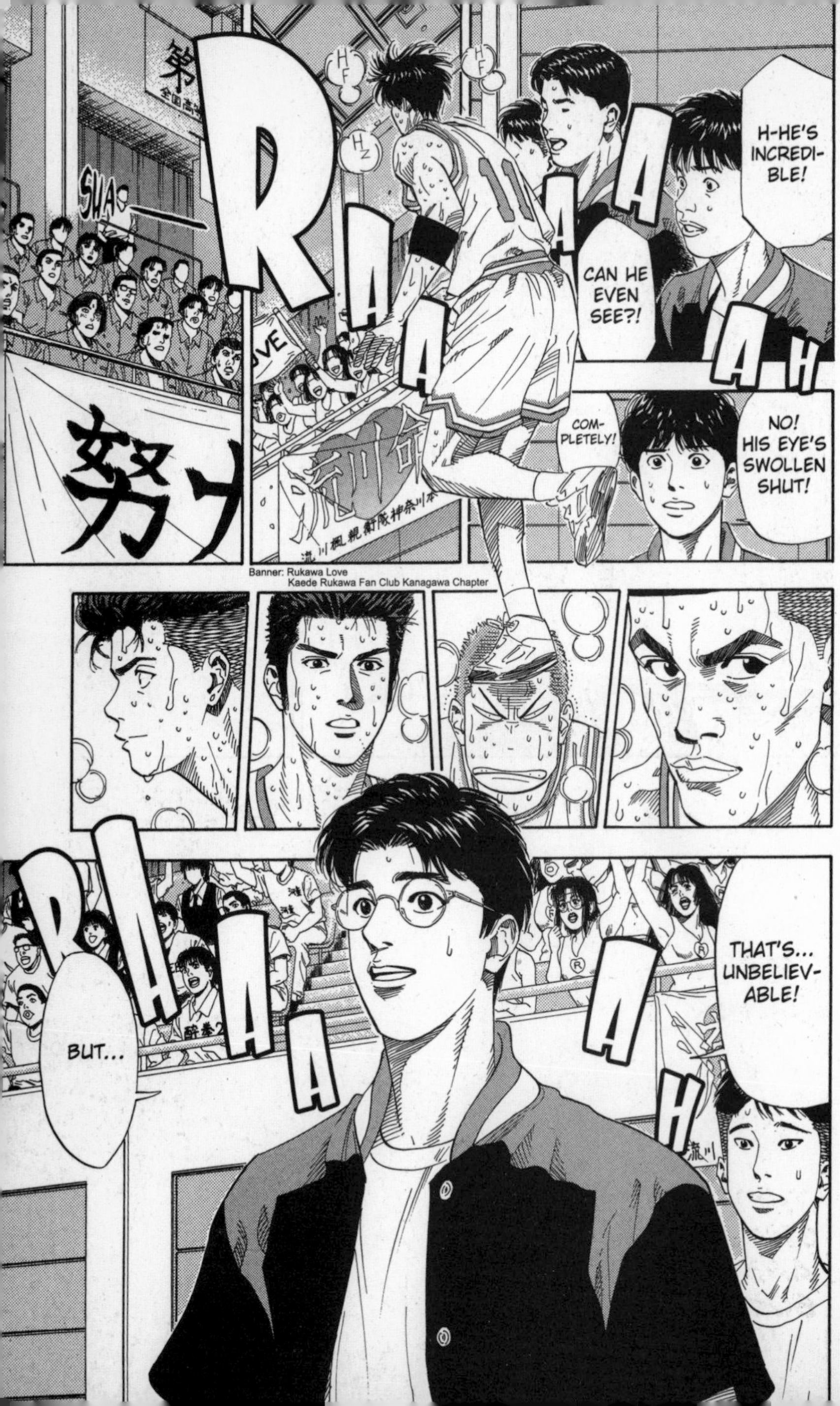
H-HE'S INCREDIBLE!
CAN HE EVEN SEE?!
NO! HIS EYE'S SWOLLEN SHUT!
COMPLETELY!
RAAAAAAAH
HF
HF
HZ
SHA
THAT'S... UNBELIEVABLE!
BUT...
RAAAAAH
Banner: Rukawa Love
Kaede Rukawa Fan Club Kanagawa Chapter

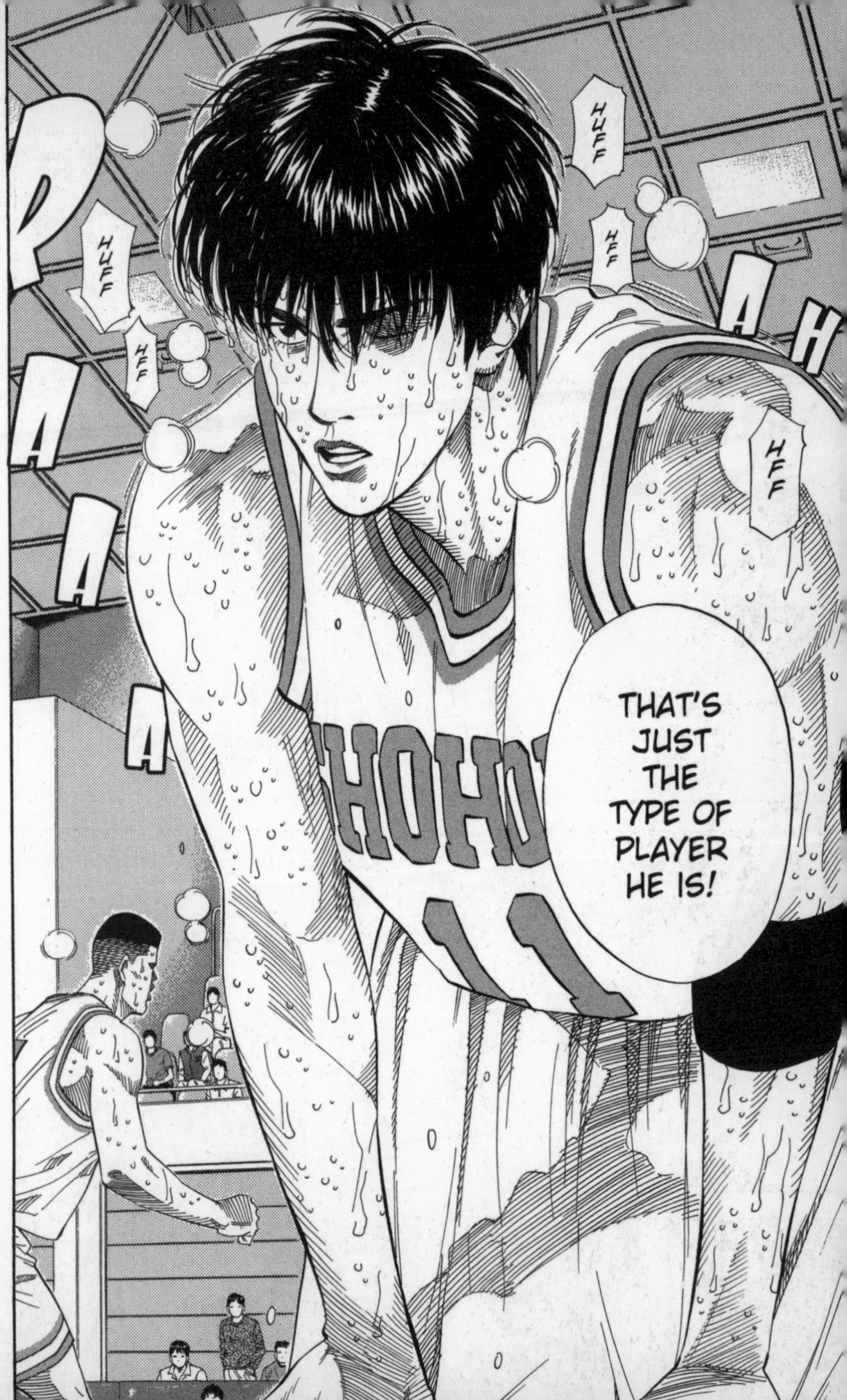
HUFF
HFF
AH
HFF
THAT'S JUST THE TYPE OF PLAYER HE IS!
HUFF
HFF
PAAAA

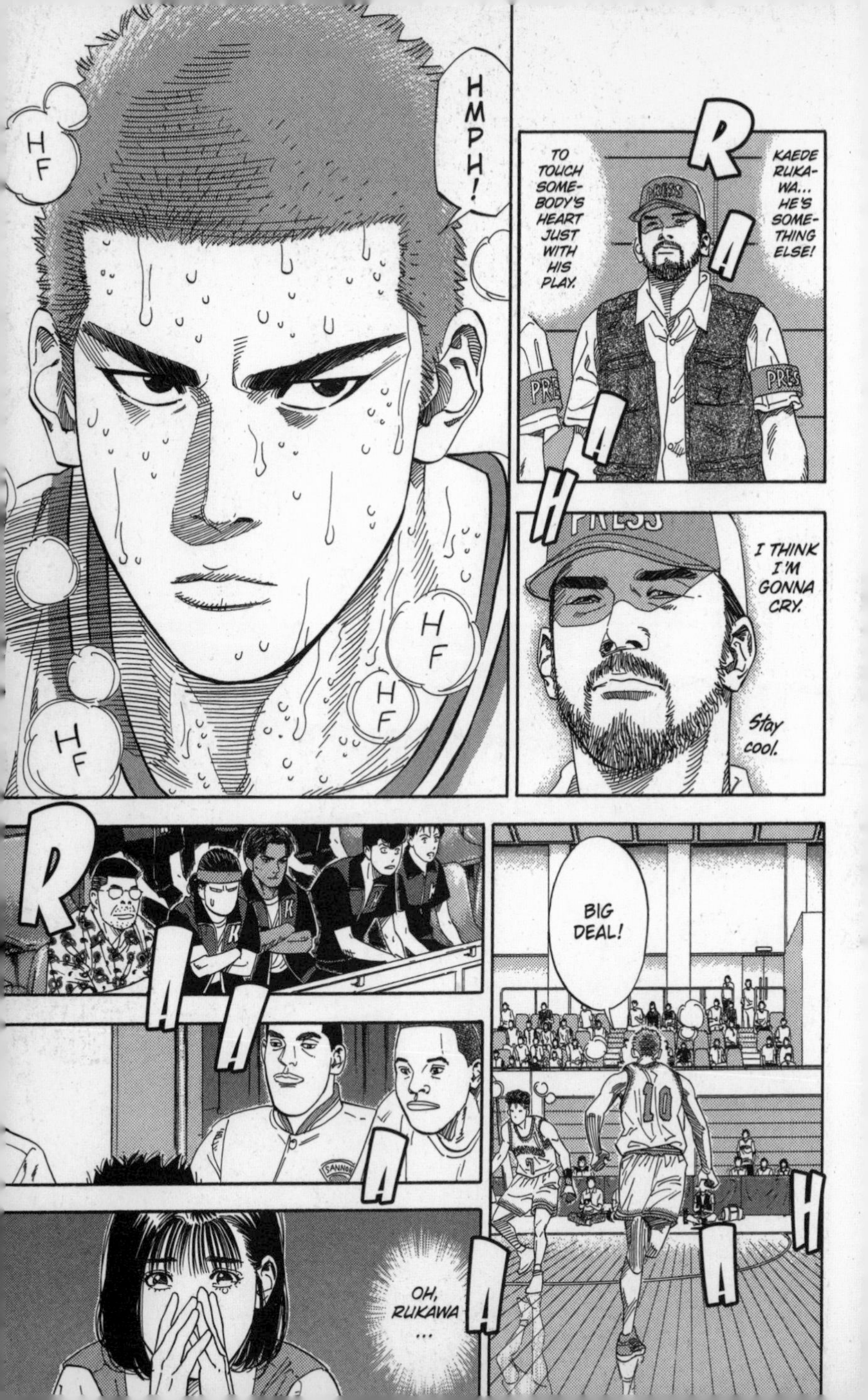
KAEDE RUKAWA... HE'S SOMETHING ELSE!
TO TOUCH SOMEBODY'S HEART JUST WITH HIS PLAY.
RAAH
I THINK I'M GONNA CRY.
Stay cool.
HMPH!
HF
HF
HF
HF
BIG DEAL!
RAAAAAAH
OH, RUKAWA ...

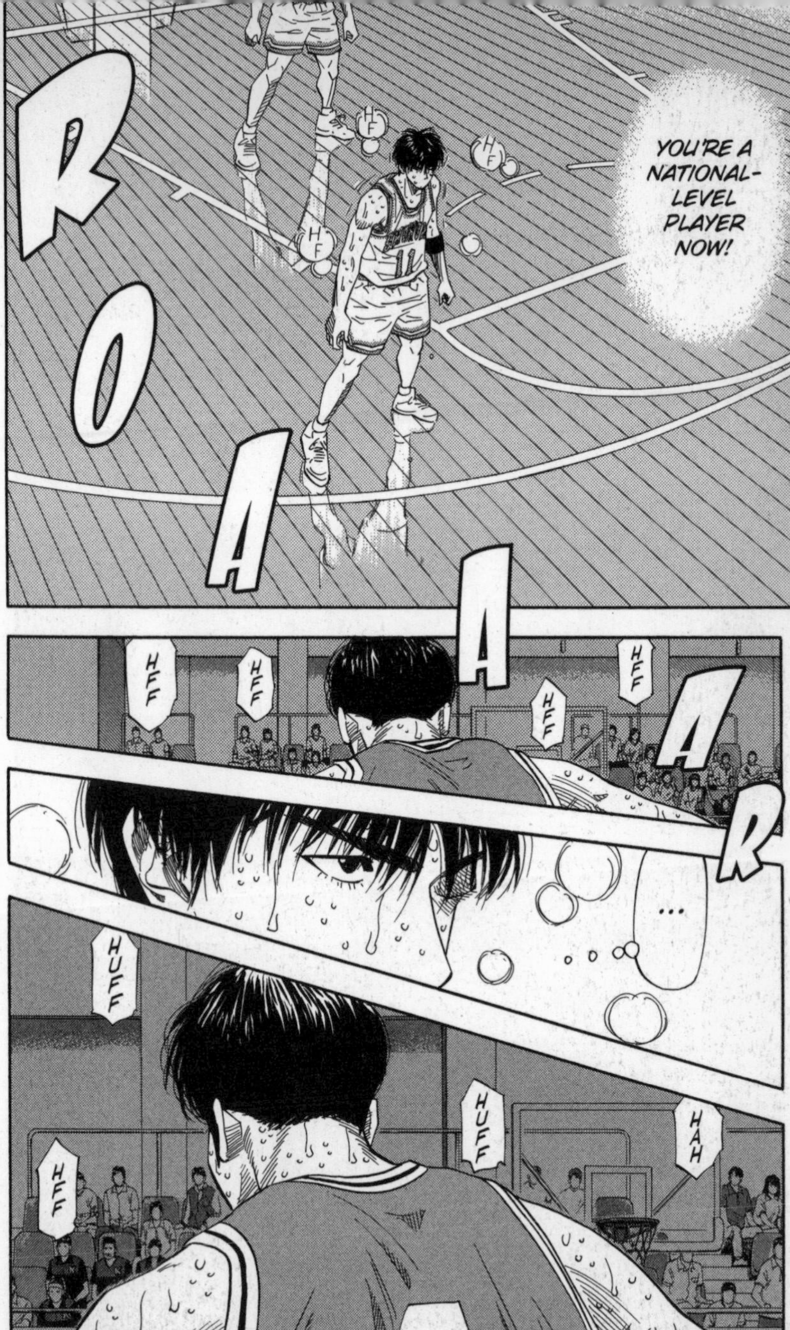
YOU'RE A NATIONAL-LEVEL PLAYER NOW!
HF
HF
HF
ROAAAR
HFF
HFF
HFF
HFF
...
HAH
HUFF
HUFF
HFF

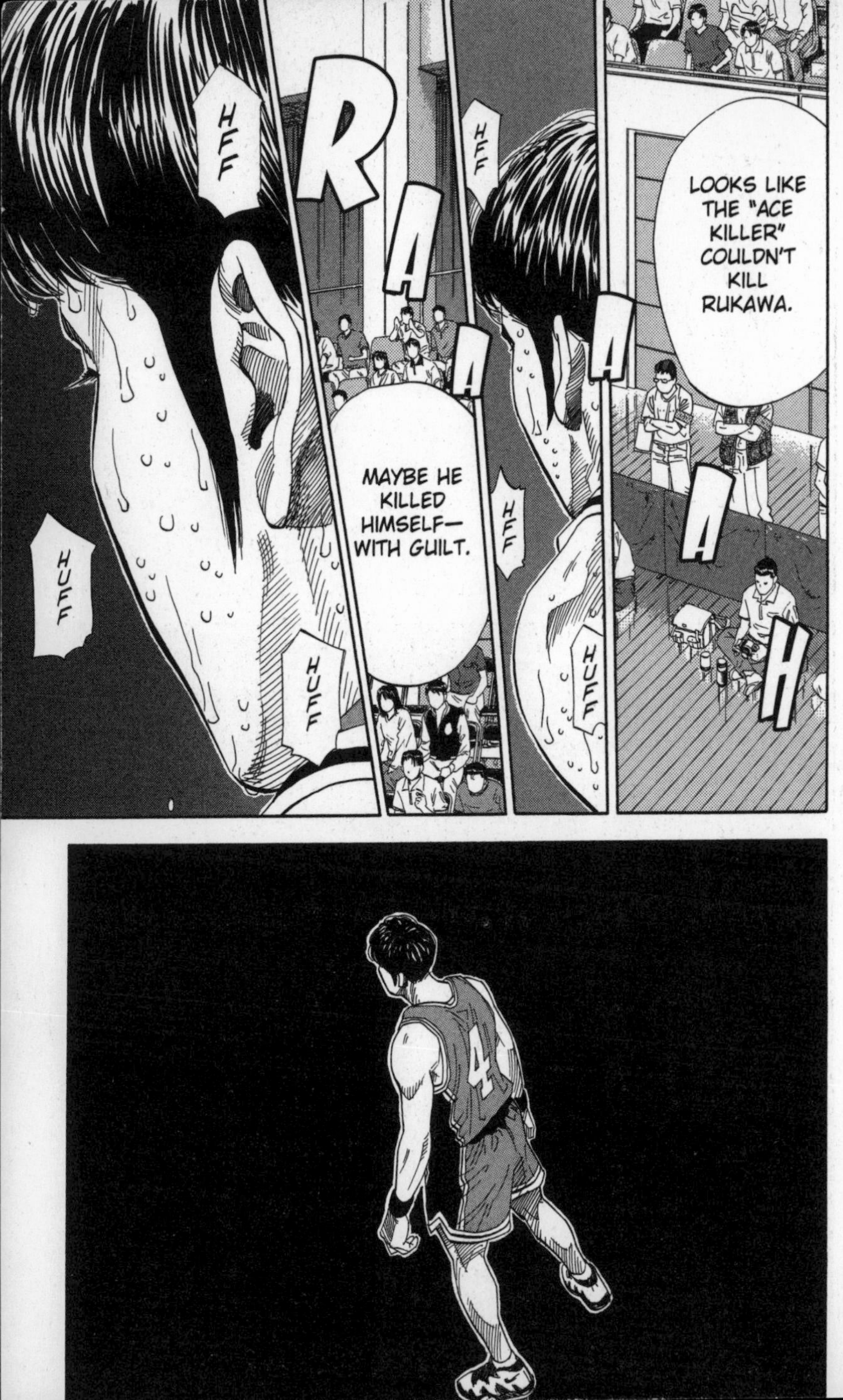
LOOKS LIKE THE "ACE KILLER" COULDN'T KILL RUKAWA.
RAAAAAH
HFF
HFF
HUFF
MAYBE HE KILLED HIMSELF— WITH GUILT.
HFF
HUFF
HUFF

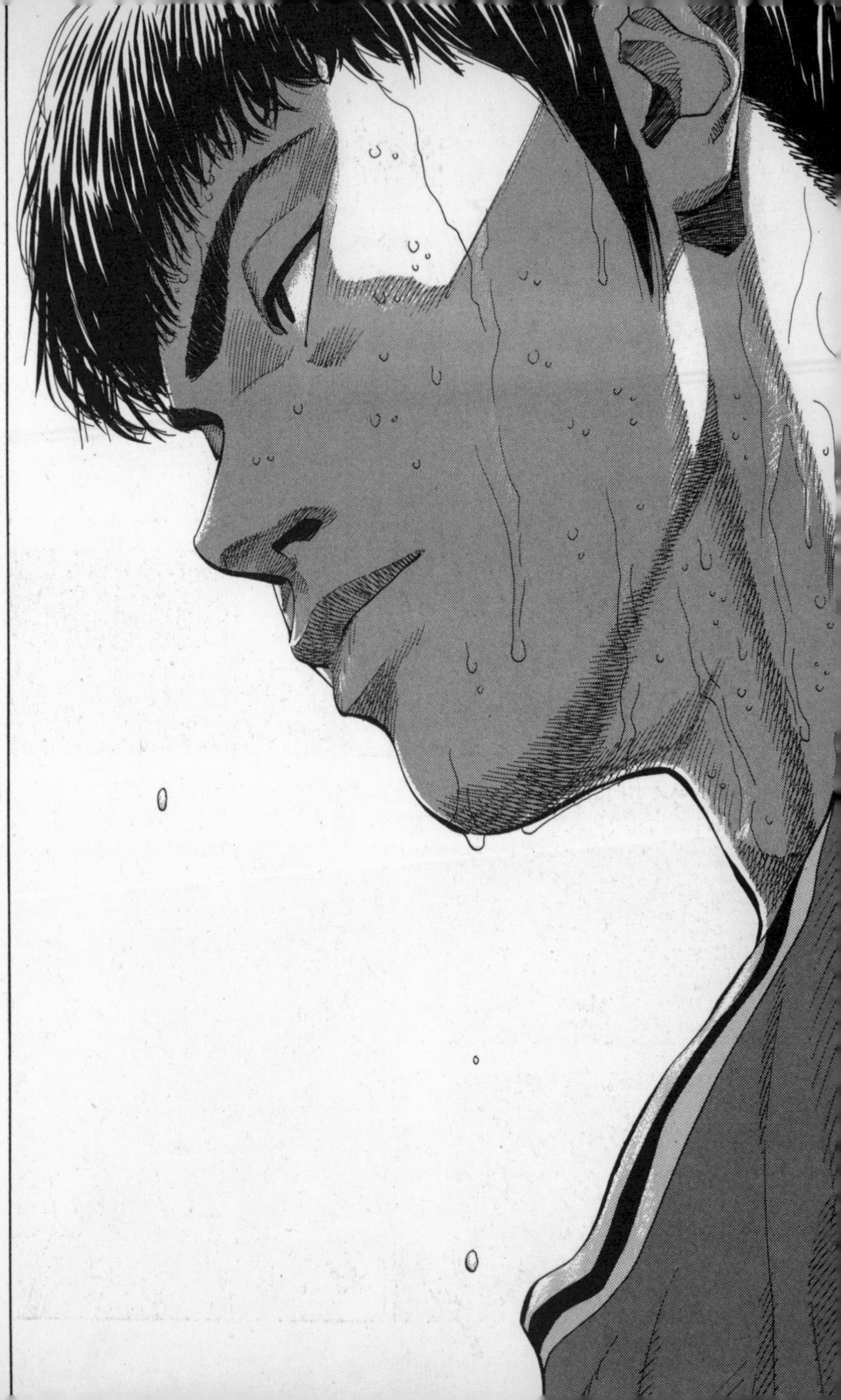

READ THIS WAY

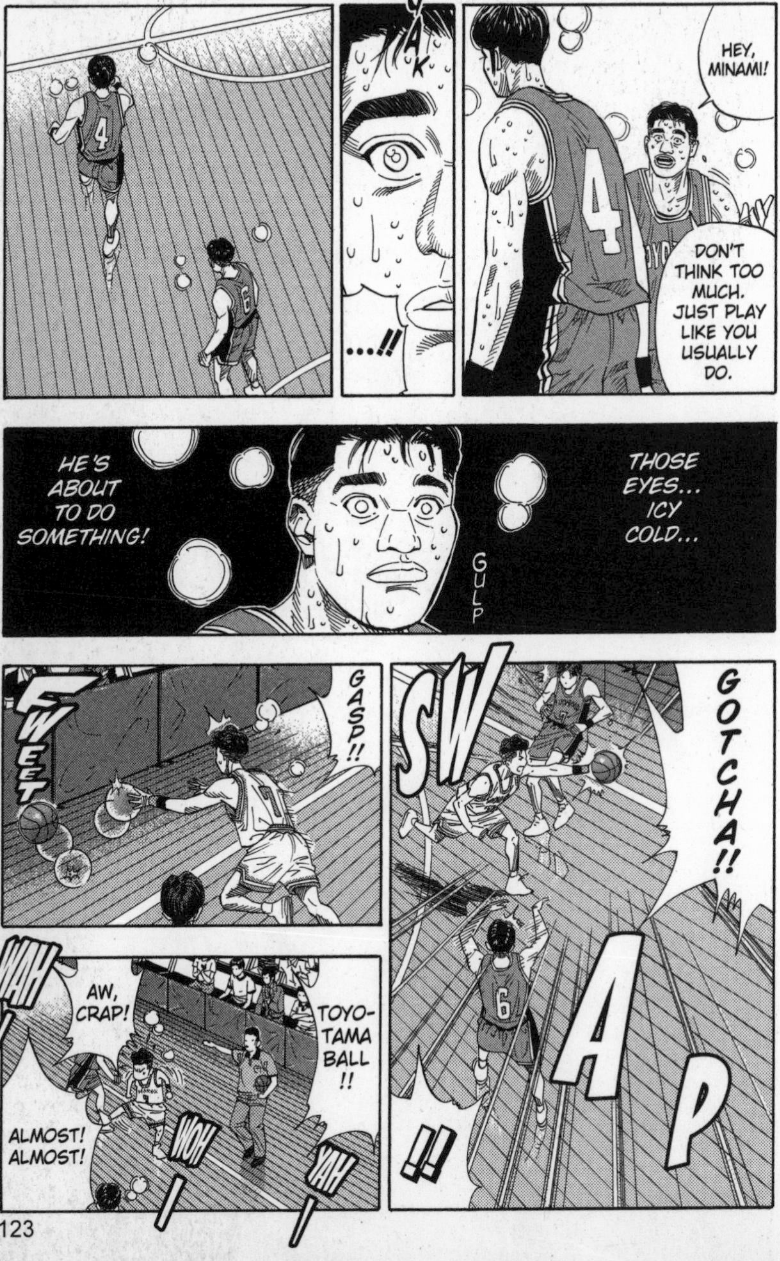

HEY, MINAMI!
DON'T THINK TOO MUCH. JUST PLAY LIKE YOU USUALLY DO.
GAK
...!!
THOSE EYES... ICY COLD...
GULP
HE'S ABOUT TO DO SOMETHING!
GOTCHA!!
SW
AP
!!
GASP!!
FWEET
TOYO-TAMA BALL!!
AW, CRAP!
WAH
WOH
YAH
ALMOST! ALMOST!

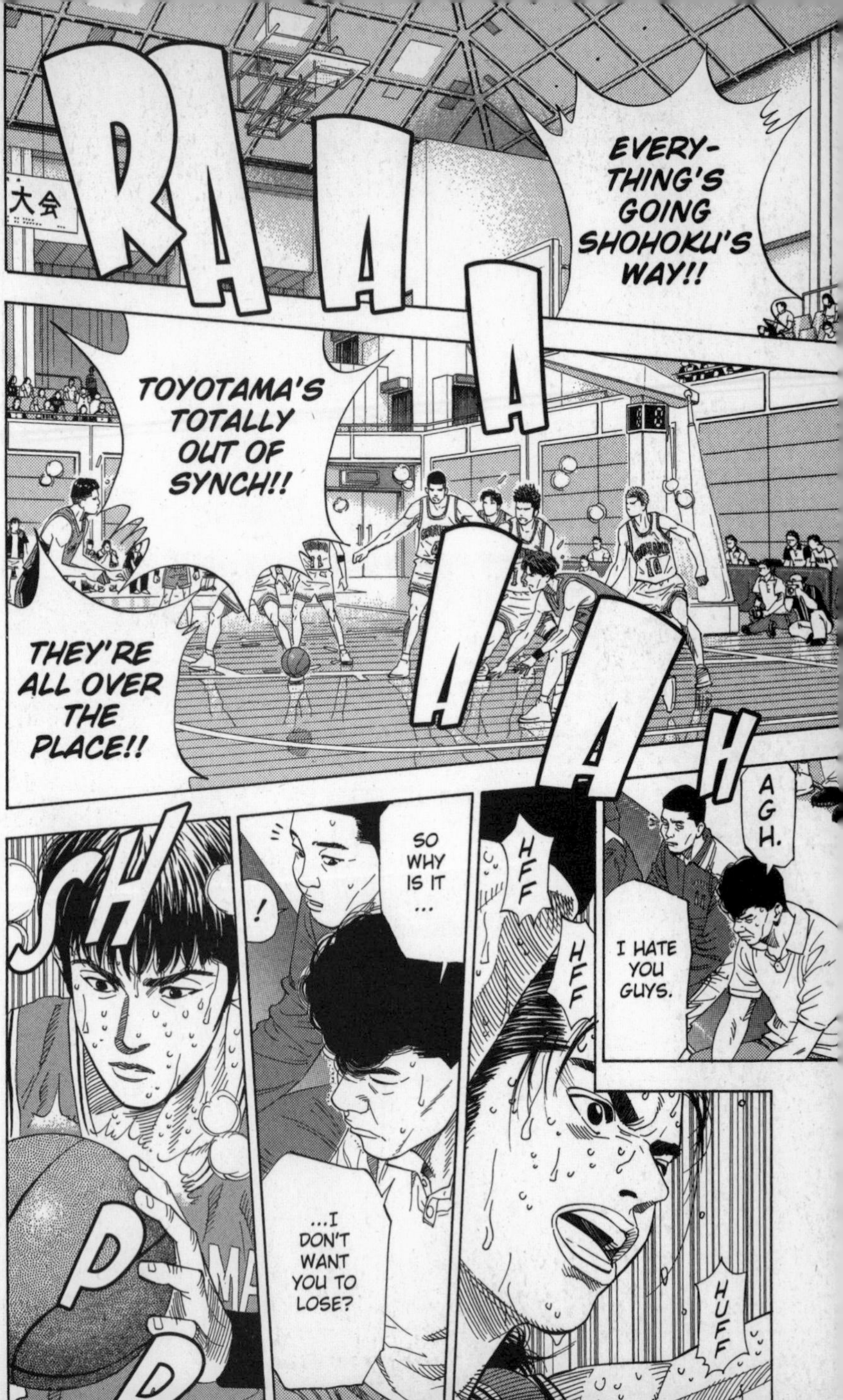
RAAAAAH
EVERY-THING'S GOING SHOHOKU'S WAY!!
TOYOTAMA'S TOTALLY OUT OF SYNCH!!
THEY'RE ALL OVER THE PLACE!!
AGH.
I HATE YOU GUYS.
HFF
HFF
HUFF
SO WHY IS IT ...
!
...I DON'T WANT YOU TO LOSE?
SH
P

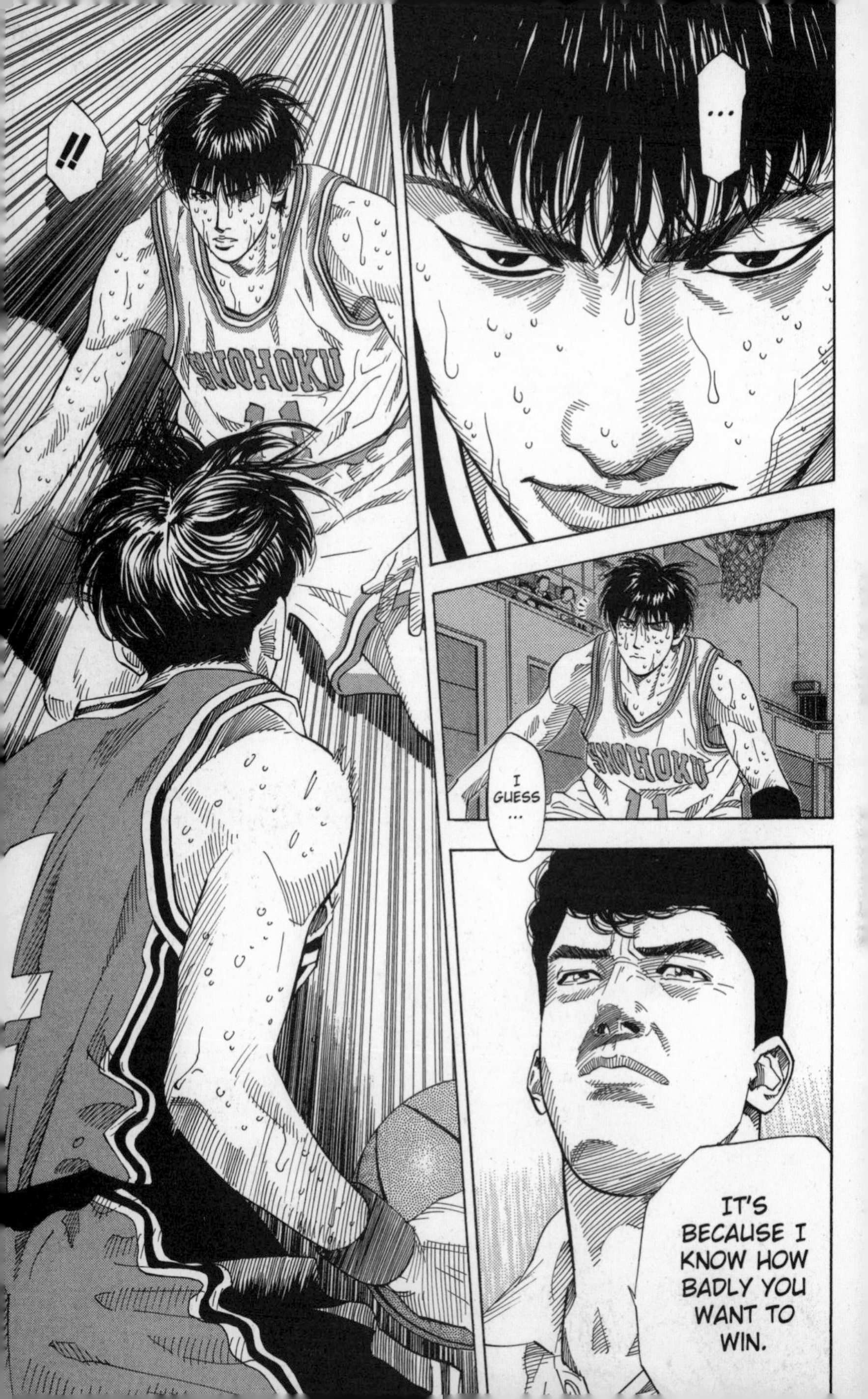
...
I GUESS ...
IT'S BECAUSE I KNOW HOW BADLY YOU WANT TO WIN.
!!

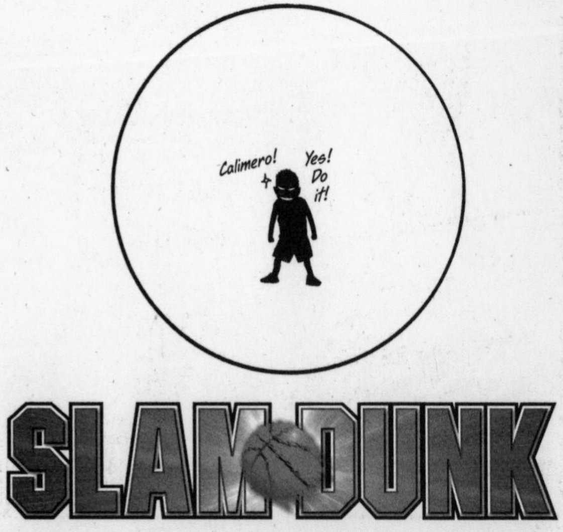
Yes! Do it!
Calimero!

SLAM DUNK

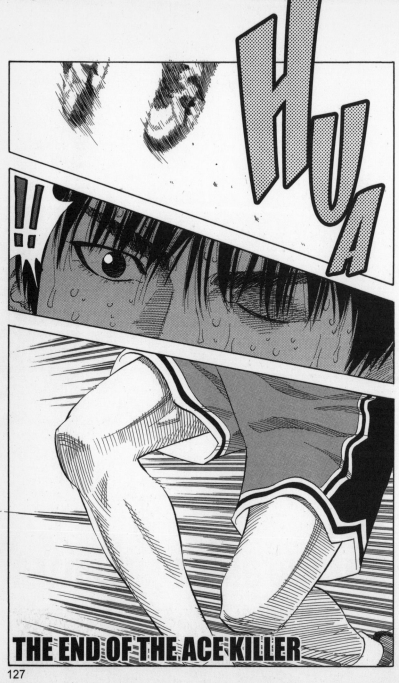

THE END OF THE ACE KILLER

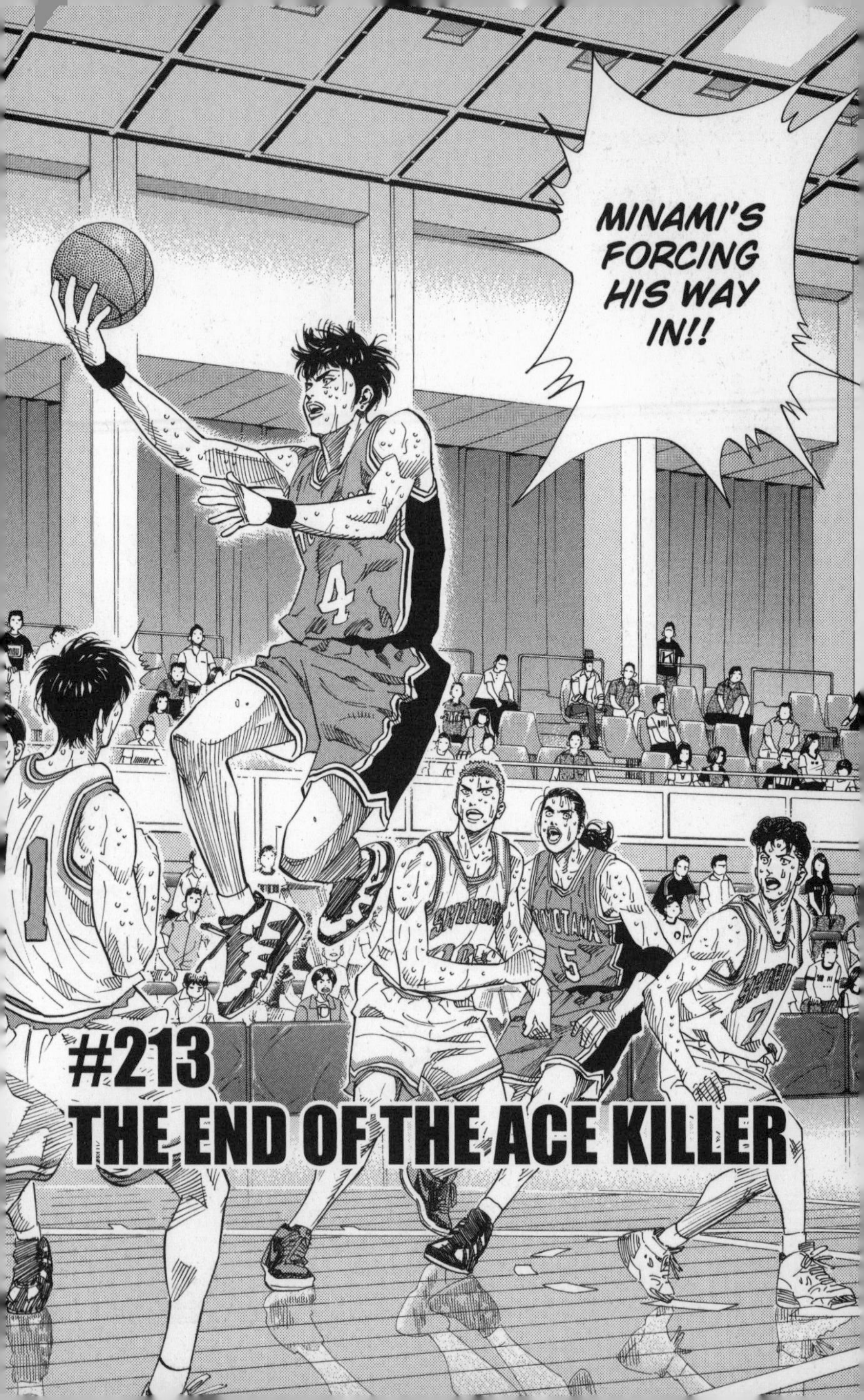
MINAMI'S FORCING HIS WAY IN!!
#213
THE END OF THE ACE KILLER

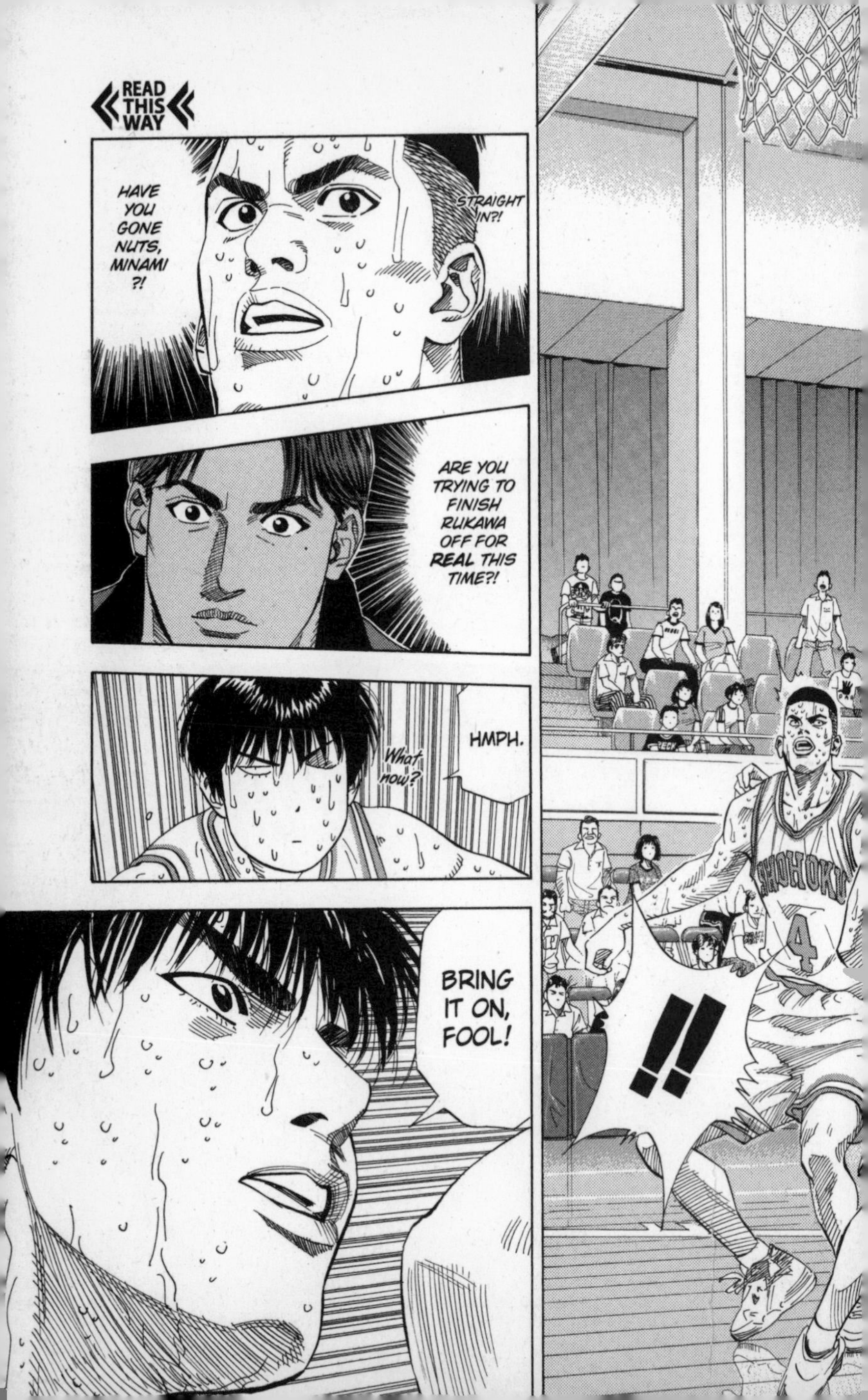
READ THIS WAY
!!
STRAIGHT IN?!
HAVE YOU GONE NUTS, MINAMI?!
ARE YOU TRYING TO FINISH RUKAWA OFF FOR REAL THIS TIME?!
HMPH.
What now?
BRING IT ON, FOOL!

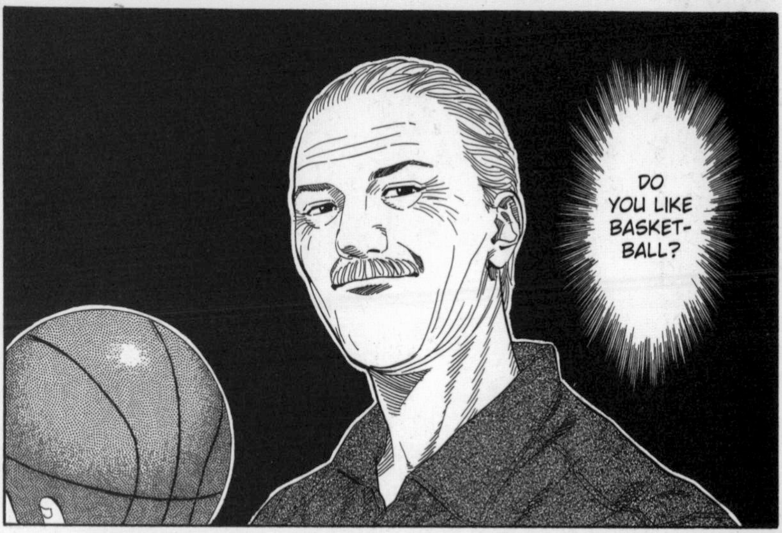
DO YOU LIKE BASKET-BALL?
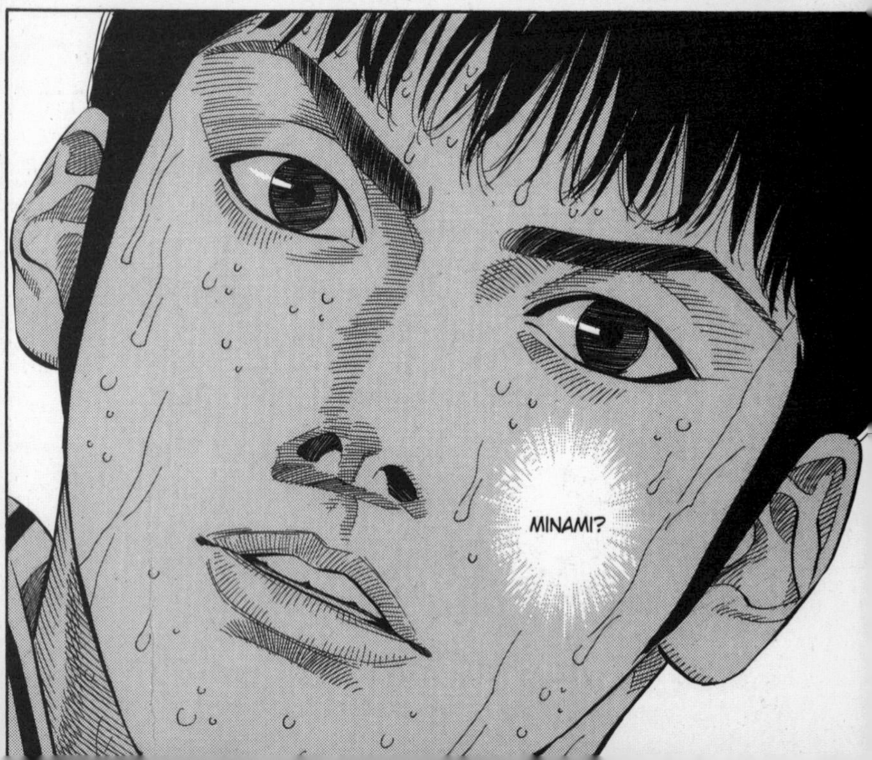
MINAMI?

READ THIS WAY

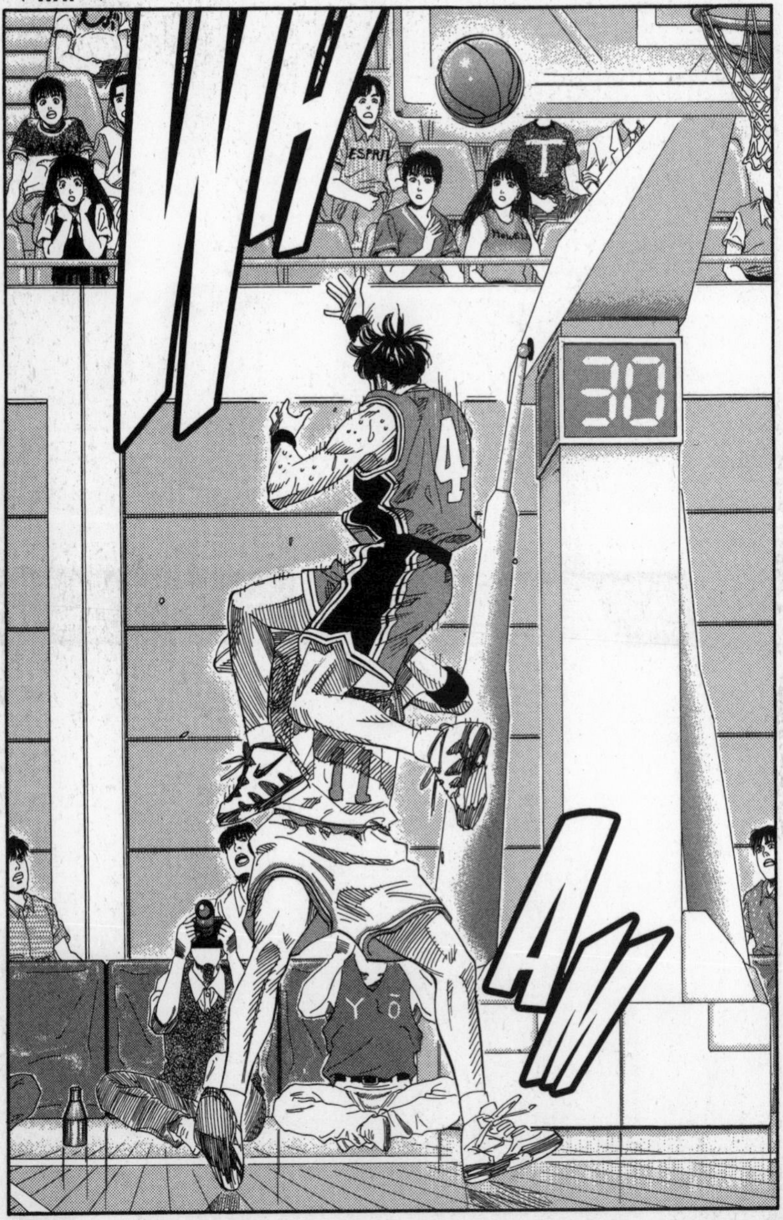
WH
AM
30

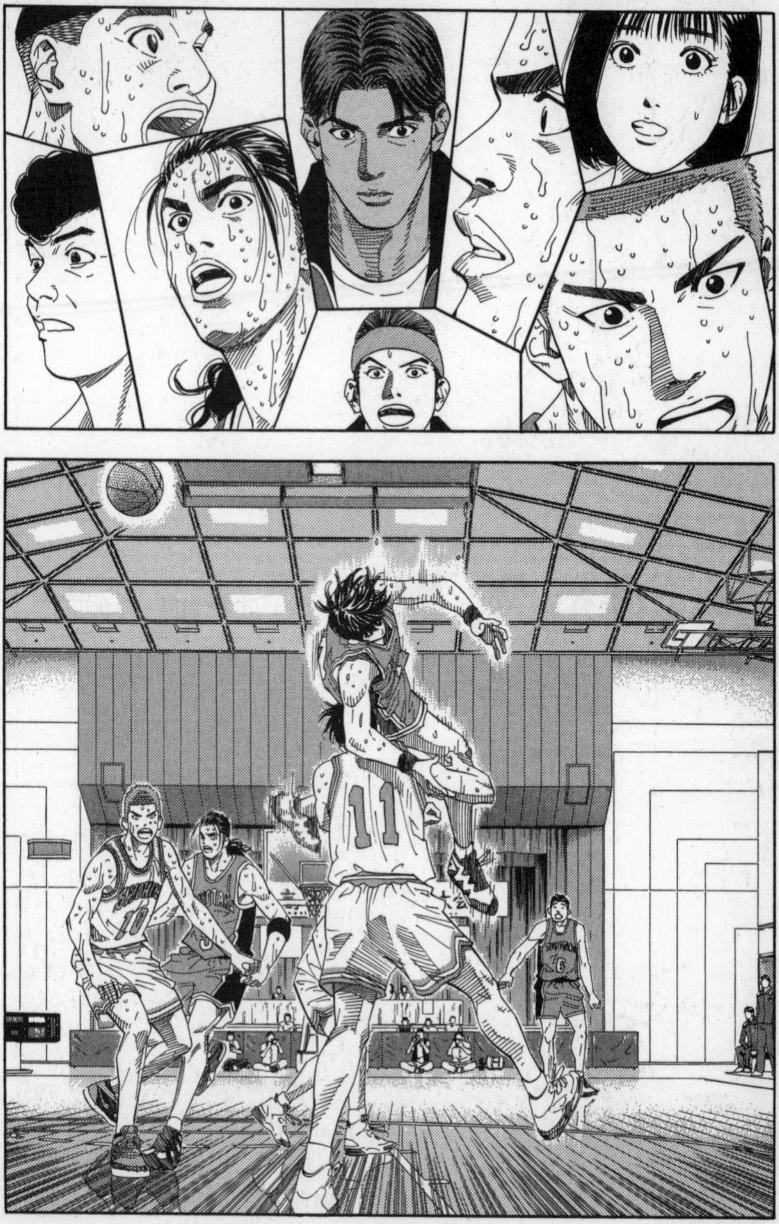

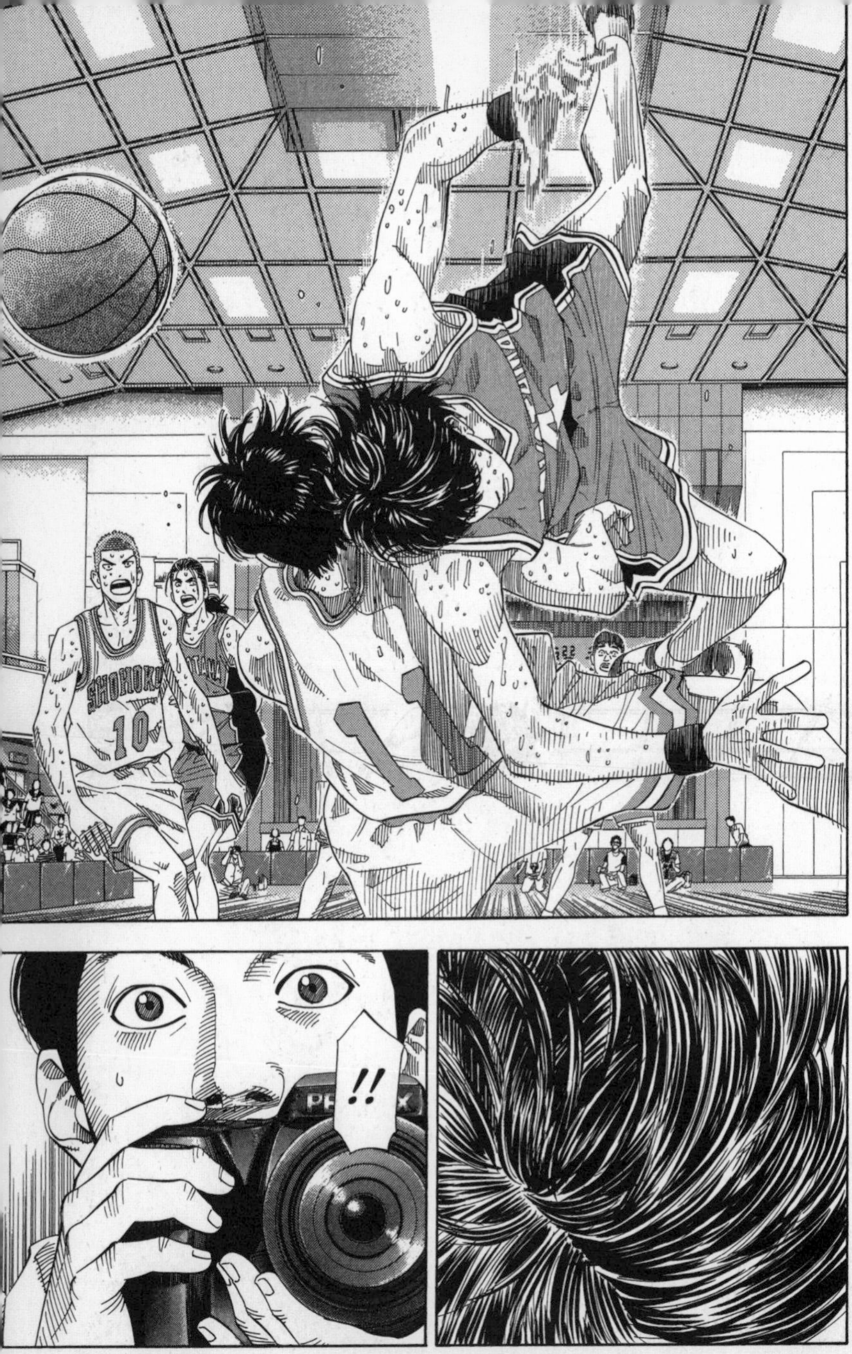
SHOHOKU
10
!!

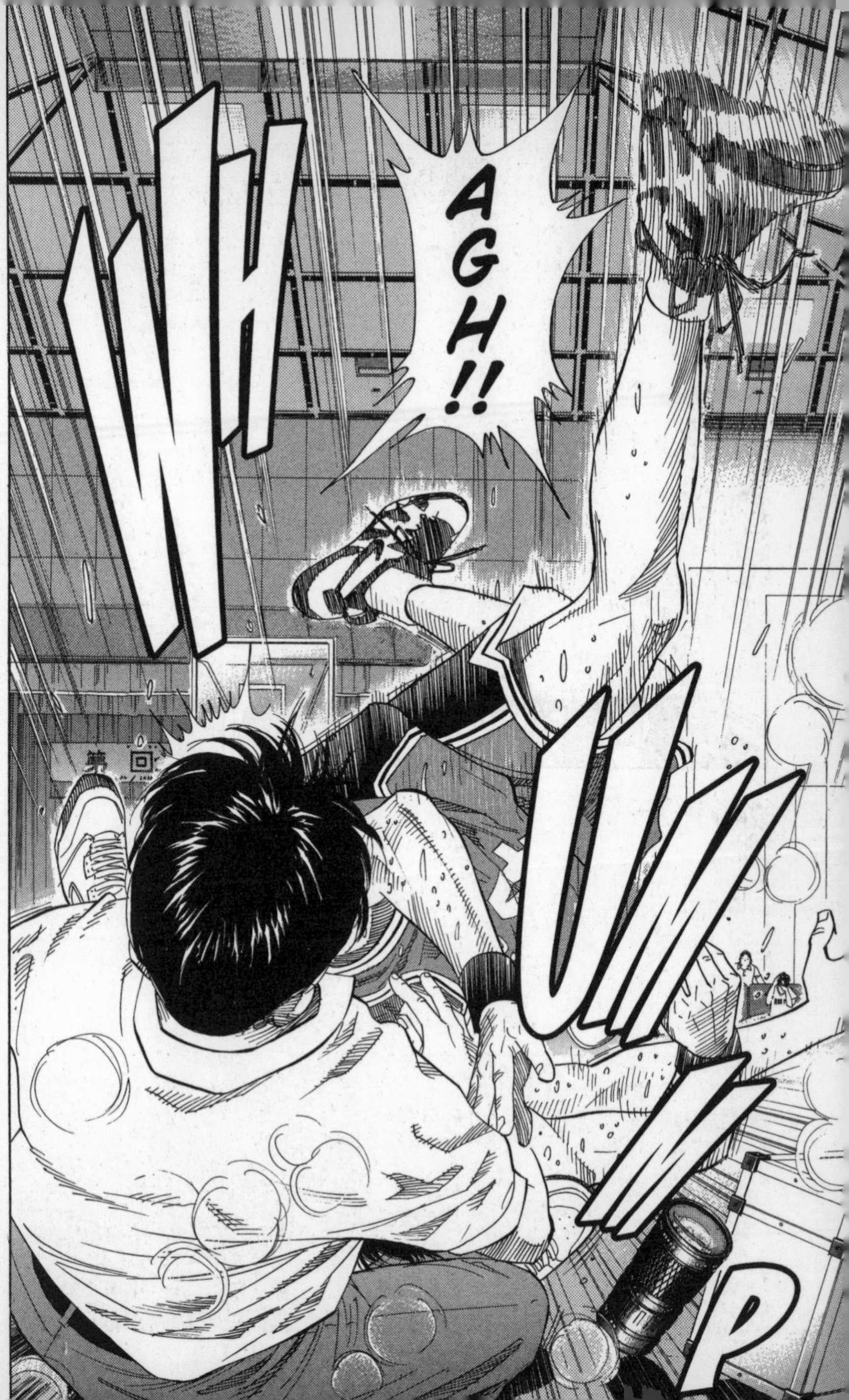
AGH!!
WHUMP

READ THIS WAY

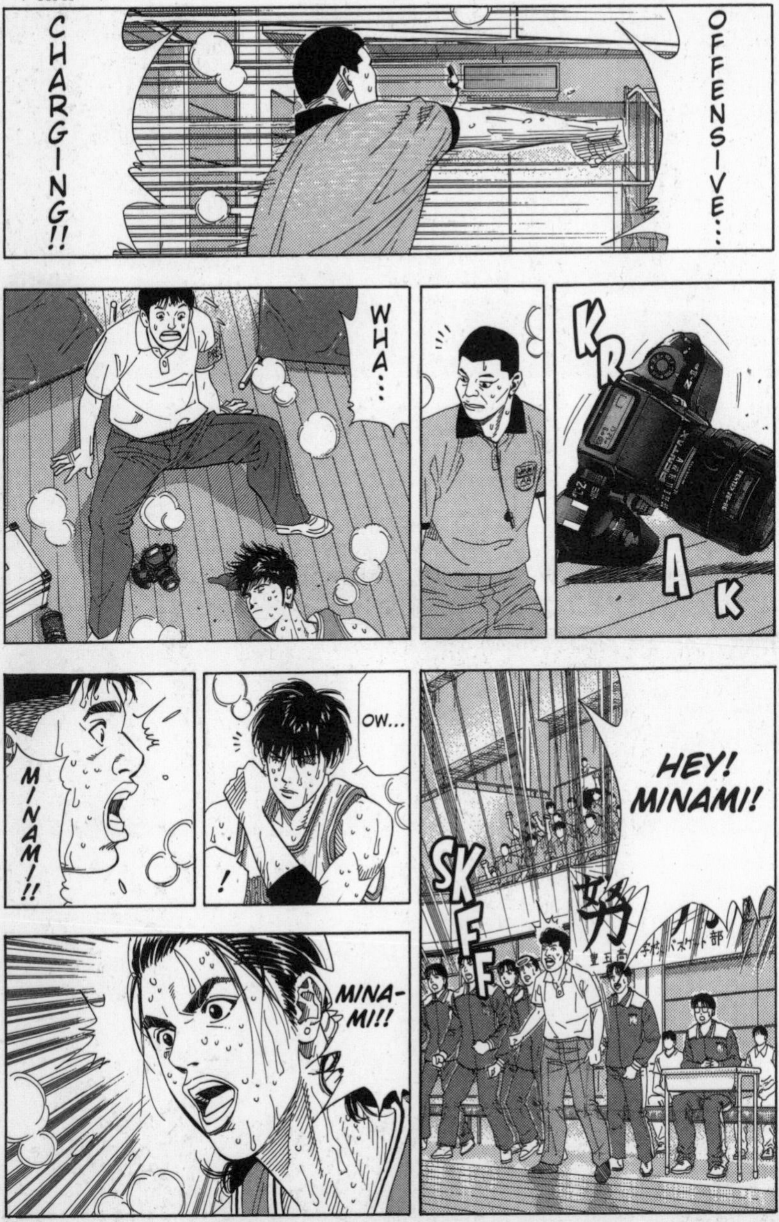
OFFENSIVE...
CHARGING!!
KRAK
WHA...
HEY! MINAMI!
SKFF
努
OW...
!
MINAMI!!
MINA-MI!!

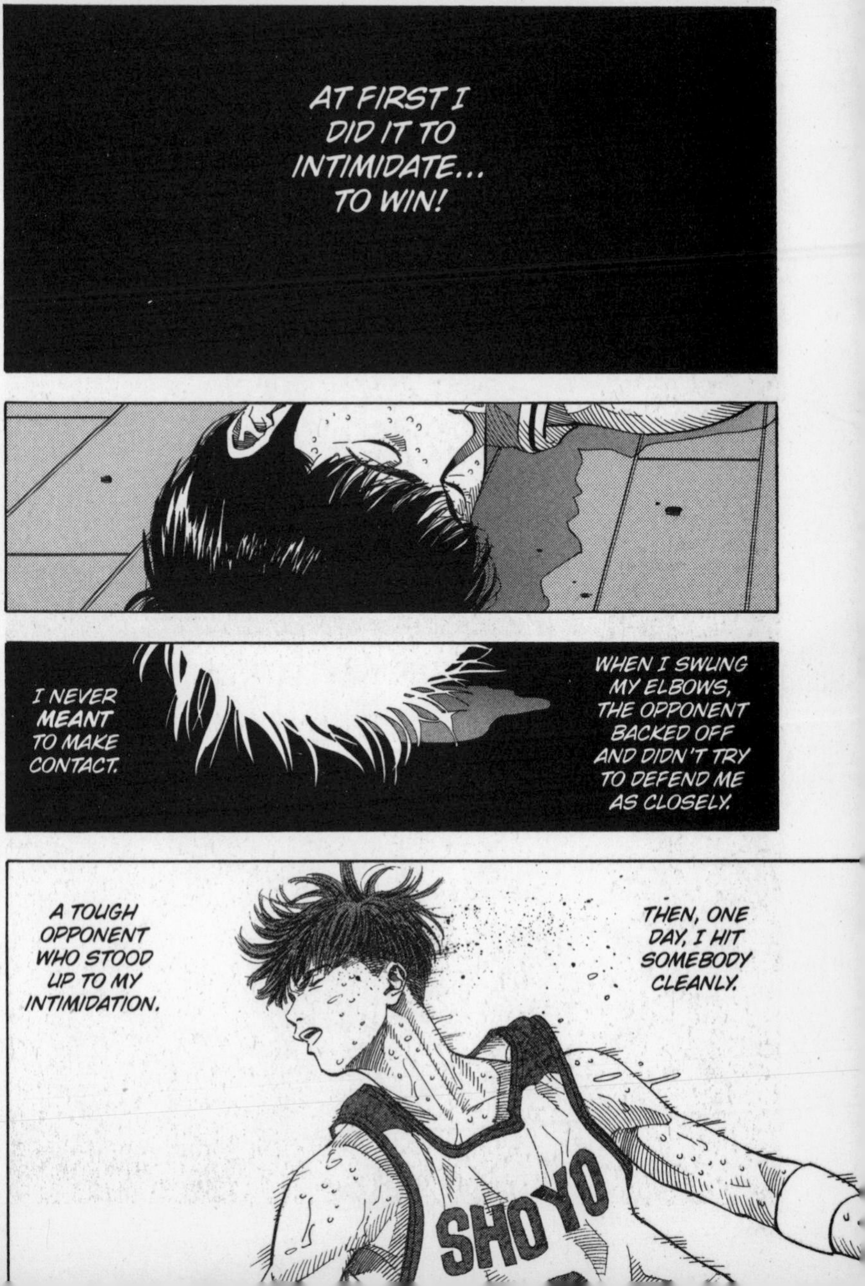
AT FIRST I DID IT TO INTIMIDATE... TO WIN!
WHEN I SWUNG MY ELBOWS, THE OPPONENT BACKED OFF AND DIDN'T TRY TO DEFEND ME AS CLOSELY.
I NEVER MEANT TO MAKE CONTACT.
THEN, ONE DAY, I HIT SOMEBODY CLEANLY.
A TOUGH OPPONENT WHO STOOD UP TO MY INTIMIDATION.
SHOYO

READ THIS WAY

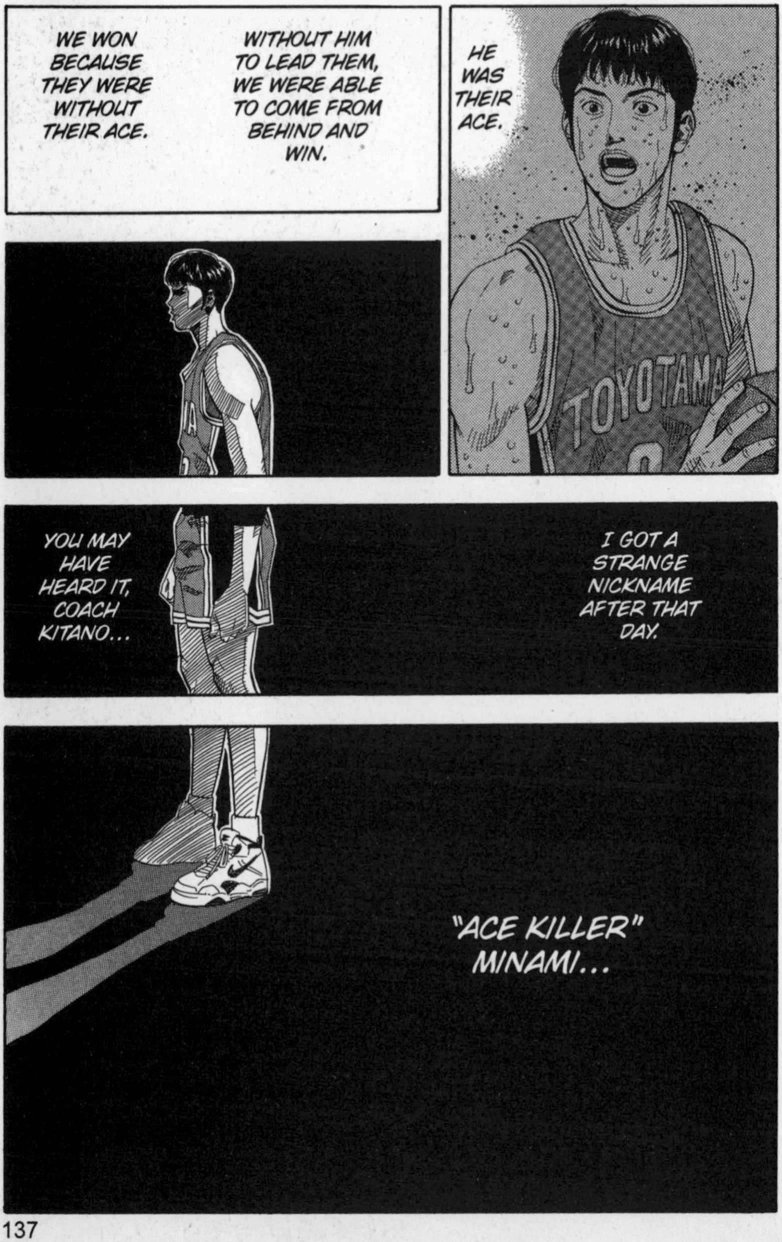
HE WAS THEIR ACE.
TOYOTAMA
WITHOUT HIM TO LEAD THEM, WE WERE ABLE TO COME FROM BEHIND AND WIN.
WE WON BECAUSE THEY WERE WITHOUT THEIR ACE.
I GOT A STRANGE NICKNAME AFTER THAT DAY.
YOU MAY HAVE HEARD IT, COACH KITANO...
"ACE KILLER" MINAMI...

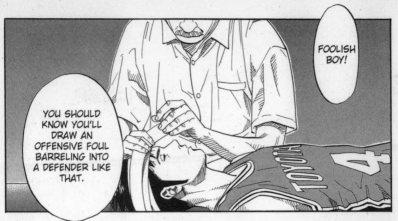

FOOLISH BOY!
YOU SHOULD KNOW YOU'LL DRAW AN OFFENSIVE FOUL BARRELING INTO A DEFENDER LIKE THAT.
TOYOTA 4
...!!
ALL RIGHT... IT WASN'T SUCH A BAD CUT.
KEY WEST
JamSessi

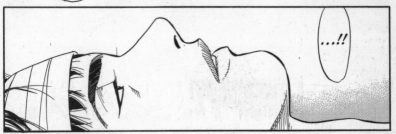

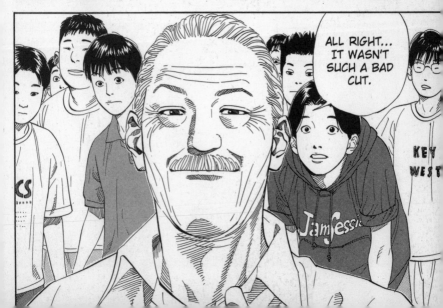

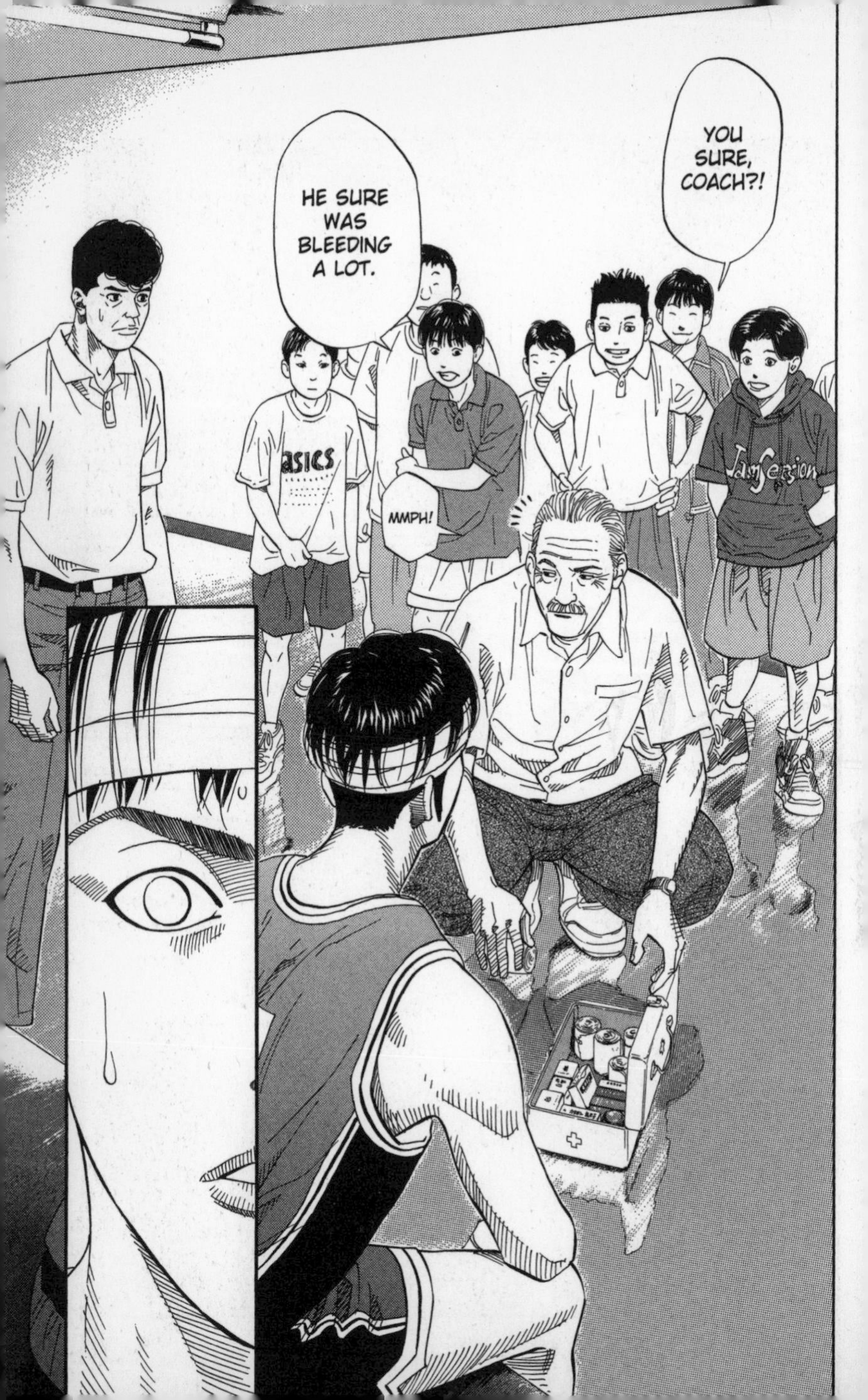
YOU SURE, COACH?!
HE SURE WAS BLEEDING A LOT.
JamSession
asics
MMPH!

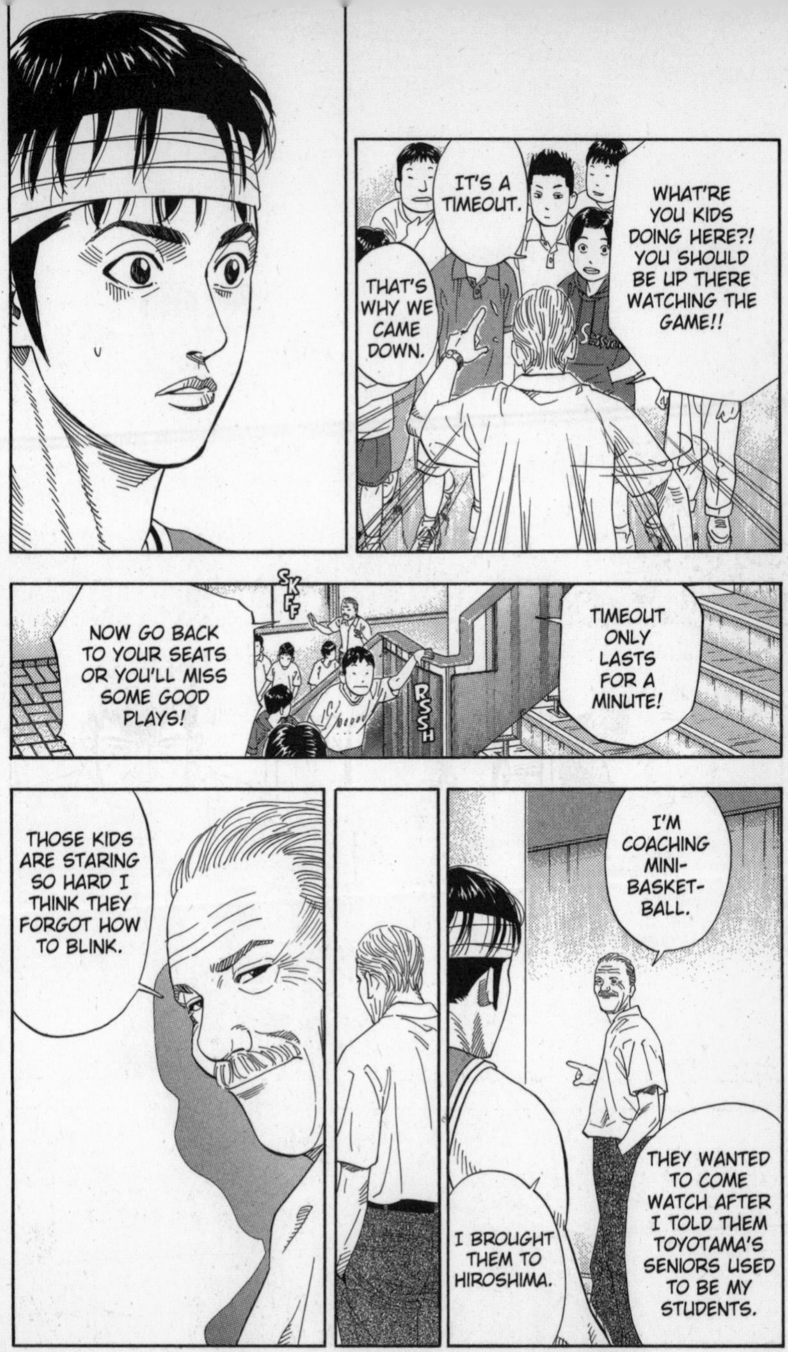
WHAT'RE YOU KIDS DOING HERE?! YOU SHOULD BE UP THERE WATCHING THE GAME!!
IT'S A TIMEOUT.
THAT'S WHY WE CAME DOWN.
TIMEOUT ONLY LASTS FOR A MINUTE!
RSSH
SKFF
NOW GO BACK TO YOUR SEATS OR YOU'LL MISS SOME GOOD PLAYS!
I'M COACHING MINI-BASKET-BALL.
THEY WANTED TO COME WATCH AFTER I TOLD THEM TOYOTAMA'S SENIORS USED TO BE MY STUDENTS.
I BROUGHT THEM TO HIROSHIMA.
THOSE KIDS ARE STARING SO HARD I THINK THEY FORGOT HOW TO BLINK.

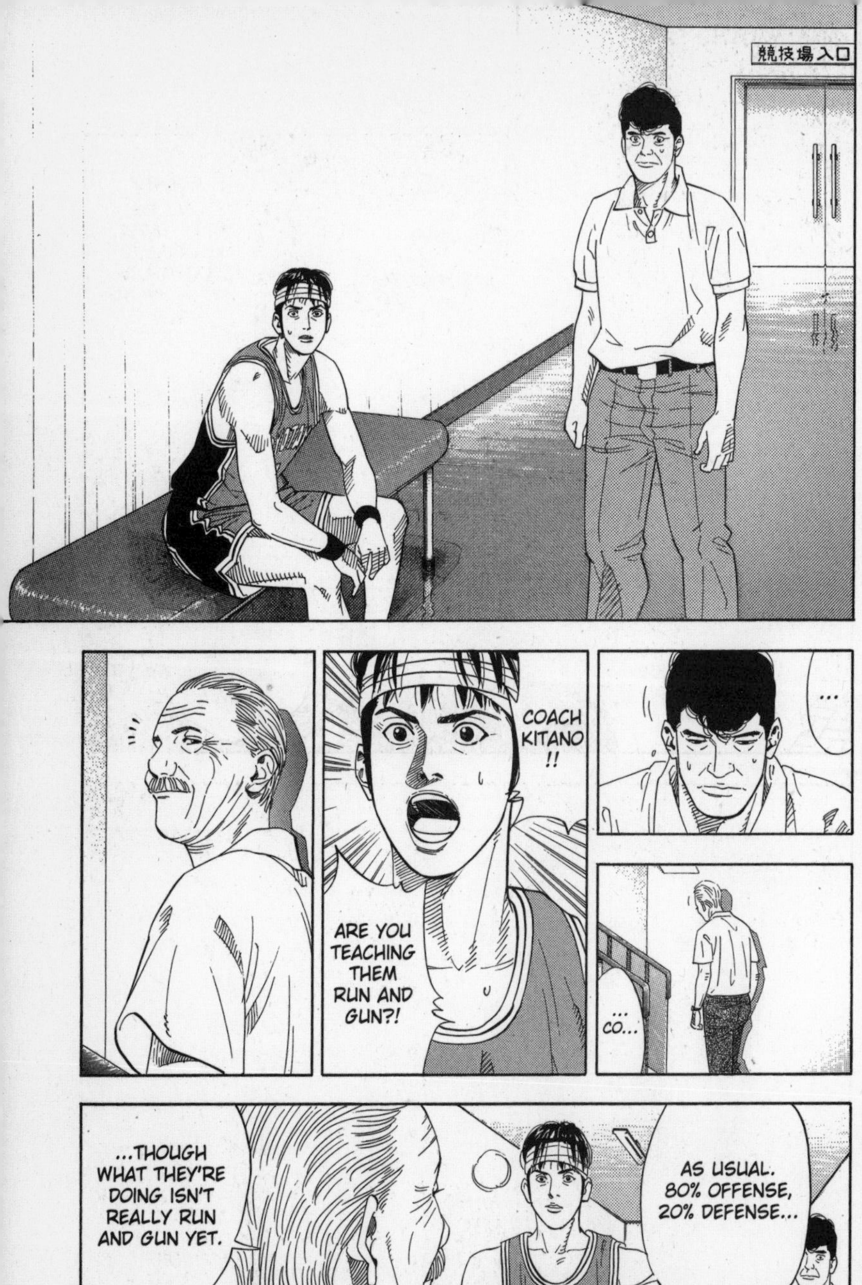
競技場入口
...
... CO...
COACH KITANO !!
ARE YOU TEACHING THEM RUN AND GUN?!
AS USUAL. 80% OFFENSE, 20% DEFENSE...
...THOUGH WHAT THEY'RE DOING ISN'T REALLY RUN AND GUN YET.
TOYOTAMA

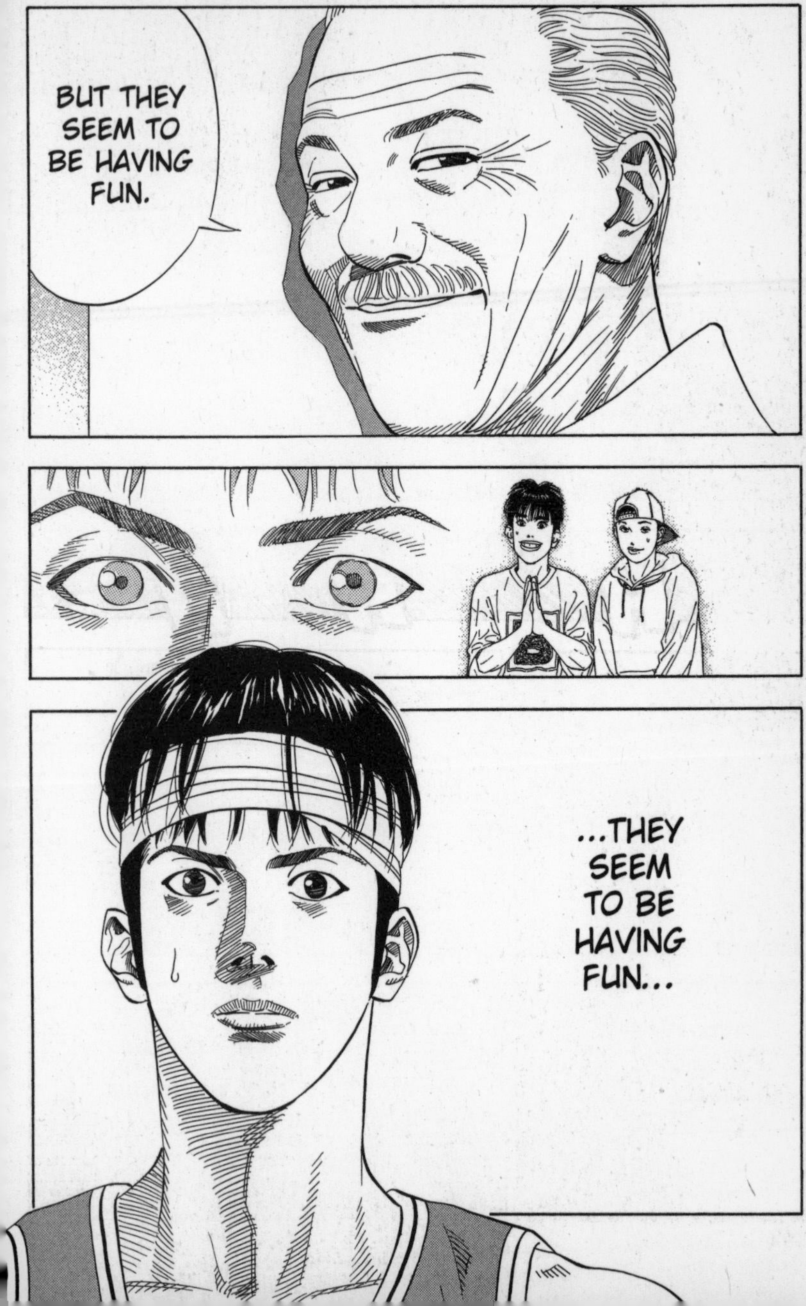
BUT THEY SEEM TO BE HAVING FUN.
...THEY SEEM TO BE HAVING FUN...

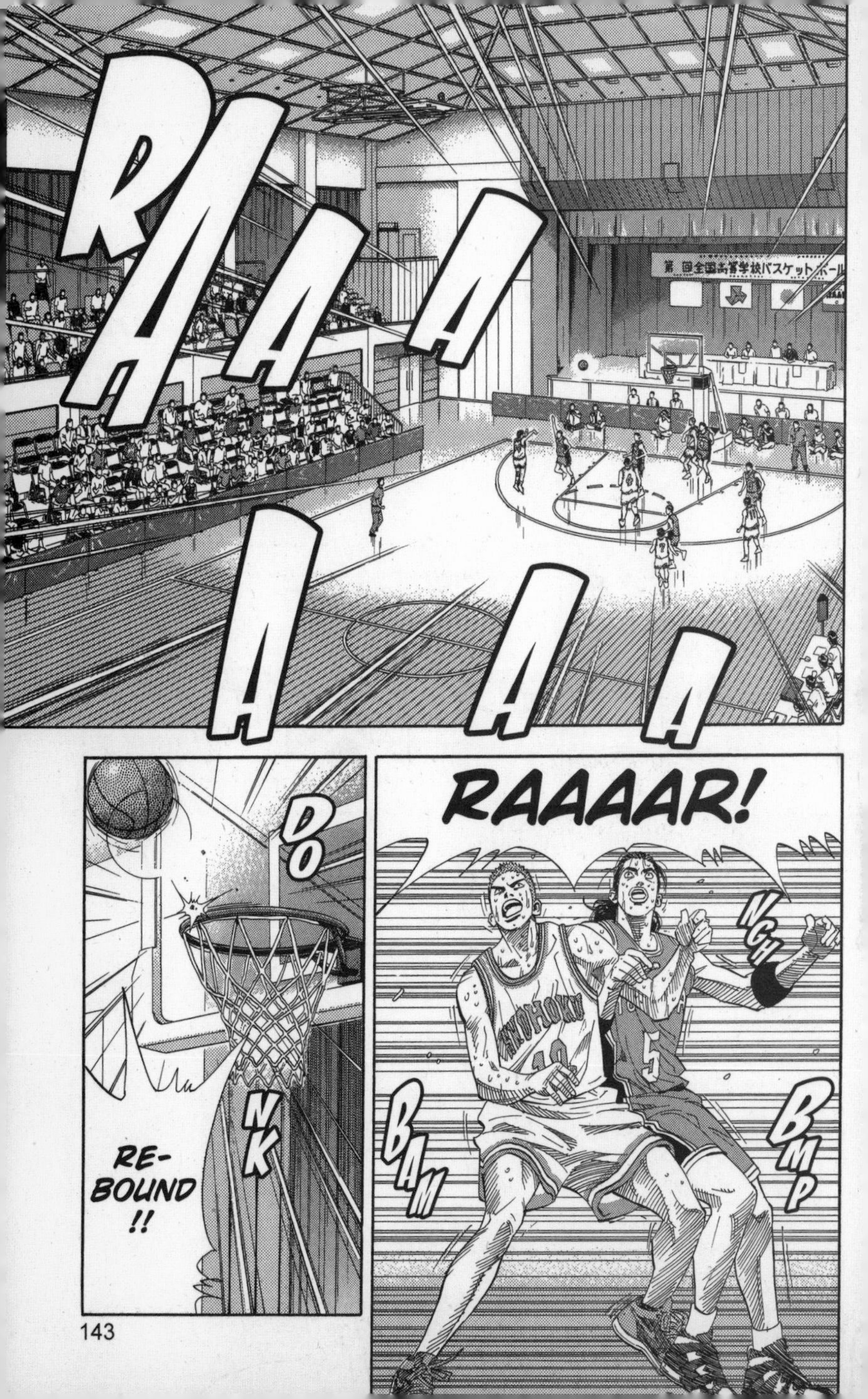
RAAA
AAA
RAAAAR!
NGH
BMP
BAM
DONK
RE-BOUND!!

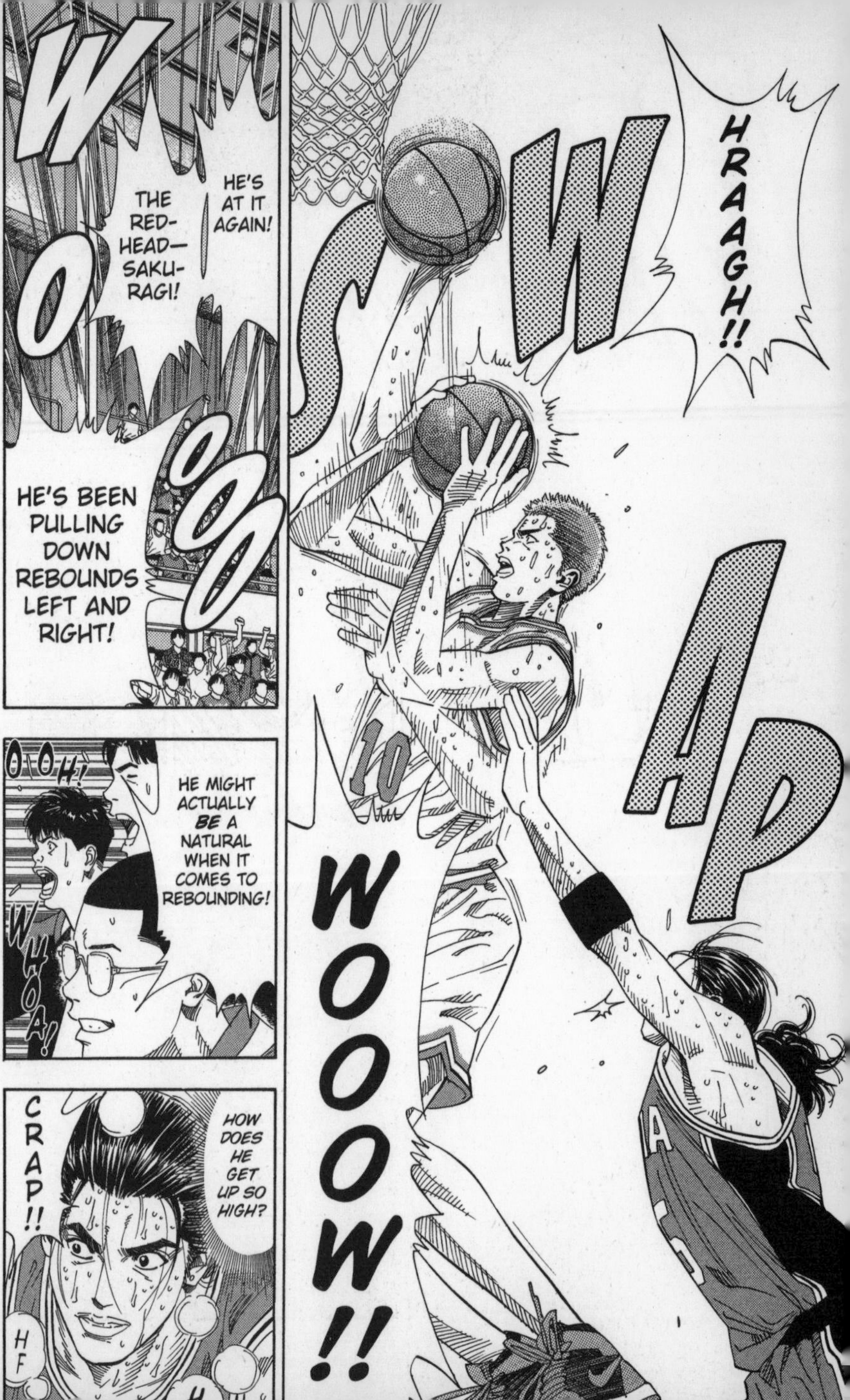
HRAAGH!!
SWAP
WOOOOW!!
WOOOO
HE'S AT IT AGAIN!
THE RED-HEAD—SAKU-RAGI!
HE'S BEEN PULLING DOWN REBOUNDS LEFT AND RIGHT!
OOH!
HE MIGHT ACTUALLY *BE* A NATURAL WHEN IT COMES TO REBOUNDING!
WHOA!
CRAP!!
HOW DOES HE GET UP SO HIGH?
HF

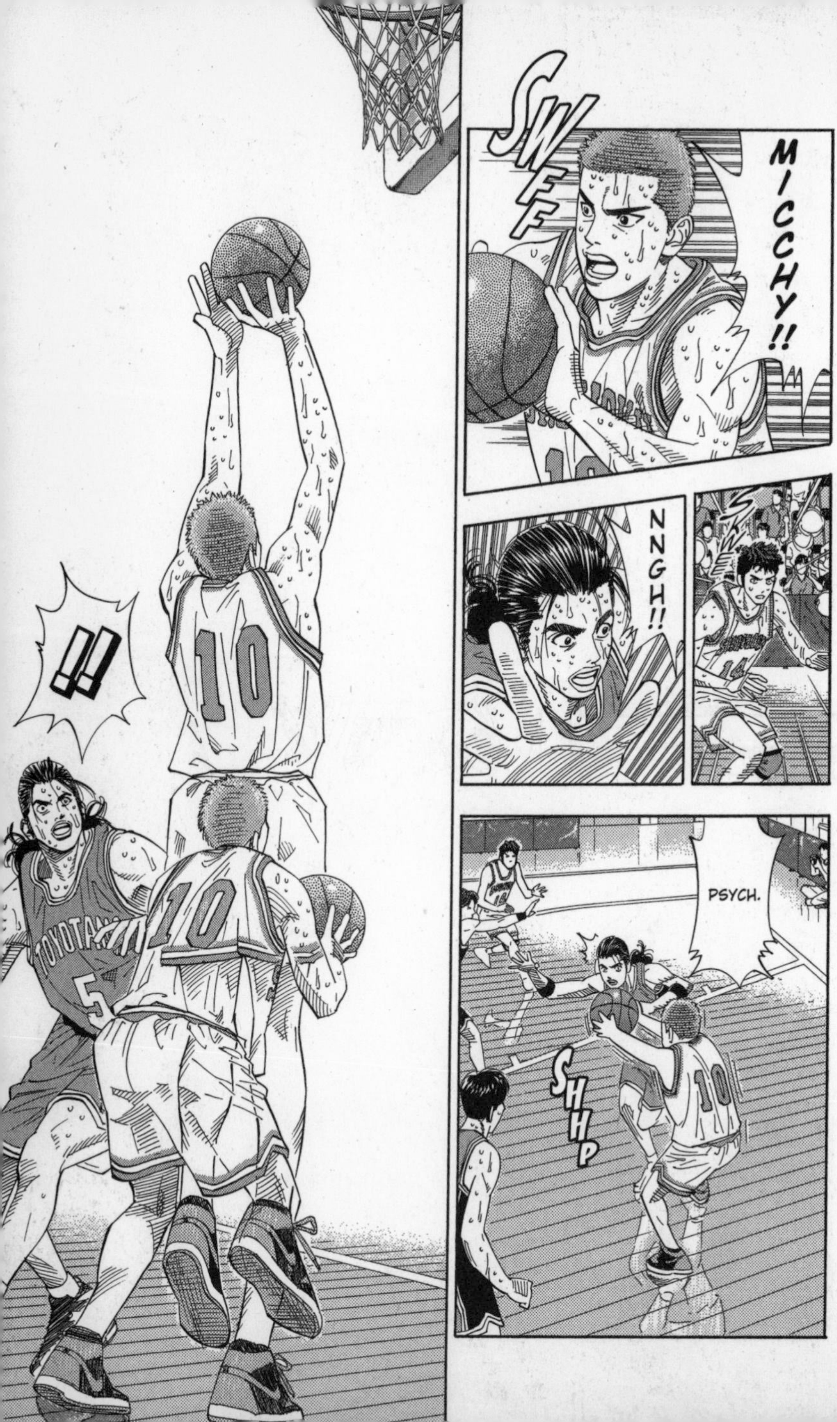
MICCHY!!
SWFF
NNGH!!
PSYCH.
SHHP
!!

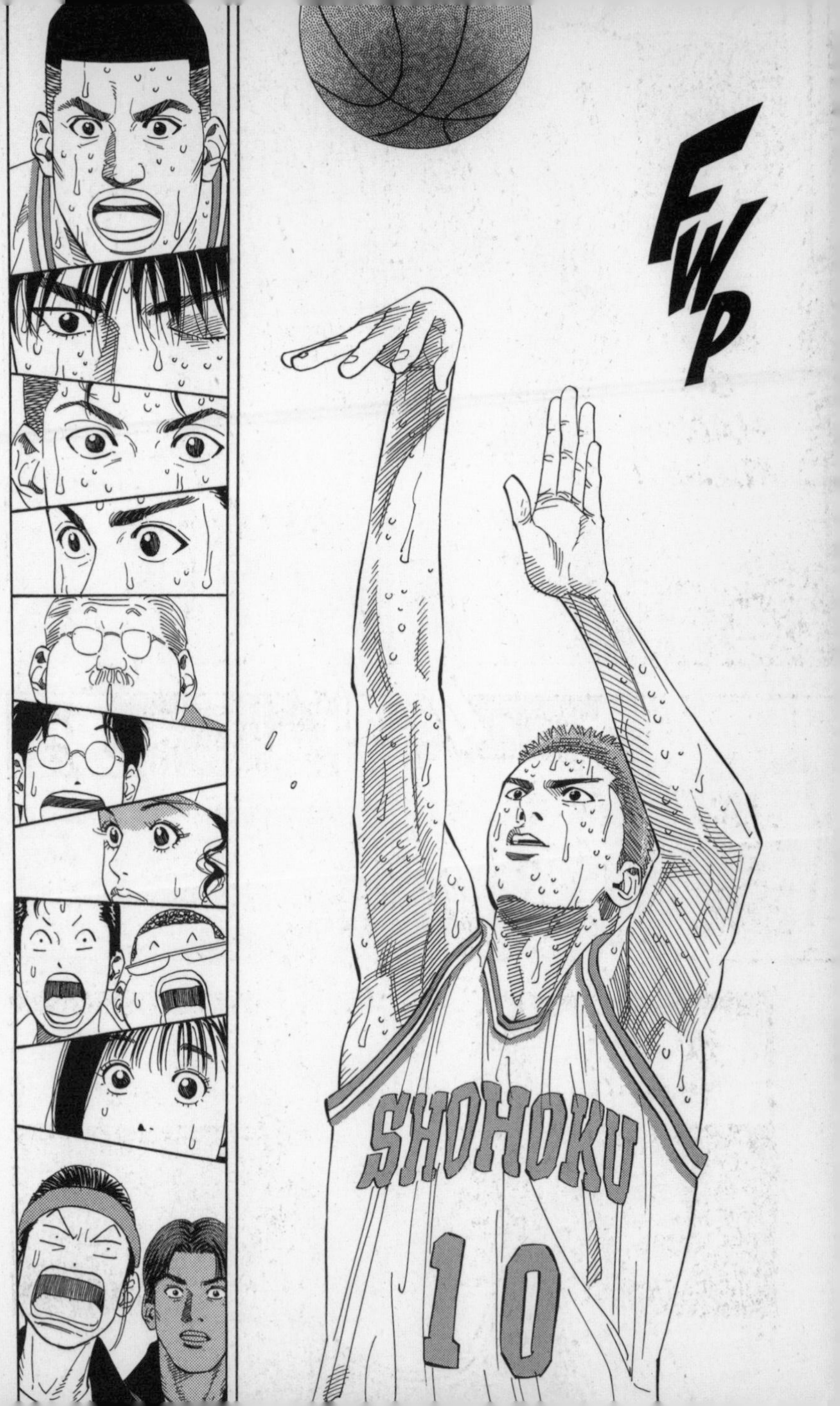
FWP
SHOHOKU
10

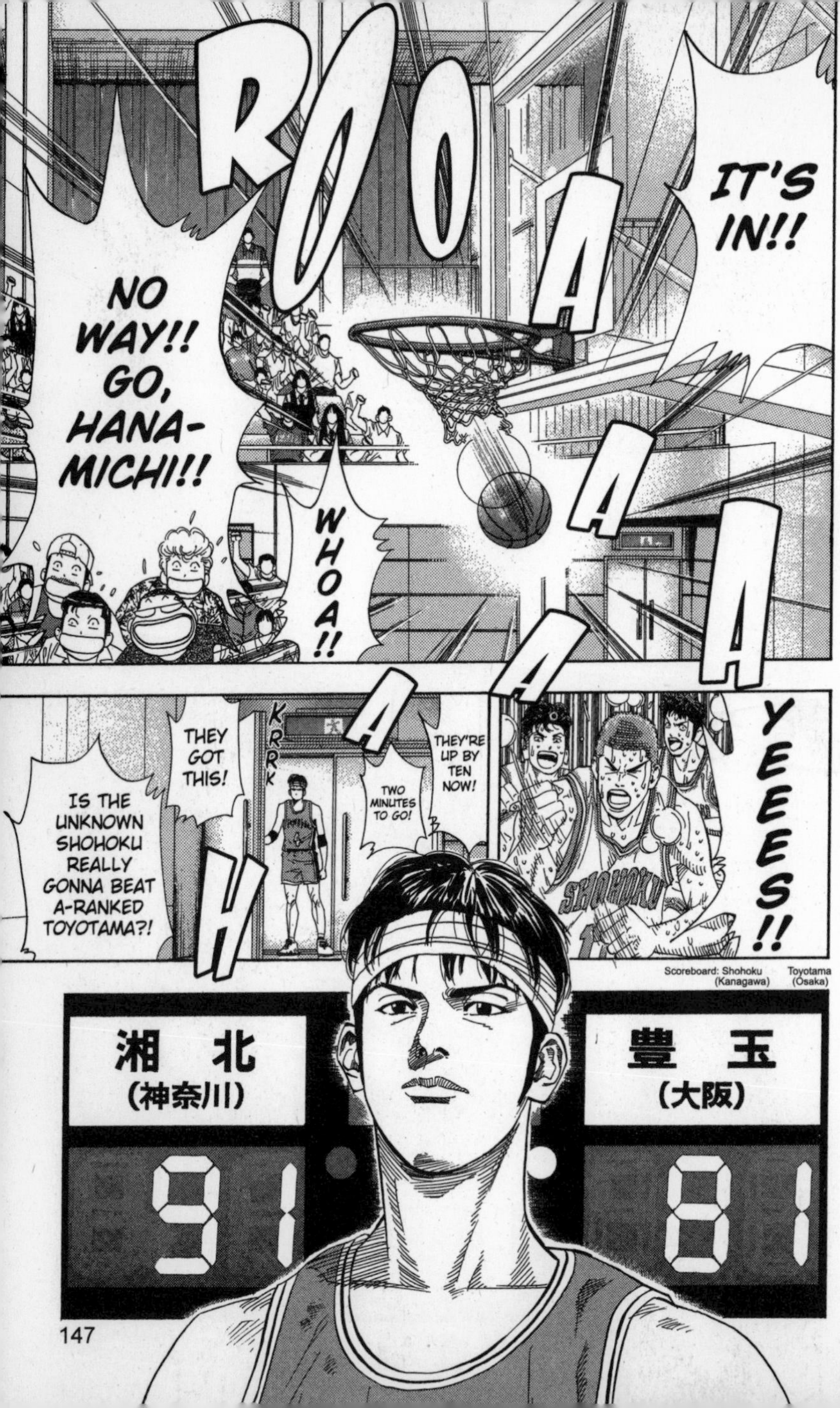
IT'S IN!!
ROOAAAAAH
NO WAY!! GO, HANAMICHI!!
WHOA!!
YEEEES!!
THEY'RE UP BY TEN NOW!
TWO MINUTES TO GO!
KRRK
THEY GOT THIS!
IS THE UNKNOWN SHOHOKU REALLY GONNA BEAT A-RANKED TOYOTAMA?!
Scoreboard: Shohoku (Kanagawa) Toyotama (Osaka)
湘北
(神奈川)
豊玉
(大阪)
91
81

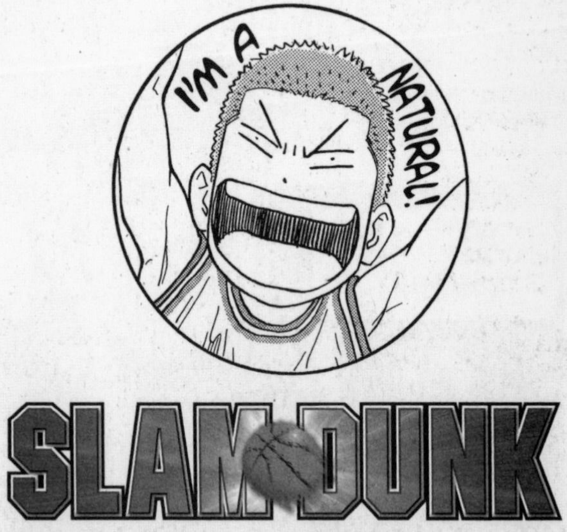
I'M A NATURAL!

SLAM DUNK

TENACITY FOR VICTORY

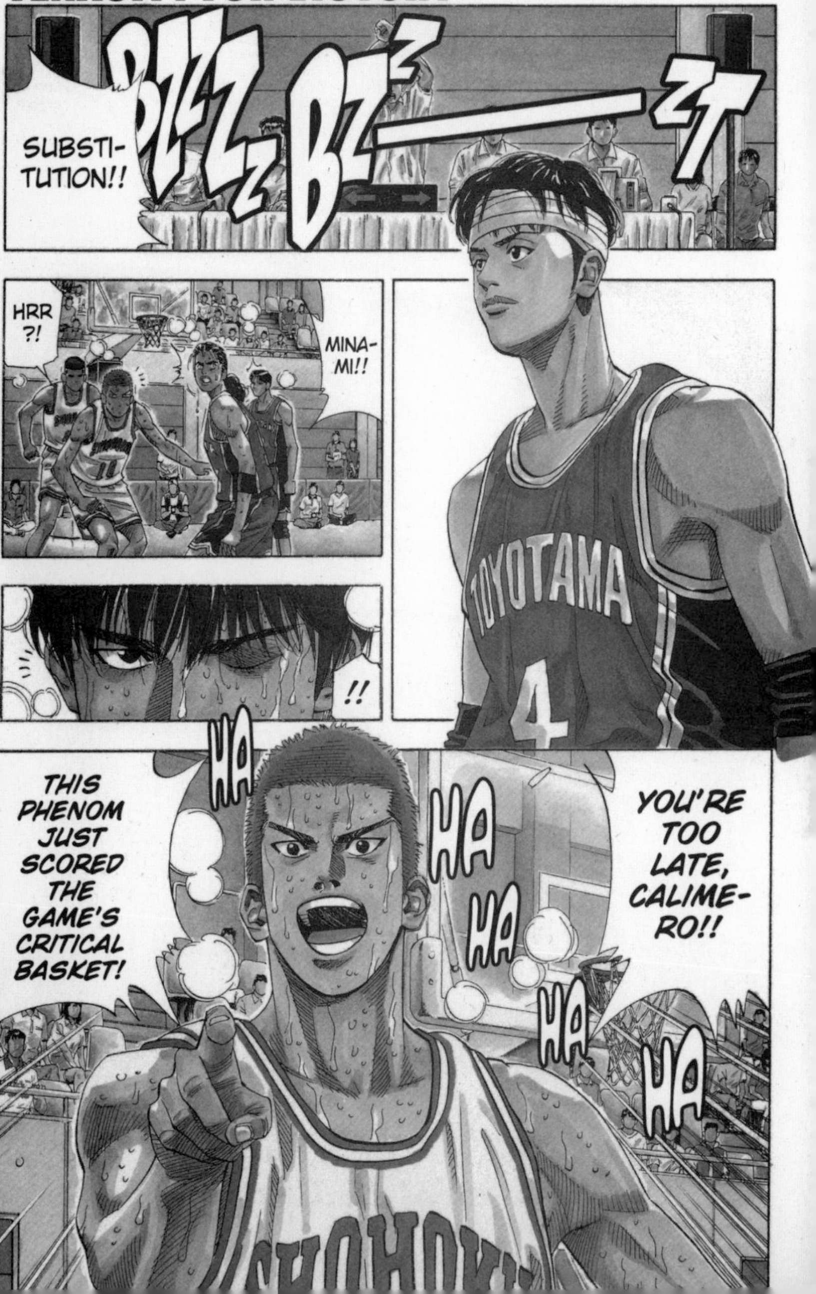

BZZZ BZZZ——ZT
SUBSTI-TUTION!!
TOYOTAMA 4
MINA-MI!!
HRR ?!
!!
HA HA HA HA HA
YOU'RE TOO LATE, CALIME-RO!!
THIS PHENOM JUST SCORED THE GAME'S CRITICAL BASKET!
SHOHOKU

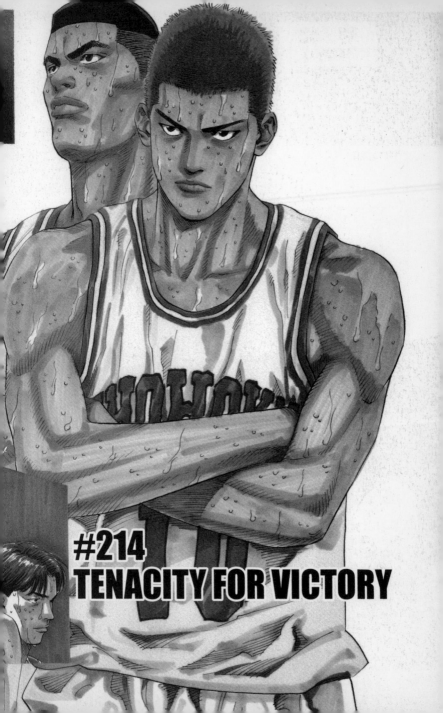

#214
TENACITY FOR VICTORY

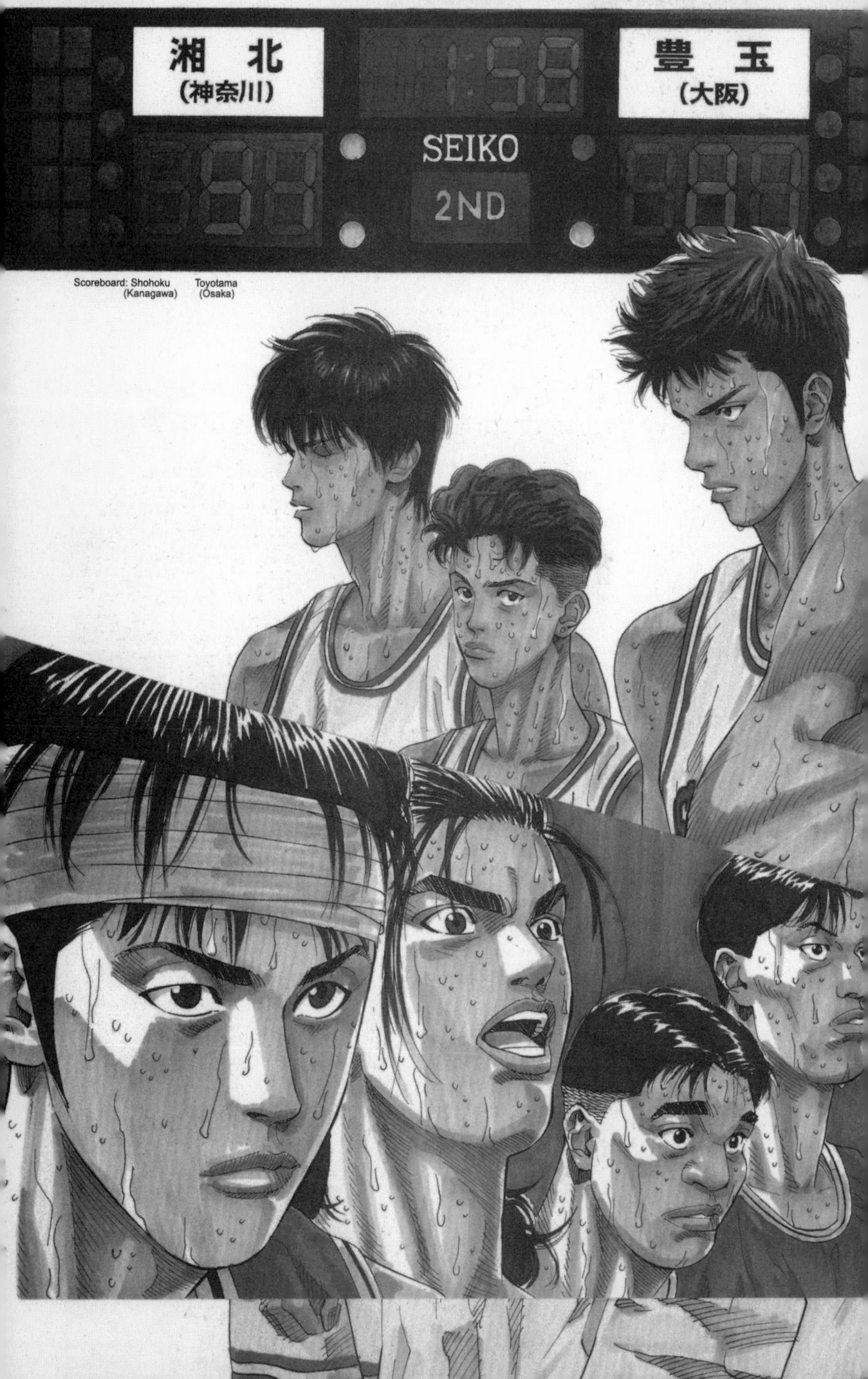
湘北
(神奈川)
豊玉
(大阪)
SEIKO
2ND
Scoreboard: Shohoku (Kanagawa) Toyotama (Osaka)

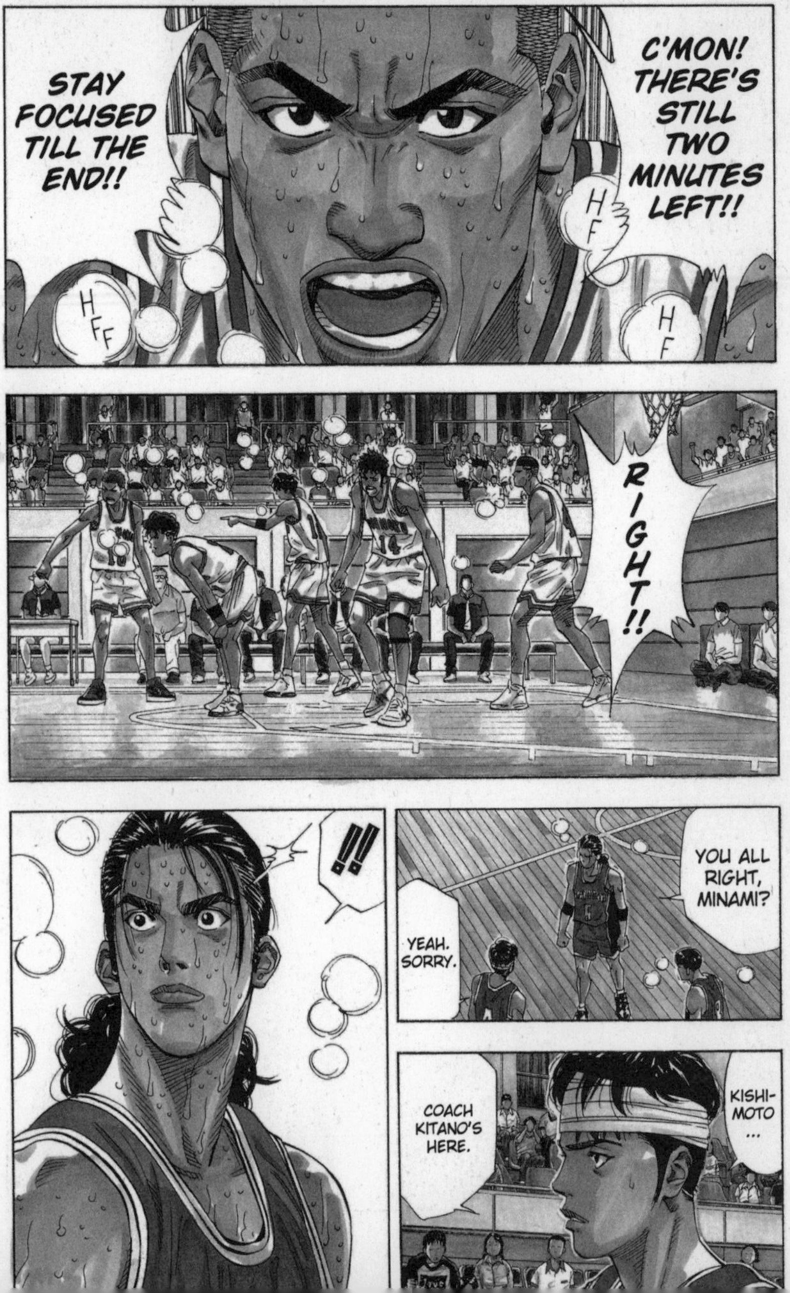
C'MON! THERE'S STILL TWO MINUTES LEFT!!
HF
HF
STAY FOCUSED TILL THE END!!
HFF
RIGHT!!
YOU ALL RIGHT, MINAMI?
YEAH. SORRY.
KISHI-MOTO ...
COACH KITANO'S HERE.
!!

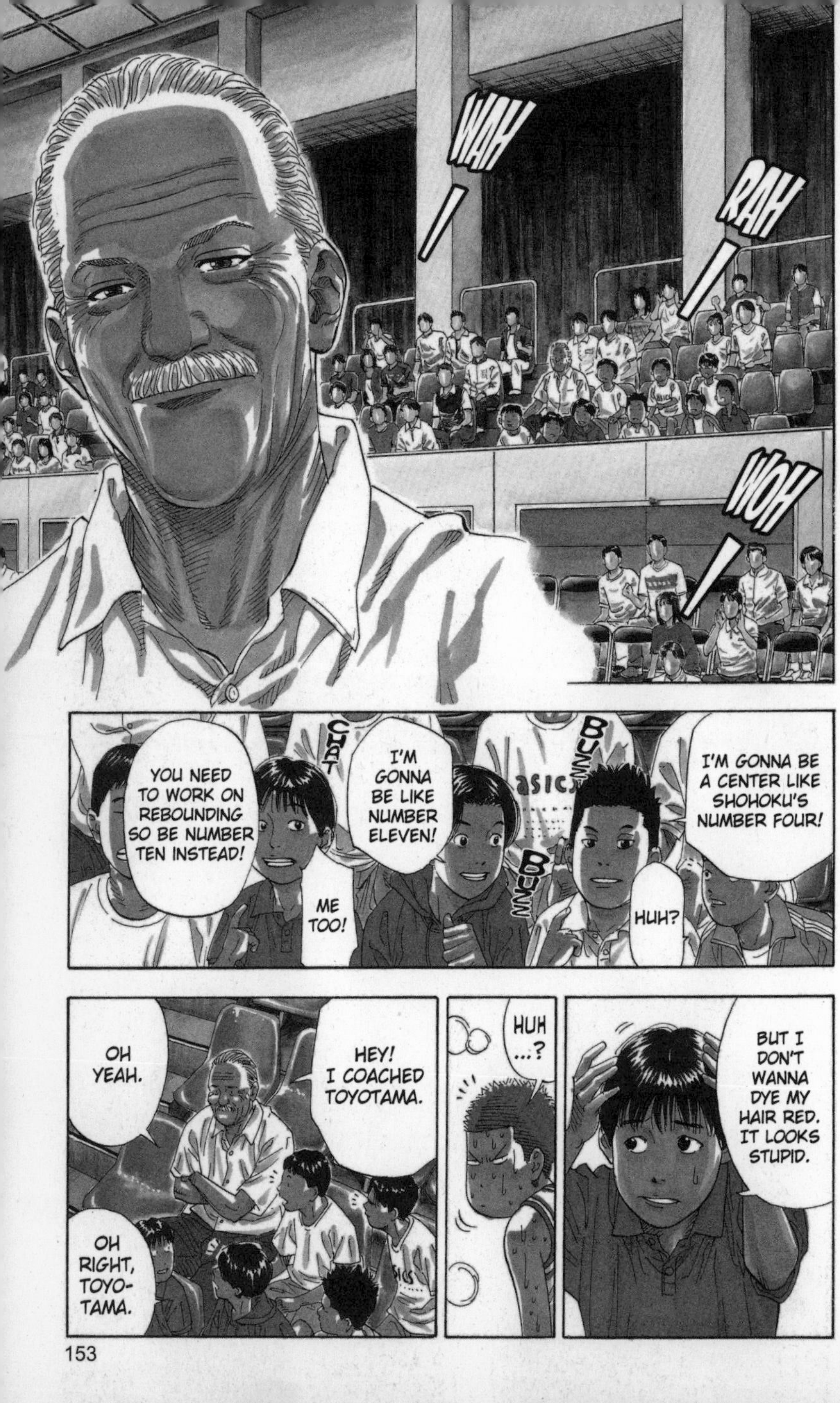
WAH
RAH
WOH
I'M GONNA BE A CENTER LIKE SHOHOKU'S NUMBER FOUR!
BUNN
BUNN
HUH?
I'M GONNA BE LIKE NUMBER ELEVEN!
CHAT
ME TOO!
YOU NEED TO WORK ON REBOUNDING SO BE NUMBER TEN INSTEAD!
BUT I DON'T WANNA DYE MY HAIR RED. IT LOOKS STUPID.
HUH ...?
HEY! I COACHED TOYOTAMA.
OH YEAH.
OH RIGHT, TOYO-TAMA.

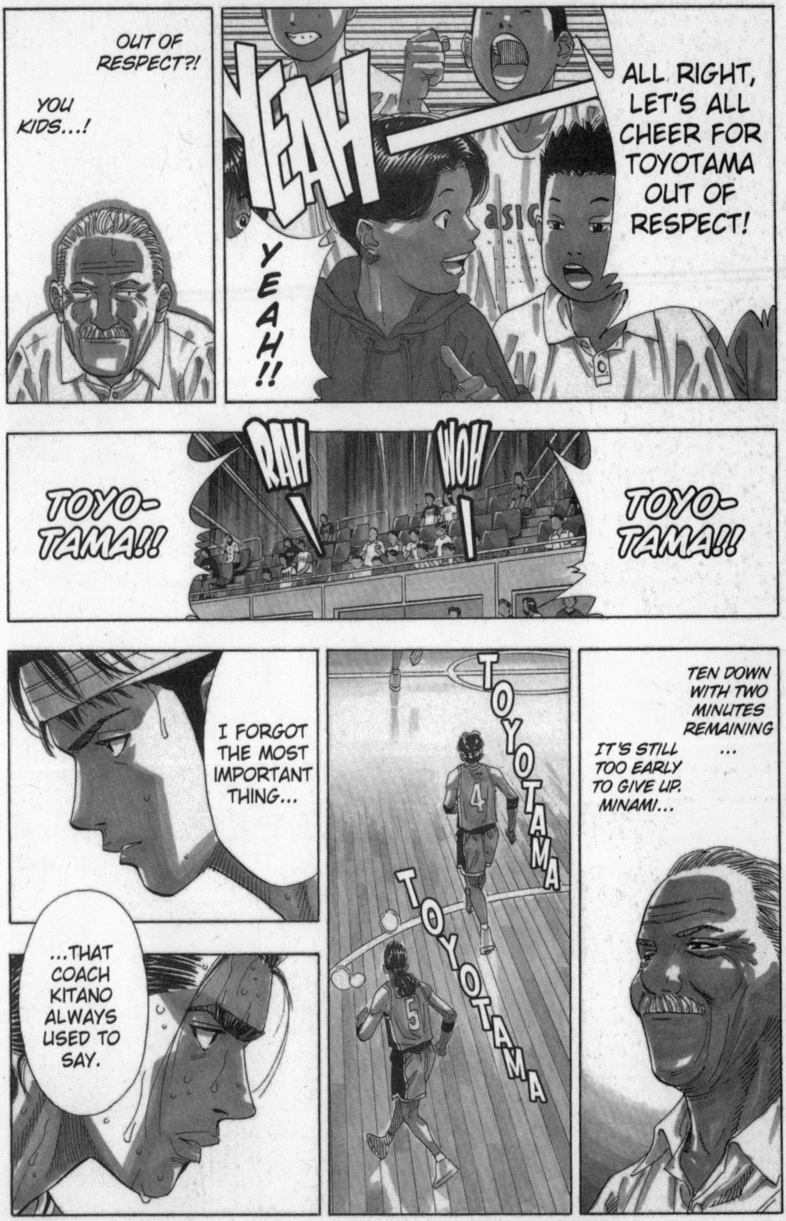
ALL RIGHT, LET'S ALL CHEER FOR TOYOTAMA OUT OF RESPECT!
YEAH
YEAH!!
OUT OF RESPECT?!
YOU KIDS...!
TOYO-TAMA!!
WOH
RAH
TOYO-TAMA!!
TEN DOWN WITH TWO MINUTES REMAINING ...
IT'S STILL TOO EARLY TO GIVE UP. MINAMI...
TOYOTAMA
TOYOTAMA
I FORGOT THE MOST IMPORTANT THING...
...THAT COACH KITANO ALWAYS USED TO SAY.

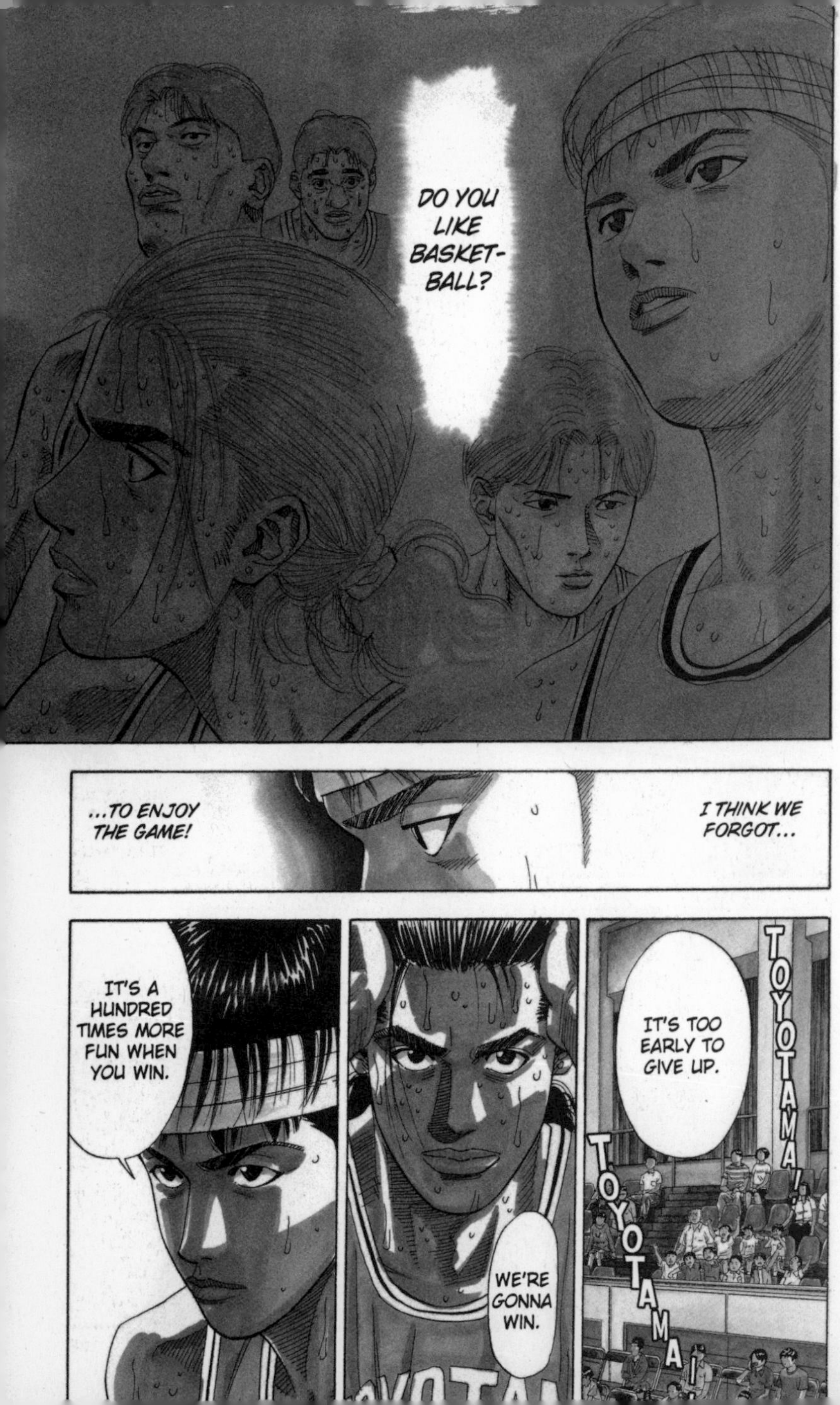
DO YOU LIKE BASKET-BALL?
I THINK WE FORGOT...
...TO ENJOY THE GAME!
TOYOTAMA!
IT'S TOO EARLY TO GIVE UP.
TOYOTAMA!
WE'RE GONNA WIN.
IT'S A HUNDRED TIMES MORE FUN WHEN YOU WIN.

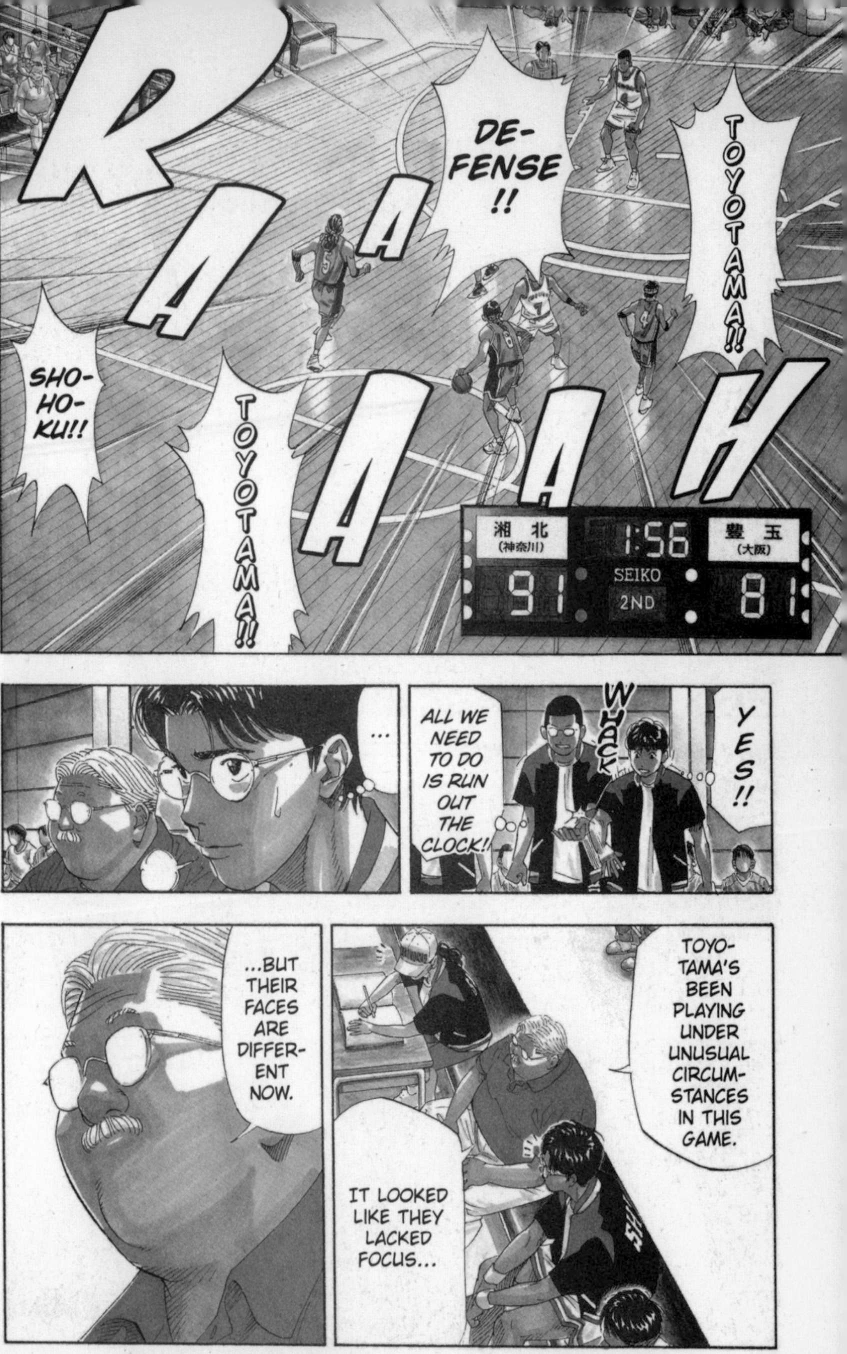
TOYOTAMA!!
DEFENSE!!
RAAAAAH
SHOHOKU!!
TOYOTAMA!!
湘北 (神奈川)
1:56
豊玉 (大阪)
91
SEIKO
2ND
81
YES!!
WHACK
ALL WE NEED TO DO IS RUN OUT THE CLOCK!!
...
TOYOTAMA'S BEEN PLAYING UNDER UNUSUAL CIRCUMSTANCES IN THIS GAME.
IT LOOKED LIKE THEY LACKED FOCUS...
...BUT THEIR FACES ARE DIFFERENT NOW.

READ THIS WAY

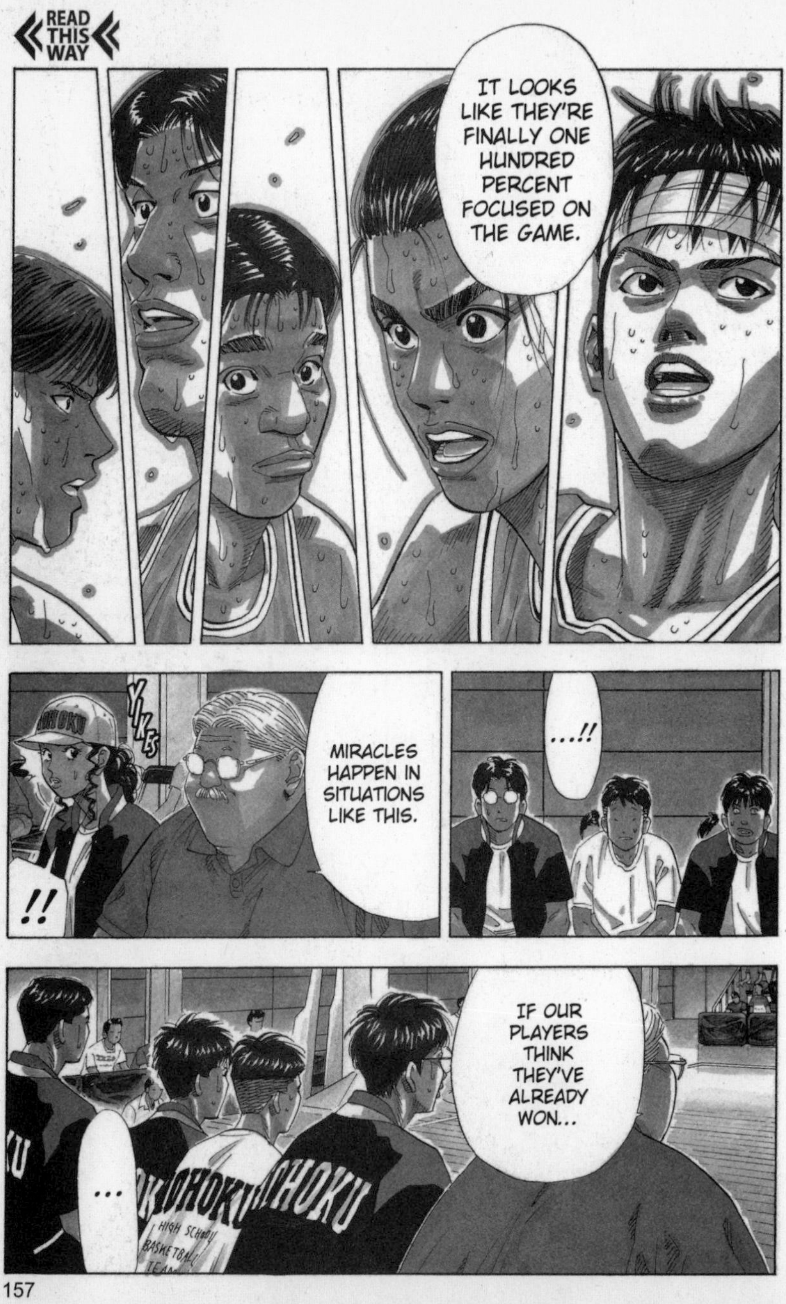
IT LOOKS LIKE THEY'RE FINALLY ONE HUNDRED PERCENT FOCUSED ON THE GAME.
...!!
MIRACLES HAPPEN IN SITUATIONS LIKE THIS.
YIKES
!!
IF OUR PLAYERS THINK THEY'VE ALREADY WON...
...

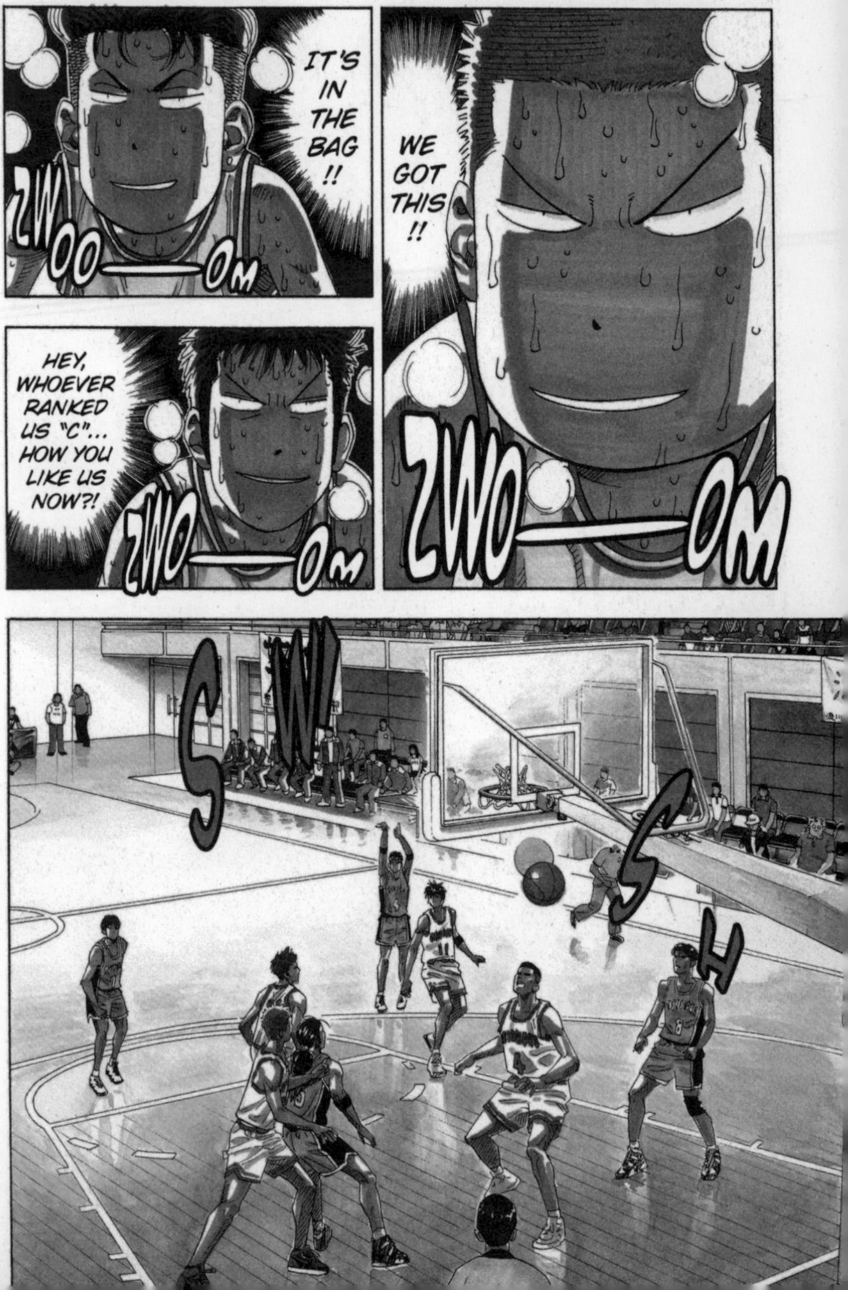
WE GOT THIS!!
ZWO—OM
IT'S IN THE BAG!!
ZWOO—OM
HEY, WHOEVER RANKED US "C"... HOW YOU LIKE US NOW?!
ZWO—OM
SWISH

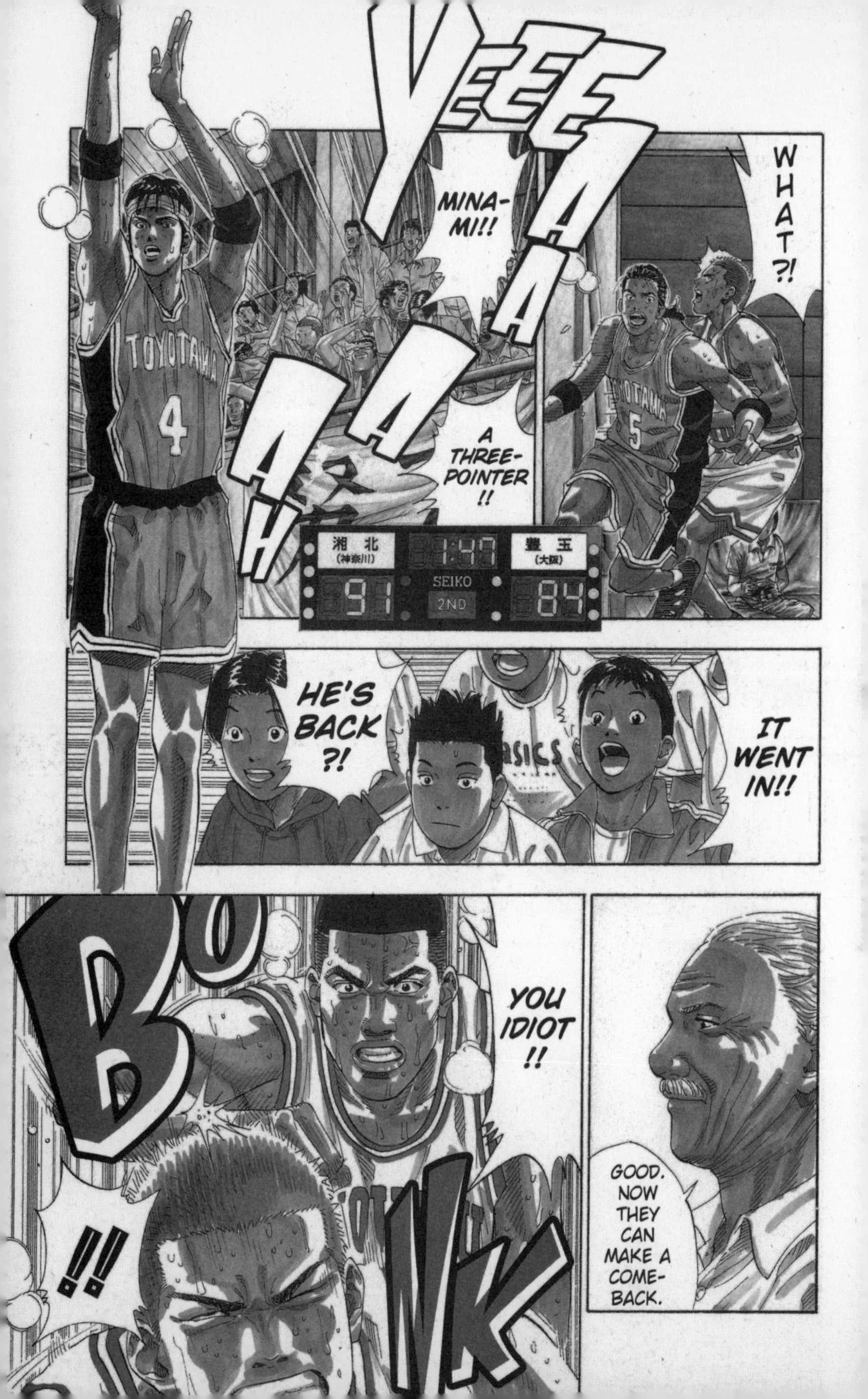
WHAT?!
MINA-MI!!
YEEEAAAAAH
A THREE-POINTER!!
湘北 (神奈川)
豊玉 (大阪)
SEIKO
2ND
91
84
IT WENT IN!!
HE'S BACK?!
GOOD. NOW THEY CAN MAKE A COME-BACK.
YOU IDIOT!!
BONK
!!

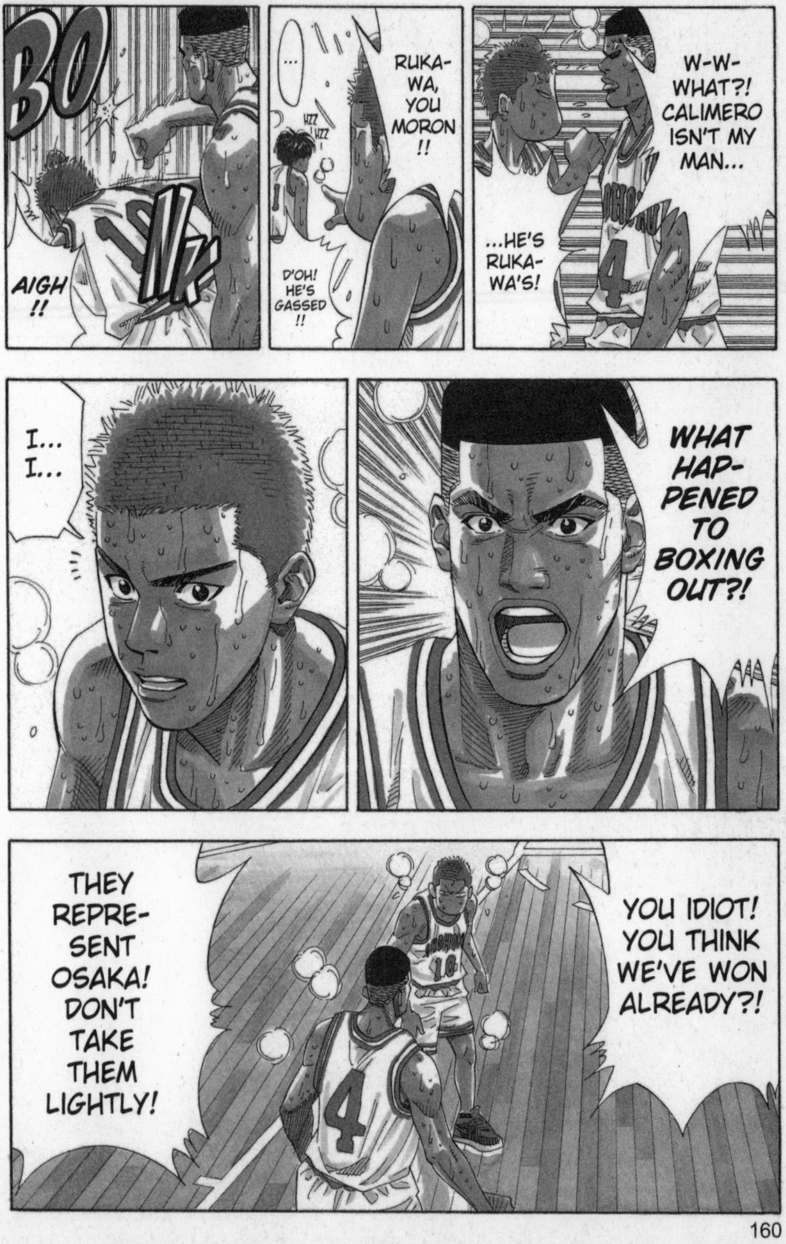
W-W-WHAT?! CALIMERO ISN'T MY MAN...
...HE'S RUKA-WA'S!
...
RUKA-WA, YOU MORON!!
HZZ HZZ
D'OH! HE'S GASSED!!
AIGH!!
WHAT HAP-PENED TO BOXING OUT?!
I... I...
YOU IDIOT! YOU THINK WE'VE WON ALREADY?!
THEY REPRE-SENT OSAKA! DON'T TAKE THEM LIGHTLY!

READ THIS WAY

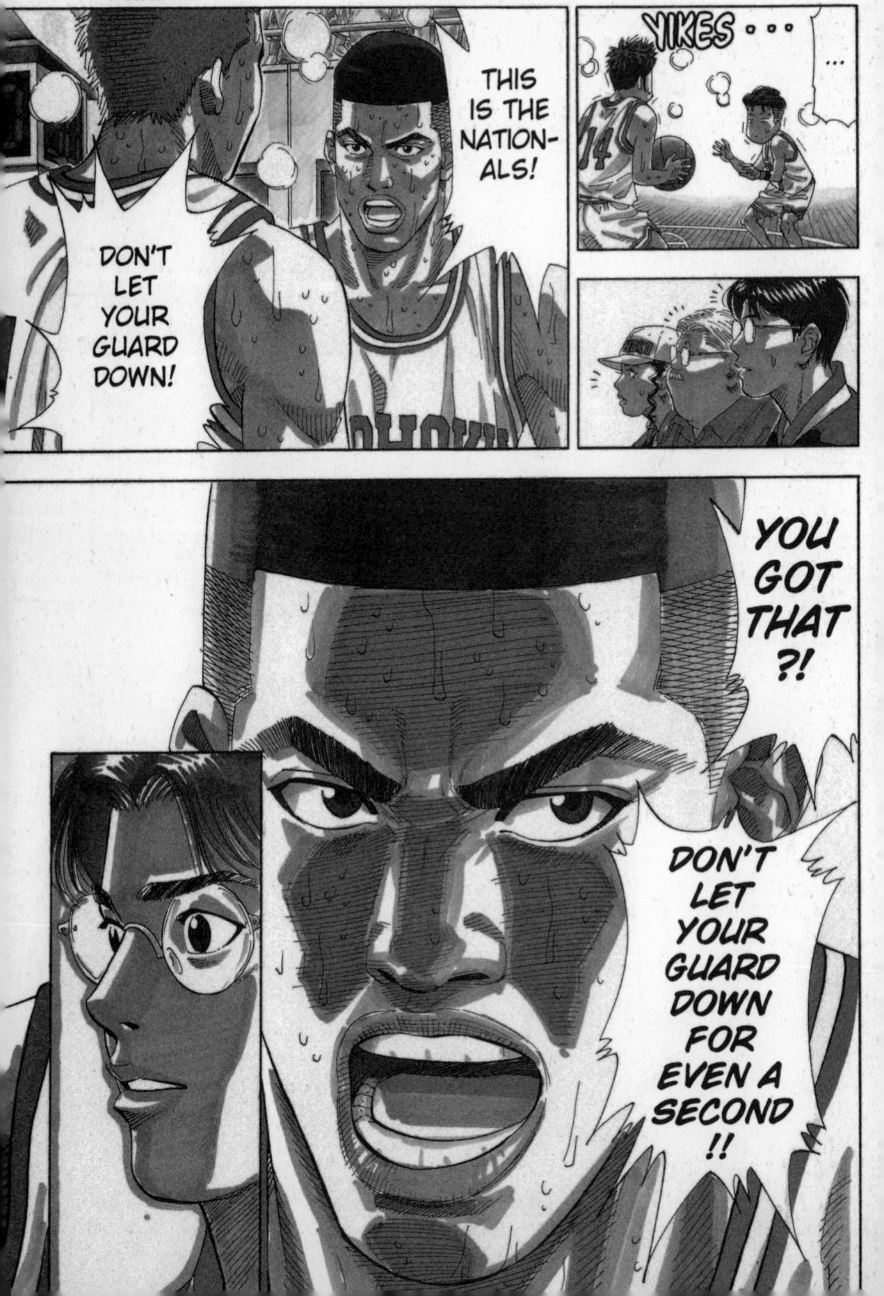
YIKES . . .
...
THIS IS THE NATION-ALS!
DON'T LET YOUR GUARD DOWN!
YOU GOT THAT?!
DON'T LET YOUR GUARD DOWN FOR EVEN A SECOND!!

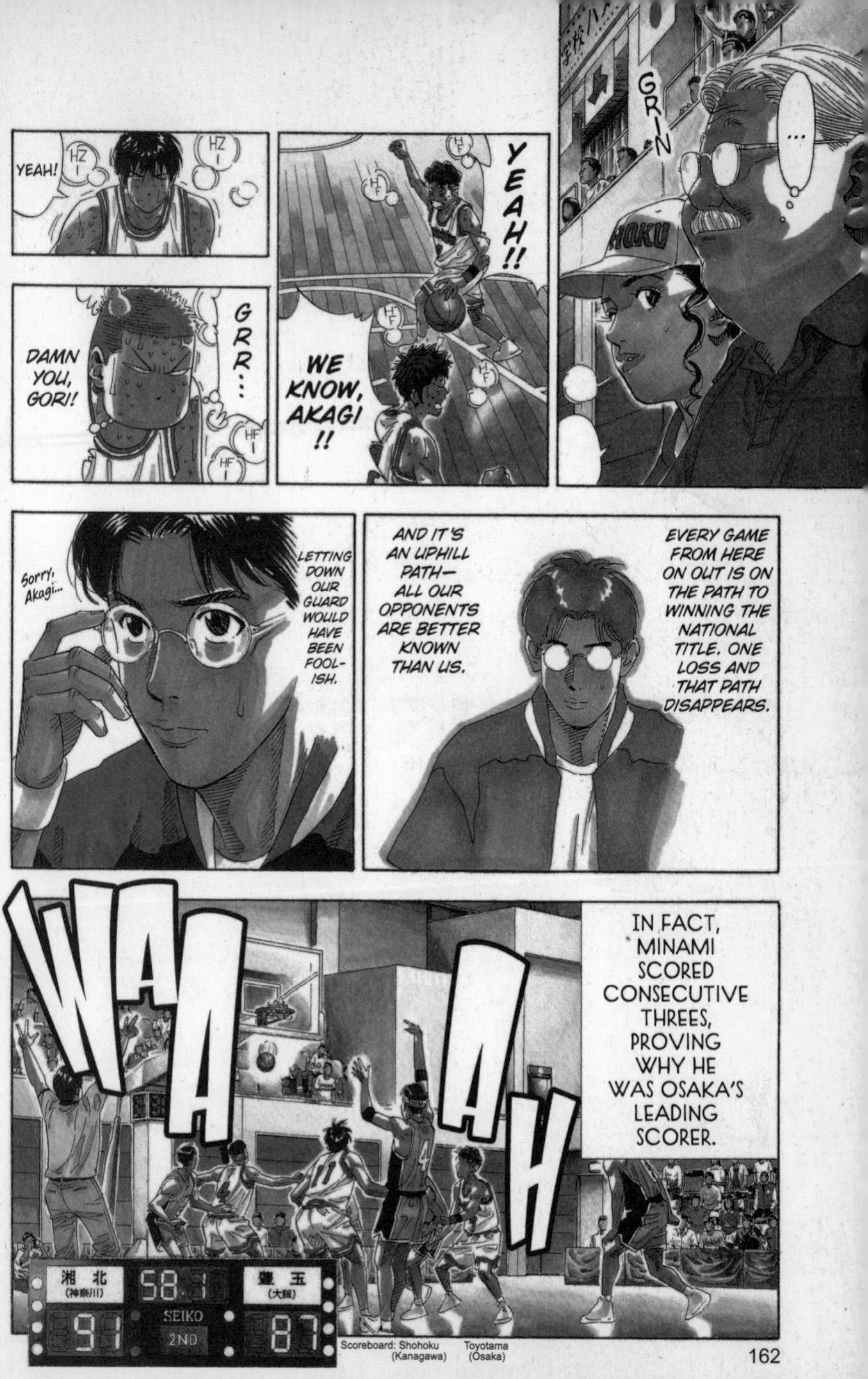
GRIN
...
YEAH!!
WE KNOW, AKAGI!!
YEAH!
HZ
HZ
HF
HF
HF
HF
DAMN YOU, GORI!
GRR...
HF
HF
EVERY GAME FROM HERE ON OUT IS ON THE PATH TO WINNING THE NATIONAL TITLE. ONE LOSS AND THAT PATH DISAPPEARS.
AND IT'S AN UPHILL PATH— ALL OUR OPPONENTS ARE BETTER KNOWN THAN US.
LETTING DOWN OUR GUARD WOULD HAVE BEEN FOOLISH.
Sorry, Akagi...
IN FACT, MINAMI SCORED CONSECUTIVE THREES, PROVING WHY HE WAS OSAKA'S LEADING SCORER.
WAAAH
湘北
(神奈川)
豊玉
(大阪)
SEIKO
2ND
91
87
Scoreboard: Shohoku (Kanagawa) Toyotama (Osaka)

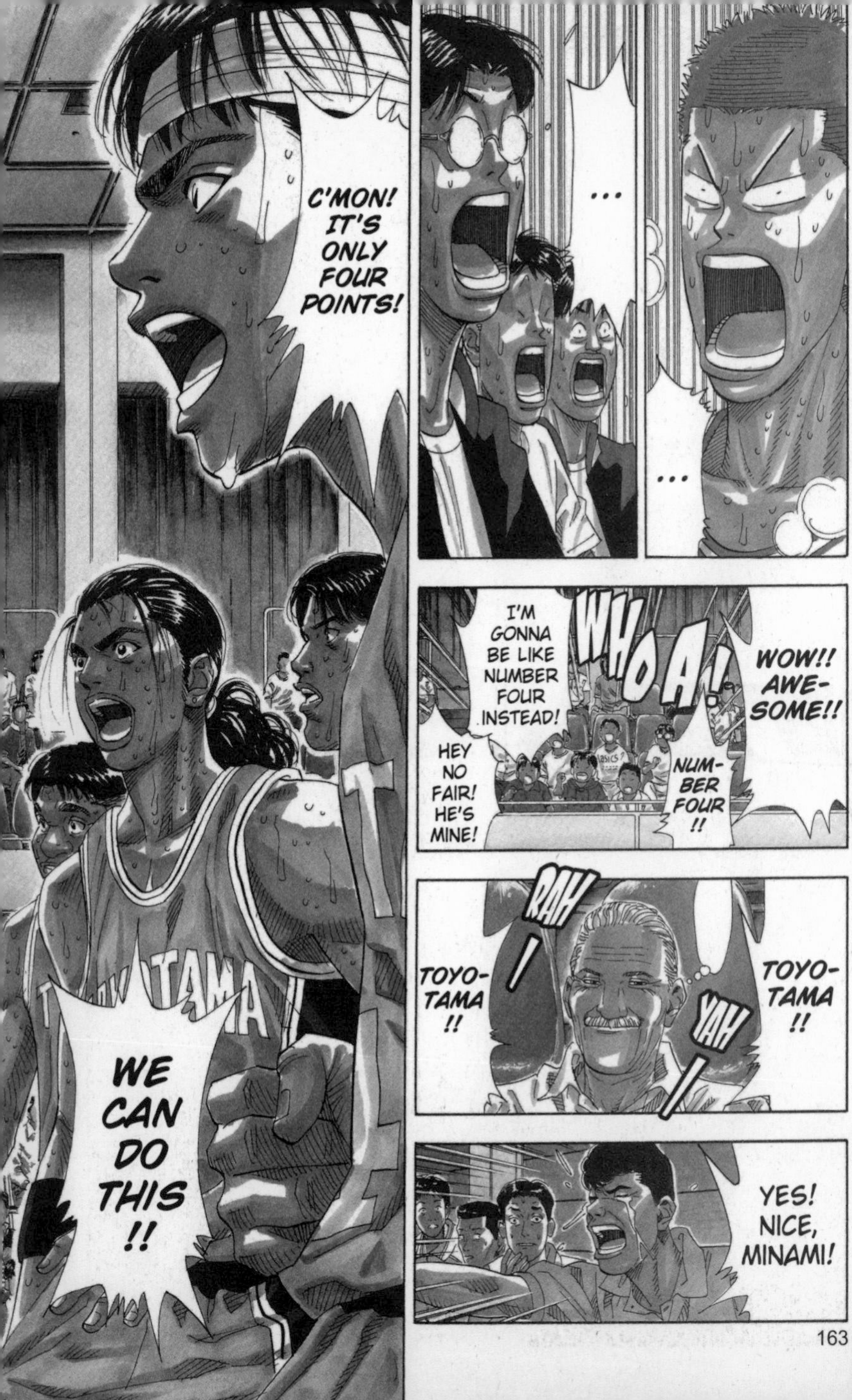
...
...
WOW!! AWE-SOME!!
WHOA!
NUM-BER FOUR!!
I'M GONNA BE LIKE NUMBER FOUR INSTEAD!
HEY NO FAIR! HE'S MINE!
TOYO-TAMA!!
RAH
YAH
TOYO-TAMA!!
YES! NICE, MINAMI!
C'MON! IT'S ONLY FOUR POINTS!
WE CAN DO THIS!!

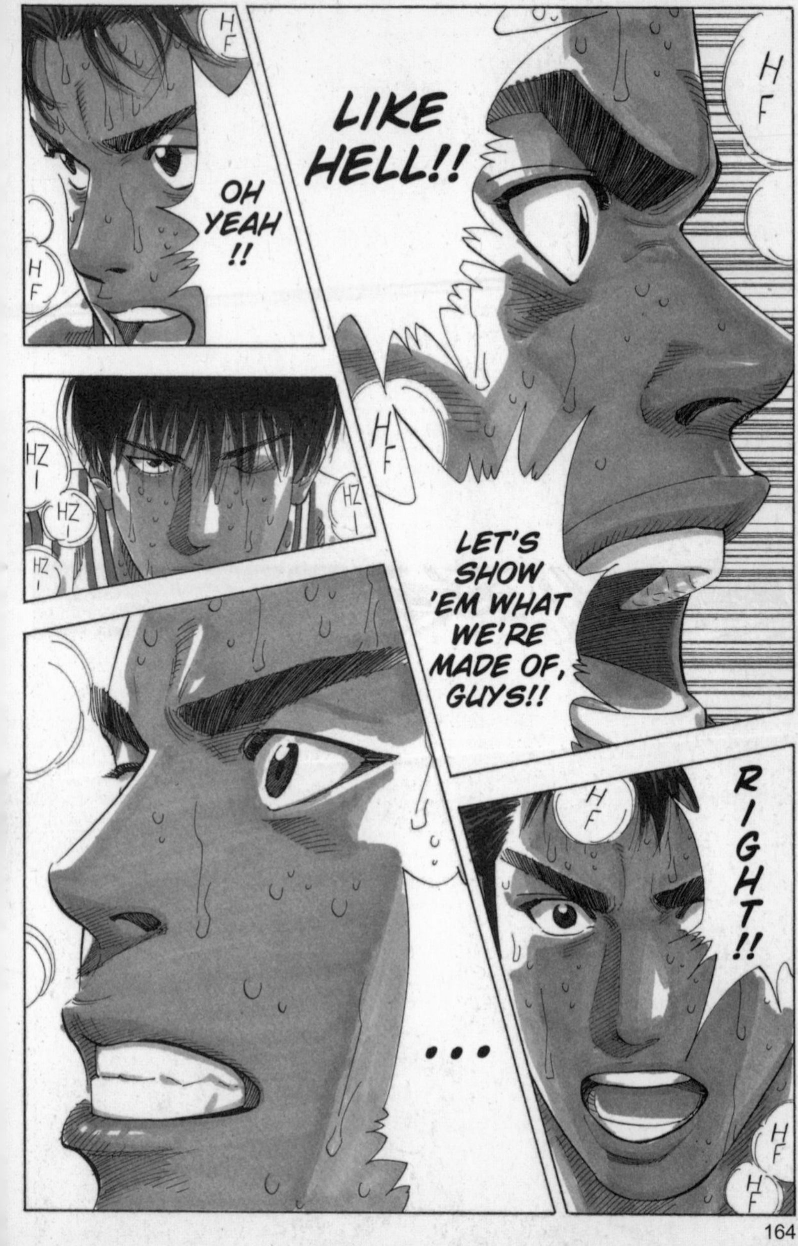
HF
LIKE HELL!!
HF
LET'S SHOW 'EM WHAT WE'RE MADE OF, GUYS!!
HF
OH YEAH!!
HF
HZ
HZ
HZ
HZ
HF
RIGHT!!
HF
HF
...

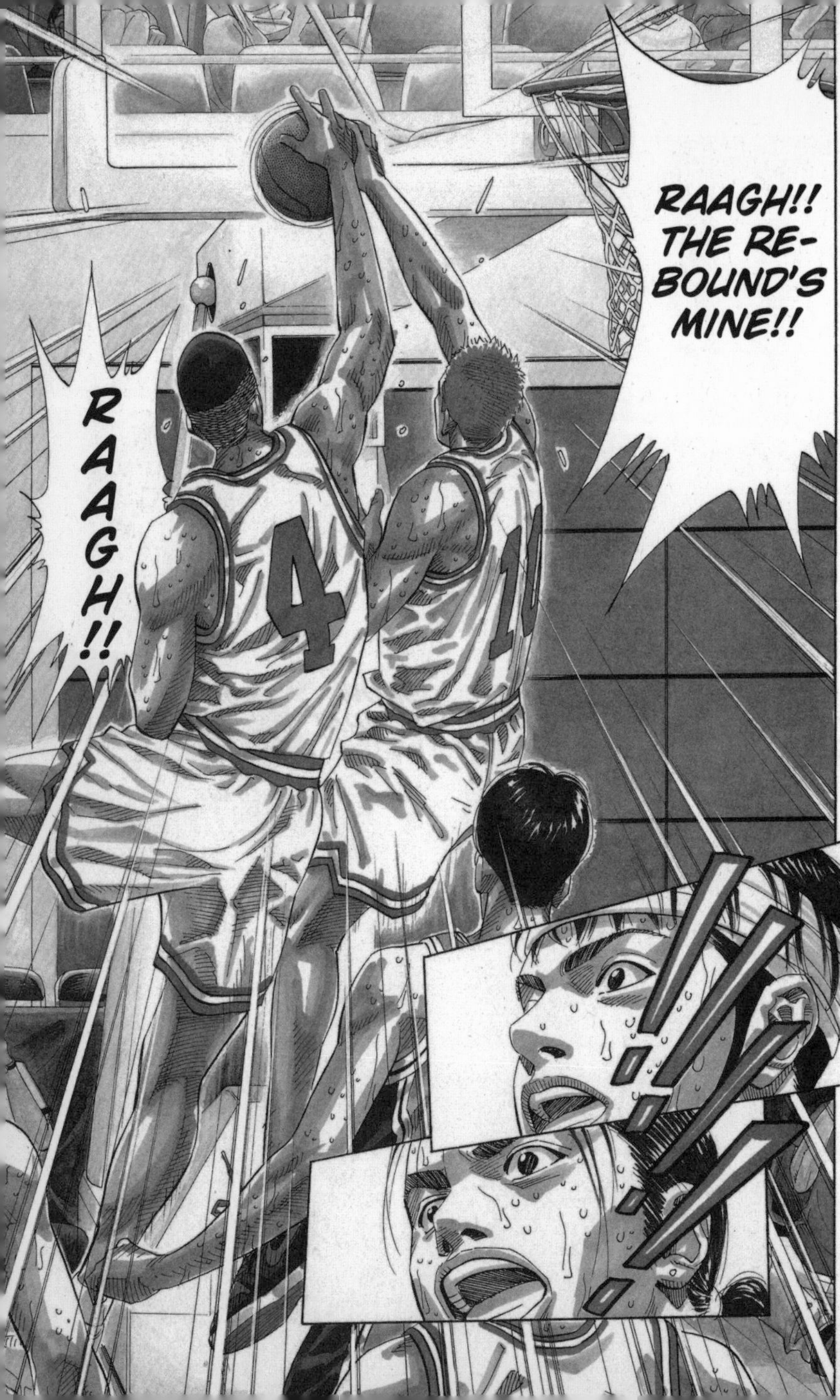
RAAGH!! THE RE-BOUND'S MINE!!
RAAGH!!

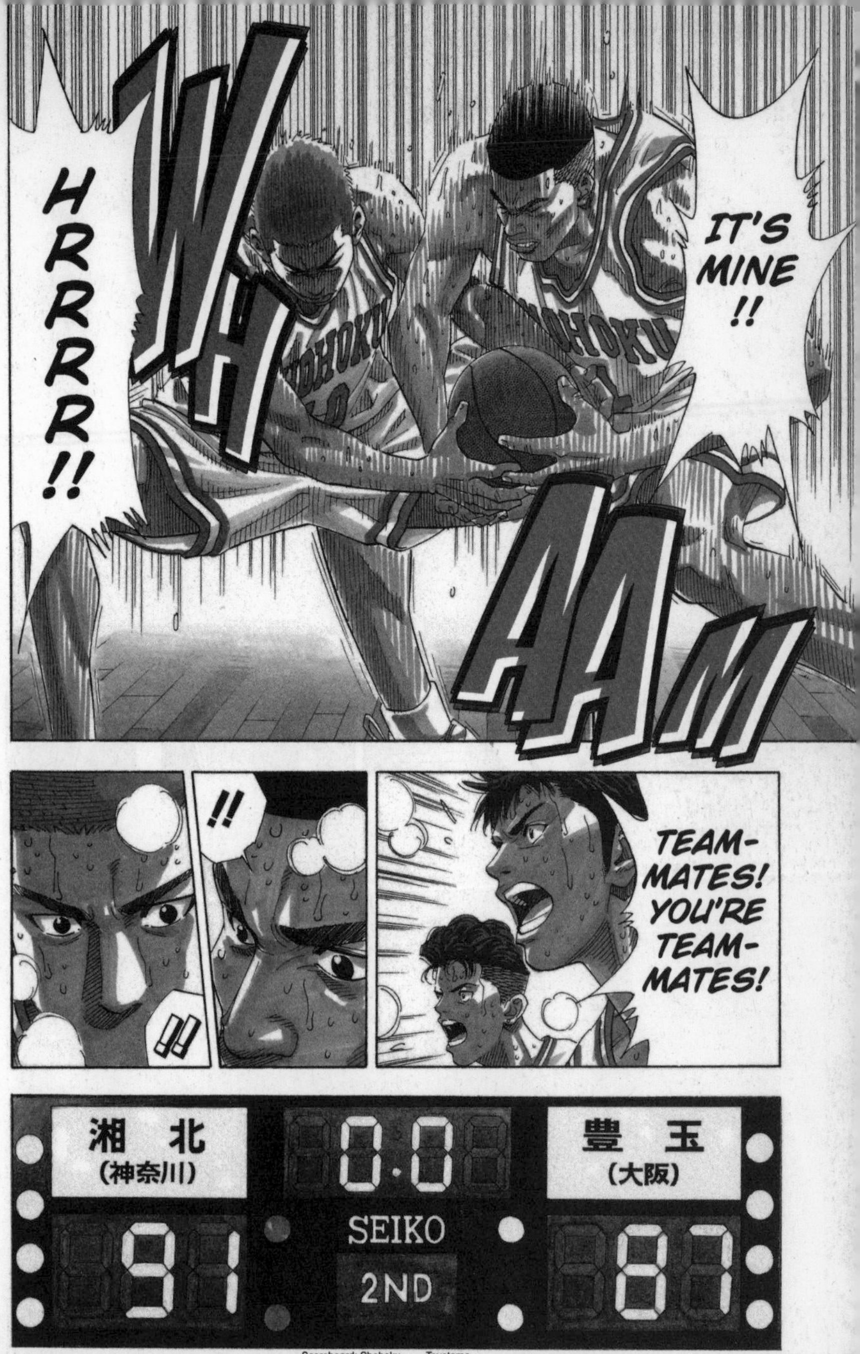
IT'S MINE!!
HRRRRR!!
WHAAM
TEAM-MATES! YOU'RE TEAM-MATES!
!!
!!
豊 玉
(大阪)
0.0
湘 北
(神奈川)
SEIKO
2ND
91
87

Scoreboard: Shohoku (Kanagawa) Toyotama (Osaka)

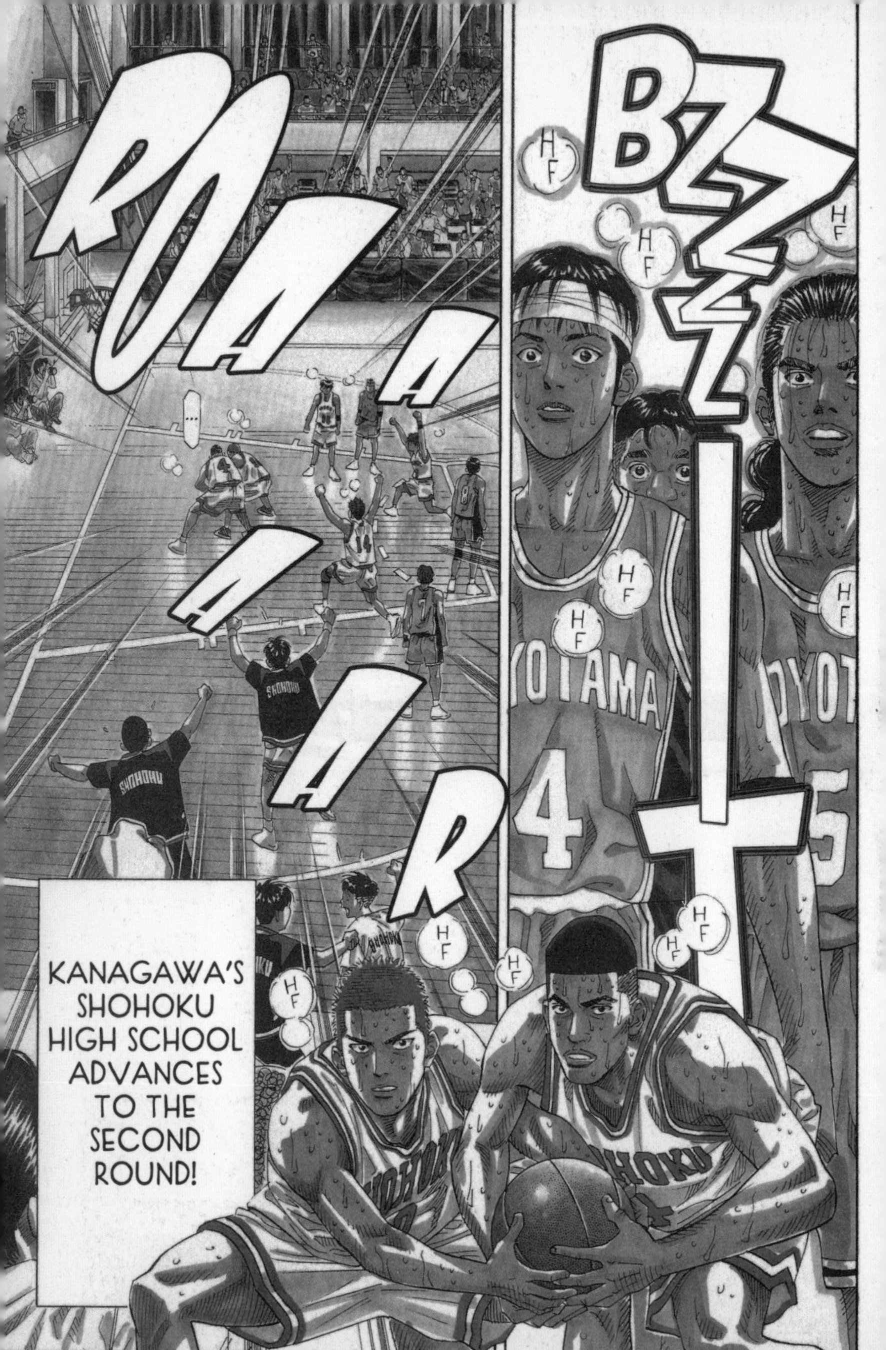
BZZZZT
HF
HF
HF
HF
HF
HF
HF
HF
ROAAAAR
...
HF
HF
HF
KANAGAWA'S SHOHOKU HIGH SCHOOL ADVANCES TO THE SECOND ROUND!

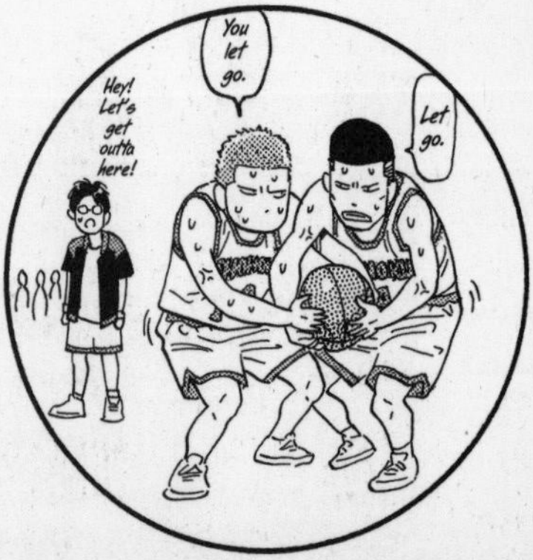
Let go.
You let go.
Hey! Let's get outta here!

SLAM DUNK

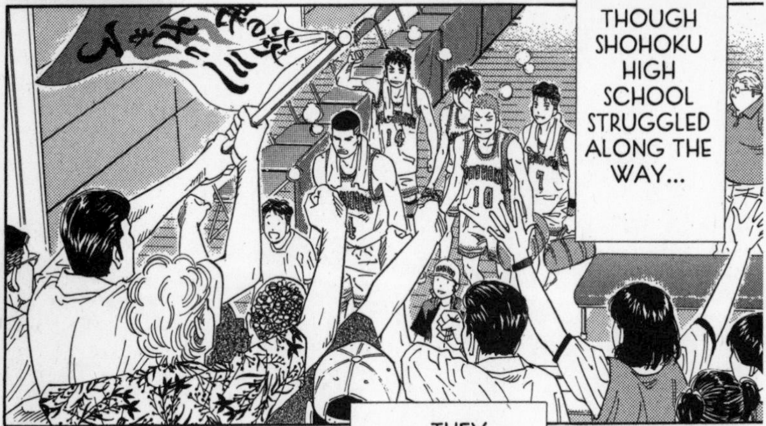
THOUGH SHOHOKU HIGH SCHOOL STRUGGLED ALONG THE WAY...
Flag: Man on Fire
Micchan

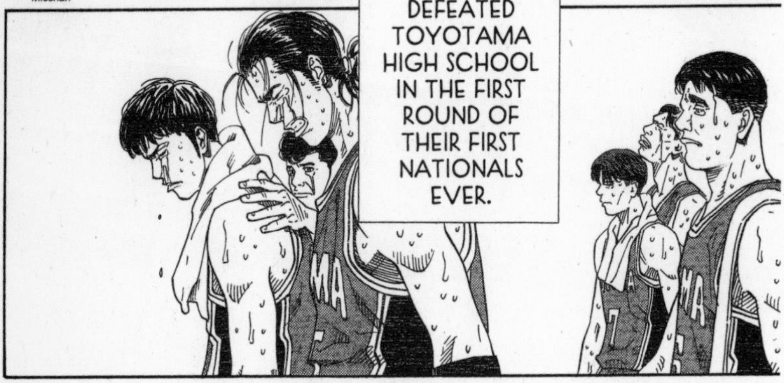
...THEY DEFEATED TOYOTAMA HIGH SCHOOL IN THE FIRST ROUND OF THEIR FIRST NATIONALS EVER.

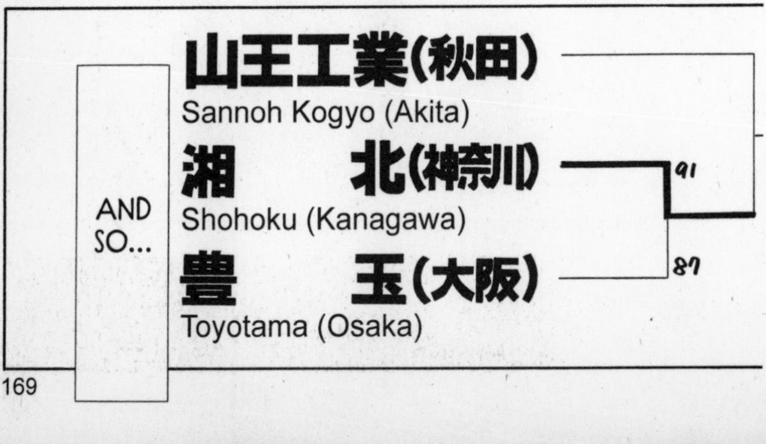
AND SO...
山王工業(秋田)
Sannoh Kogyo (Akita)
湘　北(神奈川)
Shohoku (Kanagawa)
91
豊　玉(大阪)
Toyotama (Osaka)
87

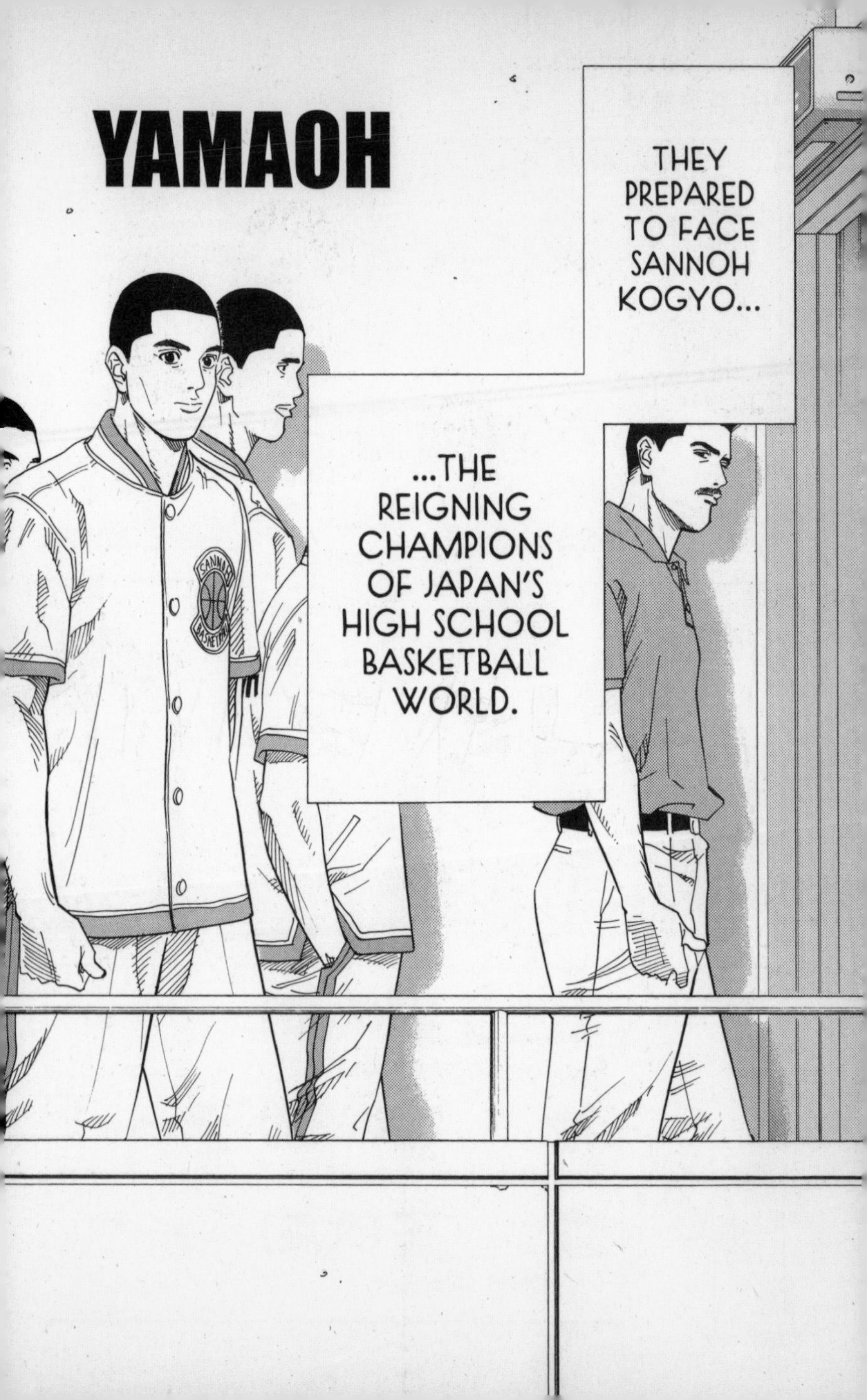
THEY PREPARED TO FACE SANNOH KOGYO...
...THE REIGNING CHAMPIONS OF JAPAN'S HIGH SCHOOL BASKETBALL WORLD.
YAMAOH

#215

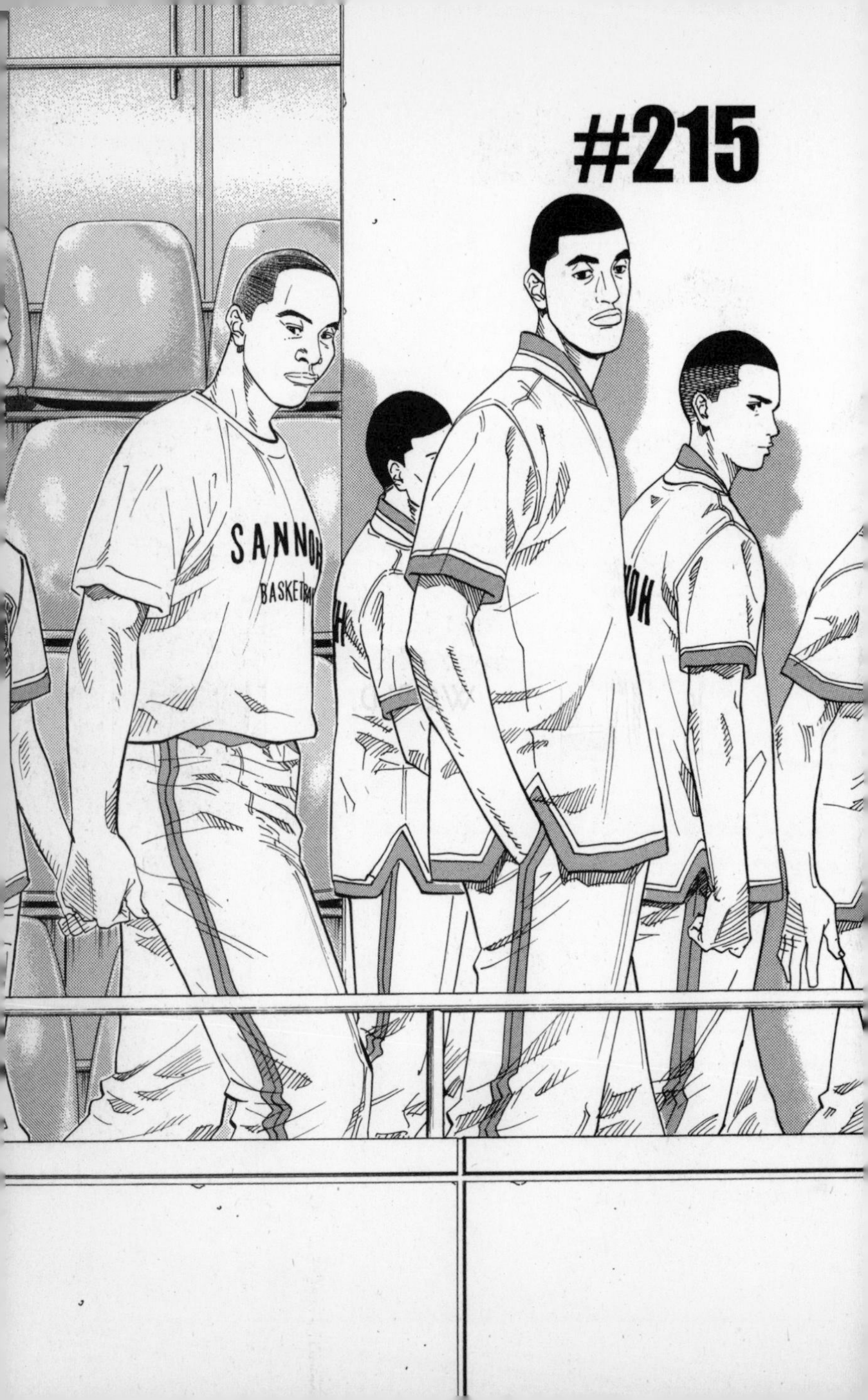
SANNOH

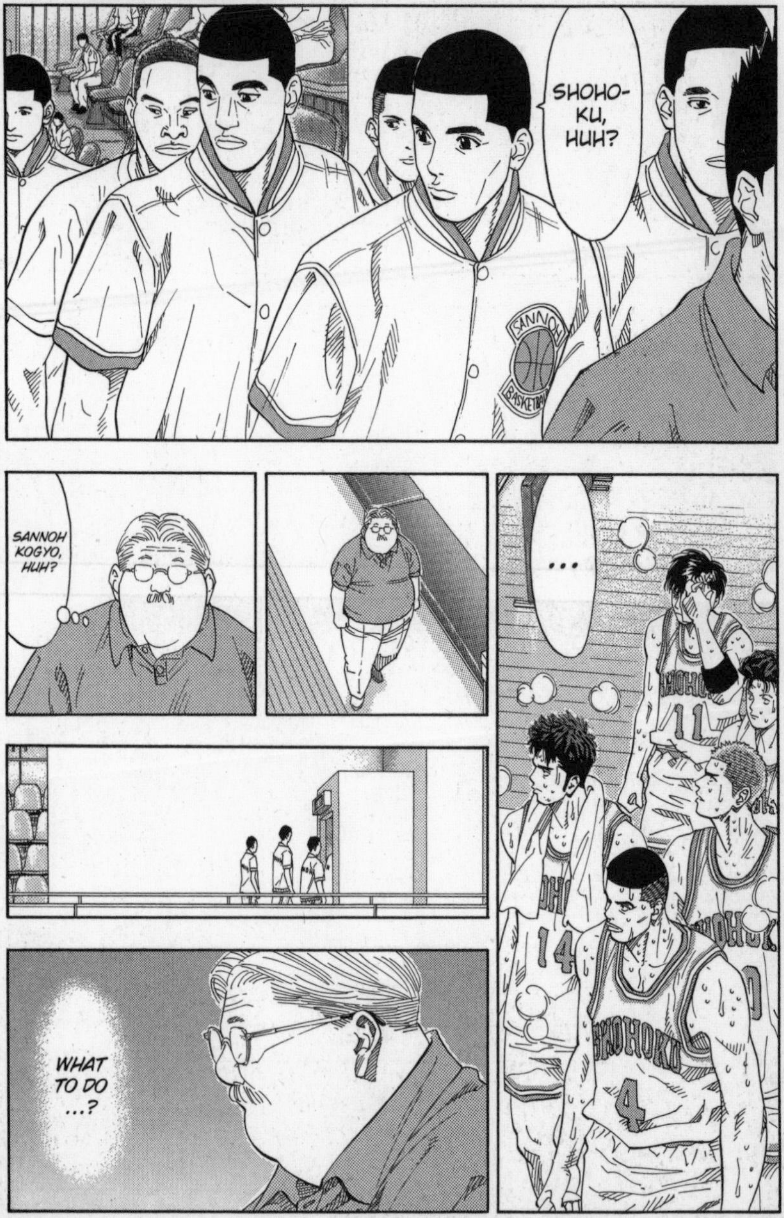
SHOHO-KU, HUH?
SANNOH
BASKETBALL
...
SHOHOKU
SANNOH KOGYO, HUH?
SHOHOKU
WHAT TO DO ...?

READ THIS WAY

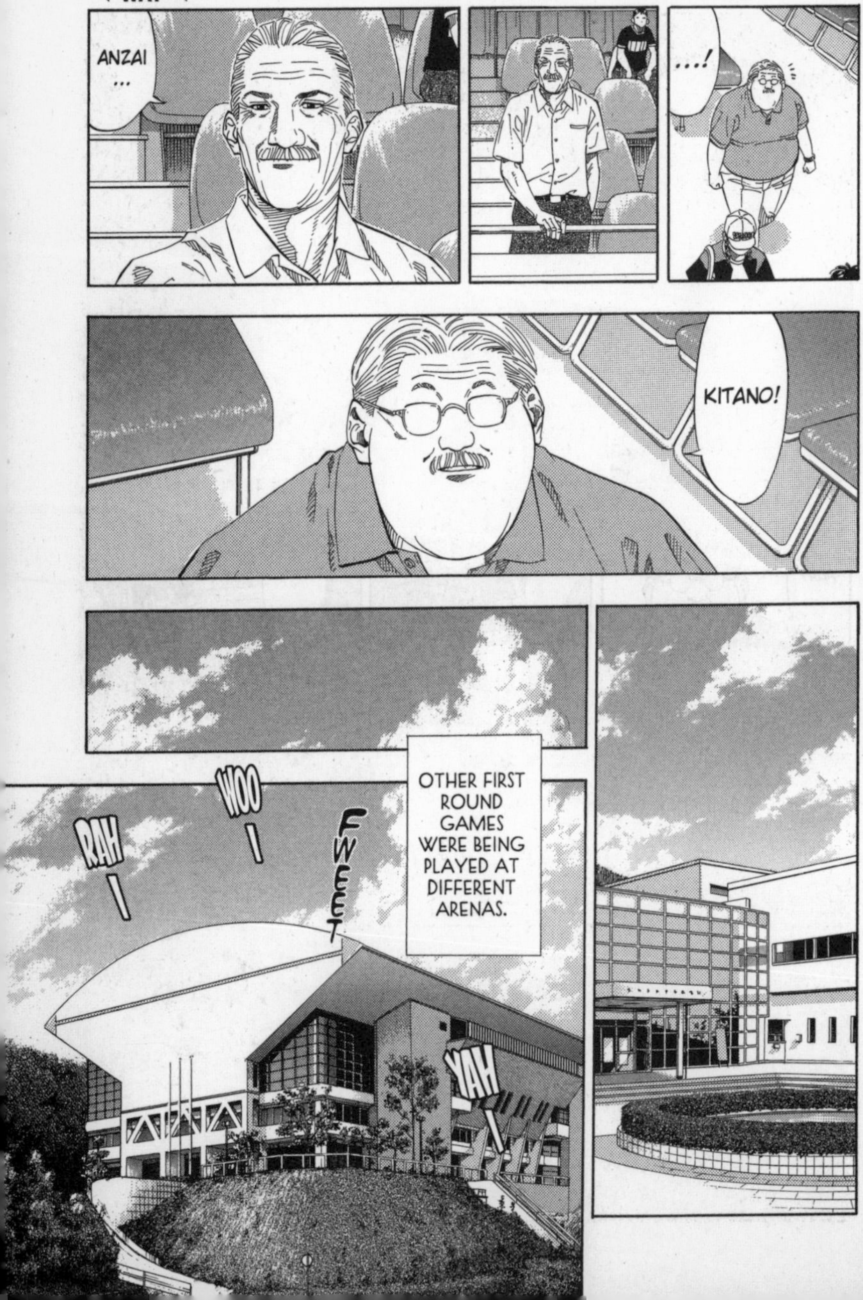
...!
ANZAI ...
KITANO!
OTHER FIRST ROUND GAMES WERE BEING PLAYED AT DIFFERENT ARENAS.
FWEET
WOO
RAH
YAH

Aiwa Gakuin (Aichi)
103 $\binom{64-27}{39-31}$ 58 Yokotama Kogyo

Daiei Gakuen (Osaka)
81 $\binom{44-22}{37-26}$ 48 Tomifusa

174

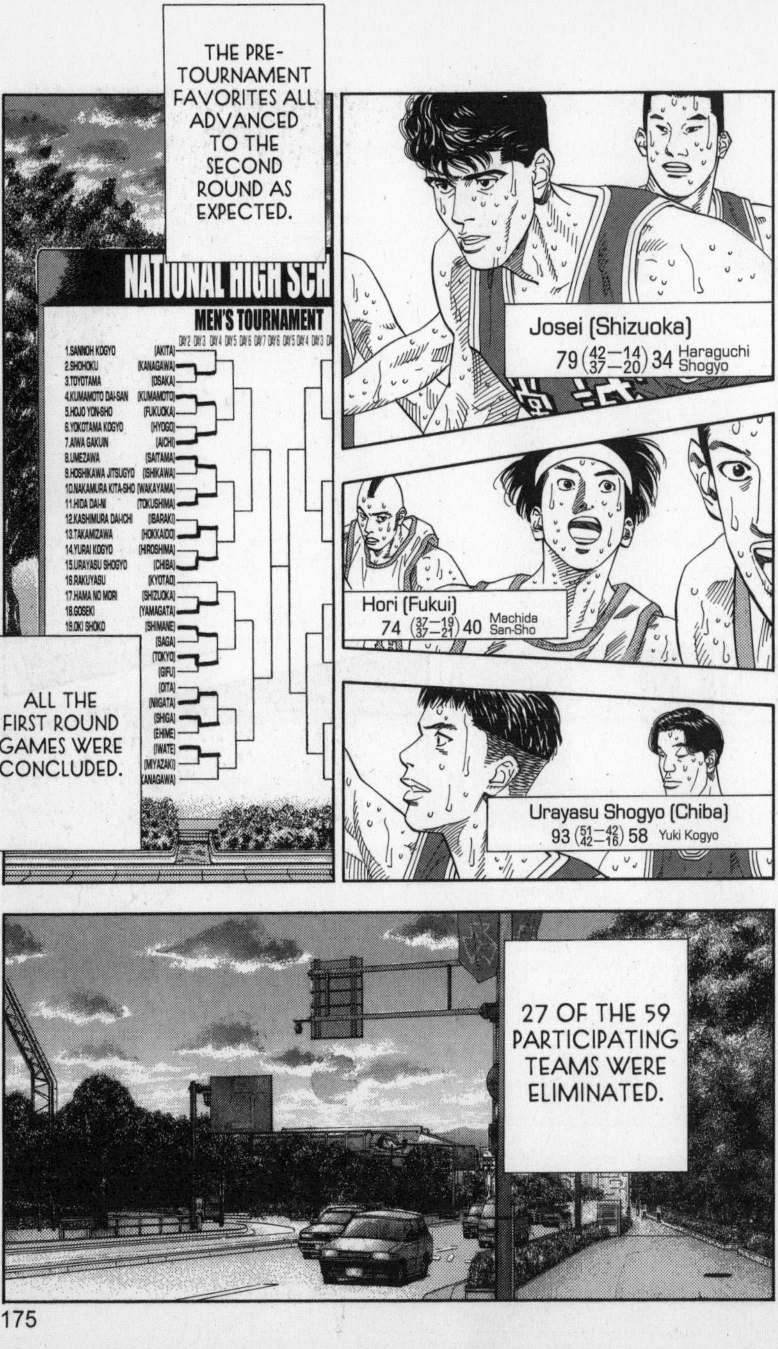
Josei (Shizuoka)
79 (42—14 37—20) 34 Haraguchi Shogyo
Hori (Fukui)
74 (37—19 37—21) 40 Machida San-Sho
Urayasu Shogyo (Chiba)
93 (51—42 42—16) 58 Yuki Kogyo
THE PRE-TOURNAMENT FAVORITES ALL ADVANCED TO THE SECOND ROUND AS EXPECTED.
NATIONAL HIGH SCH
MEN'S TOURNAMENT
DAY2 DAY3 DAY4 DAY5 DAY6 DAY7 DAY6 DAY5 DAY4 DAY3
1.SANNOH KOGYO (AKITA)
2.SHOHOKU (KANAGAWA)
3.TOYOTAMA (OSAKA)
4.KUMAMOTO DAI-SAN (KUMAMOTO)
5.HOJO YON-SHO (FUKUOKA)
6.YOKOTAMA KOGYO (HYOGO)
7.AIWA GAKUIN (AICHI)
8.UMEZAWA (SAITAMA)
9.HOSHIKAWA JITSUGYO (ISHIKAWA)
10.NAKAMURA KITA-SHO (WAKAYAMA)
11.HIDA DAI-NI (TOKUSHIMA)
12.KASHIMURA DAHCHI (IBARAKI)
13.TAKAMIZAWA (HOKKAIDO)
14.YURAI KOGYO (HIROSHIMA)
15.URAYASU SHOGYO (CHIBA)
16.RAKUYASU (KYOTAO)
17.HAMA NO MORI (SHIZUOKA)
18.GOSEKI (YAMAGATA)
19.OKI SHOKO (SHIMANE)
(SAGA)
(TOKYO)
(GIFU)
(OITA)
(NIIGATA)
(SHIGA)
(EHIME)
(IWATE)
(MIYAZAKI)
KANAGAWA)
ALL THE FIRST ROUND GAMES WERE CONCLUDED.
27 OF THE 59 PARTICIPATING TEAMS WERE ELIMINATED.

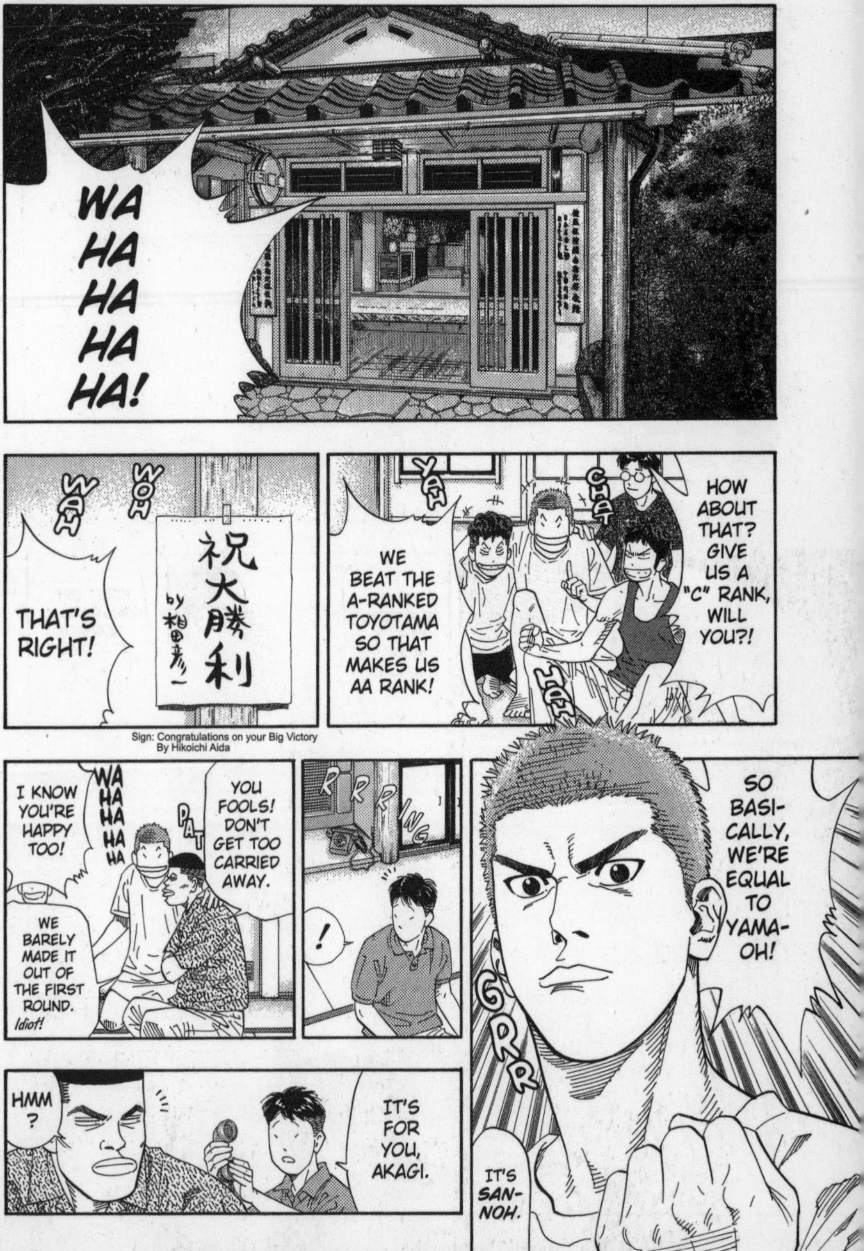
WA HA HA HA HA!
HOW ABOUT THAT? GIVE US A "C" RANK, WILL YOU?!
CHAT
YAH
WE BEAT THE A-RANKED TOYOTAMA SO THAT MAKES US AA RANK!
HEH
WOH
WAH
祝大勝利 by 相田彦一
THAT'S RIGHT!
Sign: Congratulations on your Big Victory By Hikoichi Aida
SO BASI-CALLY, WE'RE EQUAL TO YAMA-OH!
GRR
RRRING
!
YOU FOOLS! DON'T GET TOO CARRIED AWAY.
PAT
WA HA HA HA HA
I KNOW YOU'RE HAPPY TOO!
WE BARELY MADE IT OUT OF THE FIRST ROUND.
Idiot!
IT'S FOR YOU, AKAGI.
HMM?
IT'S SAN-NOH.

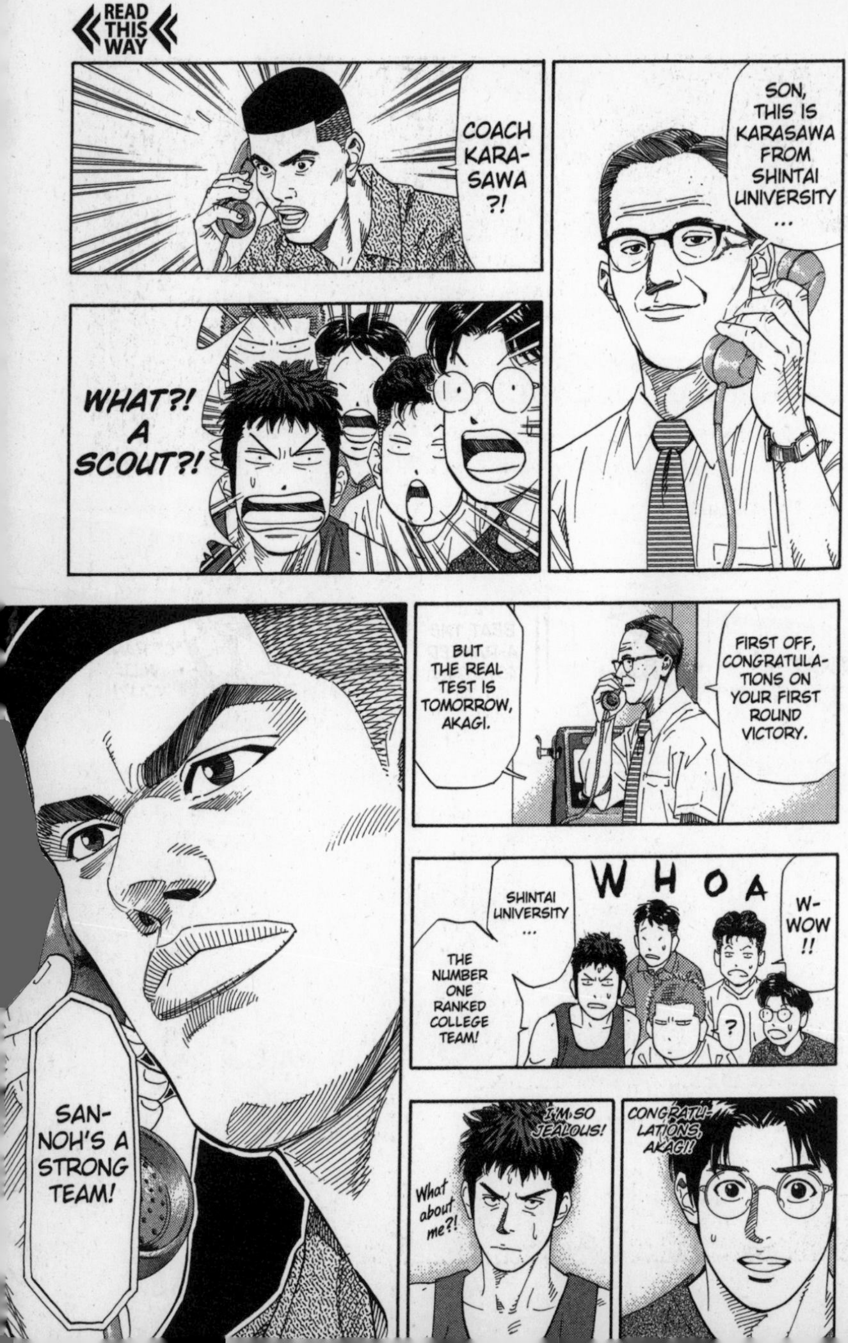
READ THIS WAY
SON, THIS IS KARASAWA FROM SHINTAI UNIVERSITY ...
COACH KARA-SAWA ?!
WHAT?! A SCOUT?!
FIRST OFF, CONGRATULA-TIONS ON YOUR FIRST ROUND VICTORY.
BUT THE REAL TEST IS TOMORROW, AKAGI.
W-WOW !!
WHOA
SHINTAI UNIVERSITY ...
THE NUMBER ONE RANKED COLLEGE TEAM!
?
CONGRATU-LATIONS, AKAGI!!
I'M SO JEALOUS!
What about me?!
SAN-NOH'S A STRONG TEAM!

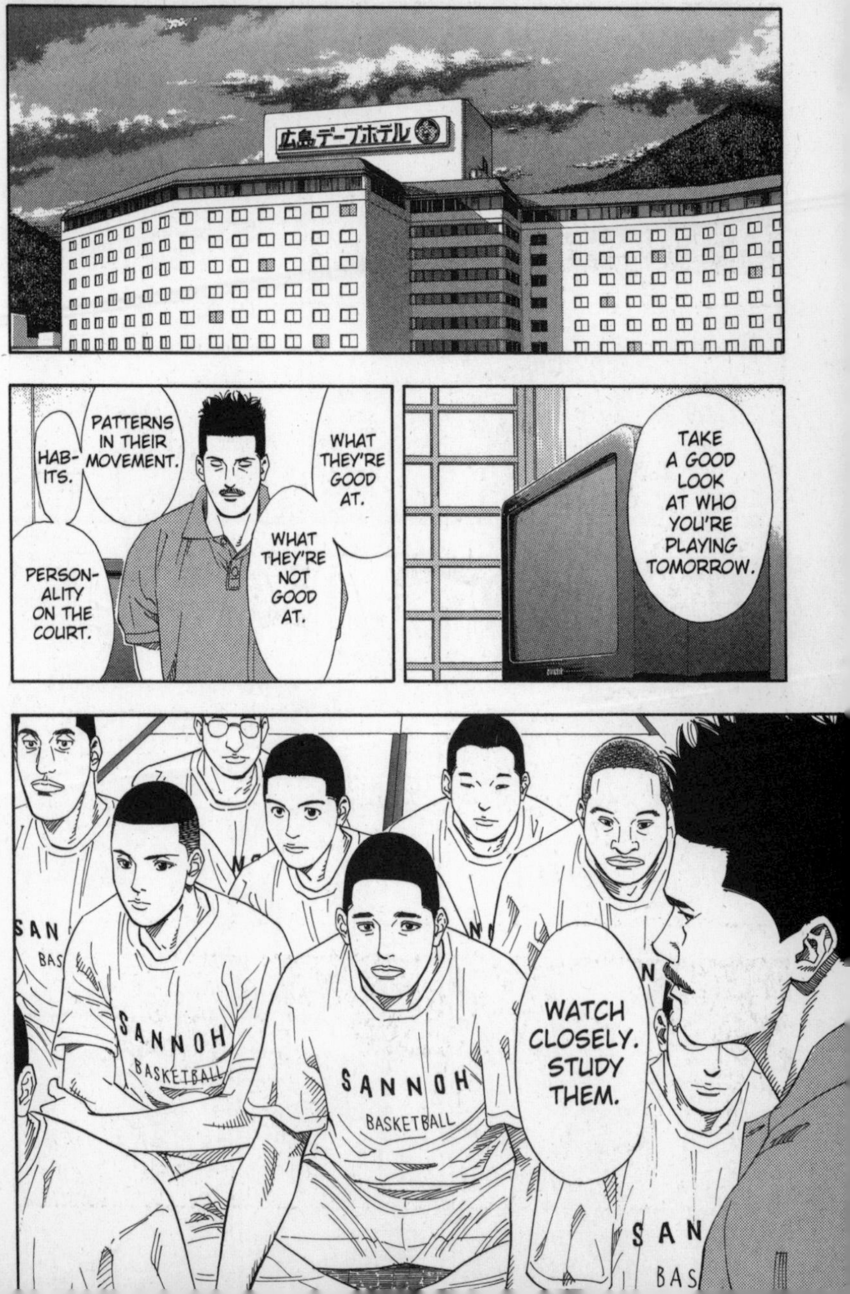
広島デーブホテル
TAKE A GOOD LOOK AT WHO YOU'RE PLAYING TOMORROW.
WHAT THEY'RE GOOD AT.
WHAT THEY'RE NOT GOOD AT.
PATTERNS IN THEIR MOVEMENT.
HAB-ITS.
PERSON-ALITY ON THE COURT.
WATCH CLOSELY. STUDY THEM.
SANNOH BASKETBALL
SANNOH BASKETBALL

READ THIS WAY

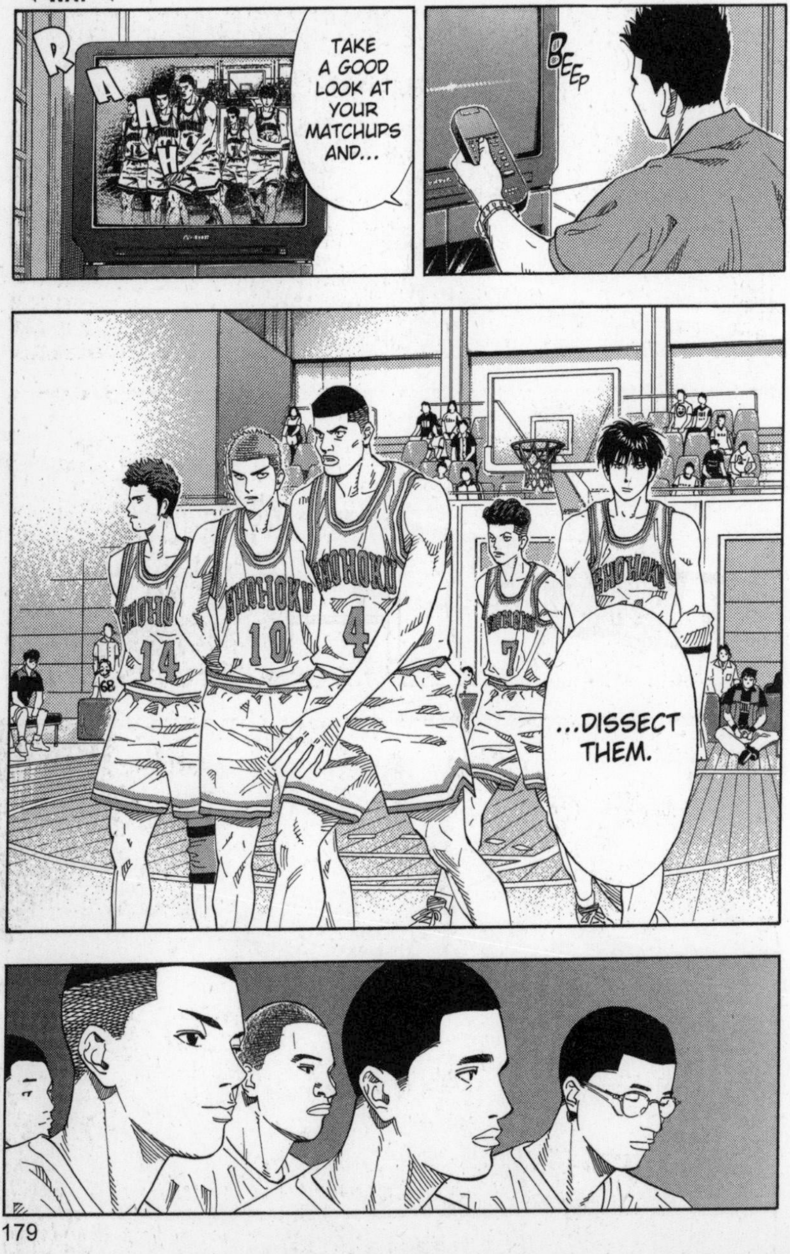
BEEP
RAAH
TAKE A GOOD LOOK AT YOUR MATCHUPS AND...
SHOHOKU
...DISSECT THEM.

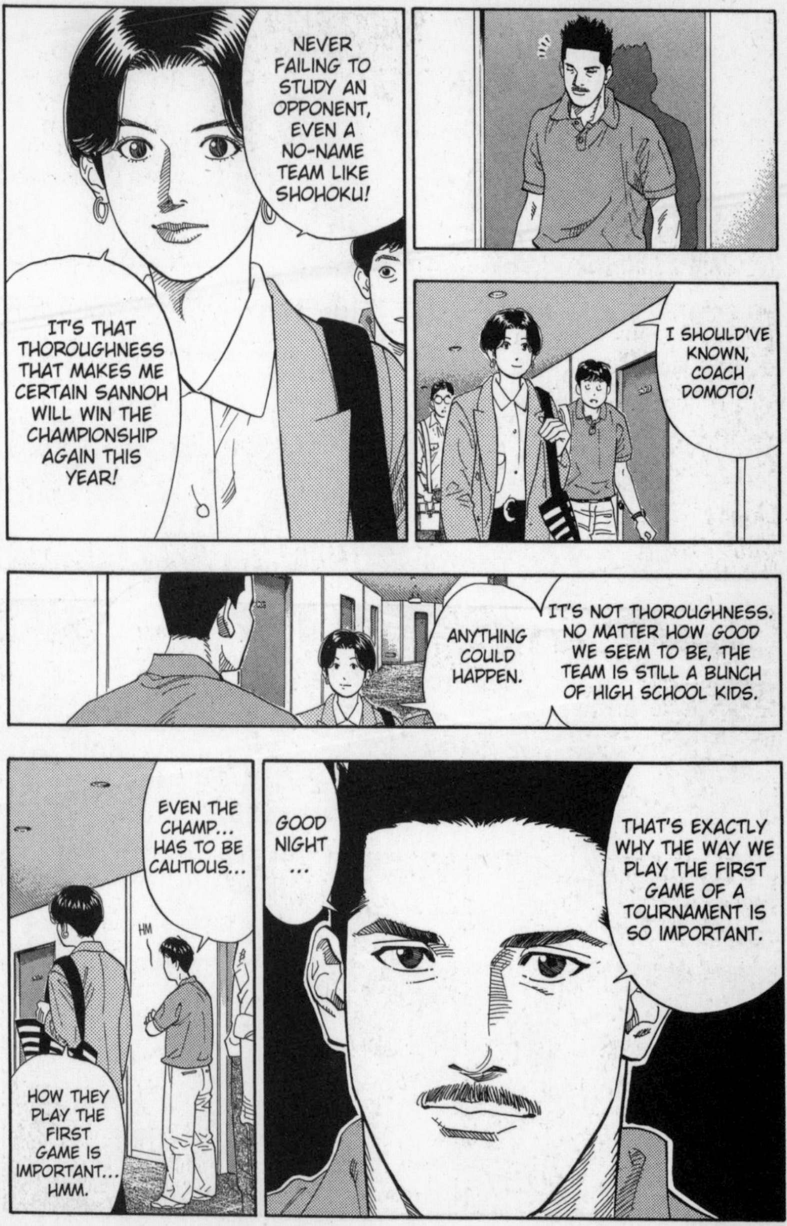

I SHOULD'VE KNOWN, COACH DOMOTO!
NEVER FAILING TO STUDY AN OPPONENT, EVEN A NO-NAME TEAM LIKE SHOHOKU!
IT'S THAT THOROUGHNESS THAT MAKES ME CERTAIN SANNOH WILL WIN THE CHAMPIONSHIP AGAIN THIS YEAR!
IT'S NOT THOROUGHNESS. NO MATTER HOW GOOD WE SEEM TO BE, THE TEAM IS STILL A BUNCH OF HIGH SCHOOL KIDS.
ANYTHING COULD HAPPEN.
THAT'S EXACTLY WHY THE WAY WE PLAY THE FIRST GAME OF A TOURNAMENT IS SO IMPORTANT.
GOOD NIGHT ...
EVEN THE CHAMP... HAS TO BE CAUTIOUS...
HM
HOW THEY PLAY THE FIRST GAME IS IMPORTANT... HMM.

READ THIS WAY

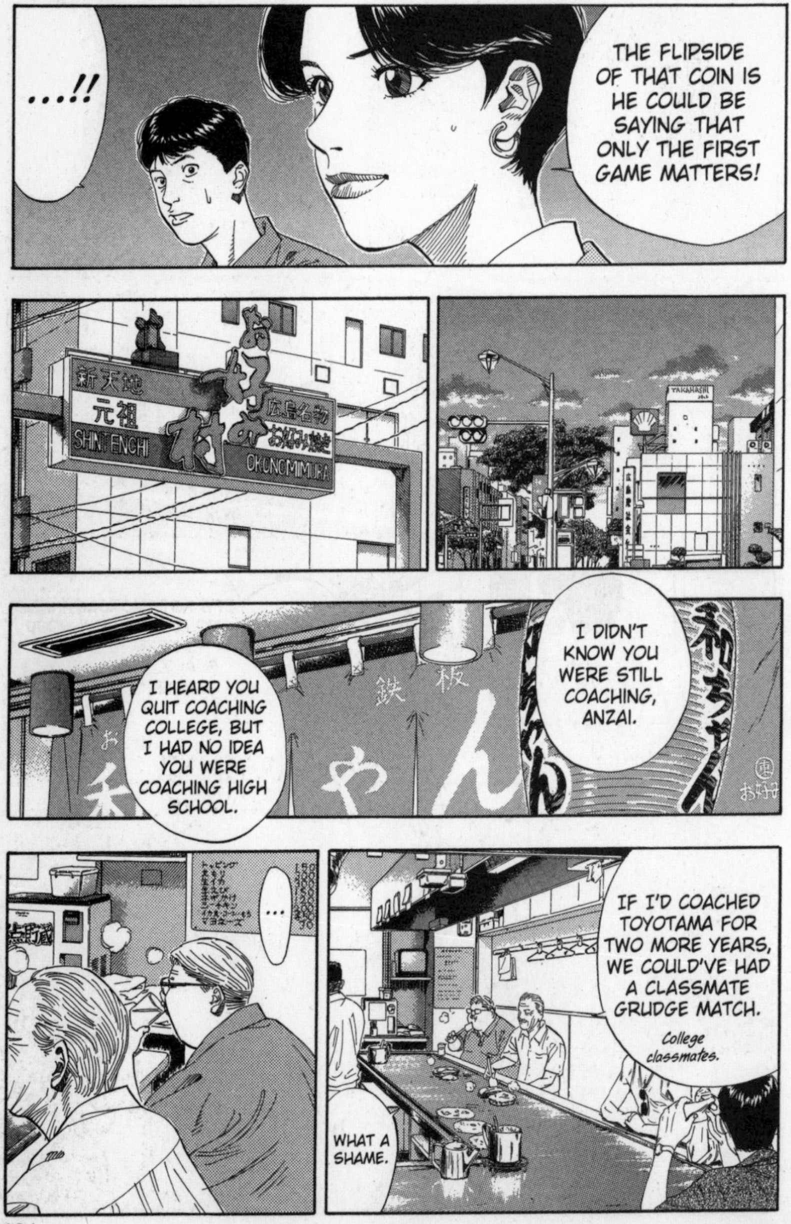
THE FLIPSIDE OF THAT COIN IS HE COULD BE SAYING THAT ONLY THE FIRST GAME MATTERS!
...!!
新天地
元祖
広島名物
SHINTENCHI
OKONOMIMURA
I DIDN'T KNOW YOU WERE STILL COACHING, ANZAI.
I HEARD YOU QUIT COACHING COLLEGE, BUT I HAD NO IDEA YOU WERE COACHING HIGH SCHOOL.
IF I'D COACHED TOYOTAMA FOR TWO MORE YEARS, WE COULD'VE HAD A CLASSMATE GRUDGE MATCH.
College classmates.
WHAT A SHAME.
...

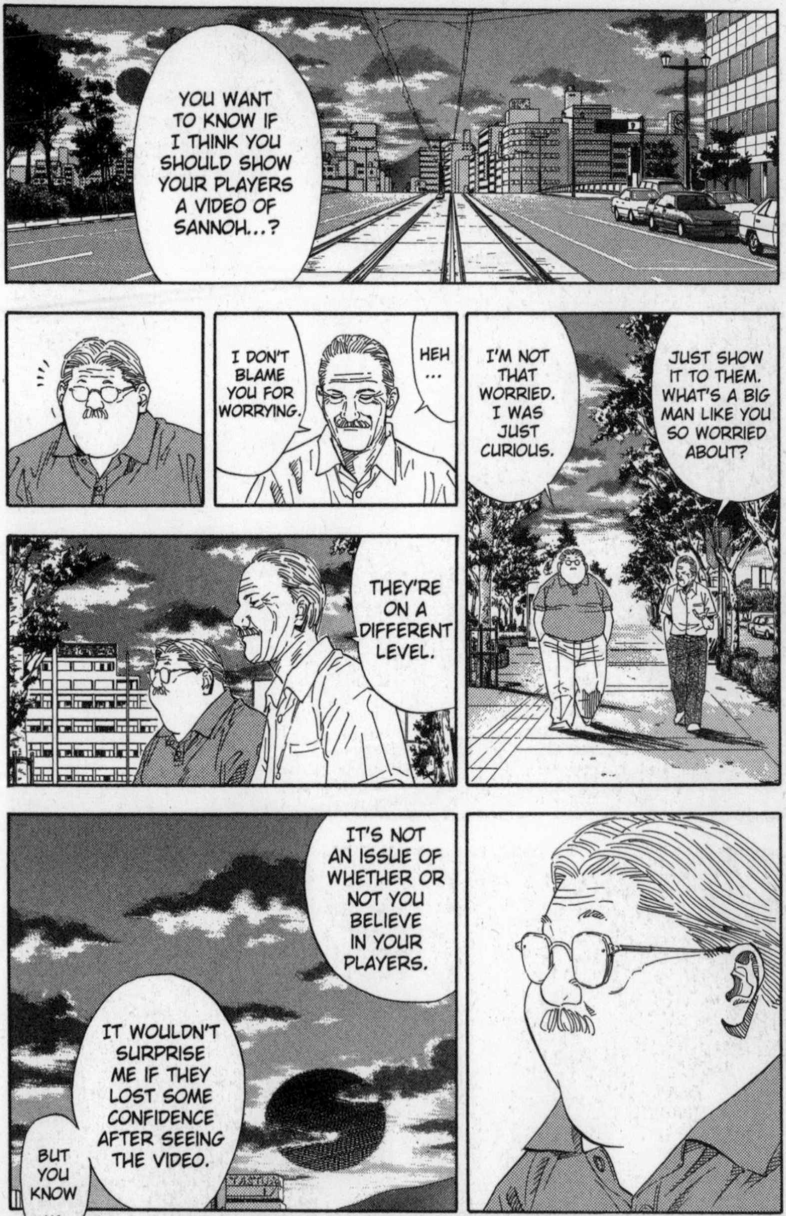
YOU WANT TO KNOW IF I THINK YOU SHOULD SHOW YOUR PLAYERS A VIDEO OF SANNOH...?
JUST SHOW IT TO THEM. WHAT'S A BIG MAN LIKE YOU SO WORRIED ABOUT?
I'M NOT THAT WORRIED. I WAS JUST CURIOUS.
HEH ...
I DON'T BLAME YOU FOR WORRYING.
THEY'RE ON A DIFFERENT LEVEL.
IT'S NOT AN ISSUE OF WHETHER OR NOT YOU BELIEVE IN YOUR PLAYERS.
IT WOULDN'T SURPRISE ME IF THEY LOST SOME CONFIDENCE AFTER SEEING THE VIDEO.
BUT YOU KNOW ...

READ THIS WAY

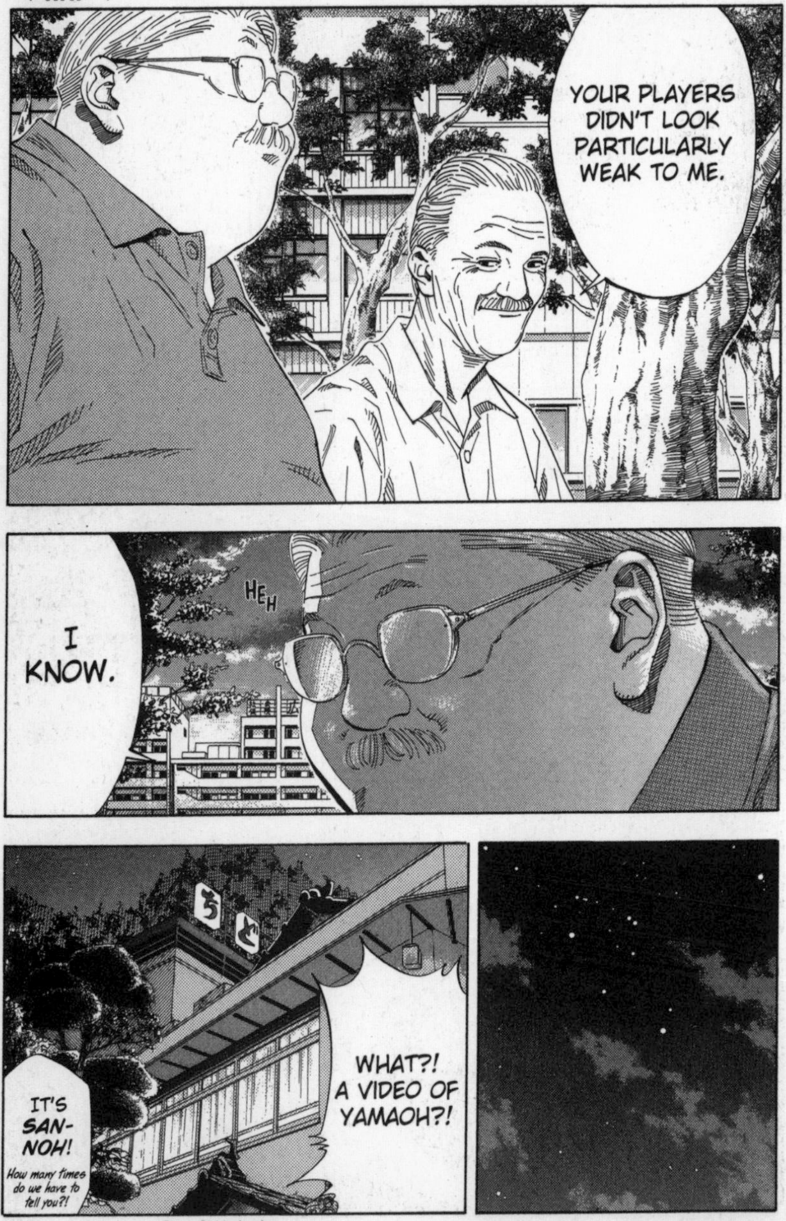

YOUR PLAYERS DIDN'T LOOK PARTICULARLY WEAK TO ME.
HEH
I KNOW.
WHAT?! A VIDEO OF YAMAOH?!
IT'S SAN-NOH!
How many times do we have to tell you?!

Sign: Chidoriso Inn

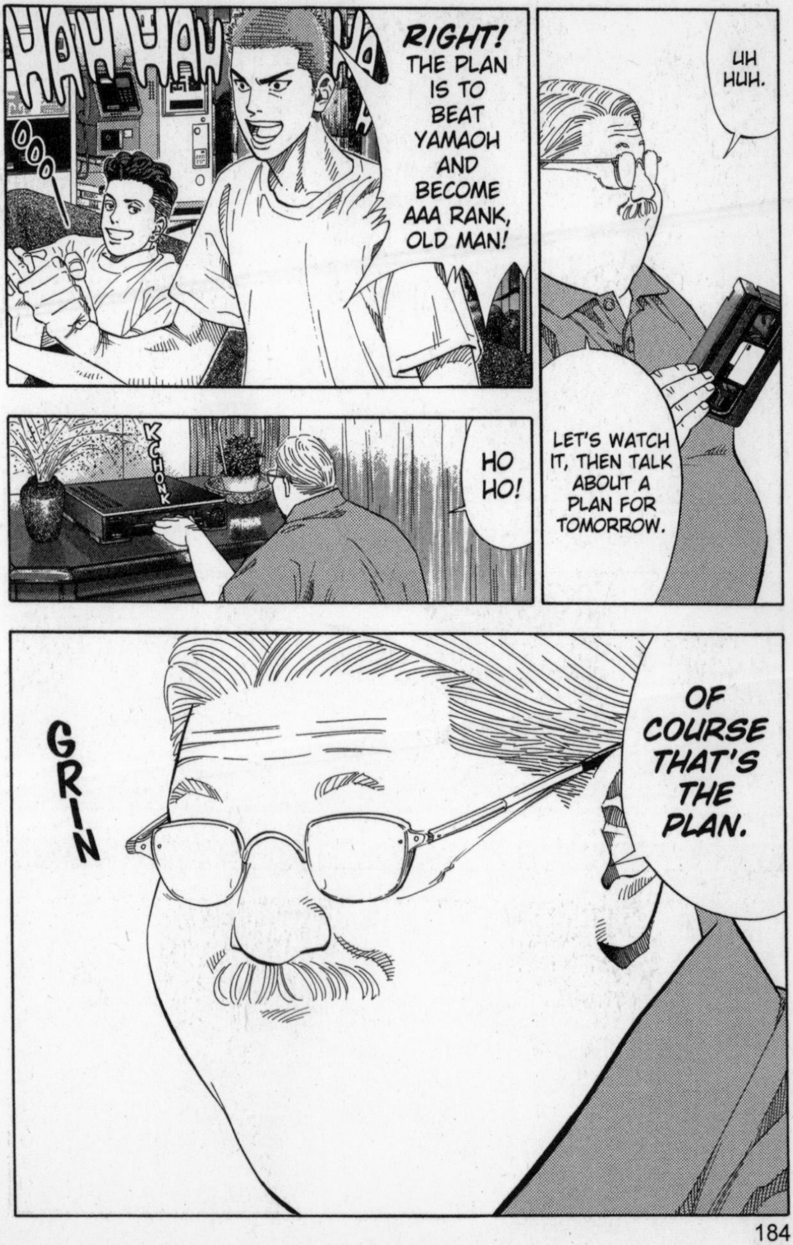
UH HUH.
LET'S WATCH IT, THEN TALK ABOUT A PLAN FOR TOMORROW.
WAH WAH WAH
OOO
RIGHT! THE PLAN IS TO BEAT YAMAOH AND BECOME AAA RANK, OLD MAN!
HO HO!
KCHONK
OF COURSE THAT'S THE PLAN.
GRIN

READ THIS WAY

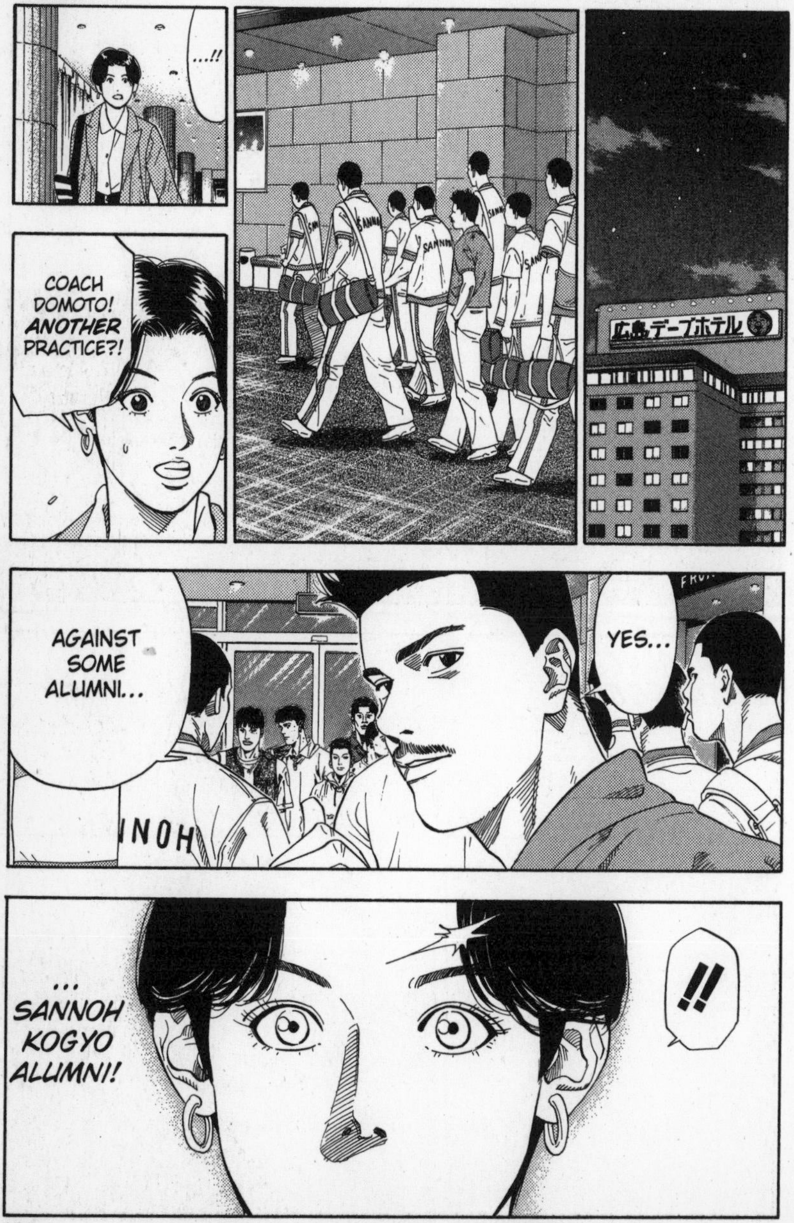

広島デーブホテル
...!!
COACH DOMOTO! ANOTHER PRACTICE?!
YES...
AGAINST SOME ALUMNI...
!!
... SANNOH KOGYO ALUMNI!

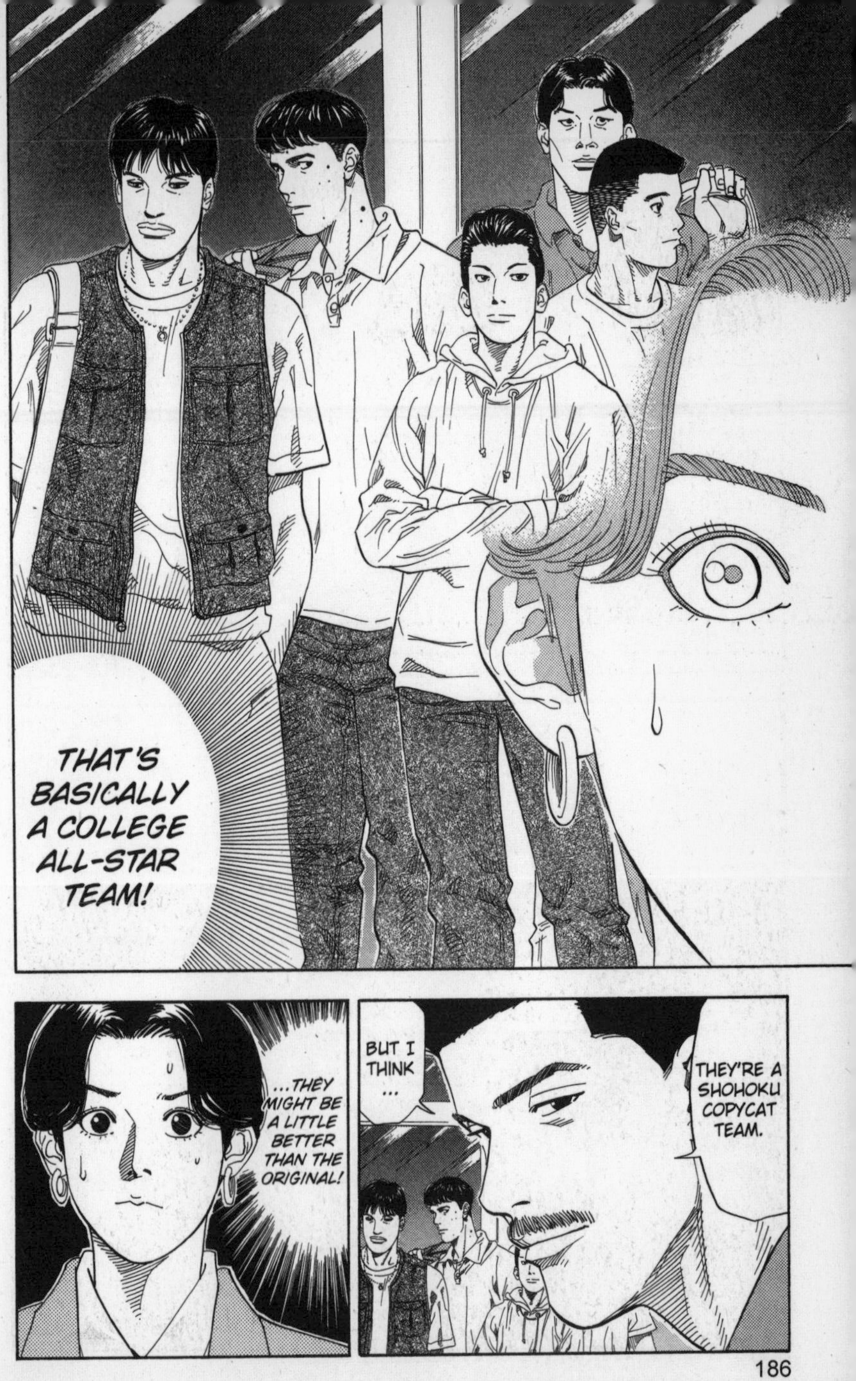
THAT'S BASICALLY A COLLEGE ALL-STAR TEAM!
THEY'RE A SHOHOKU COPYCAT TEAM.
BUT I THINK ...
...THEY MIGHT BE A LITTLE BETTER THAN THE ORIGINAL!

...

...

THE CHAMPS, SANNOH KOGYO...

THEY DON'T PLAN ON GIVING SHOHOKU EVEN A ONE PERCENT CHANCE OF WINNING!

VROON

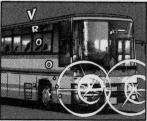

Coming Next Volume

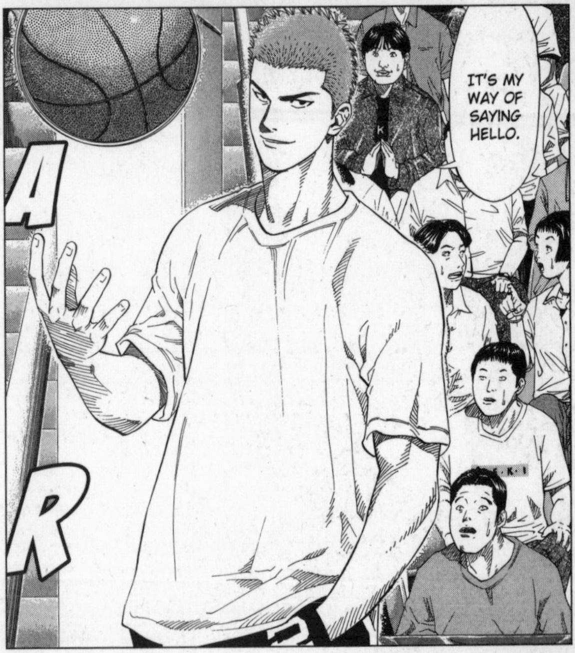
IT'S MY WAY OF SAYING HELLO.
A
R

After watching a video of Sannoh's semifinal game from the previous year, the Shohoku players, except Sakuragi of course, are feeling nervous—three of Sannoh's starters this year played on that championship team. To make things worse, the stands are filled with Sannoh supporters eager to see their favorite rack up an easy win against Shohoku. But Coach Anzai's been here before and he knows his players, instructing them to lead off with a surprise attack that lets Sannoh know that Shohoku's in the house, and they aren't going out without a fight!

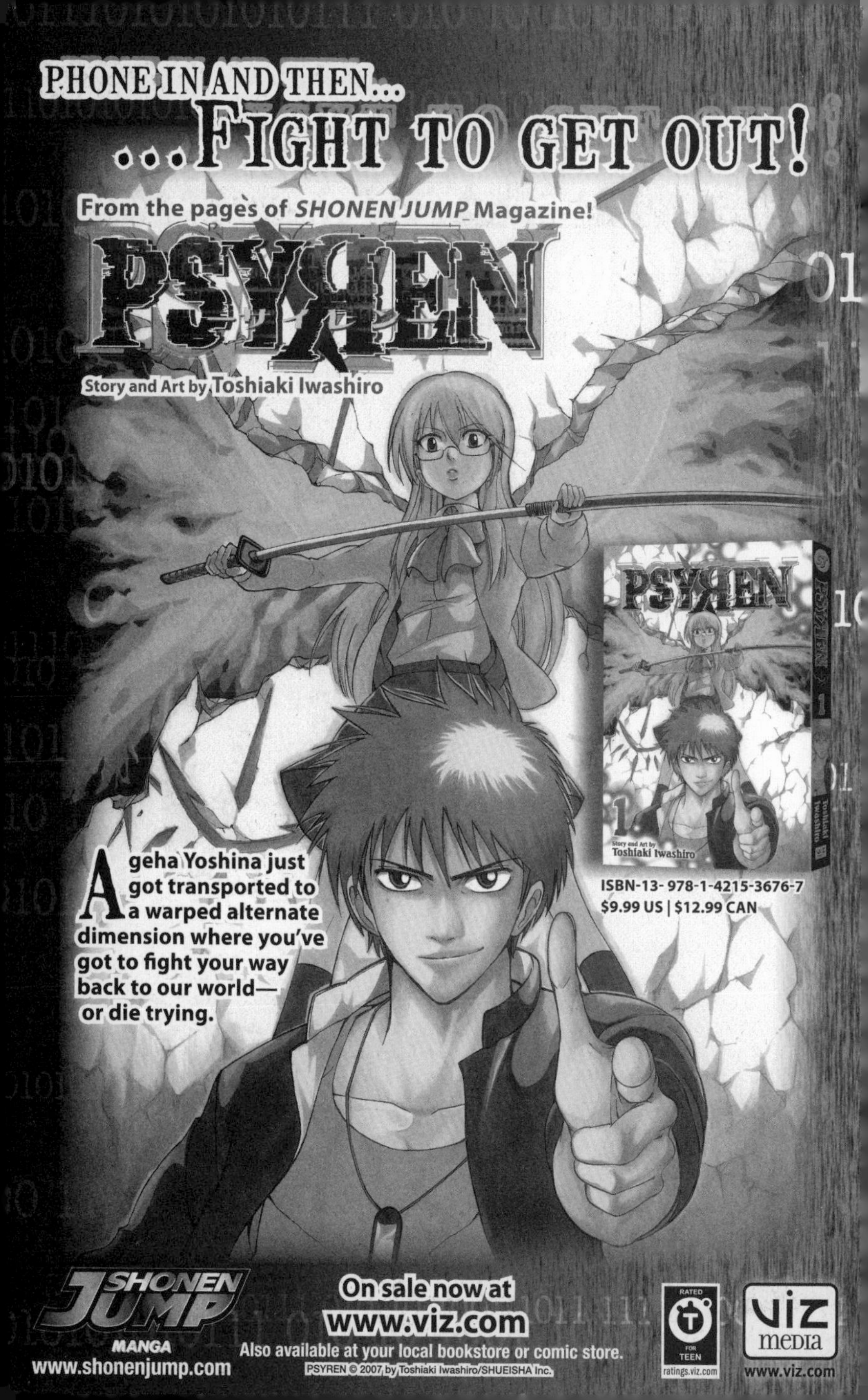

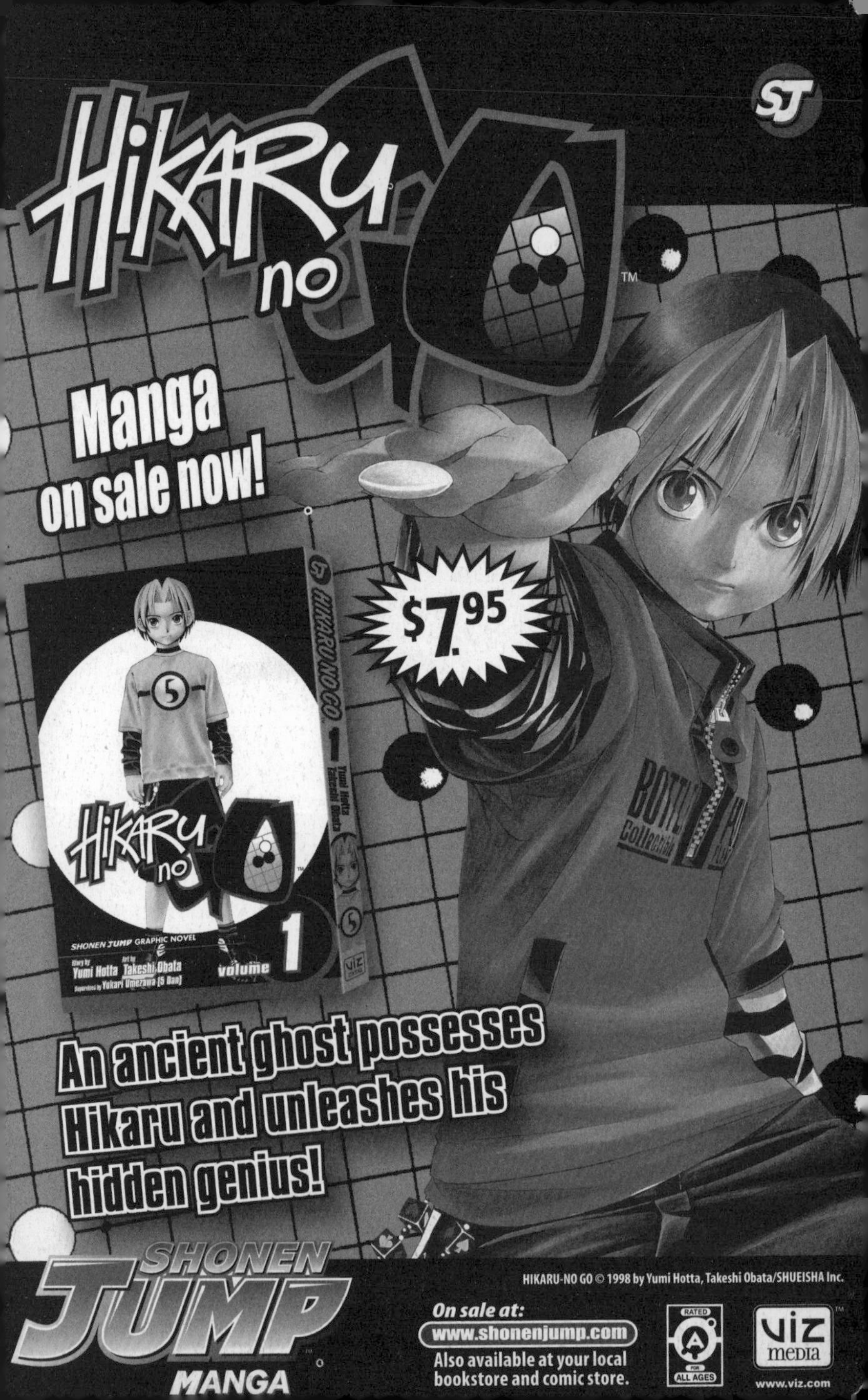

HIKARU NO GO™
Manga on sale now!
$7.95
SHONEN JUMP GRAPHIC NOVEL
Story by Yumi Hotta Art by Takeshi Obata
Supervised by Yukari Umezawa (5 Dan)
volume 1
An ancient ghost possesses Hikaru and unleashes his hidden genius!
SHONEN JUMP MANGA
HIKARU-NO GO © 1998 by Yumi Hotta, Takeshi Obata/SHUEISHA Inc.
On sale at:
www.shonenjump.com
Also available at your local bookstore and comic store.
RATED A FOR ALL AGES
VIZ media
www.viz.com

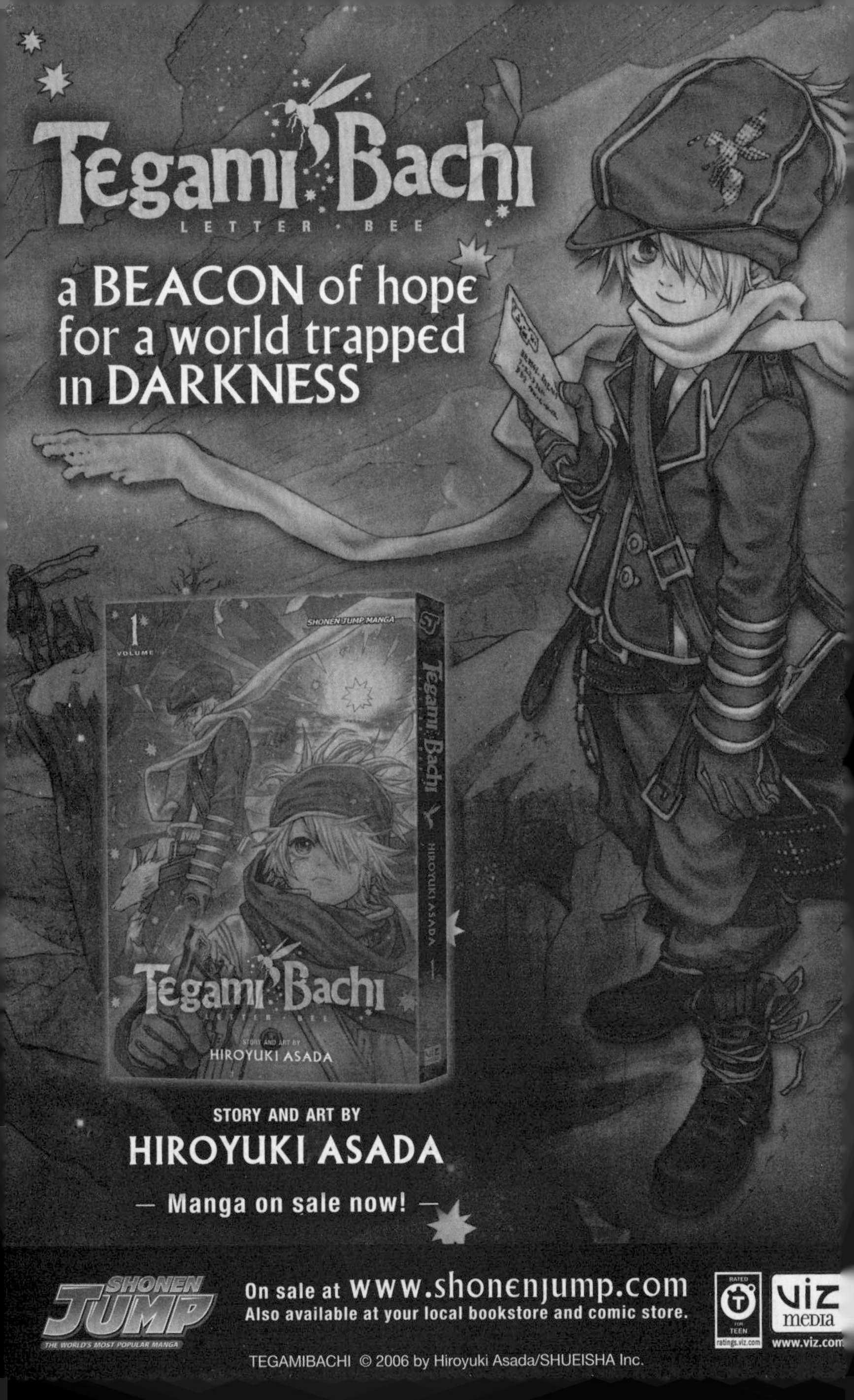
Tegami Bachi
LETTER · BEE
a BEACON of hope for a world trapped in DARKNESS
SHONEN JUMP MANGA
1 VOLUME
Tegami Bachi
LETTER BEE
STORY AND ART BY
HIROYUKI ASADA
STORY AND ART BY
HIROYUKI ASADA
— Manga on sale now! —
SHONEN JUMP
THE WORLD'S MOST POPULAR MANGA
On sale at www.shonenjump.com
Also available at your local bookstore and comic store.
RATED T FOR TEEN
ratings.viz.com
VIZ media
www.viz.com
TEGAMIBACHI © 2006 by Hiroyuki Asada/SHUEISHA Inc.

You're Reading in the Wrong Direction!!

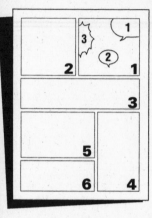

Whoops! Guess what? You're starting at the wrong end of the comic!

…It's true! In keeping with the original Japanese format, **Slam Dunk** is meant to be read from right to left, starting in the upper-right corner.

Unlike English, which is read from left to right, Japanese is read from right to left, meaning that action, sound effects and word-balloon order are completely reversed… something which can make readers unfamiliar with Japanese feel pretty backwards themselves. For this reason, manga or Japanese comics published in the U.S. in English have sometimes been published "flopped"—that is, printed in exact reverse order, as though seen from the other side of a mirror.

By flopping pages, U.S. publishers can avoid confusing readers, but the compromise is not without its downside. For one thing, a character in a flopped manga series who once wore in the original Japanese version a T-shirt emblazoned with "M A Y" (as in "the merry month of") now wears one which reads "Y A M"! Additionally, many manga creators in Japan are themselves unhappy with the process, as some feel the mirror-imaging of their art alters their original intentions.

We are proud to bring you Takehiko Inoue's **Slam Dunk** in the original unflopped format. For now, though, turn to the other side of the book and let the quest begin…!

–Editor

◀ •